INDIAN POLITICAL PARTIES ANNUAL, 2006

INDIAN POLITIAL PARTIES ANNUAL, 2006

PART II

CHRONOLOGY OF EVENTS

(1 AUGUST 2005 to 31 NOVEMBER 2005)

Dr. Mahendra Gaur

Publications

KALPAZ PUBLICATIONS

Delhi - 110052

Indian Political Parties Annual, 2006

ISBN : 81-7835-539-6 (Set)
ISBN : 81-7835-541-8 (Part II)

Published in 2006 in India by
Kalpaz Publications
C-30, Satyawati Nagar,
Delhi - 110052
e-mail : kalpaz@hotmail.com

Printed at : Salasar Imaging System, Delhi

INDIAN POLITICAL PARTIES ANNUAL, 2006

PART II

01-08-2005

(2187) Hyderabad : Five senior Congress leaders have demanded a CBI enquiry into the sale of four units of Nizam Sugars Factory to a private company alleging that irregularities took place in the transaction.

(2188) Hyderabad : Chief Minister Y. S. Rajasekhara Reddy has expressed displeasure at the absence of party MLAs and open show of differences among partymen during the Rajiv Nagara Bheri campaign launched on Saturday with an eye on the municipal elections.

(2189) Nellore : Senior vice-president of Bharatiya Janata Party (BJP) M. Venkaiah Naidu has reiterated the oft-repeated demand of the party for a uniform civil code in the country.

(2190) Nellore : BJP national secretary Bandaru Dattatreya has demanded that the Telangana Liberation Day should be celebrated officially by the State Government.

(2191) Bangalore : Confusion prevails in the Janata Dal (Secular) on the ways and means of removing Siddaramaiah as leader of the Legislature Party and Deputy Chief Minister. The confusion pertains to the timing and the venue. The party leadership has firmed up that Mr. Siddaramaiah and two others - Rural Development and Panchayat Raj Minister H.C. Mahadevappa and Textiles Minister Satish Jharkiholi - should be removed from the ministry.

(2192) Hyderabad : On the expected lines, K. Narayana has been appointed secretary of the CPI State Council, replacing Suravaram Sudhakar Reddy. The senior CPI leader was the party's assistant secretary before being elevated. The nomination comes in the light of the reluctance shown by Mr. Reddy, who is MP from Nalgonda, in holding the post. He preferred to work more actively at the national level.

(2193) New Delhi : Reiterating its stand on India-U.S. relations, the Communist Party of India (Marxist) on Sunday said the joint statement issued after the visit of Prime Minister Manmohan Singh showed the "continuation of the trend" of New Delhi being accommodated as an ally of Washington.

(2194) Bangalore : The State unit of the Bharatiya Janata Party anticipates that the Congress-Janata Dal (S) coalition Government will "fall within a week."

(2195) Shimoga : The Shimoga MP and former Chief Minister, S. Bangarappa, has urged the Government to take steps to repair the waste weir of the Ambligola reservoir in Shikaripur taluk.

(2196) Kannur : Communist Party of India (CPI) State secretary Veliyam Barghavan has said that the Congress-led Governments in the State and the Centre are serving the interests of the rich.

(2197) Kollam : Kerala Pradesh Congress Committee (KPCC) president Ramesh Chennithala has questioned the CPI(M) Polit Bureau's "silence" over the controversial SNC-Lavalin deal.

(2198) Kottayam : Kerala Congress (Joseph) chairman P.J. Joseph on Sunday called for extensive discussions on the 10-point development agenda for the State mooted by President A.P.J. Abdul Kalam during his recent visit. He urged the Chief Minister to convene an all-party meeting to prepare a comprehensive programme of action. While the KC (J) leader agreed with all the points raised by the President, he said a few components could be added to the agenda. These include a network of modern roads and railway lines, wastage disposal system, projects for biotechnology and nano technology development, inland fish culture projects and stress on organic farming.

(2199) Thiruvananthapuram : The State RSP leadership has taken strong exception to Chief Minister Oommen Chandy's statement that the RSP MP N.K. Premachandran had not suffered any injury in the police lathicharge in front of the Secretariat on July 8.

(2200) New Delhi : CPI(M) General Secretary Prakash Karat said on Sunday that the Polit Bureau of the party emphasised the importance of maintaining the country's independence in the development of nuclear technology for peaceful purposes. He was briefing the press on the two-day deliberations of the Polit Bureau.

(2201) Bhopal : The two-day training programme for State Ministers and district presidents of the Madhya Pradesh unit of the Bharatiya Janata Party concluded at Mandu near Indore on Sunday with the party president, L.K. Advani, lashing out at the United Progressive Alliance Government at the Centre saying that it should be "ashamed of the rapidly deteriorating internal security scenario." Mr. Advani said the BJP had never compromised on the national security front.

(2202) New Delhi : The Bharatiya Janata Party is all set to strongly criticise the Government for the framework agreement signed by Prime Minister Manmohan Singh with the United States President George Bush on the nuclear issue when the subject is discussed in Parliament next week.

(2203) Hyderabad : The Communist Party of India on Sunday said the Centre should tread cautiously while dealing with defence issues with the United States. The U.S. had an "aggressive defence strategy" that was designed at their will and "we should not get entangled in it," CPI general secretary A.B. Bardhan said.

(2204) New Delhi : The Communist Party of India (Marxist- Leninist) will observe August 6, sixtieth anniversary of the bombing of Hiroshima, with countrywide protests against "the worldwide military offensive of U.S. imperialism" and the Government's "strategic surrender to this American design."

(2205) New Delhi : National Democratic Alliance convenor and Janata Dal (United) president George Fernandes will seek the tabling of the "entire 700-page" Justice Phukan Commission report on the alleged Tehelka scam in Parliament on Monday. The issue will also be discussed in the NDA meeting on Monday morning, Mr. Fernandes told mediapersons here on Saturday.

(2206) New Delhi : The Delhi Industries Minister, Mangat Ram Singhal, is in the line of fire of the party high command and the Chief Minister, Sheila Dikshit, for mishandling the issue of industrial relocation as well as failure to issue a notification with regard to the areas that have more than 70 per cent industries. It is understood that the party leadership has sought a status report on the issue and the allegations made against Mr. Singhal in the Coordination Committee meeting.

(2207) Patna : The BJP today demanded quashing of the transfer order of 17 IPS officers which triggered a crisis in the administrative circle.

(2208) Pondicherry : The Pondicherry State committee of the Communist Party of India (CPI) has called for a 24-hour bandh in Pondicherry from August 3 to highlight the "suffering undergone" by students seeking admission to private medical colleges, said party secretary and MLA, N. Kalainathan.

(2209) Jaipur : The stage is set for a confrontation between farmers agitating for irrigation waters and the Bharatiya Janata Party-led Government during a "Mahapadaav" (mass sit-in) to be held at Ghadsana in Sriganganagar district of Rajasthan on Monday. Prohibitory orders imposed in Ghadsana have been extended till August 5 and all entry points to the town sealed under strict surveillance of police.

(2210) Jaipur : Rajasthan Mahila Congress president Mamta Sharma on has appealed to the State Governor, Pratibha Patil, to stall the State Government's move to outsource the services in the heritage train, Palace on Wheels (PoW). The prestige of the State was involved in the train, jointly run by the Indian Railways and the Rajasthan Tourism Development Corporation, she told the Governor.

(2211) Chennai : The Dravida Munnetra Kazhagam president, M. Karunanidhi, has appealed to the Prime Minister, Manmohan Singh, to take steps to implement the reservation policy for Other Backward Classes (OBCs) in educational institutions under the control of the Centre.

02-08-2005

(2212) Hyderabad : The Telugu Desam Party has urged Chief Minister Y.S. Rajasekhara Reddy to lead an all-party delegation to pursue the Scheduled Castes categorisation issue with the Prime Minister and the Centre instead of deputing Municipal Administration Minister Koneru Ranga Rao.

(2213) Hyderabad : The BJP has withdrawn the freedom given to the district units on seat adjustments for municipal elections and reiterated that the party will not have truck with the Telugu Desam. It said on Monday that there was no ambiguity in the State policy and the district units would not be given exemption from it.

(2214) Polavaram (West Godavari Dt.) : The Communist Party of India (Marxist) State secretary, B.V. Raghavulu, on Monday wanted a change in the design of the multi-crore Indira Sagar project facilitating reduction of its height so as to minimise human suffering and the submergence area.

(2215) Bangalore : The Janata Dal (Secular) leadership, on Monday, is believed to have decided to remove the Deputy Chief Minister, Siddaramaiah, as leader of the legislature party and elect the Revenue Minister, M.P. Prakash, in his place.

(2216) Dharwad : The Union Ministry of Water Resources is likely to clear all hurdles in the execution of two projects to divert water from the Kalasa and the Banduri nala, tributaries of the Mahadayi to the Malaprabha project.

(2217) Shimoga : The Shimoga MP and State President of the Samajwadi Party, S. Bangarappa, said here on Monday that the days of the coalition Government in the State are numbered and it will collapse sooner than expected.

(2218) Alappuzha : Kerala Pradesh Congress Committee (KPCC) president Ramesh Chennithala called on Sree Narayana Dharma Paripalana (SNDP) Yogam general secretary Vellappally Natesan at his residence in Kanichukulangara here on Monday.

(2219) Kozhikode : Bharatiya Janta Party (BJP) leaders O. Rajagopal and K. Raman Pillai will attend a programme to be held at Alakapuri auditorium on Tuesday to honour participants in the struggle waged for liberating Goa from the Portuguese rule. BJP's stand is that it was an agitation led by Bharatiya Jana Sangh (which later evolved into BJP) in 1958 that forced the then Prime Minister Jawaharlal Nehru to take military action to liberate Goa from Portuguese control and merge Goa, Daman and Diu into the Indian union. All the participants of the Goa liberation struggle who are alive will be honoured, a party spokesman said on Tuesday.

(2220) Thiruvananthapuram : The entire Opposition in the Assembly walked out on Monday alleging deep nexus between the blade mafia and the police. It accused the Government of shielding the guilty in the murder of the owner of a chit fund in North Paravur and his family in a lorry-car smash-up on the National Highway on July 20.

(2221) Thiruvananthapuram : The next United Democratic Front (UDF) liaison committee will have a new face, Dheevara Sabha leader V. Dinakaran, who has been made a special invitee to the ruling front's periodical political confabulations. Chief Minister Oommen Chandy has already informed Mr. Dinakaran about this decision, which was taken at a recent meeting of the UDF liaison committee. It was decided that more parties should be inducted into the front.

(2222) New Delhi : The Rajya Sabha on Monday approved the extension of President's rule in Bihar for another six months with Union

Home Minister Shivraj Patil backing the Governor's recommendation for dissolution of the State Assembly to avoid "Constitutional chaos." The Opposition staged a walkout after claiming that Mr. Patil's reply failed to address their concerns.

(2223) New Delhi : The Congress on Monday said the party president, Sonia Gandhi, has been in touch with the Maharasthra Chief Minster, Vilasrao Deshmukh, on the grim flood situation in Mumbai and the State.

(2224) New Delhi : The National Democratic Alliance is preparing for a stormy debate on Bihar in the Lok Sabha on Tuesday when the Government is expected to seek the approval of the House for extension of President's Rule in the State.

(2225) Bhopal : The Opposition in the Madhya Pradesh Assembly boycotted the House proceedings on Monday protesting against the Speaker's ruling to disallow discussion on two calling attention notices. This was after the Opposition had already lodged a strong protest on the issue of "BJP's election symbol" figuring in a class sixth textbook published by the State Text Book Corporation. At the end of Question Hour, the Opposition, led by the Congress members, lodged a strong protest after the leader of Opposition, Jamuna Devi, had described this as a very serious matter and accused the State BJP Government of saffronising the education. The Opposition MLAs trooped into the well of the House shouting slogans and waiving copies of the "objectionable portion" from the text book. Later, the entire opposition staged a walkout.

(2226) Pondicherry : The 24-hour bandh planned by the Communist Party of India and its allies in Pondicherry on August 4 has been postponed.

(2227) Lucknow : Even as the Mulayam Singh Yadav Government remains adamant on renaming Lucknow University (LU) after the former Uttar Pradesh Chief Minister, Chandra Bhanu Gupta, the protest of varsity teachers and students has spilled on to city roads.

03-08-2005

(2228) Cuddapah : The Telugu Desam Party is raising a hue and cry on every trivial issue with a view to tarnishing the Chief Minister Y.S.

Rajasekhara Reddy's image but has failed to gain political mileage, Congress leaders said here on Tuesday.

(2229) Hyderabad : Shiromani Akali Dal president and former Punjab Chief Minister Prakash Singh Badal along with Shiromani Gurudwara Prabhandak Committee (SGPC) president Bibi Jagir Kaur have assured committee's help for the Sikh community in the State.

(2230) Hyderabad : The Bharatiya Janata (BJP) has demanded a re-survey of Backward Class (BC) voters in a scientific manner through house-to-house verification for the municipal elections.

(2231) Hyderabad : Tribal MLAs belonging to the Congress have taken a serious exception to the campaign of Telugu Desam Party leaders on the deaths in the agency areas due to viral fevers.

(2232) Hyderabad : The Telugu Desam Party has charged the State Government with failing to take up with Volkswagen's special envoy Frank Elbe the issue of recovering the payment of Rs. 11.67 crores as equity to a bogus company and booking cases against the culprits who had siphoned off the money.

(2233) Karimnagar : Telugu Desam Party (TDP) president N. Chandrababu Naidu kicked off electioneering for the coming municipal elections by participating in road shows here on Tuesday.

(2234) Vijayawada : The internal rumblings in the TDP urban unit have been resolved with party president N. Chandrababu Naidu directing local leaders to patch up their differences and work unitedly for the coming civic elections.

(2235) Mahabubnagar : The Communist Party of India (CPI) State secretary K. Narayana accused the BJP and TRS leaders of adopting "opportunistic policies."

(2236) New Delhi : Parliament on Tuesday approved the extension of President's Rule in Bihar by another six months. The National Democratic Alliance-led Opposition staged a walkout in the Lok Sabha, which adopted the resolution by voice vote.

(2237) Bangalore : "I am the Deputy Chief Minister and Finance Minister of Karnataka and the Leader of the Janata Dal (Secular) Legislature

Party," the Deputy Chief Minister, Siddaramaiah, asserted in the Legislative Assembly on Tuesday, while hitting back against the leaders and legislators who have "removed" him from the leadership of the legislature party.

(2238) New Delhi : National Democratic Alliance members walked out of the Lok Sabha on Tuesday, demanding that the report of the Justice G.T. Nanavati Commission, which went into the 1984 anti-Sikh riots, be tabled. Speaker Somnath Chatterjee said the issue was being raised without proper notice.

(2239) Thiruvananthapuram : The Opposition on Tuesday walked out of the State Assembly alleging that the State Government had diverted for other purposes the funds received for extending relief to the victims of the tsunami onslaught of December last year.

(2240) Bangalore : The removal of the Deputy Chief Minister, Siddaramaiah, from the leadership of the Janata Dal (Secular) Legislature Party and the question mark over the fate of the Ministers, H.C. Mahadevappa and Satish N. Jarkiholi, created a furore in the Legislative Council on Tuesday.

(2241) Bangalore : Janata Dal (Secular) MLAs, who have stood by the Deputy Chief Minister, Siddaramaiah, have appealed to national leaders of the party to intervene and save the organisation in Karnataka.

(2242) Thiruvananthapuram : Leader of the Kerala Opposition V.S. Achuthanandan has observed that President A.P.J. Abdul Kalam's 10-point mission for the State ignores the agriculture and traditional industrial sectors.

(2243) New Delhi : The Congress on Tuesday emphasised that the issue of disinvestment in the Bharat Heavy Electricals Limited was put on hold till discussions to resolve the standoff was complete and sought to underline the party's commitment to public sector undertakings.

(2244) New Delhi : Senior Bharatiya Janata Party leader and former Union Minister Vijay Goel has sought an explanation from Delhi Power Minister Haroon Yusuf on why he has not allowed installation of the controversial new 'fast-running' electronic meters in his own constituency while other consumers are being forced to get their meters changed by the private power distribution companies.

(2245) New Delhi : The Lok Sabha on Tuesday witnessed an animated debate on the political stalemate in Bihar with the Government coming under fire from the Opposition for the deteriorating law and order situation under the present dispensation.

(2246) Pondicherry : P. Kannan, founder of the Puduchery Munnetra Congress (PMC) on Tuesday charged the Pondicherry Government with adopting a "chaotic and unimaginative policy taking the students seeking admission to the MBBS course in private medical colleges for a ride."

(2247) Jaipur : Communist Party of India (Marxist) politburo member Sitaram Yechury has held the Rajasthan Government responsible for the farmers' unrest over irrigation water in the northern districts of the State. The problem was not with water availability but with the management, he said and added: "The State Government's inefficiency has created the present situation."

(2248) Chandigarh : The Congress high command is understood to have inducted Devinder Singh Babla, who was expelled from the primary membership of the party in 2001, as a delegate of the local party unit executive despite sharp protests from the faction headed by the acting president, B. B. Bahl, and several other partymen.

(2249) Chennai : The Pattali Makkal Katchi founder, S. Ramadoss, on Tuesday favoured the transfer of the subject of education back to the State List from the Concurrent List.

(2250) Hyderabad : After a long delay, the Congress leadership has finally announced the constitution of executive and election committees of the Andhra Pradesh Congress Committee (APCC).

(2251) Hyderabad : The Telugu Desam Party (TDP) on Wednesday produced "documentary evidence" of irregularities in the finalisation of bids for construction of the Sripada Sagar Project (SSP-Yellampalli) on the Godavari in Karimnagar district.

(2252) Visakhapatnam : The urban district unit of the Telugu Desam Party has asked the Government and the Municipal Corporation of Visakhapatnam (MCV) to specify when the Godavari waters would be supplied to the city.

(2253) **Hyderabad :** The Telangana Rashtra Samithi (TRS) president and Union Labour Minister, K. Chandrasekhar Rao, has hinted at the possibility of a tie-up between the TRS and the Congress for the municipal polls if the leadership of the latter comes forward.

(2254) **Karimnagar :** "I did not target any employee individually. I strived to bring about attitudinal change and discipline among employees," the former Chief Minister and Telugu Desam president N. Chandrababu Naidu said while responding to employees' complaint that they were harassed during his regime.

(2255) **Bhubaneshwar :** At least 20 people, including seven policemen, were injured in a clash between policemen and protestors during a bandh in Kendrapara town of Orissa on Wednesday. The bandh call was given by Bajrang Dal in protest against the killing of a local contractor two days ago.

(2256) **Kakinada :** The Pradesh Congress chief K. Keshava Rao has ridiculed Telugu Desam Party leaders for their utterances on Volkswagen affair, describing them as ignorant of International laws and practices.

(2257) **Bangalore :** The Janata Dal (Secular) leadership on Wednesday set the ball rolling for a change in stewardship of its legislature party and the removal of the Deputy Chief Minister, Siddaramaiah, and two other Ministers, H.C. Mahadevappa and Satish Jharkiholi from office.

(2258) **New Delhi :** Members in the Lok Sabha on Wednesday took exception to judicial "encroachment and interference" into the domain of legislatures in the backdrop of the recent Supreme Court observation on the issue of "charge-sheeted" Ministers in the Union Council of Ministers. Some members suggested a discussion on the issue.

(2259) **New Delhi :** Expressing deep concern over the 'deteriorating political situation' in Nepal, nine political parties that comprise "Nepal Democracy Solidarity Committee", on Wednesday decided to mobilise national and international opinion on it.

(2260) **Bangalore :** The Working President of the State unit of the Janata Dal (Secular), H.D. Kumaraswamy, accompanied by two senior Ministers, M.P. Prakash (Revenue) and P.G.R. Sindhia (Industries), on Wednesday met the Chief Minister, N. Dharam Singh, and are believed to

(2277) New Delhi/Chennai : The Congress high command on Thursday decided to re-appoint G.K. Vasan as president of the Tamil Nadu Congress Committee even as it cleared P. Shanmugam to head the Pondicherry party unit.

(2278) Bangalore : The Bharatiya Janata Party (BJP) on Thursday continued its efforts to form a government if the upheaval in the Janata Dal (Secular) leads to the fall of the Dharam Singh Government.

(2279) Bangalore : A meeting of the Janata Dal (Secular) Legislature Party convened by the Deputy Chief Minister, Siddaramaiah, at his residence here on Thursday was postponed for want of quorum.

(2280) Bangalore : There is growing desperation in a section of the Bharatiya Janata Party leadership in the State to come to power and that too by any means, including "supping with the Congress".

(2281) Kochi : Kerala Pradesh Congress Committee president Ramesh Chennithala called on Mar Varkey Vithayathil, Major Archbishop of Ernakulam-Angamaly Archdiocese, at the Cardinal House here on Thursday.

(2282) Thiruvananthapuram : The LDF State committee has decided to register its strong disagreement to the proposed move to ban demonstrations on arterial roads in the State capital.

(2283) New Delhi : The Communist Party of India MP, Suravaram Sudhakar Reddy, has been nominated to head the Parliamentary Standing Committee on Labour. Mr. Reddy comes in place of P.K. Vasudevan Nair, who passed away last month.

(2284) New Delhi : At a Bharatiya Janata Party-sponsored discussion in the Lok Sabha, the United Progressive Alliance (UPA) and its supporting parties on Thursday urged their rivals not to politicise terror strikes. The discussion focussed on the July 5 attack on the Ram Janmabhoomi complex at Ayodhya."

(2285) New Delhi : The National Democratic Alliance on Thursday charged the United Progressive Alliance Government in the Rajya Sabha with having committed a "big blunder" by agreeing to separate the country's civilian and defence nuclear installations under the recently-signed Indo-U.S. pact.

(2286) Guwahati : A State-level convention organised by the State unit of the CPI (M) here on Thursday resolved to build a united movement to mount pressure on the Government to fulfil long-pending demands of the tea garden workers and the tea tribe community.

(2287) Jaipur : In what was meant to be a "political reply" to the farmers' agitation for irrigation water in the north Rajasthan districts, the ruling Bharatiya Janata Party on Thursday organised a public meeting in Banda village of Anupgarh tehsil in Sriganganagar district. Barring few instances of thwarted attempts to show black flags by the agitating farmers, the event passed off peacefully.

(2288) New Delhi : The Shiv Sena Parliamentary Party on Thursday asked Union Finance Minister P. Chidambaram to impress upon insurance companies to pay 50 per cent of the claim to flood victims in Maharashtra.

(2289) Pondicherry : The appointment of the senior Congress leader and former Chief Minister P. Shanmugham, as president of the Pondicherry Pradesh Congress Committee has been welcomed by the rank and file of the party. Mr. Shanmugham, who returned from his native village of Neduncadu in Karaikal on Thursday told The Hindu that he would meet the mediapersons shortly.

(2290) Kolkata : Mamata Banerjee's reported decision to resign from the Lok Sabha "is politically justified," the Leader of the Opposition in the West Bengal Assembly and Trinamool Congress leader, Pankaj Banerjee, said here on Thursday.

(2291) Coimbatore : The Bharatiya Janata Party feels that the political situation in Tamil Nadu is in a state of flux, but competition is hotting up among parties, its All-India secretary Bandaru Dattatreya told presspersons here on Thursday.

06-08-2005

(2292) Anantapur : The district unit of Communist Party of India (Marxist) has asked the Government to suspend the officials responsible for the irregularities in division of wards and identification of backward classes in the urban areas.

(2293) Hyderabad : Former Minister and TRS MLA, A. Chandra Sekhar has complained to the Chief Minister, Y. S. Rajasekhara Reddy that two

Ministers have inaugurated a drinking water scheme in his constituency, Vikarabad in Ranga Reddy district without inviting him.

(2294) Hyderabad : Senior Congress leader and MP, V. Hanumantha Rao, has expressed strong opposition to the creation of Greater Hyderabad Municipal Corporation (GHMC) by merging 12 civic bodies surrounding the City.

(2295) Karimnagar : AICC general secretary and State Congress affairs in charge, Digvijay Singh along with APCC president, K. Keshava Rao has formally launched the election campaign for the coming municipal elections by organising roadshows and meetings with the party cadre in Sircilla and Karimnagar on Friday.

(2296) Nizamambad : Telugu Desam Party president N. Chandrababu Naidu has termed the act of formation of the Telangana Jagarana Sena by the Telangana Rashtra Samithi as "political degradation and degeneration."

(2297) Vijayawada : The 14-month rule of the Congress Party was better than the nine-year rule of the Telugu Desam Party and nature is also favourable to the Congress, said speakers at the valedictory of the week-long Rajiv Nagara Bheri programme here on Friday.

(2298) Vizianagaram : The BJP will give priority to prominent personalities and those who will stay committed to the party ideology in the civic body elections, said the party's secretary, K. Haribabu, at a press conference here on Friday.

(2299) Kamareddy (Nizamabad Dt.) : The Congress party State in-charge, Digvijay Singh has said that the former Chief Minister and Telugu Desam Party president, N. Chandrababu Naidu had neglected rural economy during his nine-year rule while giving undue importance to information technology.

(2300) Sangareddy : AICC general secretary and State in charge Digvijay Singh criticised former Chief Minister Nara Chandrababu Naidu for wasting nine years running after information technology and plunging the State into backwardness.

(2301) Kamareddy (Nizamabad Dt.) : TDP president N. Chandrababu Naidu's two-day roadshow in the district ended on an upbeat note, here on Friday.

(2302) New Delhi : As part of the ongoing consensus building exercise on political reservation for women, the Government has proposed a substantial increase in the number of Lok Sabha seats and a "consequent increase" in the strength of State Assembly seats while simultaneously reserving one-third of the total legislature seats for women.

(2303) New Delhi : Lok Sabha Speaker Somnath Chatterjee on Friday took exception to reports imputing political considerations to his decision on Trinamool Congress leader Mamata Banerjee's notice for an adjournment motion.

(2304) Bangalore : On a day of fast-moving political developments, Deputy Chief Minister Siddaramaiah and two Ministers were dropped from the Council of Ministers on Friday after they refused to resign. Acting on the advice of Chief Minister N. Dharam Singh, Governor T.N. Chaturvedi relieved them of their posts. The others are Minister for Rural Development and Panchayat Raj H.C. Mahadevappa and Minister of State for Textiles Satish Jharkiholi.

(2305) Kolkata : Trinamool Congress MLAs courted arrest here on Friday after they were stopped by the police on their march from the West Bengal Assembly to Raj Bhavan. They were protesting against attempts to "muffle the voice" of party leader Mamata Banerjee in the Lok Sabha.

(2306) Bangalore : The Bharatiya Janata Party's national leadership has sent the party functionary in-charge of Karnataka affairs, Ved Prakash Goel, to the city to resolve the differences that have arisen in the State party unit over the moves to form an alternative government.

(2307) Bangalore : The All-India Mahila Congress Committee has urged the United Progressive Alliance (UPA) Government to adopt the Women's Reservation Bill without further delay.

(2308) Bangalore : The former Deputy Chief Minister, Siddaramaiah, was in an adamant mood on Friday stating that there was no need for him to resign from the office as neither the Chief Minister, N. Dharam Singh, nor the Legislative Assembly Speaker, Krishna, had asked him to do so.

(2309) Mysore : The supporters of Siddaramaiah continued their protest against his ouster from the Janata Dal (Secular) Legislature Party and staged a rail roko agitation here on Friday.

(2310) Shimoga : The reported lead taken by the Leader of Opposition in the Assembly and senior leader of the BJP, B.S. Yediyurappa, to join hands with the Janata Dal (S) with his followers to share power in the State has come as a surprise to BJP workers in Shimoga district.

(2311) Thiruvananthapuram : Communist Party of India (Marxist) State secretary Pinarayi Vijayan has taken strong exception to what he termed the Government's attempt to delay the local body elections indefinitely.

(2312) New Delhi : Bharatiya Janata Party vice-president Venkaiah Naidu and Karnataka affairs in-charge Ved Prakash Goyal met party president L.K. Advani here on Friday to discuss the political developments in the State. Several party MPs from Karnataka were present.

(2313) New Delhi : The Bharatiya Janata Party will support any of the four basic "formulas" on women's reservation: reserving one-third of the present number of seats in all legislatures; declaring one-third of all seats "double-member" constituencies with one member being a woman; increasing the strength of legislatures as proposed by the Government and then reserving one-third of all seats for women; and lastly, as the Election Commission once suggested, making it mandatory for parties to give one-third of their seats to women.

(2314) New Delhi : Accusing the Central and State governments of letting things go out of hand in the strike by employees of the Honda Motorcycle and Scooters India Ltd. (HMSI) that led to brutal police action on the agitating workers at Gurgaon, trade union leaders, mainly affiliated to the Left parties, on Friday said if the multinational companies (MNCs) want to set up shop in India, they will have to respect the Indian Constitution and obey all labour laws.

(2315) Gandhinagar : A revolt is brewing within the Gujarat BJP legislature party over the show cause notice issued to rebel leader Gordhan Jhadafiya for publicly criticising the Narendra Modi Government.

(2316) Shimla : Uproarious scenes were witnessed in the Himachal Vidhan Sabha on Friday, when the Speaker, G.R. Musafir, rejected the adjournment motion by the leader of the BJP group, Prem Kumar Dhumal, on the issues related to excessive rain and floods in the State. The Parliamentary Affairs Minister, Kaul Singh Thakur, opposing the move, said that the Government was serious about the natural calamity and the Revenue Minister would give astatement under rule 317 later in the day.

(2317) Bhopal : While the president of the Madhya Pradesh unit of Bharatiya Janata Party, Shivraj Singh Chauhan, has been caught in a controversy over his wife's godown, the Madhya Pradesh Chief Minister, Babulal Gaur, is also facing allegations that he went out of his way to patronise women considered close to him.

(2318) Kolkata : The Muzaffar Ahmed Sriti Puroskar (Memorial Award) for this year was awarded to Prof. Deb Kumar Basu for his "Essays in Environmental Economics" and Bangladeshi academician Bohranuddin Khan Jehangir for his book in Bengali "Itihas Nirmaner Dhara," on Friday. The day marked the 117th birth anniversary of the pioneer of the Communist movement in the country.

(2319) Chennai : The Union Minister for Commerce and Industry, Kamal Nath, and the Union Minister of State for Commerce and Industry, E.V.K.S. Elangovan, called on the Dravida Munnetra Kazhagam president, M. Karunanidhi, at his Gopalapuram residence here on Friday.

(2320) Chennai : Democratic Progressive Alliance MPs on Friday met the Prime Minister, Manmohan Singh, to press for Haj travel for all those who apply.

(2321) Chennai : The Puthiya Thamizhagam will organise demonstrations on August 18 in six places in the State to urge the Centre to enact a legislation that would provide reservation for Scheduled Castes/ Tribes in private sector units.

07-08-2005

(2322) Cuddapah : The Government's laxity led to irregularities in enumeration of Backward Class population and division of municipal wards, the TDP Official Spokesman M.V. Mysoora Reddy alleged on Saturday.

(2323) Hyderabad : The Telugu Desam Party has criticised, what it called, the "doublespeak" of the All-India Congress Committee general secretary, Digvijay Singh, regarding the performance of its president, N. Chandrababu Naidu .

(2324) Hyderabad : The Telangana Regional Congress Coordination Committee (TRCCC) has said that there was no opposition to the construction of Pulichintala project, provided the interests of displaced persons and the vast lime deposits are protected.

(2325) Vijayawada : The national secretariat member of the Communist Party of India (CPI) and Nalgonda MP, Suravaram Sudhakar Reddy, has said several political parties with "vested interests" are pursuing delay tactic in enacting the Women's Reservation Bill in the garb of "arriving at a consensus."

(2326) Hyderabad : The central leadership of the Congress has taken a serious view of the critical remarks made by senior party leaders against the Government.

(2327) Palakkad : Leader of the Opposition V. S. Achuthanandan has urged the State Government to take steps to prevent Tamil Nadu from diverting waters at Attumala, the main water source of Malampuzha Dam.

(2328) Sangareddy : The Union Minister of State for Rural Development and senior TRS leader, A. Narendra, on Saturday announced that the Telangana Rastra Samithi would go alone in the municipal elections.

(2329) Thiruvananthapuram : National Congress (Indira) leader K. Karunakaran has demanded an inquiry by a parliamentary committee into what he termed "misuse of the tsunami relief fund by the Oommen Chandy Government."

(2330) Bangalore : The former Deputy Chief Minister, Siddaramaiah, on Saturday declared that he will continue to espouse the cause of minorities, backward classes and Dalitsand fight for their uplift by remaining within the Janata Dal (S).Making a scathing attack on Janata Dal (S) President, H.D. Deve Gowda,Mr. Siddaramaiah demanded that he explain the reason for his ouster from the leadership of the Janata Dal (S) Legislature Party. Mr. Deve Gowda's action is unilateral, arbitrary and dictatorial, he charged.

(2331) Bangalore : Politicisation of religion and commercialisation of values has taken India away from its ethos of pluralism, veteran journalist Kuldip Nayar said here on Saturday.

(2332) Gulbarga : The former Minister and expelled Janata Dal (S) legislator, Vaijnath Patil, on Saturday termed the action of removing Mr. Siddaramaiah from the post of Deputy Chief Minister and dropping H.C.

Mahadevappa and Satish Jharkiholi from the Ministry as vindictive. He also and criticised the Congress for giving in to pressure from the Janata Dal (S) President, H.D. Deve Gowda, and dropping Mr. Siddaramaiah and his supporters from the Ministry.

(2333) Hassan : The removal of Siddaramiah and two others from the Cabinet has evoked a mixed response in Hassan. People have started calculating the impact of the action on the prospects of the Minister for Public Works and Energy, H.D. Revanna, and other five Janata Dal (Secular) MLAs in case of a snap poll. The people belonging to Kuruba and Vokkaliga communities in the district have started defending the actions of their respective leaders.

(2334) Kannur : Thalassery MLA and the Deputy Legislature Party leader of the Left Democratic Front (LDF) Kodiyeri Balakrishnan on Saturday urged the Government to take immediate steps for the development of the Malabar Cancer Centre (MCC) at Thalassery.

(2335) Kozhikode : State Janata Dal (S) president M.P. Veerendrakumar, on Saturday claimed that his party had initiated a meaningful dialogue with the Kerala Congress led by R. Balakrishna Pillai on merger of the two parties.

(2336) Thrisur : K.P. Rajendran, MLA and Communist Party of India Legislature Party leader, has alleged that the UDF Government is trying not to conduct the local body elections in September, fearing a massive debacle.

(2337) New Delhi : The Communist Party of India (Marxist-Leninist) Liberation organised protests in various parts of the country against the United Progressive Alliance Government's policy of "strategic surrender" to the U.S.

(2338) Ajmer : 'Chadar' was on Saturday offered on behalf of the former Prime Minister, Atal Bihari Vajpayee, and BJP president L.K. Advani at the tomb of Sufi saint Khwaja Moinuddin Chishti on the eve of his annual Urs.

(2339) Chennai : Tamil Nadu Congress Committee president G.K. Vasan on Saturday said that there was no room for groupism in the party and he would function above group politics.

(2340) Cuddalore : The Communist Party of India (Marxist) has urged the Tamil Nadu Government to come out with a White Paper on the tsunami relief and rehabilitation measures.

08-08-2005

(2341) Ananatapur : The Minister for Panchayat Raj and Endowments, J.C. Diwakar Reddy, has said that the Congress has a special love for minorities and implementation of five per cent reservation in the State is an indication of that.

(2342) Cuddapah : The Telugu Desam Party snapped ties with the National Democratic Alliance in order to safeguard the interests of minorities, the TDP leaders asserted here on Sunday.

(2343) Hyderabad : The Bharatiya Janata Party's Ranga Reddy district unit has opposed the decision to abolish Gaddiannaram Municipality and bring it under the proposed Greater Hyderabad Municipal Corporation (GHMC).

(2344) Hyderabad : The Union Minister of State for Rural Development, A. Narendra, has taken exception to the demand of the Telangana Regional Congress Coordination Committee (TRCCC) for a Rs. 20,000-crore package to develop Telangana.

(2345) Hyderabad : The Telugu Desam Party has demanded political reservations for minorities in the coming local body polls.

(2346) Kurnool : CPI national council member K. Ramakrishna has urged the Congress to spell out its stand on the electoral understanding in the municipal elections.

(2347) New Delhi : The Communist Party of India and the Communist Party of India (Marxist-Leninist) Liberation have called for a Bihar bandh on August 24 and invited all parties, barring the RJD and the Janata Dal (United), to join the agitation.

(2348) Bangalore : In a politically significant statement, the former Prime Minister and Janata Dal (Secular) president, H.D. Deve Gowda, has firmly ruled out any association between his party and the Bharatiya Janata Party. He said the JD(S) would stand by the commitment it gave the Congress while forming a coalition Government involving the two parties in Karnataka.

(2349) Bangalore : The President of the Janata Dal (Secular) and former Prime Minister, H.D. Deve Gowda, has appealed to party workers against being provoked by the statements and invectives being uttered against him by the former Deputy Chief Minister, Siddaramaiah, and his friends.

(2350) Gulbarga : Revenue Minister M.P. Prakash on Sunday took exception to the statement of the former Deputy Chief Minister, Siddaramaiah, casting aspersions on the Janata Dal (Secular) legislators who had signed the resolution to express lack of confidence in the latter's leadership and seeking his removal from the Deputy Chief Minister's post. He was speaking to presspersons at the helipad at the District Police Headquarters Ground in the City after conducting an aerial survey of the flood-affected regions in Bijapur, Bagalkot, Raichur and Gulbarga districts along with Chief Minister Dharam Singh and Water Resources Minister M. Mallikarjun Kharge. Mr. Prakash clarified that there has been no horse-trading as Mr. Siddaramaiah claimed.

(2351) Kannur : Kerala Pradesh Congress Committee (KPCC) president Ramesh Chennithala said here on Sunday that the Malabar Cancer Centre (MCC) at Thalassery was the victim of the Communist Party of India (Marxist)'s drive for 'amassing money.'

(2352) Thiruvananthapuram : The BJP's strategy for the upcoming local body elections would be guided by 'local factors,' party State president P.S. Sreedharan Pillai said here on Sunday.

(2353) Bangalore : The former Prime Minister, H.D. Deve Gowda, while categorically ruling out any prospect of his party, the Janata Dal (Secular), reneging on the commitment given to Congress President Sonia Gandhi with respect to its continued participation in the coalition Government in Karnataka, highlighted here on Sunday the fact that his party had joined hands with the Congress with the sole purpose of keeping the BJP out of power. "How then can the JD (S) join with the BJP at the present juncture? It will be the most unethical thing to do," he said.

(2354) New Delhi : The Communist Party of India and the Communist Party of India (Marxist-Leninist) Liberation have called for a Bihar bandh on August 24 and invited all parties, barring the Rashtriya Janata Dal and the Janata Dal (United), to join the agitation.

(2355) Jaipur : The Opposition Congress in Rajasthan is making all-out efforts to make its first "protest rally" here on August 9 a big success. The three Union Ministers hailing from the State, three former Chief Ministers and all the sitting and former party MLAs, besides a host of local leaders and activists of the party, are expected to participate in the rally.

(2356) Chandigarh : The re-appointment of B.B. Bahl as the president of the faction-ridden Chandigarh unit of the Congress by the party High Command earlier this week has evoked mixed response. Even though the party High Command had tried to broker a truce between the factions owing allegiance to Mr.Bahl and the local MP, Pawan Kumar Bansal, supporters of the latter virtually "boycotted" the installation ceremony of the former at the local Congress office here on Friday. However, a large number of partymen, mostly grassroots workers, gathered at the Tribune Chowk to welcome Mr.Bahl who was returning from New Delhi after meeting senior Central party leaders. They accorded a rousing reception to the veteran party leader at the CTCC office in Sector 35 here.

(2357) Chennai : State Governments should be given the full responsibility for all levels of education since it was their right, speakers said at a seminar on the present educational system.

09-08-2005

(2358) Hyderabad : The Congress on Monday demanded that the Telugu Desam Party president, N. Chandrababu Naidu, tender an apology to the tribals of Visakhapatnam district and various constitutional functionaries for furnishing false figures about malaria deaths in the agency areas.

(2359) Hyderabad : The Telugu Desam president, N. Chandrababu Naidu, on Monday took the unusual step of carrying to the Raj Bhavan, a vanload of petitions against the indirect municipal elections and submitting the same to the Governor, Sushil Kumar Shinde.

(2360) Vizianagaram : Bharatiya Janata Party national committee member P. V. Chalapathi Rao on Monday flayed the TDP and the Congress for "neglecting" people's welfare.

(2361) Bangalore : The Congress is conspiring to replace Governor T.N. Chaturvedi with someone who could be "manipulated" by it, and effectively bring the State under President's rule, Janata Dal (United) State President B. Somashekar has alleged.

(2362) Bangalore : The former Deputy Chief Minister Siddaramaiah has started interacting with senior leaders of the party, particularly those from the backward classes who were expelled for rebelling against the party president a few months ago.

(2363) Bangalore : Minister for Industries and Infrastructure P.G.R. Sindhia has defended the ouster of Siddaramaiah, former Deputy Chief Minister, from the leadership of the Janata Dal (S) Legislature Party and saying it was a unanimous decision of the party legislators.

(2364) Bangalore : Leader of the Opposition in the Legislative Assembly B.S. Yediyurappa on Monday called on the former Deputy Chief Minister Siddaramaiah and held talks.

(2365) Shimoga : A series of developments recently in the light of reports that Opposition Leader in the Legislative Assembly and senior Bharatiya Janata Party (BJP) leader B.S. Yediyurappa and his supporters are ready to quit the party and share power with the Janata Dal (Secular) and his subsequent volte face have put the party workers in his home district of Shimoga in a quandary.

(2366) Krishnaraja Sagar (Mandya District) : Allaying fears over the future of the coalition Government given the fluid political situation in the State, Chief Minister N. Dharam Singh on Monday down played the impact of the developments in the Janata Dal (Secular) and described them as an internal affair of that party.

(2367) Kochi : Thousands of CITU, CPI(M) and DYFI activists lined up along the red-flag-dotted road from Munambam to Chellanam in Ernakulam district's coastal belt late on Monday afternoon to a form a 'Manushya thadayana' (human bund) to press for 'saving the sea and the backwaters' and protecting the coastal people's livelihood.

(2368) Kochi : The Indian Federal Democratic Party (IFDP) has called for the resignation of Minister for Civil Supplies Adoor Prakash and action against the managing director and other officials of the Kerala State Civil Supplies Corporation.

(2369) Thiruvananthapuram : The UDF Liaison Committee has urged the Government to take steps to bring in a Goonda Act as part of its attempt to crack down on anti-social activities. The Government should think of bringing in fresh legislation if necessary, the UDF said.

(2370) Thiruvananthapuram : Kerala Pradesh Congress Committee (KPCC) media committee chairman M.M. Hassan has denied CPI(M) leader Kodiyeri Balakrishnan's allegation that KPCC president Ramesh Chennithala's 'Chaitanya Yatra' was being organised with funds mobilised from the liquor lobby.

(2371) Thiruvananthapuram : The United Democratic Front leadership has got caught in a spat with the State Election Commission over the

(2372) Thiruvananthapuram : CPI(M) State secretary Pinarayi Vijayan on Monday accused the Government of trying to 'sabotage' the elections to local bodies in the State.

(2373) New Delhi : The Bharatiya Janata Party on Monday expressed its dissatisfaction with the Action Taken Report on the Justice G.T. Nanavati Commission of Inquiry, saying it was like "sprinkling salt on the wounds" of families who had lost members in the "massacre of Sikhs" that took place in 1984.

(2374) Chandigarh : Shiromani Akali Dal president Parkash Singh Badal has described the Centre's Action Taken Report (ATR) on the Nanavati Commission's indictment of Congress leaders for organising and leading the brutal massacre of innocent Sikhs in 1984 as "a shameful governmental shield for killers and rapists."

(2375) New Delhi : Trinamool Congress leader Mamata Banerjeeon Monday said she stood by her decision to quit the Lok Sabha as "there is no official communication yet" of her resignation being rejected.

(2376) New Delhi : BJP leader Uma Bharti on Monday met Chairman of the Janata Dal (United) Parliamentary Board Sharad Yadav here to jointly raise the demand for a quota for women from Scheduled Castes, Tribes and Other Backward Communities within the overall 33 per cent reservation for women in the Women's Reservation Bill.

(2377) New Delhi : Rejecting the Action Taken Report (ATR) tabled by the Union Home Ministry in Parliament on Monday along with the Nanavati Commission report, the Bharatiya Janata Party demanded arrest of the Member of Parliament from Outer Delhi, Sajjan Kumar, and the Union Minister for NRI Affairs, Jagdish Tytler, and registration of fresh cases against them for their alleged involvement in the 1984 Sikh riots in the Capital.

(2378) New Delhi : The Municipal Corporation of Delhi (MCD) House on Monday passed a resolution demanding a Central Bureau of Investigation (CBI) probe into the alleged financial irregularities in the ongoing construction work of the Rs.110-crore modern abattoir at Ghazipur in East Delhi.

(2379) Deharadun : The Uttaranchal bandh call given by the Uttarakhand Kranti Dal (UKD) evoked a mixed response on Monday.

(2380) Chennai : The Tamil Nadu Congress Committee president, G.K. Vasan, has appealed to the people to take a pledge to oust the "anti-people" State Government on the lines of the Quit India movement launched by the Congress party in 1942 for the removal of the British Raj.

10-08-2005

(2381) Hyderabad : The Telugu Desam Legislature Party (TDLP) has warned that it would mobilise public opinion if the Government went ahead with putting irrigation projects in Telangana on the hold on the pretext that they would be included under a special Central package.

(2382) Hyderabad : The State unit of the Bharatiya Janata Party has accused the Congress and Telugu Desam Party of indulging in 'vote bank' politics with regard to reservations to Muslims.

(2383) Adilabad : The Bharatiya Janata Party (BJP) on Tuesday demanded that the Governor Sushil Kumar Shinde grant rights to tribals on the forestlands they had encroached. At a press conference here on Tuesday, former Union Minister and member of BJP's national executive committee, Ch. Vidyasagar Rao said the Governor was the custodian of all lands in tribal areas. Such an empowerment was conferred on the Governor by the V schedule sub-clause (1) of the Indian Constitution, he said. "With one stroke of pen, the Governor can benefit lakhs of tribals in the nine agency areas from Srikakulam to Adilabad," he added.

(2384) Samalkot : The Telugu Desam Party president, N. Chandrababu Naidu, got rousing reception when he put up road shows in the district on Tuesday. The spontaneous response from the public during his first day tour surprised even Mr. Naidu and the party leaders enjoyed the reception in urban areas, where municipal elections are due.

(2385) Bangalore : A Janata Dal (Secular) Minister has come out openly against the functioning of Chief Minister Dharam Singh and complained that he is interfering in the affairs of his department.

(2386) New Delhi : Parliament was adjourned on Tuesday after irate Opposition members stalled proceedings in both Houses demanding an immediate discussion on the Nanavati Commission report and the Government's Action Taken Report (ATR).

(2387) New Delhi : The Lok Sabha is expected to witness a test of strength between the Opposition and the ruling alliance on Wednesday on the issue of the Nanavati Commission report and the action taken by the Government on it. Parliament was adjourned on Tuesday after irate Opposition members stalled proceedings in both Houses demanding an immediate discussion on the report and the action taken.

(2388) Belgaum : Leader of the Opposition in the Legislative Assembly B.S. Yediyurappa has categorically said that neither he nor his party will hold talks with the Janata Dal (Secular) or its President and former Prime Minister, H.D. Deve Gowda, on forming an alternative Government in the State.

(2389) Belgaum : The State Government should lose no time in demanding an inquiry into Maharashtra Chief Minister Vilasrao Deshmukh's allegations holding Karnataka responsible for floods in that State, B.S. Yediyurappa, Leader of the Opposition in the Legislative Assembly, has said.

(2390) Davangere : Y. Nagappa, Minister for Social Welfare and Minister in-charge of Davangere district, said that Siddaramaiah, who was ousted from the post of Deputy Chief Minister and leader of the Janata Dal (Secular) legislature party, should not have organised the AHINDA conference and claimed that the backward classes, minorities and Dalits have been given "due credit" and representation in all fields. Speaking to presspersons at Harihar on Tuesday, Mr. Nagappa, who is from the same community as Mr. Siddaramaiah said that the latter is a wise person and should have thought of the consequences before organising the convention. Leaders from minorities, backward classes and Dalits are given prominence and the question of them being sidelined does not arise, he said.

(2391) Kottayam : The Kerala Congress (Secular), which held a State-level leadership camp on the development package announced by the President A. P. J. Abdul Kalam, has stressed the need to bring agriculture sector to the top of the development agenda of the State.

(2392) Palakkad : Communist Party of India (CPI) Legislature Party leader K.P. Rajendran has alleged that the State Government is delaying the filing of an appeal in the Supreme Court against the Kerala High Court order that allowed Coca-Cola to reopen its Plachimada unit.

(2393) New Delhi : The Election Commission on Tuesday reserved its orders on the plea of the former Chief Minister K. Karunakaran to register his new party as National Congress(Indira).

(2394) New Delhi : Accusing the Congress of continuously trying to appease Muslims, Bharatiya Janata Party president L K Advani on Tuesday said the latest step in this direction was giving reservation in jobs to the minority community in Congress-ruled States.

(2395) New Delhi : The Left parties on Tuesday demanded that the Manmohan Singh Government act on the specific recommendations of the Nanavati Commission, which went into the 1984 anti-Sikh riots, and also proceed against "certain persons" named in its report.

(2396) New Delhi : The Group of Ministers (GoM) charged with building a political consensus on women's reservation in legislatures carried forward the ongoing exercise on Monday and Tuesday meeting representatives of several political parties, including the Rashtriya Janata Dal, the Lok Jan Shakti Party, the Bahujan Samaj Party, the Dravida Munnetra Kazhagam and the All India Anna Dravida Munnetra Kazhagam.

(2397) New Delhi : A day after his party rejected the Opposition demand for the resignation of Union Minister Jagdish Tytler, the senior Congress leader from Delhi came under pressure to put in his papers. The Nanavati Commission found "credible evidence" against him in the 1984 anti-Sikh riots. Although there was no official word, Congress leaders in private admitted there was serious thinking, with a section in the party insisting that Mr. Tytler be asked to quit the Ministry. Party sources said its leaders broached the matter with him.

(2398) Jaipur : The Congress unleashed a major political offensive against the Bharatiya Janata Party-led Government in Rajasthan on Tuesday by holding a public rally in the State Capital. The party chose the anniversary of the Quit India Day for the move, in which speaker after speaker blamed the BJP Government for "all-pervasive lawlessness" and "all-round failure" in the State.

(2399) Deharadun : The Congress high command seems to have scotched all speculation about a change of guard in Uttaranchal by reappointing the PCC president, Harish Rawat, for a second term.

(2400) Chennai : The Bharatiya Janata Party will organise a week-long 'padayatra' from Madurai to Theni beginning July 23 to demand that Tamil Nadu be allowed to store water up to the full level of 152 feet in the Mullaperiyar dam.

(2401) Chennai : The Dravida Munnetra Kazhagam has demanded that the Election Commission take "immediate and appropriate action" against everyone responsible, including the All-India Anna Dravida Munnetra Kazhagam Ministers, for "stuffing of electoral rolls."

(2402) Chennai : The All India Anna Dravida Munnetra Kazhagam Government has not done anything worthwhile in the sectors of education, health, poverty eradication and augmentation of water sources in the last four years, the Pattali Makkal Katchi founder, S. Ramadoss, claimed here on Tuesday. He said the State's position in the four areas remained where it was four years ago. There were reports that even newly-formed States had performed better than Tamil Nadu in other sectors.

(2403) Chennai : Tamil Nadu Congress Committee president G.K. Vasan on Tuesday urged the Delimitation Commission to clear people's doubts on the ongoing delimitation process.

(2404) Madurai : The Department of Posts should not be privatised in the interest of the people and national security, the Communist Party of India (Marxist) MLA, N. Nanmaran, said on Tuesday.

11-08-2005

(2405) Guntur : The proposed reservation for the Muslims in the municipal elections will be to the disadvantage of other Backward Classes, as the seats will be cornered by Muslims, said the BJP district president Yedlapati Raghunath Babu.

(2406) Hyderabad :' The BJP will organise 'Chalo Hyderabad' programme with a rally at the Nizam College grounds here on August 18 demanding official celebration of 'Hyderabad Liberation Day' on September 17.

(2407) Hyderabad : The Congress Legislature Party (CLP) has ridiculed the Telugu Desam Party President, N. Chandrababu Naidu, for demanding that the Government bring down power tariff.

(2408) Hyderabad : A delegation of Telangana Rashtra Samithi (TRS) MLAs on Wednesday called on the Chief Minister, Y.S. Rajasekhara Reddy, and asked him to review the new excise policy.

(2409) Vizianagaram : Pradesh Congress Committee president K. Keshava Rao has refuted Opposition charges against Minister for Marketing Botcha Satyanarayana in the Volkswagen muddle at a largely attended 'Prajabheri' here on Wednesday evening.

(2410) Kakinada : The Telugu Desam Party (TDP) president and former Chief Minister N. Chandrababu Naidu has insisted on payment of "reasonable compensation" to farmers getting displaced under various irrigation projects, including the controversial Pushkara lift irrigation project.

(2411) New Delhi : The Delhi police resorted to water cannons and mild force on Wednesday to disperse a number of Akali Dal activists and victims of the 1984 massacre of the Sikhs who had gathered at Gurdwara Bangla Saheb and tried to march towards Parliament to protest against Centre's 'inaction' against the "guilty" as brought out by the Nanavati Commission report. Some protesters sustained minor injuries.

(2412) Bangalore : State Janata Dal (Secular) Vice-President C.M. Ibrahim has urged the JD(S) President H.D. Deve Gowda to resolve the differences with the former Deputy Chief Minister, Siddaramaiah.

(2413) Bangalore : The former Prime Minister and Janata Dal (Secular) President, H.D. Deve Gowda, on Wednesday held a meeting with the Congress President, Sonia Gandhi, on the political developments in the State in the aftermath of the removal of three Janata Dal (S) Ministers from the Cabinet and elevation of the Revenue Minister, M.P. Prakash, as the Deputy Chief Minister.

(2414) Mysore : The former Union Minister Murli Manohar Joshi has hinted at midterm elections to the Lok Sabha soon.

(2415) Mysore : A section of the Congress and the Janata Dal (Secular) leaders here have clarified that the struggle for the rights of backward classes, Dalits and minorities launched by AHIND is not aimed against the Vokkaliga community.

(2416) Alappuzha : The CPI(M) has been raising baseless allegations against Congress leaders with the aim of subverting the development agenda of the Oommen Chandy Government, the KPCC general secretary V.S. Sivakumar has said.

(2417) Kozhikode : President of the Kerala Pradesh Congress Committee (KPCC) Ramesh Chennithala who is now on his well-publicised Chaithanya yatra road campaign to whip up support for the UDF has dismissed as "panic reaction" the charges raised against him by the CPI(M) and the NC(I) leader K. Karunakaran.

(2418) New Delhi : The Bharatiya Janata Party on Wednesday demanded that Prime Minister Manmohan Singh "resign from the Congress" and "apologise to the nation" on behalf of his party for its involvement in the massacre of Sikhs in 1984.

(2419) Kolhapur : Five rivers - Koyana, Warana, Bhogavati, Doodhganga and Panchganga - that were in unprecedented spate and killed a dozen people and displaced thousands others and destroyed cane and soybean crops in thousands of hectares, have also sharpened differences between the Congress and NCP.

(2420) New Delhi : The Left parties on Wednesday joined the Opposition in demanding action against Jagdish Tytler, who has since resigned as Union Minister of State for Overseas Indians.

(2421) New Delhi : The Rajya Sabha was adjourned for the second consecutive day on Wednesday over the BJP-led Opposition demand for suspension of business and taking up a discussion under Rule 167 on the Nanavati Commission Report on the 1984 anti-Sikh riots and the Action Taken Report of the government. On a motion moved under Rule 167, in a matter of public interest, the decision of the House has to be made through vote, after discussion.

(2422) New Delhi : Union Minister of State for Science and Technology Kapil Sibal was on familiar turf when he rose to speak on Wednesday in the Lok Sabha during an adjournment motion on the Government's failure to act against persons indicted by the Nanavati Commission. All that was missing was the lawyer's robe. For, the lawyer-turned-politician chose to argue his case as per his first calling.

(2423) New Delhi : The Delhi Pradesh Bharatiya Janata Party has severely condemned attempts by the UPA Government at the Centre to protect those involved in the massacre of Sikhs in 1984 and demanded that Prime Minister Manmohan Singh and Union Home Minister Shivraj Patil resign immediately and the posts be handed to those who can secure justice for all the Sikhs. The demand emanated from a resolution adopted by the party unit in its monthly meeting held on Wednesday under the chairmanship of its president, Harsh Vardhan, who charged that the massacre was "Congress-sponsored".

(2424) Shimla : Uproarious scenes were witnessed in the Himachal Assembly on Wednesday when the Opposition BJP MLAs landed in the well of the House immediately after the question hour demanding a debate on corruption issue. They indulged in slogan shouting against some Ministers and demanded an inquiry into the alleged bungling in the selling of tickets during a musical programme conducted by the State Tourism Department.

(2425) Pondicherry : An all-party delegation, headed by the Leader of the Opposition in the Assembly, R.V. Janakiraman (DMK), met the Lt. Governor M.M. Lakhera, at Raj Nivas on Wednesday and presented a joint-memorandum to him seeking his intervention to relieve the students selected for admission to the private medical colleges here of their sufferings and mental agony.

(2426) Dehradun : There was widespread resentment in bureaucratic circles here on Wednesday after three ruling Congress MLAs allegedly damaged furniture following an altercation with the State Food Secretary, P. C. Sharma, in his office at the Uttaranchal Secretariat.

(2427) Chennai : Dravida Munnetra Kazhagam president M. Karunanidhi said on Wednesday that the former Prime Minister, A.B. Vajpayee's demand for the resignation of Prime Minister Manmohan Singh gave credence to the "widely held suspicion" that the Nanavati Commission was set up with "ulterior motives."

12-08-2005

(2428) Eluru : The TDP president, N. Chandrababu Naidu, on Friday demanded an explanation from the Government on its commitment towards minorities in the light of the Nanavati Commission's findings on attacks on Sikhs in Delhi after the assassination of the then prime minister, Indira Gandhi.

(2429) Eluru : TDP president N. Chandrababu Naidu on Friday sought to put up a secular face during his road show in West Godavari district.

(2430) Karimnagar : The Bharatiya Janata Party district unit alleged that the State Government was obstructing the police investigation into the bomb blast that took place in the RTC bus station complex on Tuesday for "obvious reasons".

(2431) Nalgonda : Telugu Desam activists led by the former municipal chairperson, Boyinapalli Krishna Reddy, "welcomed" the Chief Minister with slogans and banners when he went to Devarakonda road to inaugurate the works to be taken up with the Municipal and R&B funds.

(2432) Kakinada : The State Bharatiya Janata Party president N. Indrasena Reddy has lashed out at the Congress and the Telugu Desam for favouring reservations based on religion only to woo Muslim voters, unmindful of the consequences and its long ranging affect on the country.

(2433) Bangalore : President of the All-India Congress Committee and Chairman of the United Progressive Alliance Sonia Gandhi will visit the flood-affected Athani taluk of Belgaum District on Saturday. Prime Minister Manmohan Singh, who was to conduct an aerial survey of the flood-affected regions, has put off his visit.

(2434) Bangalore : The former Law Minister M.C. Nanaiah has held the former Prime Minister and Janata Dal (Secular) President H.D. Deve Gowda as being solely responsible for ouster of Siddaramaiah from the leadership of legislature party.

(2435) Bangalore : In a significant development, the Janata Dal (Secular) has virtually barred those of its members who have associated themselves with the Federation of Backward Classes, Dalits and Minorities from attending party meetings, without expelling them. They have been politely told that they are not welcome at a meeting of State office-bearers of the party to be held here on August 18. It will be attended by national party president H.D. Deve Gowda.

(2436) Belgaum : The former Prime Minister H.D. Deve Gowda has said that it is not fair for Maharashtra and Karnataka to blame each other for the floods in the two States.

(2437) Gulbarga : Leader of the Opposition in the Legislative Assembly B.S. Yediyurappa has urged the State Government to increase the compensation to be paid to farmers who lost their crops in floods to Rs. 10,000 an acre for sugarcane and Rs. 5,000 an acre for other crops.

(2438) Madikeri : The exit of Siddaramaiah from the Cabinet will have no impact on the affairs of the Kodagu Janata Dal (Secular), Kodagu unit president V.P. Aiyappa said here on Wednesday.

(2439) Mysore : The former Prime Minister and Janata Dal (Secular) President H.D. Deve Gowda is said to be keen on getting the former Union Minister V. Srinivas Prasad into the coalition Government in the State to bolster the party's prospects in Mysore region after the ouster of Siddaramaiah and H.C. Mahadevappa from the Council of Ministers.

(2440) Chitradurga : Former Deputy Chief Minister Siddaramaiah has hinted that he will take a decision about his future course of action only after getting the feedback from his supporters throughout the State.

(2441) Kochi : The general secretary of the National Congress(Indira) N. Venugopal has condemned the statement made on Wednesday by KPCC president Ramesh Chennithala denouncing K. Karunakaran.

(2442) Thiruvananthapuram : The Congress (S) MLA V C Kabeer on Thursday submitted his resignation from the State Assembly in preparation to his joining the Congress.

(2443) New Delhi : The Bharatiya Janata Party on Thursday welcomed the Election Commission's directive to delete from the electoral rolls the names of all persons against whom there were non-bailable warrants for at least six months. The BJP said the Prime Minister should convene an all-party meeting to consider legislation to prevent those chargesheeted in criminal offences from contesting elections.

(2444) New Delhi : Railway Minister Lalu Prasad had to apologise twice to Speaker Somnath Chatterjee in the Lok Sabha on Thursday as Rashtriya Janata Dal (RJD) members drew his wrath by challenging the Chair's ruling.

(2445) New Delhi : The allies of the Bharatiya Janata Party have begun demanding the resignation of Gujarat Chief Minister Narendra Modi sensing that the Congress would claim the high moral ground after the slew of "actions" it has taken in the wake of the Nanavati Commission debate in Parliament on the 1984 anti-Sikh riots.

(2446) New Delhi : The BJP-led Opposition parties on Thursday kept up pressure on the Manmohan Singh Government to immediately prosecute all those named by the Nanavati Commission on 1984 anti-Sikh riots and sought an assurance that any person involved would not be "rewarded" with political or diplomatic rehabilitation.

(2447) New Delhi : The Rajya Sabha on Thursday witnessed a flutter over a remark by BJP leader Rajnath Singh that riots can be checked within a few hours if the Chief Minister of a State is determined, provoking ruling coalition to attack him on what had happened in Gujarat under Narendra Modi.

(2448) New Delhi : Close on the heels of the former Union Minister for NRI Affairs, Jagdish Tytler, putting in his papers on Wednesday night, the Outer Delhi Member of Parliament, Sajjan Kumar, stepped down from a government post.

(2449) Srinagar : The ruling People's Democratic Party (PDP) on Thursday asked Pakistan to stop sending militants to Jammu and Kashmir if it "claims to be a well-wisher of Kashmiris."

(2450) New Delhi : The BJP Delhi Pradesh Industry Cell held a protest demonstration near Delhi Secretariat on Thursday and demanded that the Chief Minister, Sheila Dikshit, and the Industry Minister, Mangat Ram Singhal, take immediate steps to declare as industrial areas all those residential areas where industrial activity was going on in over 70 per cent of the dwelling units.

(2451) New Delhi : Warning that the poor power situation in the Capital and growing public resentment over "indifferent" functioning of the private distribution companies could cost the Congress party dearly, nearly two dozen Congress MLAs on Thursday urged the Chief Minister, Sheila Dikshit, to take effective steps to set right the situation or risk facing the wrath of harassed citizens.

(2452) Shimla : In an unusual form of protest in Himachal Assembly, the entire Opposition on Thursday staged a silent protest by squatting in the well of the House with their mouths covered with cloth. In continuation of their demand for discussion on corruption and law and order situation in the State, the BJP legislators moved to the well of the House without disturbing the proceedings.

(2453) Pondicherry : Former Chief Minister and senior Congress leader, P. Shanmugham, took charge on Thursday as president of the Pondicherry Pradesh Congress Committee following his appointment to the post by the all India Congress Committee on August 4. The 78-year-old Shanmugham replaces V. Narayanasamy, MP as president of the party.

(2454) Lucknow : Annoyed with the delaying tactics of the BSP, Uttar Pradesh Assembly Speaker Mata Prasad Pandey has set a deadline of 12 noon on Friday to the party to file written objections on commencing of the case related to defection of 13 former BSP MLAs to the ruling Samajwadi Party.

(2455) Chennai : Dravida Munnetra Kazhagam president M. Karunanidhi on Thursday said that even if it were conceded that Union Minister Jagdish Tytler resigned because of the compelling circumstances, he was better than many "insensitive persons" who were sticking to power despite being indicted by Commissions of enquiry.

13-08-2005

(2456) Cuddapah : The Telugu Desam Party president, N. Chandrababu Naidu, is proposing a third front to further his political goals and not in public interest, the CPI(M) State Committee member, G. Ramulu, said on Friday.

(2457) Eluru : The Telugu Desam Party president, N. Chandrababu Naidu, on Friday favoured emergence of a confederation of all regional parties at the national level as an alternative to the ruling United Progressive Alliance and the opposition National Democratic Alliance, both led by national parties.

(2458) Tirupati : The CPI(M) Polit Bureau member and its State general secretary, B.V. Raghavulu, has said that barring a general statement sometime ago about its intention to have an understanding with Left parties for the coming civic elections, neither the Pradesh Congress Committee nor the Congress Legislature Party has come up with any specific proposal.

(2459) Vijayawada : TDP president N. Chandrababu Naidu conducted a whirlwind roadshow in Krishna district on Friday, when he kicked off the party's campaign for the coming municipal elections. Flaying the Congress for turning "anti-people" after coming to power, Mr. Naidu appealed to the people to defeat the "corrupt Congress" in the civic elections.

(2460) Vijayawada : Alleging that there is large-scale corruption in irrigation projects, TDP president and former Chief Minister N. Chandrababu Naidu has deplored that even Sonia Gandhi is not bothered it.

(2461) Warangal : Congress and Telugu Desam Party (TDP) leaders are trying to woo Muslims in the name of reservations only for their political gains, said Bharatiya Janata Party (BJP) MLA G. Kishan Reddy.

(2462) Hyderabad : Some of the smaller regional parties supporting the United Progressive Alliance (UPA) Government at the Centre have shown interest in joining hands with the Telugu Desam-led grouping.

(2463) Kolkata : How does Gujarat Chief Minister Narendra Modi continue in office after the mass killings in Godhra for which he and his Government are responsible, Jyoti Basu, CPI(M) leader, asked on Friday. "We are satisfied with the resignation of Jagdish Tytler (in the wake of the Nanavati Commission report on the 1984 anti-Sikh riots), but how does Modi continue in office?" The Polit Bureau would decide on the party's demand on Mr. Modi, Mr. Basu said here.

(2464) New Delhi : The Central Government on Friday concluded its consultations on a Bill to provide reservation for women in legislatures with a meeting between Home Minister Shivraj Patil and women Members of Parliament from across the spectrum of political parties.

(2465) Bidar : Leader of the Opposition in the Legislative Assembly B.S. Yediyurappa criticised the Congress and the Janata Dal (Secular) of providing an insensitive, inefficient Government.

(2466) Bijapur : The districts units of the Janata Dal (Secular) in Bijapur and Bagalkot have expressed full confidence in the leadership of the former Prime Minister H.D. Deve Gowda.

(2467) Mangalore : The Bharatiya Janata Party Mangalore city unit has moved the High Court of Karnataka against the election of Mayor K. Ashraf.

(2468) Kolar : A section of Congress leaders inimical to the former Prime Minister H.D. Deve Gowda and those who were also associated with the AHIND movement on Friday used the Kolar district convention of the party to express their anger against the coalition Government in the State.

(2469) Alappuzha : National Congress (Indira) State vice-president D. Sugathan has demanded that Kerala Pradesh Congress Committee president Ramesh Chennithala withdraw his statement calling the former Chief Minister K. Karunakaran a 'Shikhandi' (eunuch) and apologise to him in a day, or face the consequences.

(2470) Malappuram : Kerala Pradesh Congress Committee (KPCC) president Ramesh Chennithala has said the Congress will enter into a dialogue with other political parties to arrive at a long-term understanding on matters of development.

(2471) Lucknow : Uttar Pradesh Assembly Speaker Mata Prasad Pandey on Friday pronounced that the June 15 application of two Samajwadi Party MLAs were maintainable for commencing the hearing in the case related to defection of 13 former BSP MLAs to the ruling SP.

(2472) Chennai : The Communist Party of India (Marxist) will continue its ties with "friendly parties" in the State to ensure the defeat of the All-India Anna Dravida Munnetra Kazhagam (AIADMK) in the next Assembly elections, the State CPI(M) secretary, N. Varadarajan, said here on Friday.

(2473) Chennai : Dravida Munnetra Kazhagam president M. Karunanidhi has written to Prime Minister Manmohan Singh requesting him to adopt the report of the Parliamentary Standing Committee on the Reservation Bill, 2004 "without any dilution."

(2474) Chennai : "The Congress high command is for continuing the existing Democratic Progressive Alliance in the State for the next Assembly election as the objective is to defeat the All-India Anna Dravida Munnetra Kazhagam Government," G.K. Vasan, the Pradesh Congress Committee president, said here on Friday.

(2475) Chennai : The Democratic Progressive Alliance (DPA) will always support the cause of Telugu-speaking people, Dravida Munnetra Kazhagam deputy general secretary M.K. Stalin has said.

14-08-2005

(2476) Karimnagar : The MIM will not forge alliance with any political party in the forthcoming municipal elections and contest all seats independently and expand its base in the State, said the Hyderabad MP and MIM leader, Asaduddin Owaisi, here on Saturday.

(2477) Vijayawada : It was a day of endless wait for TDP urban unit leaders on Friday. Even followers and sympathisers of TDP had to wait late into the night to hear their party president and former Chief Minister N. Chandrababu Naidu.

(2478) Hyderabad : The former Chief Minister and Telugu Desam president, N. Chandrababu Naidu, has deplored the Supreme Court judgment abolishing reservations in private colleges. He has urged the Prime Minister, Manmohan Singh, to convene an all-party meeting to discuss as to how the reservation policy in these institutions can be restored.

(2479) Hyderabad : The former Chief Minister and Telugu Desam president, N. Chandrababu Naidu, has deplored the Supreme Court judgment abolishing reservations in private colleges.

(2480) New Delhi : Accusing the Delhi Government and the Delhi Jal Board of succumbing to pressure from the World Bank and taking up privatisation of the Capital's water resources and water distribution, the National Council of the Communist Party of India has demanded a rollback of the move and threatened to release documents about the "secret deal" if the issue is not addressed urgently.

(2481) Chennai : The Democratic Progressive Alliance (DPA), led by the Dravida Munnetra Kazhagam, on Saturday urged the Centre to bring forward "suitable amendments to law" to ensure continuance of the present reservation system for self-financing professional colleges in the private sector.

(2482) Belgaum : President of the All-India Congress Committee and Chairperson of the United Progressive Alliance Sonia Gandhi has promised that adequate relief will be provided to the States that have been affected by heavy rainfall and floods.

(2483) Gulbarga : Congress leaders at a party workers' rally in Gulbarga on Saturday hinted at an imminent mid-term election.

(2484) Mangalore : The Communist Party of India Marxists (CPI-M) will launch a ten-day nationwide "food, land and employment campaign" from September 9. The rally will be held along the coastal zone and will culminate in Mangalore on September 19.

(2485) Mysore : In a significant development, senior Congress leaders and supporters of the former Deputy Chief Minister, Siddaramaiah, separately met the former Union Minister, V. Srinivas Prasad, at his residence here on Saturday evening, in an apparent effort to prevent Mr. Prasad from joining the Dharam Singh-led coalition Government in Karnataka as a Janata Dal (Secular) Minister.

(2486) Raichur : Leader of the Opposition in the Legislative Assembly B.S. Yediyurappa has said that the Bharatiya Janata Party will resort to agitations if the Government fails to pay adequate compensation for loss of crops and property in the flood-hit areas in north Karnataka.

(2487) Shimoga : Leader of the Opposition in the Legislative Council D.H. Shankaramurthy said here on Saturday that the Government should file a review petition in the Supreme Court challenging its ruling quashing the allocation of seats in private colleges to the Government.

(2488) Kozhikode : Responding quickly to complaints from its supporters in foreign countries, senior leaders of the Indian Union Muslim League (IUML) have decided to stage demonstrations to press for cheaper facilities for international journeys.

(2489) Palakkad : Kerala Pradesh Congress Committee (KPCC) president Ramesh Chennithala has said that a leadership meeting of the party has been convened in Muvattupuzha on August 17 to discuss the issue regarding the Supreme Court verdict on unaided private colleges.

(2490) Palakkad : The former AICC general secretary Vayalar Ravi, MP, has said that the "Judiciary cannot go beyond the purview of the Constitution. They can interpret the law but cannot become the law-makers."

(2491) Thiruvananthapuram : State secretary of the Communist Party of India (Marxist) Pinarayi Vijayan has said that the United Democratic Front Government, which could not do anything worthwhile for the development of the State and had wasted the last four years of its tenure, is incapable of implementing the President's proposals for helping the State progress.

(2492) Thiruvananthapuram : Congress Working Committee (CWC) member and the former Chief Minister of Kerala A.K. Antony said the Supreme Court verdict on self-financing professional colleges did not take into consideration the social reality prevailing in Kerala's education sector.

(2493) Thiruvananthapuram : National Congress (Indira) district general secretary Thampanoor Satish has warned Kerala Pradesh Congress Committee president Ramesh Chennithala against deriding the former Chief Minister K. Karunakaran and NC(I) K. Muraleedharan.

(2494) Thiruvananthapuram : The former Union Minister and BJP leader O. Rajagopal on Saturday urged the Union Government to enact a new legislation during the current session of Parliament to address the social issues involved in the verdict of the Supreme Court on self-financing colleges.

(2495) Malappuram : A brief meeting Chief Minister Oommen Chandy had with Indian Union Muslim League (IUML) State president Syed Mohammedali Shihab Thangal at the latter's Kodappanakkal house at Panakkad near here on Friday has sparked off speculations about the Muslim League's stand on implementing the Narendran Commission report.

(2496) Chennai : Tamil Nadu Chief Minister Jayalalithaa has strongly condemned the assassination of the Sri Lankan Foreign Minister, Lakshman Kadirgamar.

(2497) New Delhi : The Left parties on Saturday said the United Progressive Alliance Government should bring forth a legislation to ensure that private professional educational institutions conformed to certain norms concerning admission, with the Communist Party of India describing the Supreme Court judgment on the autonomy of such institutions as "retrograde."

(2498) New Delhi : The Polit Bureau of the Communist Party of India (Marxist) has condemned the assassination of Lakshman Kadirgamar. Describing him as a "champion of ethnic harmony," the CPI(M) said Mr. Kadirgamar strove tirelessly for establishing peace in Sri Lanka. "He was a vigorous campaigner for the betterment of relations between Sri Lanka and India. A distinguished statesman, Kadirgamar was known for his benevolence and warmth."

(2499) New Delhi : Unhappy with the priorities of the United Progressive Alliance Government, the Communist Party of India on Saturday announced it would observe an all-India "implementation of CMP" day. At the end of its three-day National Council meeting, party general secretary A.B. Bardhan said the UPA Government should implement the priorities laid down in the Common Minimum Programme. The National Rural Employment Guarantee Bill should be introduced and passed after removing the "dilution".

(2500) Ludhiana : The National Democratic Alliance (NDA) will not seek the resignation of Prime Minister Manmohan Singh over the 1984 anti-Sikh riots as it will be "stretching it a little too far," NDA convener George Fernandes has said.

(2501) Mumbai : UPA chairperson and Congress president, Sonia Gandhi on Saturday visited the deluge and disease-hit parts of Mumbai and also the flood-affected villages of Kolhapur and Sangli districts of Maharashtra and Athani in neighbouring Karntaka.

(2502) New Delhi : Social activists, academicians and political leaders on Saturday asked the Government to ensure that the rights of workers are properly safeguarded particularly under the changing economic scenario when multinational companies are setting up shops in India. They also denounced a section of media for calling hapless Honda workers as lumpens and rioters, and said that they were mere workers fighting for their rights and opposing exploitation.

(2503) Chennai : Even while calling for a legislation at the national level to ensure social justice for the poor and continuation of the government quota in unaided higher educational institutions, PMK founder leader S. Ramadoss on Saturday urged democratic and political organisations to start a major struggle to bring back the benefits students enjoyed earlier.

15-08-2005

(2504) Guntur : The TDP president, N.Chandrababu Naidu, asking the Government to reduce power tariff is a perfect example of double standard, said the Andhra Pradesh Congress Committee vice-president, Mohammad Jani. He told reporters here on Sunday that the current situation in the power sector was a result of the previous Government's hasty decisions to please the World Bank. The Andhra Pradesh State Electricity Board (APSEB), which was a pioneer in electricity generation and a model organisation for other States, was destroyed as a result of the TDP Government's policies, he alleged.

(2505) Hyderabad : Varavara Rao, former CPI (Maoist) emissary, has asked the Government to declare a ceasefire and create an atmosphere conducive for resumption of talks.

(2506) Hyderabad : The Republican Party of India, Andhra Pradesh Backward Classes Welfare Association and State committee of Students' Federation of India have demanded passing of a separate legislation by Parliament to tide over the crisis arising out of the Supreme Court ruling. Three RPI leaders, M.V.Suryanarayana, vice-president, and G. Gnaneshwar and B.Suresh Kumar, general secretaries, in a statement issued here on Sunday said the judgment was against the Constitution. They demanded a constitutional amendment to restore the quota to students belonging to weaker sections.

(2507) Hyderabad : Union Minister of State for Rural Development A. Narendra on Sunday took up with the Chief Minister Y.S. Rajasekhara Reddy, the "injustice" to police officers of Telangana in the implementation of GO 610.

(2508) Hyderabad : Communist Party of India (CPI) State secretary K. Narayana on Sunday said there was no proposal yet from the Congress on a possible tie-up with it in the coming municipal elections.

(2509) Hyderabad : The Telugu Desam Party has urged the Governor to reconsider the decision to grant mercy for Congress leader G. Venkata Reddy, who was serving life-term in connection with a murder case.

(2510) Mancherial (Adilabad Dt.) : State Government representatives were hard put to defend the allegation made by the Bharatiya Janata Party (BJP) regarding 'manipulation' of figures relating to the ayacut of the Rallivagu medium irrigation project in Adilabad district.

(2511) Bangalore : The relationship between the Congress and the Janata Dal (Secular) has changed for the better in recent days, particularly after the last three meetings between Congress president Sonia Gandhi and Janata Dal (Secular) president H.D. Deve Gowda.

(2512) Belgaum : Janata Dal (Secular) district unit president Ashok Pujari said on Sunday that the party is prepared to test its strength among the backward classes, Dalits and minorities and propose to the State leadership to convene a conference of these sections in Hubli.

(2513) Gulbarga : Karnataka Pradesh Congress Committee President M. Mallikarjun Kharge has appealed to people to vote the party to power in the next Assembly elections. Speaking at a party rally in Gulbarga on Saturday, he said comprehensive development of the State is possible only if the ruling party has a clear majority in the Assembly. "We were forced to go enter a coalition as the result of the previous Assembly elections was not in favour of a particular party. Let us hope this is not repeated next time and the Congress gets a clear majority," he said.

(2514) Mysore : Even as M. Rajasekhara Murthy, Bharatiya Janata Party MP, arrived here on Sunday to meet the former Union Minister V. Srinivas Prasad and jointly announce their plans, the Congress began, albeit belatedly, to woo the two veteran leaders.

(2515) Kochi : Leader of the Opposition V.S. Achuthanandan has said that the United Democratic Front (UDF) Government is trying to protect the culprits in the controversial SNC Lavalin deal.

(2516) Thiruvananthapuram : Revolutionary Socialist Party (RSP) State secretary T.J. Chandrachoodan has accused the United Democratic Front Government of having diverted a substantial portion of the tsunami funds to meet its political ends with an eye on the upcoming local body elections.

(2517) Malappuram : National Congress (Indira) leader K. Muraleedharan has accused the Indian Union Muslim League (IUML) of playing hide-and-seek in the matter of Narendran Commission report.

(2518) New Delhi : Accusing the Sheila Dikshit Government of delaying the issuing of a notification for declaring 14 residential areas having more than 70 per cent industry as industrial clusters, the Delhi Pradesh Congress Committee president, Ram Babu Sharma on Saturday decried the delay and sought immediate action on the issue as it was causing anxiety and concern among the lakhs of workers and unit holders.

(2519) New Delhi : Blaming the Delhi Government for the poor power situation in the Capital and harassment of lakhs of consumers, former Union Minister Vijay Goel on Sunday demanded that the Central Vigilance Commission probe the privatisation of the power sector in Delhi so that people get to know the truth about why the State Government sold the public utility at a throw away price.

(2520) Pondicherry : The Pattali Makkal Katchi parliamentary party leader, M. Ramadass, convened a meeting here on Sunday with leaders of political parties, representatives of the State Women's Commission, voluntary organisations and women's fora to seek their views on the proposed Bill on reservation for women in legislatures and Parliament.

(2521) Lucknow : The BJP on Sunday lashed out at the Samajwadi Party Government for pushing Uttar Pradesh into an unprecedented power crisis, owing to privatisation of power sector and growing corruption in the bureaucracy.

(2522) Chennai : DMK president M. Karunanidhi, general secretary K. Anbazhagan, and other State-level functionaries on Sunday briefed party speakers on issues to be highlighted at public meetings in the prevailing political scenario in the State and at the national level.

(2523) Vellore : The Pattali Makkal Katchi will launch an agitation if the Tamil Nadu Government does not withdraw the ban on recruitment, party founder S. Ramadoss said here on Sunday.

(2524) Pondicherry : Congress MP V. Narayanasamy on Sunday urged the high command to take action against a section of party legislators and workers who, he alleged, transgressed the limits of discipline by resorting to a series of demonstrations and issuing press statements against him during his tenure as president of the party's Pondicherry unit.

16-08-2005

(2525) Hyderabad : Andhra Pradesh Congress Committee president K. Keshava Rao has decried the Supreme Court judgment against reservations in private and unaided colleges and urged the Government to take its legal fight against it to the logical end.

(2526) Hyderabad : Bharatiya Janata Party State president N. Indrasena Reddy has called for opposing religion-based reservations and the parties, which are supporting them.

(2527) Hyderabad : Political parties across the spectrum expressed shock at the gunning down of the Congress MLA from Makthal, C. Narsi Reddy and eight others. Stunned Congress party leaders described it as a "dastardly act."

(2528) Hyderabad : The Telugu Desam Party president, N. Chandrababu Naidu, on Monday went into introspection mode wondering if the fruits of development achieved during the 58 years of independence had reached all sections of people.

(2529) Bangalore : Top leaders of the Bharatiya Janata Party (BJP), Rashtriya Swayamsevak Sangh (RSS) and organisations affiliated to the sangh on Monday paid homage to H.V. Seshadri, leader and thinker of the RSS, who died here on Sunday.

(2530) Kozhikode : The Narendran panel recommendations continue to be a worrying factor for the Indian Union Muslim League (IUML) leadership as it begins preparing the ground for elections to local bodies.

(2531) New Delhi : Underlining the need for a comprehensive model law to tackle communal violence, the Communist Party of India (Marxist) has suggested that the Centre should take the initiative and consult all States on this.

(2532) Dehra Dun : A number of ruling Congress MLAs including the Food and Civil Supplies Minister, Pritam Singh, on Monday urged the Chief Minister, Narayan Dutt Tiwari, to suspend the Food and Civil Supplies Secretary, P. C. Sharma, for having allegedly used 'casteist' words against the party MLA, Pradeep Tamta. Mr Tamta has filed an FIR under the SC/ ST Act against Mr Sharma and his staff.

17-08-2005

(2533) Hyderabad : Even as talk on re-imposition of ban on Maoists gains momentum, AICC general secretary and Andhra Pradesh in-charge

Digvijay Singh has said that the party has left it for the State Government to take a decision on the issue.

(2534) Bangalore : Minister for Rural Water Supply B. Sathyanarayana has said the former Deputy Chief Minister Siddaramaiah will be expelled from the Janata Dal (Secular) if he continues to level allegations against national party president H.D. Deve Gowda.

(2535) Bangalore : Following Karnataka Pradesh Congress Committee (KPCC) President M. Mallikarjun Kharge's "no" to the proposed China jaunt to be undertaken by a team of corporators of the Bangalore Mahanagara Palike (BMP), the Congress members are planning to persuade him to permit them to take up the tour.

(2536) Kottayam : The Kerala Congress(Jacob) leader Johnny Nellore on Tuesday said that T.M. Jacob would function as the Legislature Party leader of the National Congress(Indira) in the Assembly after the merger of the two parties scheduled for August 21 at Kollam. Mr. Nellore would be the deputy leader.

(2537) Thiruvananthapuram : The National Congress (Indira) is gearing up for the local bodies elections. The party has convened three regional seminars to discuss its strategies for the elections from Thursday onwards.

(2538) New Delhi : Ahead of the introduction decision of the United Progressive Alliance Government to introduce the National Rural Employment Guarantee Bill in the Lok Sabha on Thursday, the Left parties have urged the Centre to make some changes in it to further strengthen the social security measure.

(2539) Gandhinagar : In an apparent show of strength, dissidents in the Gujarat unit of the Bharatiya Janata Party assembled at the residence of the former Chief Minister, Keshubhai Patel, here on Tuesday ostensibly to "enquire" about his wife's health.

(2540) Mumbai : Shiv Sena chief Bal Thackeray and other leaders are trying to settle differences between the supremo's son and party executive president Uddhav Thackeray and his cousin and party leader Raj Thackeray.

(2541) New Delhi : Underlining the need for a comprehensive model law to tackle communal violence, the Communist Party of India (Marxist) has suggested that the Centre should take the initiative and consult all States on this.

18-07-2005

(2542) Guntur : The Backward Class enumeration list is full of irregularities and has been done in an arbitrary manner, alleged the Bharatiya Janata Party (BJP) Guntur urban unit president, Devarajan Kidambi.

(2543) Hyderabad : The State CPI(M) and the CPI on Wednesday opposed the re-imposition of ban on the Maoists saying it was a useless step while the Telugu Desam saw in the move confusion in the Government's stand.

(2544) Hyderabad : In a bid to mount pressure on the State Government to officially organise the Hyderabad Liberation Day celebrations on September 17, the Bharatiya Janata Party city unit is organising a public meeting here on Thursday.

(2545) Hyderabad : The Telugu Desam Legislature Party (TDLP) on Wednesday expressed surprise at the way the Central Bureau of Investigation has arrested only Ashok Jain and left others in the "Volkswagen scam".

(2546) Hyderabad : The Communist Party of India (Marxist) State committee has cautioned the Government against taking structural adjustment loan from the World Bank, saying it is "ridden with conditionalities harmful to people."

(2547) Khammam : The Telugu Desam Party chief, N. Chandrababu Naidu, was given a rousing welcome as he entered the town at 7.30 pm - five hours behind schedule on Wednesday. The road show was greeted by unprecedented turnout of crowds all the way. People came in large numbers on to the poorly lit streets as he reached the Nayabazar college centre with a convoy of about 400 cars and jeeps.

(2548) Nellore : The Polit Bureau member of the Telugu Desam Party and Rajya Sabha member, Lal Jaan Basha, has appealed to the people to "introspect" the performance of Congress and TDP in the State and realise as to who safeguarded the minorities.

(2549) Bangalore : A.K. Antony, All-India Congress Committee General Secretary in-charge of the State, has ruled out midterm elections in the State and echoed Janata Dal (Secular) President H.D. Deve Gowda by stating that the Congress too is equally committed to the smooth running of the coalition Government. Mr. Gowda had said that his party will not disturb the coalition set-up.

(2550) New Delhi : Union Minister and Telangana Rashtra Samiti president, K. Chandrasekhara Rao, deplored the decision of the Andhra Pradesh Government to re-impose ban on naxalites and demanded that it be revoked immediately. Reacting to the State Government's decision, the Union Minister said the move was not good since it would give scope for violation of human rights. "It will be in the interest of society, people and the Government to lift the ban and restart talks," Mr. Rao said here on Wednesday.

(2551) New Delhi : Members of Parliament belonging to the Democratic Progressive Alliance in Tamil Nadu on Wednesday presented a memorandum to Prime Minister Manmohan Singh demanding a Central legislation to provide reservation for Scheduled Castes, Scheduled Tribes and other Most Backward Classes in unaided higher educational institutions.

(2552) New Delhi : A number of the Bharatiya Janata Party's MPs from Gujarat who are against Narendra Modi continuing as Chief Minister have begun blaming the current general secretary in-charge of Gujarat affairs, Om Prakash Mathur, for dissatisfaction among the party MLAs as well as a majority of the State MPs with the Modi government.

(2553) Mumbai : Shiv Sena executive president Uddhav Thackeray and his cousin Raj Thackeray patched up after a meeting with party chief Bal Thackeray and other leaders here on Wednesday. There have been hectic efforts since Tuesday to end the crisis in the Shiv Sena which arose after Mr. Raj made comments on the party leadership.

(2554) Bangalore : In the wake of the Supreme Court's decision against imposing reservation on private professional education institutions, both the Union and State governments must evolve legislation to ensure socio-economic equity, especially for students coming under the 34 categories of reservation, the Janata Dal (United) has demanded.

(2555) Bangalore : Minority and Dalit leaders warned AHIND leaders, particularly the former Union Minister C.M. Ibrahim and the former Deputy

Chief Minister Siddaramaiah at a convention organised at the Janata Dal (S) office here on Wednesday that the people would not tolerate any more insulting remarks against the former Prime Minister H.D. Deve Gowda who was responsible for their rise in public life.

(2556) Bangalore : Charging that the Government had totally failed in tackling the flood situation and providing relief to the people, the Bharatiya Janata Party announced here on Wednesday that it would launch an indefinite dharna from August 22 in Belgaum demanding speedy relief works in the affected areas.

(2557) Bijapur : S. Bangarappa, former Chief Minister, on Wednesday demanded that crop loans taken by those affected by floods be waived.

(2558) Davangere : Siddaramaiah, former Deputy Chief Minister, has taken exception to the recent verdict of the Supreme Court that there can be no quota and reservation in private unaided professional colleges. He has called upon the Union Government to bring in legislation providing for reservation in such colleges.

(2559) Kochi : Members of Parliament from the State have failed to pressure the Centre to include the Kerala Self-Financing College Act in the Ninth Schedule of the Constitution, Kerala Pradesh Congress Committee (KPCC) president Ramesh Chennithala has said.

(2560) Thiruvananthapuram : The Kerala Congress faction led by R. Balakrishna Pillai has decided to fight the upcoming local body elections on Janata Dal (Secular) symbol. A decision to this effect was arrived at discussions between Mr. Pillai and JD(S) State president M. P. Veerendrakumar here on Wednesday. The decision is subject to approval by the Left Democratic Front (LDF) leadership.

(2561) Panur : The Indian Union Muslim League (IUML) has claimed credit for the sanctioning of various developmental activities in the Pannyannur grama panchayat area here.

(2562) New Delhi : The Left parties on Wednesday urged the Centre to bring in legislation during the winter session of Parliament to ensure reservation in unaided professional colleges, in the wake of the August 12 Supreme Court order.

(2563) Chennai : Janata Party president Subramanian Swamy said on Wednesday that those responsible for the assassination of Sri Lankan

Foreign Minister Laxman Kadirgamar should be brought to justice by resolve and without ambivalence. The retaliation must be "in a language that terrorists understand," he said in a statement.

(2564) New Delhi : A number of the Bharatiya Janata Party's MPs from Gujarat who are against Narendra Modi continuing as Chief Minister have begun blaming the current general secretary in-charge of Gujarat affairs, Om Prakash Mathur, for dissatisfaction among the party MLAs as well as a majority of the State MPs with the Modi government.

(2565) New Delhi : The decks have been cleared for the introduction of the much-awaited National Rural Employment Guarantee Bill on Thursday. The Lok Sabha will take it up for consideration and passage, amid clear indications of support across the political spectrum for the social security measure.

(2566) New Delhi : Pointing a finger at Congress leaders in the Municipal Corporation of Delhi, the Bharatiya Janata Party on Wednesday alleged bungling amounting to Rs.17crores in purchase of school uniforms for nearly 9 lakh children studying in primary schools of the civic body.

(2567) Gandhinagar : In an apparent show of strength, dissidents in the Gujarat unit of the Bharatiya Janata Party assembled at the residence of the former Chief Minister, Keshubhai Patel, here on Tuesday ostensibly to "enquire" about his wife's health.

(2568) Pondicherry : The Karaikal-based Cauvery Delta Farmers Legal Action Committee has urged the Territorial Administration to pay an incentive of Rs. 750 for each bag of paddy procured from farmers in Karaikal area.

(2569) Pondicherry : Founder of the Puduchery Munnetra Congress P. Kannan has called for Central legislation to protect students belonging to the weaker sections of society and enable them to get admission into privately-run professional colleges.

(2570) Pondicherry : A meeting of coordination committee of all political parties held here on Wednesday urged the Centre to enact legislation to ensure quota for students of Scheduled Castes, Scheduled Tribes, Backward Classes and other weaker sections in privately-managed professional colleges .

(2571) Vellore Preparations : for the Dravida Munnetra Kazhagam's Vellore zonal conference slated for August 27 and 28 are going on in full swing under the supervision of Durai Murugan, Principal Secretary of the party.

19-08-2005

(2572) Cuddapah : The CPI State Secretariat member, T. Lakshminarayana, on Thursday demanded that the Central and State Governments tackle naxalism as a political and socio-economic problem.

(2573) Hyderabad : Several top leaders of the Bharatiya Janata Party (BJP) and about 4,000 activists were arrested by the city police here on Thursday when they attempted to storm the Secretariat wanting the State Government to officially organise the Hyderabad Liberation Day celebrations on September 17.

(2574) Hyderabad : Representatives of recognised political parties on Thursday urged the State Election Commission (SEC) to ensure that elections to chairperson posts of municipalities and corporations be held immediately after the election of ward members.

(2575) Karimnagar : The Telangana Rashtra Samithi district unit has refuted the allegations levelled by Congress leaders that the Telangana Jagarana Sena (TJS) is reportedly involved in destruction of plaques of various development works taken up by the Minister for Sports, M Satyanarayana Rao.

(2576) Kurnool : The State Secretariat member of CPI and convener of Minority cell, Aziz Pasha, advocated literacy among Muslim for eradication of poverty.

(2577) Thiruvananthapuram : Leader of the Opposition V. S. Achuthanandan has taken strong exception to Chief Minister Oommen Chandy's stand that he had no knowledge about the Justice V. Bhaskaran Nambiar Commission report on the Brahmapuram deal.

(2578) Bangalore : The virtual bar imposed by the Congress on its members attending the conventions of backward classes, minorities and Dalits has placed the leaders who were till now active in organising them, in a quandary.

(2579) Bangalore : The Janata Dal (Secular) in the background of the removal of Siddaramaiah, H.C. Mahadevappa and Satish Jharkiholi from the Ministry on Thursday expressed solidarity with the former Prime Minister and President of the party, H.D. Deve Gowda, with all the leaders and legislators vouching that they would stand by their leader.

(2580) Bijapur : The former Chief Minister S. Bangarappa on Thursday urged the Union Government to ensure that the State Governments strictly adhere to the Central Water Commission norms on impounding water in dams.

(2581) Bijapur : The President of the State unit of the Samajwadi Party S. Bangarappa on Thursday said he saw no threat to his party from the movement launched by former Deputy Chief Minister Siddaramaiah under the banner of Alpasankhyataru, Hindulidavaru mathu Dalitaru (AHIND).

(2582) Bangalore : A crucial meeting of the office-bearers of the Janata Dal (Secular) Karnataka State unit here on Thursday unanimously passed a resolution authorising national party president H.D. Deve Gowda to initiate disciplinary action against the former Deputy Chief Minister Siddaramaiah, two former Ministers H.C. Mahadevappa and Satish Jarkiholi and several legislators. Mr. Siddaramaiah and the others have been accused of anti-party activities.

(2583) Davangere : The former Deputy Chief Minister Siddaramaiah said on Wednesday that Mahima Patel, Chennagiri MLA and secretary general of the Janata Dal (Secular) will leave the camp of former Prime Minister and Janata Dal (S) leader H.D. Deve Gowda and join his faction.

(2584) Jog Falls (Shimoga District) : Chief Minister N. Dharam Singh said here on Thursday that what the All-India Congress Committee general secretary A.K. Antony had said on Congress leaders and party workers participating in the AHIND conference to be held in Tumkur on Saturday is final. "I have nothing to add to it."

(2585) Kochi : Communist Party of India (Marxist-Leninist) (CPI(ML) leader K.N. Ramachandran has said that his party welcomes the 'ideological conflict' within the Communist Party of India (Marxist) CPI(M).

(2586) Thiruvananthapuram : The National Congress (I) leader K. Karunakaran, on Thursday claimed that seven political parties have come forward offering to cooperate with his party.

(2587) **Thiruvananthapuram :** The CPI(M) deputy legislature party leader Kodiyeri Balakrishnan has demanded a 'white paper' on the way the Government had handled the cases relating to self-financing professional college admissions and fees.

(2588) **New Delhi :** Terming the Free and Compulsory Education Bill, 2004 "discriminatory," Communist Party of India secretary D. Raja on Thursday said it only sought to legitimise inequality in society and the bias suffered by the weaker sections.

(2589) **New Delhi :** Congress president and United Progressive Alliance chairperson Sonia Gandhi on Thursday described the tabling of the National Rural Employment Guarantee Bill in the Lok Sabha as a "historic occasion."

(2590) **New Delhi :** Bharatiya Janata Party leader Uma Bharti has written to party president L.K. Advani, demanding that the party discuss the proposed women's reservation bill thoroughly before taking a stand on it.

(2591) **New Delhi :** The "replace Narendra Modi" demand of a sizeable section of the Bharatiya Janata Party in Gujarat was on Thursday carried to the residence of former Prime Minister Atal Bihari Vajpayee when former Chief Minister Keshubhai Patel, leading the dissident group, met him on Thursday along with other senior Gujarat leaders of the BJP.

(2592) **Pondicherry :** The PMK Parliamentary party leader, M.Ramadass, has called upon the Union Human Resources Development (HRD) Minister to bring in a comprehensive legislation to declare reservation to protect the students belonging to weaker and downtrodden and backward classes in getting admission to professional colleges.

(2593) **Pondicherry :** The Pondicherry Government should file a review petition in the Supreme Court to ensure continuance of quota for students in private unaided professional institutions.

(2594) **Pondicherry :** Secretary of Pondicherry State committee of the All-India Anna Dravida Munnetra Kazhagam (AIADMK) A. Anbalagan, MLA, has called upon the Union Territory administration to emulate Tamil Nadu Government in urging the Centre to bring in legislation on quota in unaided private medical and engineering colleges.

(2595) Pondicherry : The Secretary of the Pondicherry AIADMK, A. Anbalagan, MLA, leading a team of residents of Uppalam Assembly constituency, returned to the Director of the Civil Supplies department, K. Elumalai on Thursday a large number of 'yellow colour' ration cards distributed to the families "without assessing" their true economic conditions.

(2596) Lucknow : The Congress today slammed the Uttar Pradesh government for its alleged failure in dealing with Japanese encephalitis (JE) in eastern parts of the state, which has so far claimed 93 lives.

(2597) Chennai : The Pattali Makkal Katchi on Thursday demanded that Chief Minister Jayalalithaa take steps for enacting a law to take over the administration and properties of deemed universities in the State.

(2598) Bangalore : A crucial meeting of the office-bearers of the Janata Dal (Secular) Karnataka State unit here on Thursday unanimously passed a resolution authorising national party president H.D. Deve Gowda to initiate disciplinary action against the former Deputy Chief Minister Siddaramaiah, two former Ministers H.C. Mahadevappa and Satish Jarkiholi and several legislators. Mr. Siddaramaiah and the others have been accused of anti-party activities.

(2599) Tirupur : Welcoming the Central Government's decision to bring a Bill to protect quotas in the self-financing professional institutions, the Tamil Nadu unit of the Bharatiya Janata Party urged the State to start engineering colleges at all district headquarters.

20-08-2005

(2600) Karimnagar : The Union Minister for Labour and Employment, K. Chandrashekhar Rao, has reiterated that he will sacrifice his life for the cause of Telangana and will not compromise on the issue.

(2601) Nalgonda : Accusing the Congress Government of mishandling the extremism problem, Telugu Desam president N. Chandrababu Naidu on Friday demanded that it come out with a white paper on the issue.

(2602) Ongole : Andhra Pradesh Congress Committee president K. Keshava Rao has said the Congress will align with the CPI, the CPI(M), the TRS and the MIM in the coming municipal elections and expressed confidence that they will together win 75 per cent of the municipal chairmen and ward councillor posts.

(2603) Vijayawada : Rajiv Gandhi wanted to make use of technology for the benefit of the poor and he was not a hitech man like some others, but favoured "appropriate technology," said the Andhra Pradesh Congress Committee president, K.Kesava Rao, here on Friday.

(2604) Kamareddy (Nizamabad Dt.) : Union Minister of State for Rural Development A. Narendra has condemned the re-imposition of ban on the CPI (Maoist) and also the arrest of Revolutionary Writers' Association leaders - P. Varavara Rao and G. Kalyan Rao.

(2605) Siddipet : Telangana Rashtra Samiti president and Union Minister for Labour and Employment K. Chandrasekhar Rao on Friday claimed that all obstacles to the formation of a separate

(2606) Bellary : Sushma Swaraj, senior Bharatiya Janata Party (BJP) leader and former Union Minister, performed Sri Varamahalakshmi puja at the residence of B.K. Srinivasmurthy, a leading physician, here on Friday.

(2607) Bellary : Bharatiya Janata Party president L.K. Advani, and party leader Sushma Swaraj were all praise for the Reddy brothers, Karunakar Reddy, MP, Somashekar Reddy, Mayor, Bellary City Corporation, and Janardhan Reddy, President of district unit of BJP, for taking up constructive activities for the welfare of the people.

(2608) Gulbarga : The former Union Minister and Convener of the National Democratic Alliance George Fernandes on Friday took serious exception to the statement of the former Union Minister Jagdish Tytler casting aspersions on the findings of the Justice Nanavati Commission.

(2609) Shimoga : Leader of the Opposition in the Legislative Assembly B.S. Yediyurappa admitted what he called his "folly" before party workers here on Thursday in having raised a storm in Bharatiya Janata Party (BJP) circles by claiming that the BJP was ready to form a Government with the help of the Janata Dal (Secular).

(2610) Kozhikode : A. Kunhikoya Thangal, secretary-general of the Lakshadweep unit of the Janata Dal(United), has alleged that the Lakshadweep administration has been neglecting the needs and aspiration of the people of the island.

(2611) Thiruvananthapuram : Prime Minister Manmohan Singh will address the KPCC general body on September 3. The KPCC general body will be held at the new KPCC office that would be inaugurated by Congress president Sonia Gandhi on August 27.

(2612) Kolkata : Veteran Marxist leader and Communist Party of India (Marxist) Polit Bureau member Jyoti Basu on Friday hinted at the Left parties reviewing their decision to suspend their participation in the Coordination Committee meetings with the United Progressive Alliance (UPA).

(2613) New Delhi : Not satisfied with the response by the Election Commission (EC), a delegation of senior Rashtriya Janata Dal (RJD) leaders submitted a memorandum to the President, Abdul Kalam, expressing "serious concern" over the sharp decline in voting percentage in the previous Bihar Assembly elections. The delegation sought his intervention to ensure that no person who was registered as a voter in the electoral rolls was deprived of his/her right to vote.

(2614) New Delhi : Recalling his experience in the riots that took place after Indira Gandhi's assassination, the former Communist Party of India (Marxist) general secretary, Harkishan Singh Surjeet, says the West Bengal Government was forced to issue shoot-at-sight orders because some political bigwigs were trying to create mayhem in the State. However, "we of the CPI(M) are proud of the fact that the Left Front Government of West Bengal protected Sikh lives all over the State," writes Mr. Surjeet in the latest issue of People's Democracy.

(2615) Bellary : Internal security has been jeopardised under the Congress-led United Progressive Alliance (UPA) Government at the Centre, the Leader of the Opposition in the Lok Sabha and Bharatiya Janata Party (BJP) president, L.K. Advani, said here on Friday.

(2616) Kasaragod : Communist Party of India (Marxist) general secretary Prakash Karat has said that the Left parties will strengthen its relationship with the United Progressive Alliance even as they continue to uphold their independent stance on various issues.

(2617) New Delhi : The Delhi Bharatiya Janata Party on Friday asked the Union Home Minister, Shivraj Patil, to take effective steps immediately to improve the worsening law and order situation in the Capital and instil confidence among the people, especially women who are feeing insecure under the present regime.

(2618) Shimla : Political leaders belonging to the ruling Congress party as well as the Opposition parties are studying the ramifications of the judgment delivered by a Division Bench of the Himachal Pradesh High Court here quashing the appointment of eight Chief Parliamentary Secretaries and four Parliamentary Secretaries appointed by the Virbhadra Singh Government.

(2619) Bhopal : Following the decision of the Hubli Additional District and Session's Court last Tuesday to uphold the former Madhya Pradesh Chief Minister, Uma Bharti's discharge by a lower court in a decade-old criminal case, Bharti loyalists here have started demanding her reinstallation as the State Chief Minister.

(2620) Chennai : Are self-financing colleges providing higher education as a service, as cited in judicial pronouncements asked the Pattali Makkal Katchi founder, S. Ramadoss, at a demonstration here on Friday.

21-08-2005

(2621) Guntur : There is no blanket ban on the media and the Government expects the journalists only to be responsible, sensitive while discharging their duty, Andhra Pradesh Congress Committee president K. Keshava Rao has said.

(2622) Guntur : The Bharatiya Janata Party (BJP) will field its candidate in every ward of all the municipalities in the State in the coming elections, former Union Minister Bandaru Dattatreya has said.

(2623) Khammam : Bharatiya Janata Party (BJP) leader Ch. Vidhayasagar Rao on Saturday said that the Indira Sagar project (Polavaram) was implemented in violation of all the rehabilitation and resettlement norms.

(2624) New Delhi : Bharatiya Janata Party president L.K. Advani on Saturday ordered the suspension of the former Rajasthan Governor, Madan Lal Khurana, from the party for "gross indiscipline." Mr. Advani stripped him of all official duties on the recommendation of the general secretaries. Party leaders hinted that Mr. Khurana could be expelled if he did not apologise.

(2625) Bangalore : Bharatiya Janata Party (BJP) national general secretary H.N. Ananth Kumar has asked the Centre to direct public sector banks to reduce the interest rate on farm loans from nine per cent to six per cent.

(2626) Bangalore : President of Janata Dal (United) George Fernandes and President of the party's State unit B. Somashekar have said that the State Government has failed to provide succour to the flood affected people of Belgaum, Bijapur, Gulbarga and Bagalkot districts. The Janata Dal (U) leaders undertook an extensive tour of the four districts over the past two days and received a large number of representations from the people whose houses were washed away and crops damaged.

(2627) Hassan : The coalition Government in the State will outlive the political crisis it is facing. AHIND (Alpasankhyataru, Hindulidavaru mattu Dalitaru) conventions will not destabilise the Janata Dal (Secular), national president of the party H.D. Deve Gowda has said.

(2628) Tumkur : A convention of Alpasankhyataru, Hindulidavaru mathu Dalitaru (AHIND) here on Saturday passed a resolution condemning the style of functioning of H.D. Deve Gowda, Janata Dal (Secular) President, and H.D. Kumaraswamy, Working President of the State unit of the Janata Dal (S).

(2629) Kochi : The ensuing panchayat elections have triggered another round of merger among splinter groups of political parties. Pre-election time is usually the time for realignments and mergers in the State.

(2630) Kottayam : Kerala Pradesh Congress Committee president Ramesh Chennithala has said that the party will soon set up district-level committees for selection of candidates for the forthcoming local body elections.

(2631) Palakkad : Leader of the Opposition V.S. Achuthanandan has demanded that the State Government implement the order of the Pollution Control Board (PCB) to close down the Coca-Cola bottling plant at Plachimada immediately.

(2632) Pathanamthitta : Kerala Pradesh Congress Committee president Ramesh Chennithala has demanded a probe into the source of the assets valued at Rs.4,600 crores of the Communist Party of India (Marxist) State unit.

(2633) Thiruvananthapuram : National Congress (Indira) leader K. Karunakaran has said that he is confident that his party will have an understanding with the CPI(M) and the LDF for panchayat elections.

(2634) New Delhi : The Communist Party of India (CPI) has said that it will not stand in the way World Bank loans, but it was opposed to the conditions imposed as in the in the loan offer made to the Delhi Government for water sector reforms.

(2635) New Delhi : Left parties and like-minded organisations on Saturday spoke out against the ban on the Communist Party of India (Maoist) and demanded that the arrested writers of Andhra Pradesh be released immediately.

(2636) New Delhi : Left parties will soon take up the issue of relocation of slum-dwellers with Prime Minister Manmohan Singh.

(2637) Ahmedabad : BJP national president L. K. Advani on Saturday praised the performance of the Gujarat Government led by Narendra Modi giving an indication to the party dissidents that he was in no mood to entertain their demand for a change of leadership in the State.

(2638) New Delhi : Senior Bharatiya Janata Party leader Madan Lal Khurana on Saturday asked the party president, L.K. Advani, to remove Gujarat Chief Minister Narendra Modi immediately in order to redeem the party's image that had been badly affected due to Gujarat riots, thereby emulating the example set by Prime Minister Manmohan Singh on the issue of Sikh riots.

(2639) Pondicherry : The dawn-to-dusk bandh called by the AIADMK in Pondicherry on Saturday evoked a near total response with all privately run buses remaining off the roads. The bandh was organisd by the party to mark its protest against the 'non cooperative stand of the managements of the two privately run medical colleges in admitting students to MBBS course despite the order of the Supreme court to fill all the 100 seats in each of them on the basis of merit list of the Centralised Admission committee (CENTAC).

(2640) Chandigarh : The Shiromani Akali Dal has decided to launch a movement called "Sarab Sanjhi Insaf Muhim" (People's Movement for Justice) to fight for the rights and interests of the victims of the 1984 anti-Sikh violence that followed the assassination of then Prime Minister Indira Gandhi.

(2641) Chennai : Dravida Munnetra Kazhagam (DMK) president M. Karunanidhi on Saturday called upon the United Progressive Alliance (UPA) Government to act swiftly on vital issues such as according reservation to women in Parliament and State Assemblies.

(2642) Theni : Thousands of Dravida Munnetra Kazhagam party men, led by the party's agriculture labourers' wing secretary, K.P. Ramalingam, staged a demonstration before the District Employment Office in Theni town on Saturday, pressing various demands, including raising the storage level to 152 feet in Periyar dam.

22-08-2005

(2643) Anantapur : The Bharatiya Janata Party (BJP) has alleged that the Congress Government has opted for indirect elections to municipalities fearing reverses.

(2644) Hyderabad : Communist Party of India (Marxist) MP Penumalli Madhu has urged Finance Minister K. Rosaiah to reduce the Value-Added Tax imposed on items of mass consumption like coffee, tea and footwear - chappals - from the existing 12.5 per cent to 4 per cent in line with other States.

(2645) Hyderabad : The Telangana Rashtra Samithi and the Telugu Desam Party on Sunday opposed Chief Minister Y.S. Rajasekhara Reddy's request for Rs. 25,000-crore Central assistance for irrigation projects in the State.

(2646) Nellore : The Telugu Desam Party (TDP) has sought the immediate suspension of the Revenue Divisional Officer, Nellore, Venkataramana Reddy, and other staff responsible for the alleged enrolment of 'bogus voters', in the forthcoming corporation elections.

(2647) New Delhi : Reviving the controversy that the Sangh Parivar appeared to have buried, former Prime Minister Atal Bihari Vajpayee on Sunday said Pakistan founder Mohd Ali Jinnah was secular initially but was later responsible for the Partition.

(2648) Kochi : The National Congress (Indira) has entered into electoral pacts in some civic bodies, including two Corporations, with like-minded parties, NC(I) leader K. Karunakaran has said.

(2649) Belgaum : The Leader of the Opposition in the Legislative Assembly, B.S. Yediyurappa, on Saturday alleged that the officials are swindling money meant for providing relief to the flood-affected victims in the district.

(2650) **Hassan :** Regretting the verdict of the Supreme Court granting absolute rights to private professional colleges to admit students in medicine, engineering, and other professional courses without government interference, the former Prime Minister and national President of the Janata Dal (Secular) H.D. Deve Gowda said here on Sunday that it is imperative for the Union Government to introduce a Bill in Parliament or pass an ordinance to reintroduce reservation in self-financing institutions.

(2651) **Bangalore :** Bharatiya Janata Party leader and former Union Minister Rajnath Singh has demanded immediate implementation of the farmers' crop insurance scheme in all States and steps taken to bring down the interest rate on agricultural loans to less than 5 per cent.

(2652) **Pathanamthitta :** Kerala Pradesh Congress Committee president Ramesh Chennithala has alleged that the claim of National Congress(Indira) leader K. Karunakaran that his party would align with the LDF in the coming local body polls was like "attending a marriage feast without getting invitation for the same."

(2653) **Thiruvananthapuram :** The Opposition Left Democratic Front (LDF) has decided to face next month's local bodies elections without altering its composition, but also keep its options open on local level tie-up with the National Congress (Indira) to avert UDF victory in specific wards.

(2654) **Thrissur :** Indian National League (INL) State secretary P.M.A. Salam has said that his party is not particular on joining the Left Democratic Front (LDF) and that the question of alliances will be decided by the party depending on the political conditions prevailing during the elections.

(2655) **New Delhi :** In a move to bring about a consensus on the Women's Reservation Bill, providing for one-third reservation in Parliament and State Legislatures, the United Progressive Alliance Government has called a meeting of the constituents and the supporting parties on Monday that could pave the way for a forward movement.

(2656) **New Delhi :** Senior Left party leaders along with several political activists and Dalit rights workers on Sunday urged the Congress-led United Progressive Alliance (UPA) Government to pass a Bill in Parliament ensuring reservation for Dalit students and those belonging to backward classes in unaided private colleges.

(2657) Gandhinagar : BJP president L.K. Advani's praise for Gujarat Chief Minister Narendra Modi's "achievements" and his Government's performance does not seem to have discouraged party dissident MLAs from campaigning for a change of leadership in the State.

(2658) Pondicherry : Chief Minister N. Rangasamy has called upon the coordination committee of political parties headed by the Dravida Munnetra Kazhagam to drop its plan to observe a bandh in the Union Territory on August 23 to focus the grievances of students aspiring to study the MBBS course in privately medical colleges here.

(2659) Jaipur : The ruling Bharatiya Janata Party in Rajasthan has shown a credible performance in the recent civic bodies elections by winning 1,319 of the 3,096 wards which went to the polls in this round. The main Opposition in the State, the Congress, is closely behind its rival with victories in 1,044 wards.

(2660) Lucknow : Political parties in Uttar Pradesh, including ruling coalition ally Congress, on Sunday demanded a probe into the alleged land scam even as Chief Minister Mulayam Singh Yadav ruled out any irregularities in the allotment of plots by the Lucknow Development Authority (LDA),

(2661) Lucknow : The Congress on Sunday urged Uttar Pradesh Governor T. V. Rajeswar to cancel the ongoing Panchayat polls in the State, alleging large- scale irregularities in electoral rolls and misuse of Government machinery by the ruling Samajwadi Party,

(2662) Dehra Dun : Seventeen Bharatiya Janata Party MLAs, including the Leader of the Opposition, Matwar Singh Kandari, were arrested while marching to the Chief Minister's residence on Sunday morning. They have decided not to seek bail and continue in custody till the Chief Minister, Narain Dutt Tiwari, apologized for the drastic police action.

(2663) Kolkata : The need to ban the Communist Party of India (Maoist) in West Bengal has not arisen now, veteran Marxist leader Jyoti Basu said here on Sunday.

(2664) Madurai : The All-India Anna Dravida Munnetra Kazhagam (AIADMK) is trying to divert the attention of people from the coming Assembly elections by making sudden announcements, Tamil Nadu Congress Committee president G.K. Vasan has said.

(2665) Salem : "The leadership of the Tamil Nadu Congress Committee, instead of confining their activities to Sathyamurthy Bhavan should reach out to the people of Tamil Nadu," the Congress leader and Union Minister of State for Commerce and Industry, E. V. K. S. Elangovan said on Sunday. Hoping that the TNCC President Mr. G. K. Vasan would function well as the party's chief in Tamil Nadu, Mr. Elangovan, talking to reporters here, said the party should take up the issues of the people and launch agitations.

23-08-2005

(2666) Hyderabad : An understanding between the two major Communist parties on seat adjustments for the municipal elections is expected to be finalised in a week, according to CPI State secretary K. Narayana.

(2667) Hyderabad : The Telugu Desam Legislature Party has asked the Congress Government to tell the people what it has done for the State in 15 months of its rule here.

(2668) Gandhinagar : A Minister in the Narendra Modi Cabinet in Gujarat, Baukubhai Ugad, known to be close to the dissident leader, Keshubhai Patel, has sought the State party president, Vajubhai Vala's "permission" to quit the Ministry.

(2669) Belgaum : Any possible "third front" should have an independent economic agenda that strengthens the Indian economy, the former Prime Minister, H.D. Deve Gowda, has said.

(2670) Hassan : Expressing dissatisfaction over the announcement of Rs. 300 crores as interim relief by the Union Government from the National Calamity Contingency Fund (NCCF) for rehabilitation of people in the flood-affected areas in the State, Janata Dal (Secular) Presidnt and former Prime Minister, H.D. Deve Gowda, has urged Prime Minister Manmohan Singh to increase the relief.

(2671) New Delhi : The Centre on Monday promised all assistance to the Karnataka Government to meet the situation caused by heavy rain and floods and said as per latest estimates the State put its loss at Rs. 2,079 crores.

(2672) Alappuzha : The former Chief Minister A.K. Antony has said the State Government should take the lead to ensure that the proposed Central legislation on private unaided professional colleges should guarantee 50 per cent of the seats to meritorious students and government fee for these seats.

(2673) Alappuzha : The decision of the Left Democratic Front (LDF) to go in for local-level alliances with the National Congress (Indira) and other parties in the local body elections is a proof of its eroding confidence, Kerala Pradesh Congress Committee president Ramesh Chennithala said here on Monday.

(2674) Palakkad : Some top Kerala Congress (Mani) leaders, including one State secretariat member and State executive committee member, have joined the Kerala Congress (Joseph) group.

(2675) Thiruvananthapuram : The Bharatiya Janata Party (BJP) will raise the controversial SNC Lavalin and Brahmapuram deals in Parliament, party vice-president Venkaiah Naidu has said.

(2676) New Delhi : Even as the Government fielded two ministers in the Lok Sabha to address the issues raised by Bharatiya Janata Party (BJP) leader Kalyan Singh during the discussion on the National Rural Employment Guarantee Bill 2004, the Opposition on Monday sought an assurance from Finance Minister P. Chidambaram that funds would be made available for this "revolutionary" programme.

(2677) New Delhi : Uproarious scenes were witnessed in the Rajya Sabha on Monday, causing disruption for nearly 15 minutes as Bharatiya Janata Party members objected to a question hour reference to a textbook on Ramakrishna Paramhans.

(2678) New Delhi : The Opposition has given notice for another adjournment motion, on the transfer recommendation involving Bihar Governor Buta Singh.

(2679) New Delhi : The Telugu Desam Party on Monday urged the Centre to convene an all-party meet and introduce a Constitutional amendment Bill to provide social justice to the weaker sections of society in the wake of the recent Supreme Court order abolishing state quota and reservation in private unaided professional educational institutes.

(2680) New Delhi : Senior Bharatiya Janata Party leader and former Delhi Chief Minister Madan Lal Khurana on Monday received the show-cause notice served on him by the party high command for acts of "gross indiscipline" and he busied himself consulting his supporters on the future plan of action. However, it is learnt that Mr. Khurana has made it clear that he is not going to quit the party with which he had been associated for the past 50 years.

(2681) Patna : Strongly favouring quotas for scheduled castes and tribes in private sector jobs and educational institutions not receiving financial assistance from the government, the JD-U today assailed the UPA government for its 'equivocal' stand on the issue.

(2682) Pondicherry : The Pondicherry State unit of the All India Anna Dravida Munnetra Kazhagam (AIADMK) will soon file a petition in Madras High Court seeking its directives to the two privately run unaided medical colleges here to admit students under the government quota in spite of the institutions having become 'deemed universities'. The two institutions, Vinayaka Mission at Karaikal and Aarupadai Veedu Medical College in Pondicherry, are refusing to admit students under the government quota on the grounds that they were 'deemed universities.'

(2683) Jaipur : The election results from 126 civic bodies involving 32 lakh urban voters in Rajasthan have come as a shot in the arm for Chief Minister Vasundhara Raje. The ruling Bharatiya Janata Party has managed to get control over an unprecedented number of 81 civic bodies, including the municipal corporation of Ajmer, by electing its chairpersons.

(2684) Chennai : The Dravida Munnetra Kazhagam has cautioned against raising "a number of problems" in Parliament and Legislative Assemblies when the issue of reservation for women is being considered.

24-08-2005

(2685) Visakhapatnam : The State Government should immediately annul its agreement with the private company on bauxite mining as it would destroy the life of Girijans, demanded the Chintapalli MLA, G. Demudu, of CPI, on Tuesday.

(2686) Hyderabad : Bharatiya Janata Party's (BJP) State unit has urged the Government to withdraw the proposal to create Greater Hyderabad in the wake of a stay given on it by the High Court.

(2687) Bangalore : The Bharatiya Janata Party (BJP) State unit appears to be heading for trouble within days of the "patch-up" brought about between the two factions by party's Senior Vice-President M. Venkaiah Naidu. It is learnt that one faction is keen that the formula should be implemented in letter and spirit while the other is eager to wriggle out of the "pact".

(2688) Bangalore : Leader of the Opposition in the Legislative Assembly B.S. Yediyurappa has said that the Government has totally failed in its attempts to handle the flood situation and provide relief to the people. He demanded that Chief Minister N. Dharam Singh lead an all-party delegation to New Delhi to seek more funds for relief measures from the Centre.

(2689) Dharwad : H. Vishwanath, Congress leader, has ruled out the possibility of AHIND (Alphasankhyakataru, Hindulidavaru and Dalitaru) emerging as a political party.

(2690) Kollam : The Chaithanya Yatra led by Kerala Pradesh Congress Committee (KPCC) president Ramesh Chennithala was given a rousing reception at Ochira in Kollam district on Tuesday. Mr. Chennithala was formally received by District Congress Committee president Sooranad Rajashakaran and KPCC general secretary K.C. Rajan.

(2691) Kottayam : In spite of initial hiccups, the merger talks between the LDF partner, Kerala Congress (Joseph) and the NDA partner, Indian Federal Democratic Party, is progressing at a fast pace, leaders from both parties have said.

(2692) Malappuram : Countries should unite on the basis of their littoral proximity as man-made boundaries have become irrelevant in today's world, said V. Suryanarayanan, senior professor from the Centre for South and South-East Asian Studies, University of Madras.

(2693) New Delhi : The Congress on Tuesday termed the Supreme Court's observations in regard to the apex court's decision on 'quotas and reservation' in unaided private educational institutions as "unfortunate".

(2694) New Delhi : Home Minister Shivraj Patil on Tuesday assured the Rajya Sabha that the Government would respect the Supreme Court judgment striking down the Illegal Migrants (Determination by Tribunals) Act.

(2695) New Delhi : Prime Minister Manmohan Singh has expressed confidence that the Women's Reservation Bill will be passed in Parliament.

(2696) New Delhi : Bharatiya Janata Party president L.K. Advani noted on Tuesday that although the party had virtually given a "blank cheque" to the Government on reservation for women in legislatures, there were differences on the issue among the constituents of the ruling United Progressive Alliance and its supporting parties.

(2697) New Delhi : Communist Party of India (Marxist) leader Sitaram Yechury on Tuesday opened his oratorical innings in the Rajya Sabha by initiating a short duration discussion on the state of agriculture, poverty and unemployment in the light of the mid-term appraisal of the Tenth Five Year Plan.

(2698) Pondicherry : The Pondicherry based Multi Party Action Committee headed by the Dravida Munnetra Kazhagam has called upon the Centre and the State government to derecognise Vinayaka Mission at Karaikal and the Aarupadai Veedu Medical college in Pondicherry (the two privately run unaided medical colleges) for their continued 'refusal' to admit students under the government quota in MBBS course. These institutions had taken the stand that as 'deemed universities' they were not bound to admit students sponsored by the State government.

(2699) Pondicherry : The dawn-to-dusk bandh called by the DMK-led multi party action committee on Tuesday to condemn the 'non cooperative attitude' of the private unaided medical colleges in admitting students under the government quota threw normal life out of gear. All transport services, autos and tempos were off the roads and shops and establishments also remained closed.

(2700) Madurai : A 'padayatra' led by the BJP State president C.P. Radhakrishnan from Madurai to Cumbum, demanding immediate steps to restore the water level of Mullaperiyar dam to 152 feet, began on Tuesday.

(2701) Vellore : Dravida Munnetra Kazhagam treasurer Arcot N.Veerasamy on Monday urged the Election Commission to take legal action against the "All India Anna Dravida Munnetra Kazhagam Ministers who submitted 13 lakh bogus applications" during the voters list revision process in Tamil Nadu.

(2702) New Delhi : MDMK general secretary Vaiko on Tuesday met Prime Minister Manmohan Singh and impressed on him the need for amending the Payment of Bonus Act to increase the bonus ceiling.

25-08-2005

(2703) Hyderabad : The State unit of the Bharatiya Janata Party has urged Chief Minister Y. S. Rajasekhara Reddy to declare September 17 as "Hyderabad Liberation Day" and organise official programme.

(2704) Hyderabad : The Bharatiya Janata Party has finally announced that it will have no truck with any party for the municipal elections.

(2705) Hyderabad : The Chief Minister, Y.S. Rajasekhara Reddy, has positively responded to the PCC proposal to rationalise the property tax structure in municipalities.

(2706) Kurnool : The CPI(M) State secretary, B.V. Raghavulu, has urged the Government to concede the justified demands of Government employees over pay revision.

(2707) Tirupati : The Communist Party of India (CPI) has lashed out at the Government for its "lopsided policies."

(2708) Gudivada : The raging controversy over the suicide by a farmer Moshe at Pedapalaparru of Mudinepalli mandal in Krishna district is apparently snowballing into a showdown between the Government and the Telugu Desam Party. An eerie silence gripped the town on Wednesday with about 300 policemen descending on it to keep the situation under control, even as TDP activists are fully geared to "meet any eventuality," including the arrest of local MLA Kodali Srivenkateswara Rao (Nani).

(2709) New Delhi : The Centre is sympathetic to the demand for a separate Telangana state but is yet to receive a resolution to this effect from the Andhra Pradesh Assembly, Union Home Minister Shivraj Patil said in the Rajya Sabha on Wednesday.

(2710) Chennai : Chief Minister Jayalalithaa on Wednesday suggested an addition of 33 per cent seats to all elected bodies to ensure a consensus over the Women's Reservation Bill.

(2711) **New Delhi :** At a meeting chaired by Prime Minister Manmohan Singh here on Wednesday, almost all National Democratic Alliance constituents and other Opposition parties favoured implementation of the Election Commission (EC) formula for increasing women's representation in Parliament and State assemblies

(2712) **Thiruvananthapuram :** Alleging attempts by the Government to confound the confusion surrounding the upcoming local body elections, CPI(M) State secretary Pinarayi Vijayan has called upon the State Election Commission to notify the elections without any further delay.

(2713) **New Delhi :** Pakistan High Commissioner Aziz Ahmed Khan on Tuesday told a delegation of Janata Dal (U) leaders that Sarabjit Singh, sentenced to death by Pakistani courts, could file a review petition in the country's Supreme Court and present a mercy plea to President Pervez Musharraf.

(2714) **Bangalore :** The Minister for Tourism and president of the Backward Classes wing of the State Janata Dal (Secular), D.T. Jayakumar, on Wednesday lashed out at the former Deputy Chief Minister, Siddaramaiah, and pooh-poohed his being compared with Devaraj Urs.

(2715) **Gulbarga :** The leader of the Opposition in the Legislative Assembly B.S. Yediyurappa on Wednesday demanded the State Government to release Rs. 500 crores from its funds to increase the compensation to the farmers who had lost standing crops and to the people who lost their houses in the rain and floods in Belgaum, Bagalkot, Bijapur, Gulbarga, Raichur and Kodagu districts.

(2716) **Gulbarga :** Leader of Opposition in the Legislative Assembly B.S. Yediyurappa on Wednesday urged the State Government not to succumb to pressure from the Maharashtra Government and release water from the Alamatti Dam.

(2717) **Toranagal (Bellary District) :** "AHIND meets have not rattled us. Our convention in different parts of the State is not to counter AHIND meets but to strengthen the party and induct all those who had left it," H.D. Kumaraswamy, Working President of the State unit of Janata Dal (Secular), has said.

(2718) Kozhikode : The Communist Party of India (Marxist-Leninist) (CPI(ML) Red Flag has condemned the attempts to put down Marxist-Leninist (ML) movements and alleged its real objective was to crush the rising dissent against globalisation and 'anti-people' policies of Central and State Governments.

(2719) Palakkad : Former Union Minister and BJP leader O. Rajagopal has demanded that the State Government get the clearance of the Union Government and the Defence Ministry for the proposed Dubai Internet City (DIC) project since major defence installations are located in Kochi.

(2720) Thiruvananthapuram : The all-party meeting convened by the Government here on Wednesday to discuss the utilisation of tsunami relief funds and Central move to enact a legislation to govern admissions and free structure in self-financing professional colleges was only partially successful.

(2721) New Delhi : The Election Commission on Wednesday disapproved the name of National Congress (Indira) given by K. Karunakaran for his newly-floated party holding that it was capable of creating confusion in the minds of the general public and the electorate with the Indian National Congress.

(2722) New Delhi : There is a move to bring about radical changes in the Bharatiya Janata Party constitution that would bring in the concept of "collective leadership" as opposed to the present "presidential system" under which the party president is all-powerful and nominates the entire team of central office-bearers and most of the national executive members.

(2723) New Delhi : Pitching for "course correction" in the economic reforms policy to benefit the poor, the Left parties on Wednesday cautioned that inequitable growth could lead to social unrest.

(2724) New Delhi : The Communist Party of India on Wednesday demanded the removal of Bihar Governor Buta Singh and a probe by the Central Bureau of Investigation into corruption charges in flood relief in the State among other issues.

(2725) Srinagar : Extending full support to the ongoing peace process, Communist Party of India (Marxist) general secretary Prakash Karat on Wednesday asked the Centre to come up with clear initiatives to resolve the Kashmir issue. He advocated dialogue with all political forces in Jammu and Kashmir.

(2726) New Delhi : The former Gujarat Chief Minister, Keshubhai Patel, and Gujarat BJP MPs in his camp met senior party leaders here on Wednesday to lobby for the removal of Narendra Modi as Chief Minister.

(2727) New Delhi : Delhi Bharatiya Janata Party president Harsh Vardhan on Wednesday wrote to Reliance Energy chairman Anil Ambani asking him to withdraw the 10 per cent power tariff hike in the Capital failing which the party would be forced to launch an agitation.

(2728) New Delhi : Congress MPs from Punjab on Wednesday urged the Centre to ensure prompt payment of compensation to the relatives of those killed in the 1984 anti-Sikh riots and said the quantum and nature of compensation should be the same for the affected families throughout the country.

(2729) New Delhi : Describing the recent legislations on Right to Information and Employment Guarantee Scheme as "historic", the All-India Congress Committee general secretary in charge of frontal organisations, Ashok Gehlot, on Wednesday said Youth Congress activists would fan across the country to spread awareness about the two schemes and ensure that the benefits percolate to the targeted groups and sections.

(2730) Lucknow : Uttar Pradesh women's Congress on Wednesday held protest demonstrations at all the district headquarters against the alleged hard stance by some political parties over the proposed Women's Reservation Bill.

26-08-2005

(2731) Hyderabad : The Bharatiya Janata Party has alleged irregularities in voters' list and demanded holding of all-party meetings in municipalities and corporations to discuss various civic poll issues.

(2732) Hyderabad : The State committee of the Communist Party of India (Marxist) has asked the State Government to announce a special package of Rs. 5,000 crores for the current year for the development of the Telangana region.

(2733) Hyderabad : The Telugu Desam Legislature Party on Thursday demanded dismissal of the Deputy Superintendent of Police who threatened the party's Gudivada MLA, Kudali Sri Venkateswara Rao alias Nani, at gunpoint.

(2734) Nellore : The Telugu Desam Party (TDP) president, N. Chandrababu Naidu, has come down heavily on the Congress party for its "anti-people" and "anti-farmer" policies and appealed to people, to teach it a befitting lesson in the coming municipal polls.

(2735) Chennai : DMK president Karunanidhi on Thursday wanted 33 per cent reservation for women to be implemented before taking up the demand for a quota for Backward Classes and Most Backward Classes within the overall reservation.

(2736) New Delhi : An "oust Munda" campaign has been launched by dissident Ministers from Jharkhand. They have been camping here for the past several days to meet senior Bharatiya Janata Party leaders to complain against the "style of functioning" of Chief Minister Arjun Munda.

(2737) New Delhi : Congress president Sonia Gandhi on Thursday accused the Bharatiya Janata Party and its allies of going back on their earlier stand on the women's reservation bill, but said efforts to build a consensus would continue.

(2738) Bangalore : Bharatiya Janata Party (BJP) leader and Leader of the Opposition in the Legislative Assembly B.S. Yediyurappa said on Thursday that party State unit President Jagadish Shettar and he will visit New Delhi on August 29 and urge party MPs to pressure the Centre to sanction at least Rs. 1,000 crores immediately for flood relief work. They will call on the former Prime Minister Atal Bihari Vajpayee and BJP President L.K. Advani and apprise them of the flood havoc. He said the Centre and the State have failed to undertake relief operations and even the sanctioned funds are yet to be made over to the districts concerned. Of an estimated loss of Rs. 3,200 crores, the Centre should chip in with at least Rs. 1,000 crores immediately.

(2739) Thiruvananthapuram : Leader of the Opposition V. S. Achuthanandan has sought a probe by an Assembly committee into what he termed corruption in public sector Kerala Minerals and Metals Limited (KMML).

(2740) Thiruvananthapuram : CPI State secretary Veliyam Bhargavan has said that his party does not see the party led by K. Karunakaran, tentatively named National Congress (Indira) as an untouchable and would have local level tie-up with it to defeat the UDF in the upcoming local body elections.

(2741) Thiruvananthapuram : K. Muraleedharan, today made it clear that his party would not have any kind of alliance with the Indian Union Muslim League and would try for a tie-up with the Left parties to defeat the United Democratic Front and other communal parties.

(2742) New Delhi : The Communist Party of India (Marxist) on Thursday charged that the Bharatiya Janata Party's move to withdraw support to any proposal to reserve one third seats for women "as sabotaging" the United Progressive Alliance Government's move to bring the Bill to Parliament. "It is indeed shocking that the BJP should execute such an about turn when only a few days ago the BJP had made a public commitment to support either of the two proposals to ensure one third seats for women," the CPI (M) Polit Bureau said in a statement.

(2743) New Delhi : Differences in political ideology between the Bharatiya Janata Party and its key ally, Janata Dal (United), came to fore in the Lok Sabha on Wednesday when Nitish Kumar strongly advocated that benefits of reservation be extended to Scheduled Castes who convert to Islam and Christianity, a proposal that did not go down well with the BJP.

(2744) New Delhi : Delhi Pradesh Congress Committee president Ram Babu Sharma on Thursday described the passage of the Rural Employment Guarantee Bill in Parliament as a historic step that would change the face of villages of the country.

(2745) Srinagar : Extending full support to the ongoing peace process, Communist Party of India (Marxist) general secretary Prakash Karat on Wednesday asked the Centre to come up with clear initiatives to resolve the Kashmir issue. He advocated dialogue with all political forces in Jammu and Kashmir.

(2746) Jaipur : A few workers of the Communist Party of India (Marxist-Leninist) were injured when the police resorted to a lathi-charge at Buhana town in Jhunjhunu district of Rajasthan on Thursday.

(2747) Villupuram : While favouring reservation for women in legislatures, the Pattali Makkal Katchi on Thursday insisted that one-third allocation must be made within the existing set-up, without increasing the number of seats.

27-08-2005

(2748) Hyderabad : A delegation of Telugu Desam leaders met the Defence Minister, Pranab Mukherjee, at Delhi on Thursday and demanded immediate elections to Secunderabad Cantonment Board and abolition of octroi and toll tax there.

(2749) Hyderabad : The Telugu Desam Party on Friday charged the Chief Minister, Y. S. Rajasekhara Reddy, with carrying a "false propaganda" that the party was coming in the way of building irrigation projects.

(2750) Vijayawada : National vice-president of the Bharatiya Janata Party M. Venkaiah Naidu, on Friday, reiterated the party's commitment to its Hindutva agenda and called upon the rank and file to be prepared for Parliament elections any moment in view of the "prevalent political instability at the Centre."

(2751) Sangareddy : The Union Minister of State for Rural Development, A. Narendra, who was here to participate in the Janmashtami celebrations told reporters that there is no need of a State Assembly resolution for the formation of a separate State, if the Union Government wishes to grant it to the people of Telanagana.

(2752) Nellore : Telugu Desam Party president N. Chandrababu Naidu has warned those officials who are reportedly toeing a political line in discharge of their duties.

(2753) New Delhi : Jharkhand Chief Minister Arjun Munda got a reprieve on Friday after dissident Bharatiya Janata Party MLAs "agreed" to work under his leadership. General secretary Rajnath Singh thrashed out an agreement at a three-hour meeting between the warring factions at his house here. Five Independent MLAs also attended the meeting.

(2754) New Delhi : The Bharatiya Janata Party will raise in the Rajya Sabha on Monday the issue of Nalini Chidambaram, wife of Union Finance Minister P. Chidambaram and senior advocate in the Madras High Court, taking up a case for the Income Tax Department in the Court.

(2755) Patna : Bahujan Samaj Party chief and former Uttar Pradesh Chief Minister Mayawati on Friday ruled out alliance with any party in Bihar and asserted that her party would contest the coming Assembly polls in the State on its own.

(2756) Davangere : Chief Minister N. Dharam Singh has said that the Congress will strive to come to power on its own in the next elections and declared that the party "will be strengthened at all levels."

(2757) Kochi : The Indian Federal Democratic Party (IFDP), a constituent of the Bharatiya Janata Party-led National Democratic Alliance (NDA) at the Centre, has decided to merge with the Kerala Congress(J) led by P.J. Joseph.

(2758) Mysore : Leader of Opposition in the Legislative Assembly B.S. Yediyurappa has accused the Congress of preparing the ground for mid-term polls in the State.

(2759) Davangere : President of the Karnataka Pradesh Congress Committee M. Mallikarjun Kharge on Friday said that the Congress is ready to admit the ousted Deputy Chief Minister and Janata Dal (Secular) leader Siddaramaiah into the party.

(2760) Thiruvananthapuram : Leader of the Opposition V. S. Achuthanandan has questioned the appropriateness of the Government decision to float the National University of Advanced Legal Studies (NUALS) in the self-financing sector with Chief Justices of the Supreme Court and the Kerala High Court in key positions in its governance structure, but the Government itself enjoying little power to control its functioning.

(2761) Thiruvananthapuram : Secretary of the Aall India Congress Committee (AICC) Tom Vadakkan on Friday said that the United Progressive Alliance Government proposed to bring in legislation on self-financing professional institutions that would reinvent the wheel in terms of social justice, besides clearing ambiguity that would make judicial interpretation easy.

(2762) Balaramapuram : The 'Chaithanya Yatra' has paved the way for the resurrection of the Indian National Congress in Kerala, torn by factional feuds in recent years, said Ramesh Chennithala, president, Kerala Pradesh Congress Committee (KPCC).

(2763) Bangalore : The Left parties will participate in the Coordination Committee meetings with the United Progressive Alliance (UPA) only if the Government changes its stand on the disinvestment of 'Navaratna' public sector undertakings such as Bharat Heavy Electricals Ltd.

(2764) New Delhi : The Bharatiya Janata Party (BJP) on Friday described as "wrong and baseless" Congress president Sonia Gandhi's charge that the BJP had changed its stand on the Women's Reservation Bill.

(2765) Chennai : Janata Party president Subramanian Swamy has demanded the resignation of Finance Minister P. Chidambaram over the appointment of his wife Nalini Chidambaram as a Government counsel in the Income Tax Tribunal.

(2766) Bangalore : Communist Party of India (Marxist) general secretary Prakash Karat on Friday called on the former Prime Minister and Janata Dal (Secular) president, H.D. Deve Gowda, at his residence here.

(2767) New Delhi : Suggesting that the Delhi Development Authority (DDA) confine itself to only regulatory functions and discontinue acting as "the regulator, promoter and planner", the Congress Member of Parliament from New Delhi, Ajay Maken, has written to Union Urban Affairs Minister Ghulam Nabi Azad asking the Government to transfer power of land to the Government of Delhi, which he said was "closer to the ground realities of land use in the Capital".

(2768) New Delhi : The Leader of the Opposition in the Delhi Assembly, Jagdish Mukhi, has demanded a Central Bureau of Investigation probe into privatisation of the erstwhile Delhi Vidyut Board in the light of the glaring irregularities pointed out in its working in the recently released CAG report. Speaking at a press conference here, Dr. Mukhi said he had submitted a memorandum in this regard to Prime Minister Manmohan Singh.

(2769) Bhopal : The Madhya Pradesh unit of the Women's Congress on Friday submitted a memorandum to the State Governor, Balram Jakhar, and held a demonstration near the Congress headquarters here in protest against increasing incidents of rape and other crimes being committed against women and girls in the State.

(2770) Chennai : The ruling All-India Anna Dravida Munnetra Kazhagam (AIADMK) and the Dravida Munnetra Kazhagam-led Democratic Progressive Alliance (DPA) appear to be vying with each other to garner the support of women self-help groups (SHGs).

(2771) Chennai : The Marumalarchi Dravida Munnetra Kazhagam and Puthiya Thamizhagam have welcomed the agreement to prepare a detailed project report on the interlinking of Ken and Betwa rivers.

(2772) Chennai : The Dravida Munnetra Kazhagam president, M. Karunanidhi, on Friday said it had now become clear that the party's complaint to the Election Commission on the massive inclusion of bogus voters was true.

28-08-2005

(2773) Hyderabad : The TDP president N. Chandrababu Naidu said the Government lacks foresight on the construction of irrigation projects, as clearances for many of them have not been obtained.

(2774) Nalgonda : Central Committee member of the Communist Party of India (Marxist) V. Srinivasa Rao has said the CPI(M) does not have any problem in working with the Bharatiya Janata Party and the Telangana Rashtra Samithi to achieve comprehensive development of the Telangana region.

(2775) Thiruvananthapuram : Congress president Sonia Gandhi said on Saturday that though the Congress and the Left parties were together at the national level in the ideological fight against communal forces, represented by the BJP and the Sangh Parivar, the Left was its main opponent in Kerala.

(2776) Thiruvananthapuram : The Kerala Pradesh Congress Committee's (KPCC) long wait for the opening of the party's new office ended on Saturday with Congress president Sonia Gandhi inaugurating it.

(2777) Singapore : The West Bengal Chief Minister, Buddhadeb Bhattacharjee, has affirmed that the Left parties in India "are changing" their political view of the world and "are trying to change [the] mindset" of workers.

(2778) Bangalore : Janata Dal (Secular) President H.D. Deve Gowda has urged Chief Minister N. Dharam Singh to take complete charge of flood relief works and ensure that funds provided by the Centre are appropriately used.

(2779) Bijapur : Decks have been cleared for the launch of the Shiv Sena's State unit here on Sunday under the leadership of Pramod Muthalik, convenor of Bajrang Dal for south India.

(2780) Tumkur : H.D. Kumaraswamy, Working President of the State unit of the Janata Dal (Secular), said on Saturday that he will accept the challenge by R.L. Jalappa, MP and former Union Minister, for an inquiry by the Central Bureau of Investigation into the assets owned by the families of Mr. Jalappa and H.D. Deve Gowda, Janata Dal (S) President.

(2781) Davangere : Chief Minister N. Dharam Singh on Saturday compared the district-level workers' conferences of his party being held all over the State to "military preparations" and said the move is aimed at preparing the party to face the elections any time.

(2782) Kottayam : The merger move between the Left coalition partner Kerala Congress (J) and the NDA ally Indian Federal Democratic Party (IFDP) was cemented here on Saturday with leaders of the two parties jointly announcing the merger and their future course of action. The merger will be formalised here on September 5.

(2783) Pathanamthitta : CPI(M) State committee member Thomas Issac has alleged that the World Bank was trying to 'popularise' globalisation throughout the country with the help of non-Governmental organisations under the cover of decentralisation of power.

(2784) Thiruvananthapuram : Former Chief Minister A. K. Antony and KPCC president Ramesh Chennithala, who addressed the Congress rally in the capital city this evening, were unanimous in their view that Oommen Chandy would return as Chief Minister of Kerala in 2006.

(2785) Thiruvananthapuram : Congress president Sonia Gandhi on Saturday endorsed the Kerala Pradesh Congress Committee's strong anti-CPI (M) positions by demarcating the party's national imperatives in forging an alliance with Left parties and its priorities in the State where it is in "aggressive opposition" to them.

(2786) Thrissur : General secretary of the Communist Party of India (Marxist) Prakash Karat has said that his party 'rebuffs and refutes' all the allegations levelled against CPI(M) State secretary Pinarayi Vijayan on the

SNV Lavalin issue. Addressing a public meeting organised by the Thrissur CPI(M), Mr. Karat said, "We cannot respond to a preliminary report of the Accountant General. Let the final report of the Comptroller of Auditor General (CAG) come. Then we will make our stand clear."

(2787) Jamnagar : Even as dissidents in the Gujarat BJP Legislature Party continued to cold-shoulder him, party national president L.K. Advani virtually issued an invitation to them for "talks" to redress their "grievances."

(2788) Guwahati : Congress MPs from Assam belonging to both Houses have appealed to the Prime Minister for the introduction of a bill in the winter session for creation of an upper House for the Assam Legislature.

(2789) Pune : A "deliberate" attempt was being made to show non-reforms in labour laws as an "impediment" to attracting FDI (foreign direct investment) and this was not acceptable to the Left parties, CPI-M Polit Bureau member and MP Brinda Karat said here on Saturday.

(2790) Kolkata : Rebel Trinamool Congress leader and former Kolkata Mayor Subrata Mukherjee on Saturday joined the Congress after he broke away from the party, which he had demanded should ally with the Congress.

(2791) New Delhi : The issue of the electricity meters coupled with Chief Minister Sheila Dikshit's remark on Friday asking consumers to swallow the bitter pill of power tariff hike is threatening to snowball into a major crisis in the Congress Party. Two senior leaders, Pervez Hashmi and Subhash Chopra, have written to Ms. Dikshit and the AICC general secretary in charge of Delhi, Ashok Gehlot, seeking an emergency meeting of the Congress Legislature Party (CLP) to discuss the situation arising out of the strong public resentment against the increase in power tariffs.

(2792) Chennai : Tamil Nadu Congress Committee president G.K.Vasan on Saturday criticised the State Government for its "attempt to politicise" the functioning of self-help groups.

(2793) Vellore : The two-day zonal conference of the Dravida Munnetra Kazhagam, which began at Perumugai near here on Saturday, has demanded a White Paper from the State Government on allocations for implementing orders and announcements made in the wake of the Lok Sabha elections and the target period fixed by the Government for the same to clear the doubts about the financial administration of the Jayalalitha Government.

29-08-2005

(2794) Hyderabad : The Andhra Pradesh Congress Committee will take a decision soon on whether Chief Minister Y.S. Rajasekhara Reddy should campaign for the coming municipal elections in the State or not.

(2795) Hyderabad : Eight Left parties have accused the Congress Government of following the diktats of the World Bank and vowed to wage a united struggle against globalisation and privatisation.

(2796) Hyderabad : The Telugu Desam Legislature Party (TDLP) has demanded that the Government roll back power tariff before holding memorial meetings like the one organised here on Sunday by the Congress and Left parties.

(2797) Karimnagar : Communist Party of India floor leader in the Assembly, Chada Venkat Reddy has urged upon the State Government not to succumb to World Bank diktats and strive to fulfil all election promises.

(2798) Nellore : The Telugu Desam Party (TDP) has reiterated its charge that the officials in the district were indifferent towards its complaints regarding alleged bungling of voters in the forthcoming municipal elections.

(2799) Vijayawada : National vice-president of the Bharatiya Janata Party (BJP) M. Venkaiah Naidu, on Sunday, said the result of the municipal elections would be a litmus test to know the outcome of severing relations between the BJP and the Telugu Desam Party (TDP).

(2800) Vijayawada : The presidents and secretaries of TDP urban and district units as well as three-member committees constituted for municipalities will reach Hyderabad to have a comprehensive meeting with the TDP president N. Chandrababu Naidu on Monday, ahead of the civic elections.

(2801) Hyderabad : The Andhra Pradesh Congress Committee (APCC) has asked its district leaders to forge alliances with friendly political parties to keep anti-TDP and anti-BJP vote intact in the coming municipal elections.

(2802) Tumkur : The former Prime Minister, H.D. Deve Gowda, here on Sunday urged United Progressive Alliance Chairperson Sonia Gandhi and Prime Minister Manmohan Singh to give a "new shape to the third-level economic reforms in a way helpful to economically weaker sections."

(2803) New Delhi : The resentment against her Government over the latest increase in power tariffs notwithstanding, Delhi Chief Minister Sheila Dikshit has also come under fire for her criticism of the Parliamentary Standing Committee report on Power and Privatisation in Delhi. The Member of Parliament from South Delhi, Vijay Kumar Malhotra, has decided to move a breach of privilege motion against Ms. Dikshit in the Lok Sabha on Monday.

(2804) Bijapur : Hundreds of Sangh Parivar members, mostly activists of the Vishwa Hindu Parishat and Bajrang Dal, joined Shiv Sena here on Sunday.

(2805) Mysore : Over 50 Janata Dal (Secular) MLAs will join former Deputy Chief Minister Siddaramaiah if the Congress re-inducts him into the coalition Government by snapping links with former Prime Minister and Janata Dal (S) President H.D. Deve Gowda, rebel Janata Dal (S) leader A.K. Subbaiah has claimed.

(2806) Tumkur : Speakers at the Janata Dal (Secular) Workers' Convention here on Sunday singled out for attack S.M. Krishna, Maharashtra Governor; Siddaramaiah, former Deputy Chief Minister; and C.M. Ibrahim, former Union Minister.

(2807) Udupi : The meeting of the Bharatiya Janata Party (BJP) MPs, MLAs, MLCs and party office- bearers of the three coastal districts of Udupi, Dakshina Kannada and Uttara Kannada held here on Sunday urged the Union and State Governments to take steps to set up the Rs. 21,000-crore ONGC project in Mangalore.

(2808) Kozhikode : Growing political camaraderie between Left parties and the National Congress (Indira) could be witnessed in the next few days with leaders of the parties planning to hold one-on-one talks for the coming three-tier local body polls in Kozhikode district.

(2809) Pathanamthitta : The CPI(M) State secretariat member Thomas Isaac, MLA, has said the Left Democratic Front (LDF) will revive the

People's Plan Campaign which was discontinued mid-way by the United Democratic Front (UDF) Government, if it comes back to power.

(2810) Thiruvananthapuram : Kerala Pradesh Congress Committee (KPCC) president Ramesh Chennithala has regretted the delay in the Vigilance investigation in the SNC Lavalin deal and has expressed hope that it will be completed in six months as promised by Chief Minister Oommen Chandy.

(2811) Thiruvananthapuram : The CPI(M) State secretariat has pointed out there are several grey areas in the Memorandum of Agreement (MoA) exchanged between the State Government and Dubai Internet City (DIC), promoters of the Smart City project.

(2812) Bhavnagar : BJP national president L.K. Advani on Sunday cautioned the dissidents in Gujarat that he would not allow anyone to come in the way of Chief Minister Narendra Modi in leading the State on the path of progress.

(2813) Kolkata : In the backdrop of West Bengal Chief Minister Buddhadeb Bhattacherjee's high-profile visit to Indonesia and Singapore to woo foreign investors to the State, the CPI(M) would discuss the issue threadbare at its Polit Bureau and Central Committee meetings in Delhi early next month.

(2814) Patna : It will be tea for more than 50,000 RJD workers with their supremo and Railway Minister, Lalu Prasad, who would be formally elected president for the fifth successive term on Monday, starting September 5 for a better footing in the Assembly elections.

(2815) New Delhi : Even as Chief Minister Sheila Dikshit reportedly issued "another" warning to the Reliance Energy chairman, Anil Ambani, the Delhi Electricity Regulatory Commission (DERC) on Sunday made it clear that the private discoms as well as the State-owned Transco had asked for a massive hike in the power tariffs but it toned down their claims to a great extent relieving the consumers of a heavy financial burden.

(2816) Patna : The Lok Janshakti Party (LJP) on Sunday accused the Congress of creating confusion by stating that the coming Bihar Assembly election would be contested under the banner of UPA.

(2817) Chandigarh : The Haryana Chief Minister Bhupinder Singh Hooda, Deputy Chief Minister Chander Mohan and President of the Haryana unit of the Congress and former Chief Minister Bhajan Lal on Sunday congratulated Prime Minister Manmohan Singh and Congress President Sonia Gandhi for getting the National Rural Employment Guarantee Act, 2005 passed in the Parliament.

(2818) Pondicherry : The Pondicherry unit of the All India Anna Dravida Munnetra Kazhagam (AIADMK) has through a resolution adopted at its workers meeting in Lawspet near here on Sunday called upon the Union Territory Administration to start afresh a survey of economic status of the people so that there would be fair identification of the families living below poverty line group for distribution of "red colour" ration cards to them.

(2819) Pondicherry : The founder leader of the Pattali Makkal Katchi (PMK), S. Ramadoss, has announced that the volunteers of the party in Pondicherry will stage a demonstration by raising slogans 'non stop' (thodar muzhakka aarpaattam) in front of the Assembly premises here on September 16 to urge the Pondicherry administration to introduce reservation for Most Backward Class (MBC) in employment also.

(2820) Bhopal : The Bharatiya Janata Party President, L.K. Advani has expressed the hope that Pakistan would meet its commitment to combat global terrorism by acting positively on India's demand for the extradition of those wanted in criminal cases, including Dawood Ibrahim.

(2821) Jaipur : Members of Parliament from Rajasthan have expressed concern over the delay in according international status to the Sanganer airport, near here, despite an announcement to this effect in the Lok Sabha. The MPs have pointed out that neither the notification for the purpose has been issued, nor the funds have been allocated for the airport's expansion so far.

(2822) Kolkata : The former Kolkata Mayor, Subrata Mukherjee, on Saturday joined the Congress after he broke away from the Trinamool Congress, which he had demanded should ally with the Congress.

(2823) Vellore : The welfare schemes announced by Chief Minister Jayalalithaa in the last few months were prompted by "fear of defeat of the

All-India Anna Dravida Munnetra Kazhagam in the Assembly elections," in the wake of the party's debacle in the May 2004 Parliamentary elections,

(2824) Vellore : The last zonal conference of the Dravida Munnetra Kazhagam ended here on Sunday, with leaders of the party and its allies calling upon the cadres to work cohesively to ensure the victory of the Democratic Progressive Alliance in the coming Assembly elections.

30-08-2005

(2825) Hyderabad : The two-day strategy meet of the Andhra Pradesh Congress Committee (APCC) for the Municipal elections concluded here on Monday, with a call to its cadres not to foreclose options for alliances with friendly political parties in their over-enthusiasm. The party should join hands with secular forces to defeat the TDP and the BJP. It has also decided to opt for a common manifesto to promise a holistic development of urban centres.

(2826) Hyderabad : No sooner did the State Election Commission issue the municipal election schedule, than the top Telugu Desam leaders went into a huddle on Monday to discuss election strategies and selection of candidates.

(2827) Hyderabad : The Chief Minister Y. S. Rajasekhara Reddy has said that he was not a "forerunner" for the coveted post of Congress Working Committee (CWC) Member.

(2828) Karimnagar : Former Union Minister and BJP senior leader Ch. Vidyasagar Rao called upon the TRS president and Union Minister K. Chandrasekhar Rao to pay his obeisance and pray to the Bharatiya Janata Party for the formation of separate Telangana State.

(2829) Ongole : The Telugu Desam Party wants to select candidates for the municipal elections based on their track record, their acceptability to the people and highlight the development the party had achieved in the towns during its reign. The TDP had won Ongole, Markapur and Kandukur municipalities in the elections held in 2000, while the Congress-I could win only Chirala Municipality in Prakasam district.

(2830) Visakhapatnam : The Telugu Desam Party has questioned "the silence" of people's representatives of the ruling Congress over the inordinate delay in the completion of the Godavari water scheme, though the city has been facing a severe water shortage for the past few months.

(2831) Warangal : TDP leaders condemned the remarks made by the leaders of TRS district unit against their leader N. Chandrababu Naidu on his visit to the district on August 31.

(2832) Sangareddy : Political parties in Medak district have decided to intensify their campaign following the notification by the State Election Commission (SEC).

(2833) Patna : Rashtriya Janata Dal supremo and Railway Minister Lalu Prasad soon after his election as the party chief for the fifth successive time, said his party would win in the coming elections but charged that his Cabinet colleague and LJP chief Ram Vilas Paswan was indirectly helping the National Democratic Alliance.

(2834) Thiruvananthapuram : The Congress MLAs would play an important role in forging local level seat adjustments with coalition partners and other like-minded groups that subscribe to the UDF policies in the coming local bodies election.

(2835) Bangalore : In an oblique reference to the reported statement of Janata Dal (Secular) leader H.D. Deve Gowda in Tumkur on Sunday, the former Deputy Chief Minister Siddaramaiah on Monday said, "There is no need make efforts to bring down the Government as it is set to fall on its own."

(2836) Chitradurga : Senior Congress leader and former Union Minister C.K. Jaffer Sharief said here on Sunday that the Alpasankhyataru Hindulidavaru mattu Dalitaru (AHIND) movement is not apolitical anymore and it is being used to serve the political interests of a few people who are out of power.

(2837) New Delhi : Bharatiya Janata Party General Secretary Ananth Kumar and Leader of the Opposition in State Assembly B.S. Yediyurappa, who are reportedly having an uneasy political relationship, on Monday jointly called on party President L.K. Advani.

(2838) Pathanamthitta : The Left Democratic Front (LDF) and the Naticnal Congress (Indira) have alleged large-scale manipulation in the draft voters' list for Pathanamthitta municipality, which was under preparation at the DTP centre of the Kudumbasree Mission in Pathanamthitta.

(2839) Thiruvananthapuram : General secretary of the Kerala Pradesh Congress committee (KPCC) K. Sudhakaran, MLA, on Monday hit out at the State Election Commission alleging that the SEC had failed to prepare the State for free and fair elections to the local bodies.

31-08-2005

(2840) Nedumbassery : Bahujan Samaj Party (BSP) leader Mayawati on Monday asked for separate reservation for women belonging to weaker sections under the proposed Women's Reservation Bill.

(2841) Chennai : The Communist Party of India(Marxist) general secretary, Prakash Karat, on Monday said that his party had "serious criticisms" of the military cooperation agreement and also the "overall approach and content" of the recent joint statement signed at the end of the Prime Minister Manmohan Singh's visit to the United States.

(2842) New Delhi : For once Finance Minister P. Chidambaram found himself on the back foot on issues of propriety and conflict of interest, raised in the Rajya Sabha by the All-India Anna Dravida Munnetra Kazhagam member, N. Jothi, with regard to his wife, Nalini Chidambaram's role as counsel to the Income Tax Department.

(2843) Kolkata : Asserting that the Left was not adopting double standards on the issue of economic reforms, West Bengal Chief Minister Buddhadev Bhattacharjee said on Monday that his Government would take advantage of the Centre's "Look East" policy to attract foreign direct investment (FDI).

(2844) New Delhi : Under pressure from her party legislators over the strong public resentment against the Capital's private power distribution companies in view of the latest increase in power charges, a beleaguered Delhi Chief Minister Sheila Dikshit has convened a meeting of the Congress Legislature Party (CLP) on Tuesday evening. Fireworks are expected at the meeting with the stage being set for a confrontation between the agitated MLAs and the Chief Minister on the issue.

(2845) Shimla : The Congress on Monday lost the by-election from a much-hyped Municipal Corporation ward here in the State Capital.

(2846) Pondicherry : Cadres of the Communist Party of India (Marxist) will picket Central and State Government offices here on September 13, demanding that the Government solve the problems of the poor, landless farmers and unemployed youth and that the public distribution system be toned up.

(2847) Lucknow : Challenging the claim of Uttar Pradesh Chief Minister Mulayam Singh Yadav about the Samajwadi Party reaffirming its supremacy in the recently held Panchayat elections, the BJP on Monday said 48 per cent victorious gram pradhans belonged to it. Terming the results as a mandate against the SP-led Government in the State, the BJP state unit said despite the party not participating in the polls directly, the victory could well be attributed to the party. Addressing newspersons here, BJP spokesman H.N. Dixit said the party had fared commendably in eastern and central districts while in Rampur party-supported candidates emerged clear winners.

(2848) Chennai : The message emerging from the last of the Dravida Munnetra Kazhagam's (DMK) zonal conferences is unambiguous - there is no time to be lost in reaching out to the people.

01-09-2005

(2849) Hyderabad : The Bharatiya Janata Party has accused the State Government of violating the election code by issuing ration cards and urged the State Election Commission to instruct the Government not to take up any programmes for influencing voters.

(2850) Hyderabad : Bharatiya Janata Party has welcomed the statement of Telugu Desam president, N. Chandrababu Naidu, that his party would have no truck with it in future.

(2851) Hyderabad : The Congress Legislature Party (CLP) on Wednesday accused TDP president N. Chandrababu Naidu of attempting to resurrect its political fortunes by resorting to false campaigns. He was doing so in desperation following the declining image of his party, it added.

(2852) Nizamabad : The Bharatiya Janata Party has accused the Congress and the Telugu Desam Party of vying with each other to appease Muslims to secure votes in the municipal elections.

(2853) Vijayawada : With leaders at the top echelons of the Left parties camping in the city to 'realise' the desire - they shared with Chief Minister

Y.S. Rajasekhara Reddy - of forging an alliance with the Congress in the elections, talks between both sides seem to be boiling down to an amiable settlement.

(2854) Visakhapatnam : Former president of Bharatiya Janata Party Bangaru Laxman indicated on Wednesday that the present party president, L.K. Advani, might prefer to quit the party post and continue as Leader of the Opposition in Lok Sabha.

(2855) Warangal : Ruling out a truck with the BJP in the ensuing municipal elections, the TDP president, N Chandrababu Naidu, exuded confidence that his party would fare better despite an alliance between the Congress, TRS and Left parties.

(2856) Udupi : The head of the State unit of Shiv Sena, Pramod Mutalik, on Wednesday said that a substantial number of Bharatiya Janata Party (BJP) MLAs were supporting the Shiv Sena in the State.

(2857) Thiruvananthapuram : The BJP on Wednesday alleged that the UDF Government's performance over the last one year was marked by abject failure on all fronts.

(2858) Thiruvananthapuram : The KPCC president Ramesh Chennithala today alleged that the CPI(M) and the LDF leadership have built bridges with the BJP in the State via the erstwhile IFDP leader P.C. Thomas.

(2859) Thiruvananthapuram : Leader of the Opposition V. S. Achuthanandan has alleged corruption involving at least Rs.75 crores in the award of contract for supply of DI pipes to be used in the Rs.1,787-crore JBIC-aided drinking water supply scheme.

(2860) New Delhi : The Election Commission of India on Wednesday approved the registration of the newly-floated party of the breakaway Karunakaran faction of the Congress in Kerala as 'Democratic Indira Congress (Karunakaran).'

(2861) Malappuram : Democratic Indira Congress (Karunakaran) leader M.P. Gangadharan here on Wednesday underscored the importance of an alliance with the Left Democratic Front (LDF).

(2862) New Delhi : The Bharatiya Janata Party has made it clear that it will strongly oppose foreign direct investment in the retail trade and that it hoped the Government would not decide on this issue between now and the winter session of Parliament when the issue could be discussed in detail on the floor of the House.

(2863) New Delhi : The Janata Dal (United) has taken exception to the Rashtriya Swayamsevak Sangh's criticism of its leader, Nitish Kumar, for suggesting reservation for Dalits who have converted to Christianity and Islam. Mr. Kumar was criticised in an editorial in the Organiser, an RSS mouthpiece.

(2864) Chennai : Janata Party president Subramanian Swamy has called for an investigation by the Central Bureau of Investigation into charges against Union Finance Minister P. Chidambaram, his wife, Nalini Chidambaram and son Karthi Chidambaram.

(2865) New Delhi : The Delhi unit of the Congress was thrown into turmoil on Wednesday with the Member of Parliament from New Delhi, Ajay Maken, reportedly demanding resignation of Chief Minister Sheila Dikshit for "mishandling the power crisis" and going ahead with the anti-people step of offering subsidy to private distribution companies at the cost of the taxpayer's money.

(2866) Chennai : Tamil Nadu Congress Committee president G.K. Vasan has criticised Chief Minister Jayalalithaa for demanding the resignation of Union Finance Minister P. Chidambaram.

(2867) Chennai : Dravida Munnetra Kazhagam president M. Karunanidhi on Wednesday charged the State Government with considering it "infra dig" to invite transport corporation employees for talks on their demands, including wage revision.

(2868) Chennai : Marumalarchi Dravida Munnetra Kazhagam general secretary Vaiko on Wednesday said his party was ready to accept any formula for passing the Women's Reservation Bill.

02-09-2005

(2869) Hyderabad : The Bharatiya Janata Party (BJP) president N. Indrasena Reddy lashed out at the Telugu Desam Party chief, N. Chandrababu Naidu and wanted him to spell out his party's ideology.

(2870) Hyderabad : Andhra Pradesh Congress Committee president K. Keshava Rao has lashed out at Telangana Rashtra Samithi president K.

Chandrasekhara Rao for his criticism of Chief Minister Y. S. Rajasekhara Reddy.

(2871) Hyderabad : The Telugu Desam Party has said that the Chief Minister, Y. S. Rajasekhara Reddy, should convey his views against creation of more States to the AICC President, Sonia Gandhi, and ask for severance of ties with the Telangana Rashtra Samithi.

(2872) Thiruvananthapuram : The Democratic Indira Congress (DIC) (Karunakaran) has staked claims to the seats contested by the Congress in the last local bodies elections in its seat adjustment dialogues with Left parties. In return, it has agreed not to stake a claim to the posts of presiding officers of the local bodies, particularly district panchayats, municipalities, and corporations after the elections. Since this is an issue that has to be sorted out on the basis of the outcome, the party has decided not to dispute it and concede the ground despite the fact that the nature of alliance would have a bearing on the control over the local bodies.

(2873) New Delhi : The Telangana Rashtra Samiti has once again raised the pitch against the Andhra Pradesh Chief Minister Y.S. Rajasekhara Reddy, and said it is considering the attitude of the latter and the party may think of quitting the United Progressive Alliance.

(2874) Bangalore : The Janata Dal (Secular), to make up for the setback in Mysore district on account of the revolt by the former Deputy Chief Minister Siddaramaiah, on Thursday admitted the former Congress MLA for Hunsur Chikkamadu and a large number of workers from other parties.

(2875) Bangalore : The Maharashtra Government has indulged in unethical and clever practices to build up make-believe evidence against the State to demand an undue share of Krishna waters under Scheme B of the Bachawat Tribunal Award, Leader of the Opposition in the Legislative Assembly B.S. Yediyurappa has alleged.

(2876) Mangalore : The Karnataka unit of the Shiv Sena will grow from strength to strength and there are promises from 38 MLAs in the State to join the party, founder chief of the Shiv Sena Karnataka Unit Pramod Muthalik said on Thursday.

(2877) Palakkad : Kerala Pradesh Congress Committee (KPCC) president Ramesh Chennithala has said his party will have no alliance with the Bharatiya Janata Party (BJP) in the local bodies elections.

(2878) Thiruvananthapuram : Leader of the Opposition V. S. Achuthanandan has alleged a conspiracy involving Industries Minister V. K. Ebrahim Kunju's office and top leaders of the Muslim League to 'impose' a Rs.250-crore pollution control project on public sector Travancore Titanium Products (TTP) Limited in total disregard for the recommendations of the Supreme Court Monitoring Committee and the Kerala State Pollution Control Board.

(2879) Thiruvananthapuram : Democratic Indira Congress (DIC) (Karunakaran) president K. Muraleedharan on Thursday said that Congress president Sonia Gandhi's intervention in the Election Commission case regarding a name for his party proved that she continued to harbour fears about it as a political force.

(2880) New Delhi : Congress president Sonia Gandhi used the first meeting of the National Integration Council (NIC) in 13 years to celebrate India's diversity and assert that it should not be allowed to divide the country under any circumstances. Reiterating her party's commitment to combating communalism and terrorism at the meeting here on Wednesday, she also made out a strong case for sustained involvement of civil society in nation-building on the premise that it was the best safeguard against social strife, sectarianism and violence.

(2881) New Delhi : The Bharatiya Janata Party Councillors have flayed Chief Minister Sheila Dikshit for agreeing to share the subsidy in order to rollback the hike in power tariffs. Demanding that the private distribution companies should take the entire burden, senior BJP councillor Vijender Kumar Gupta has termed the "arrangement" as a conspiracy between the Congress Government and the discoms to siphon off the public money.

(2882) New Delhi : With the battle lines having been drawn within the Delhi unit of the Congress, the party leader in charge of Delhi affairs, Ashok Gehlot, on Thursday announced convening of the Coordination Committee meeting on September 8 to discuss various issues including the power crisis and industrial relocation. The decision to convene the meeting comes hot on the heels of a confrontation between the Chief Minister's camp and loyalists over the issue of rollback of the increase in power tariffs and the demand by one of the party leaders Ajay Maken for resignation of Ms. Dikshit throwing the party into a crisis.

(2883) New Delhi : There seems to be no respite for Chief Minister Sheila Dikshit on the power front with two-dozen MLAs reportedly writing to Congress president Sonia Gandhi and various All-India Congress Committee leaders seeking a "review" of the Delhi Cabinet's decision to offer a 5 per cent subsidy to make up for the losses of the private distribution companies as part of the rollback formula for the recent power tariff increase.

(2884) Chennai : There would be practical problems if political parties are required to allot one-third of the constituencies to women, Dravida Munnetra Kazhagam president M. Karunanidhi said here on Thursday.

(2885) Villupuram : The Pattali Makkal Katchi has underscored the need for a national movement to revive awareness about the significance of reservation in legislature, education and employment.

03-09-2005

(2886) Hyderabad : The Congress party has charged the Telugu Desam Party with adopting an anti-poor stand by opposing the distribution of ration cards during the municipal elections.

(2887) Hyderabad : As the last date for filing nominations for municipal elections is approaching, the Communist Party of India (Marxist) is not fully confident of the Left reaching an understanding with the Congress in at least a couple of corporations and some municipalities.

(2888) Kakinada : The Bharatiya Janata Party (BJP) has lost heavily for sailing blindly with the Telugu Desam Party (TDP) all these years and the party workers are totally disillusioned, according to the former State party president, P.V. Chalapathi Rao.

(2889) New Delhi : The Telangana Rashtra Samiti (TRS) on Friday announced it would go it alone in the coming municipal elections in Andhra Pradesh.

(2890) Bangalore : B.S. Yediyurappa, Leader of the Opposition in the Legislative Assembly, has accused the State Government of suppressing and acquiescing with the directive issued by the Centre to store water only up to 509.1 m in the Alamatti Dam across the Krishna till September 30. He has demanded that the Centre withdraw the directive immediately.

(2891) Bellary : S. Prasannakumar, general secretary of the Communist Party of India (Marxist) has accused the Congress-led United Progressive Alliance Government at the Centre of succumbing to pressures of the World Bank in adopting anti-labour policies, among other things.

(2892) Hubli : Pramod Mutalik, the president of the State unit of the Shiv Sena, which was launched in the State recently, is confident that the party will emerge a rallying point for the Hindutva forces in Karnataka.

(2893) Thiruvananthapuram : Kerala Pradesh Congress Committee president Ramesh Chennithala on Friday demanded a probe into the utilisation of the Rs. 10.54-crore Swiss aid under the People's Plan programme during the LDF rule.

(2894) Thiruvananthapuram : The RSP leadership has asked P.C. Thomas, MP, to forswear links with the BJP before he becomes part of the LDF.

(2895) Malappuram : The Indian Union Muslim League (IUML) leadership has accused the Left Democratic Front (LDF) of entering into an "unholy alliance" with the Bharatiya Janata Party (BJP) to single out the League in the coming local bodies elections.

(2896) Thiruvananthapuram : Prime Minister Manmohan Singh on Friday urged all sections outside the electoral process, be it in Assam, Jammu and Kashmir or Andhra Pradesh, to shun violence and take the path of dialogues to resolve issues.

(2897) New Delhi : The former Defence Minister and Bharatiya Janata Party (BJP) leader, Jaswant Singh, on Friday criticised the United Progressive Alliance (UPA) Government for referring nearly three dozen defence purchases to the Central Bureau of Investigation (CBI), as "this amounted to political vendetta and would cause anxiety among bureaucrats and defence officials negotiating major defence deals."

(2898) New Delhi : The Communist Party of India (Marxist) on Friday made it clear that the Left parties would resume participation in the United Progressive Alliance-Left coordination committee meetings only after a "categorical announcement" by the Government that there would be no disinvestment in 'navratna' PSUs.

(2899) New Delhi : The Communist Party of India (Marxist) on Thursday said it was "disturbed" by the decision of the Centre to go ahead with the bidding process to facilitate privatisation of the Mumbai and Delhi Airports and demanded it be stopped pending resolution of critical issues.

(2900) New Delhi : Even as the dissident MLAs claimed to have got the signatures of nearly two dozen legislators as part of their campaign to take on Chief Minister Sheila Dikshit, some loyalist MLAs on Friday denied having anything to do with the latest letter-writing initiative on the issue of providing subsidy to the Capital's private power distribution companies and said they were completely behind the Chief Minister.

(2901) New Delhi : The Leader of the Opposition in the Delhi Assembly, Jagdish Mukhi, has welcomed the decision of the Chief Vigilance Commissioner to initiate an enquiry into privatisation of the erstwhile Delhi Vidyut Board and urged Prime Minister Manmohan Singh to refer the case to the Central Bureau of Investigation.

(2902) New Delhi : Backed by some "revealing documentary evidence" provided by the Member of Parliament from New Delhi, Ajay Maken, indicating "unlawful gains" given to the Capital's private power distribution companies, senior party leaders, including Members of Parliament and Congress Working Committee members on Friday decided to write to Congress president Sonia Gandhi "complaining" against the Chief Minister, Sheila Dikshit, for her continued defiance of the party and its leaders.

(2903) Chennai : Communist Party of India national secretary D. Raja on Friday said the United Progressive Alliance (UPA) Government, supported by the Left parties, would complete its term.

(2904) Chennai : Tamil Nadu Congress Committee president G.K. Vasan, has criticised Chief Minister Jayalalithaa for demanding immediate suspension of dredging work for the Sethusamudram project.

04-09-2005

(2905) Hyderabad : TDP president N. Chandrababu Naidu said here on Saturday that it was improper on the part of the TRS president, K.

Chandrasekhar Rao, to have called on the Virasam leader, Varavara Rao, in Chanchalguda jail considering that he was a Union Minister.

(2906) Hyderabad : The APCC president, K. Keshava Rao, has advised TDP president N. Chandrababu Naidu to cultivate 'a healthy respect' for democratic norms.

(2907) Hyderabad : The Telugu Desam Party is of the view that pre-election alliances or the lack of such arrangements among major players in the coming municipal elections will have no significant impact on the final outcome.

(2908) Hyderabad : Union Labour Minister and Telangana Rashtra Samithi president K. Chandrasekhar Rao on Saturday called on former CPI (Maoist) emissaries - Varavara Rao and G. Kalyan Rao - at the Chanchalguda jail, here, where they are detained following a ban imposed on Maoists.

(2909) Nellore : State president of the Bharatiya Janata Party N. Indrasena Reddy has demanded a white paper on provision of civic amenities in various municipalities, as promised by the Congress party's manifesto.

(2910) Warangal : Senior CPI leader Puvvada Nageshwar Rao has ruled out any alliance with the Telangana Rashtra Samithi in the coming municipal elections.

(2911) Sangareddy : Union Minister of State for Rural Development and TRS leader A. Narendra announced that his party would decide its future plan of action after September 8, heeding to the request of Union Minister for Agriculture Sharad Pawar.

(2912) Bijapur : The former Prime Minister H.D. Deve Gowda said here on Saturday that he saw enough reason behind the Centre's directive to Karnataka to reduce the water level in the Alamatti Dam to 509.1 metres till September 30.

(2913) Bangalore : All-India Congress Committee General Secretary Margaret Alva on Saturday expressed confidence that the Women's Reservation Bill, providing for 33 per cent reservation for women in Parliament and legislatures, would be passed despite initial hurdles.

(2914) Bijapur : Former Prime Minister H.D. Deve Gowda on Saturday completed the tour of the flood-affected districts of Belgaum, Bijapur and Bagalkot. He sought immediate commencement of rehabilitation programme for people living in low-lying habitations along the Krishna and the Bhima.

(2915) Gulbarga : Karnataka Pranta Raitha Sangha and Communist Party of India (Marxist) on Saturday took exception to Union Minister for Water Resources Priyaranjan Dasmunshi writing to Karnataka to take steps to reduce the water level in the Alamatti dam to 509 metres on humanitarian grounds to "prevent flooding of some areas in Maharashtra."

(2916) Tumkur : Senior Congress leaders on Saturday criticised Janata Dal (Secular) President H.D. Deve Gowda for what they called misusing the name of Congress president Sonia Gandhi for his own political advantage in the State.

(2917) Chitradurga : H.D. Kumaraswamy, Working President of the Janata Dal (Secular) State unit, has challenged leaders of AHIND to come out with at least one instance to substantiate their allegations of nepotism and anti-backward class attitude levelled against former Prime Minister and party President H.D. Deve Gowda.

(2918) Kochi : The BJP State president P. S. Sreedharan Pillai has said that there would be no truck with the LDF or the UDF in the ensuing elections to the local bodies.

(2919) Palakkad : Democratic Indira Congress (Karunakaran) president K. Muraleedharan has said that the Indian Union Muslim League (IUML) has lost its secular tradition and political integrity because of the stand it has taken on issues like the Marad violence and the Kannur speech of (its State general secretary) P.K. Kunhalikutty.

(2920) New Delhi : The Delhi State Committee of the Communist Party of India (Marxist) on Saturday staged a protest march here against the burning down of 50 houses of Dalits at Gohana in Sonepat on August 31.

(2921) New Delhi : Sensing growing differences within the National Democratic Alliance and possible parting of ways of some of its constituents, the Communist Party of India (Marxist) feels that in such a situation the party should expand its base to fill the vacuum.

(2922) New Delhi : The announcement of four-phase polling in October-November to the Bihar Assembly received a mixed response with the Congress, the Communist Party of India and the Nationalist Congress Party suggesting a compact schedule during November.

(2923) Patna : Rashtriya Janata Dal supremo and Railway Minister Lalu Prasad and Congress general secretary Digvijay Singh on Saturday welcomed the announcement of four-phase elections to the Bihar Assembly.

(2924) New Delhi : The Bharatiya Janata Party and the Janata Dal (United) on Saturday once again reiterated their demand that Bihar Governor Buta Singh be recalled as free and fair elections with him in the Raj Bhavan would not be possible.

(2925) New Delhi : Terming the recent announcement of rollback of the 10 per cent power tariff hike by Delhi Chief Minister Sheila Dikshit as a victory for the people of the Capital, former Union Minister Vijay Goel on Saturday sought an assurance from the Delhi Government that power tariffs would not be hiked during the coming years.

(2926) New Delhi : Seeking to set the record straight, Delhi Chief Minister Sheila Dikshit is understood to have written to Congress president Sonia Gandhi on Saturday explaining the sequence of events that led to the rollback of the 10 per cent increase in the power tariffs. She has reportedly given details of attempts by the party to derail a government that had been running successfully and efficiently for almost seven years.

(2927) Pondicherry : A resolution adopted at the meeting of the office bearers of Pondicherry State committee of the All India Anna Dravida Munnetra Kazhagam (AIADMK) here on Saturday condemned the 'failure of the Chief Minister' to participate in the recent National Development Council meeting in Delhi.

(2928) Chennai : Dravida Munnetra Kazhagam president M. Karunanidhi on Saturday criticised Chief Minister Jayalalithaa for her demand to stop dredging operations of the Sethusamudram Ship Canal Project (SSCP).

(2929) Madurai : The elected members of the constituent parties of Democratic Progressive Alliance (DPA) rallied behind the Union Minister of Shipping, T.R. Baalu, justifying the ongoing dredging operation for the Sethusamudram Ship Channel Project.

05-09-2005

(2930) Hyderabad : The Communist Party of India State council has urged Chief Minister Y.S. Rajasekhara Reddy to announce a one-time settlement scheme for clearing the pending crop loans in cooperative banks. This should be done in the interests of farmers affected by the construction of the flood flow canal in Karimnagar district.

(2931) Hyderabad : The Telugu Desam Party has criticised the Government for deciding to accept the cheque for Rs. 11.67 crores without recovering the amount first from those who allegedly duped it. In a press release, the party general secretary, Ch. Ayyanna Patrudu, and MLA, V. Keshav, said it the decision was unfortunate.

(2932) Nizamabad : The Telugu Desam MLA and former chief engineer, Sana Maruthi, has alleged that the Congress Government is deliberately neglecting the irrigation projects in backward Telangana region and the delay in completion of the Guthpa lift scheme in Nizamabad district is an example for it.

(2933) Visakhapatnam : CPI(M) MP Midiam Babu Rao on Sunday found fault with the State Government for signing a memorandum of understanding (MoU) with the Jindal Group for setting up an alumina plant and refinery in the district without consulting tribals and their representatives.

(2934) Hyderabad : Union Labour Minister and Telangana Rashtra Samithi (TRS) president K. Chandrasekhar Rao has indicated that he and his colleague - Union Minister of State for Rural Development A. Narendra - will pull out of the United Progressive Alliance (UPA) Government but will continue to extend it outside support.

(2935) Bangalore : Janata Dal (Secular) leader H.D. Deve Gowda, who is being targeted by leaders of the Federation of Dalits, Minorities and Backward Classes, on Sunday drew support and praise from the former Law Minister L.G. Havanur, who headed the first Karnataka Backward Classes Commission.

(2936) Shimoga : The Shimoga MP and President of the State unit of the Samajawadi Party S. Bangarappa said here on Saturday that able leadership is the basic requirement for any country to prosper.

(2937) Thiruvananthapuram : Leader of the Opposition V.S. Achuthanandan has flayed the Government for not accepting the food and cloth consignment sent from Dubai for distribution among the tsunami-hit in the State.

(2938) New Delhi : West Bengal Chief Minister Buddhadeb Bhattacharjee got an endorsement from the CPI (M) Central Committee on Sunday after he gave clarifications on his statements on foreign investment and related issues during his recent visit to Singapore and Indonesia.

(2939) New Delhi : Union Minister and Lok Jan Shakti Party (LJP) chief Ram Vilas Paswan said his party would not field candidates in the seats held by the Congress even if it contested in an alliance with the Rashtriya Janata Dal (RJD) in the coming elections.

(2940) Nadi (Fiji) : Lok Sabha Speaker Somnath Chatterjee has been appointed to a 11-member body of the Executive Committee of the Commonwealth Parliamentary Association (CPA) to choose a new Secretary General.

(2941) New Delhi : The Communist Party of India's general secretary, A.B. Bardhan, and the Communist Party of India (Marxist) Central committee member, E. Balanandan, have demanded review of the Electricity Act-2003 and its implementation.

(2942) Chennai : Dravida Munnetra Kazhagam president M. Karunanidhi on Sunday criticised Chief Minister Jayalalithaa for staying away from the Prime Minister's programmes in the city.

(2943) Pondicherry : The Tamil Nadu Chief Minister, Jayalalithaa's sudden opposition to the Sethusamudram project was "unwarranted" and her reason seeking a stop to the project was "not convincing," CPI leader D Raja said.

06-09-2005

(2944) Hyderabad : The Congress Legislature Party (CLP) has termed the Telugu Desam Party (TDP) petition to the State Election Commission against the implementation of the PRC recommendations anti-employee.

(2945) Hyderabad : APCC president K. Keshava Rao has called upon the protagonists of Telangana to join hands with the Congress in the civic elections "in the best interest of Telangana."

(2946) Hyderabad : The Telugu Desam Party president, N. Chandrababu Naidu, on Monday charged the Congress Government with resorting to politically vindictive actions to browbeat the Opposition.

(2947) New Delhi : The prices of petrol and diesel are likely to be raised on Tuesday. Despite Left objections, Prime Minister Manmohan Singh has indicated that the Cabinet will consider the issue on Tuesday to deal with the immediate crisis created by the surging world oil prices .

(2948) Kottayam : The merger between the LDF partner Kerala Congress (Joseph) and the NDA member Indian Federal Democratic Party (IFDP) was formalised at a special function here on Monday.

(2949) Bangalore : Both Prime Minister Manmohan Singh and Congress President Sonia Gandhi have been evincing special interest in the development and prosperity of Karnataka, according to Chief Minister N. Dharam Singh.

(2950) Bangalore : Now it is the turn of the Bharatiya Janata Party (BJP) to organise a convention of Scheduled Castes, Scheduled Tribes and slum dwellers.

(2951) Bangalore : Janata Dal (Secular) President H.D. Deve Gowda on Monday told party MLAs who intend to join the Congress to emulate the example of the former Chief Minister S. Bangarappa, who resigned from the Lok Sabha after quitting the Bharatiya Janata Party (BJP).

(2952) Malappuram : Chief of the Naval Staff Admiral Arun Prakash has underscored the need for a shift in the security and foreign policies towards self-interest and pragmatism. It is time the country overcame its internal security challenges and started looking beyond its shores with forces, which have transnational capabilities and contingency plans to match.

(2953) New Delhi : The Bharatiya Janata Party would lodge a formal complaint with the Election Commission against Bihar Governor Buta Singh for alleged violation of the model code of conduct.

(2954) New Delhi : The Bharatiya Janata Party has demanded the dismissal of a member of the Securities and Exchange Board of India (SEBI) for predicting that Sensex will cross the 16,000-mark in the coming months. It has expressed surprise at the Finance Ministry's "inaction. "

(2955) New Delhi : The Congress on Monday refused to reciprocate the Lok Jan Shakti Party's decision not to field candidates against it in the Bihar Assembly elections, saying the third alternative forged by the LJP would eat into secular votes.

(2956) New Delhi : The Communist Party of India (Marxist) on Monday deplored the use of violence by the monarchy in Nepal against the peaceful demonstration in Kathmandu that led to large-scale arrests. It urged the Manmohan Singh Government not to support the regime of King Gyanendra.

(2957) Rae Bareli : Congress president Sonia Gandhi and her son and party MP Rahul Gandhi on Monday visited the district hospital here to meet patients suffering from Japanese encephalitis.

(2958) New Delhi : The opposition Bharatiya Janata Party on Monday lambasted the ruling Congress leadership in the Municipal Corporation of Delhi for insulting teachers by not attending Teachers' Day function in the Capital.

(2959) Tambaram : members of the AIADMK took out a rally here on Monday to protest against the reported attempts made by Union Minister for Shipping, Road Transport and Highways T.R. Baalu to scuttle development works initiated by the State government and the Pallavaram Municipality.

(2960) Chennai : "If [oil] prices are raised again it will be regrettable," Dravida Munnetra Kazhagam president M. Karunanidhi said on Monday. Answering questions from presspersons here, he agreed that news on the need for raising the price of petroleum products was coming in.

07-09-2005

(2961) Hyderabad : The coordination committee formed by the AICC to interact with the Government in ensuring the implementation of the party programmes would begin its on-the-spot study of the ground realities from November.

(2962) Hyderabad : The Bharatiya Janata Party will contest over 2,000 seats in the coming municipal elections.

(2963) Hyderabad : The Andhra Pradesh Congress Committee has urged the AICC president, Sonia Gandhi, to nominate all 21 members of the Congress Working Committee (CWC) instead of holding elections to the posts.

(2964) Hyderabad : Castigating the Central and State Governments for the latest hike in petroleum prices, the Telugu Desam Party president, N. Chandrababu Naidu, demanded that the duties/taxes component constituting two-thirds of their prices, be brought down.

(2965) Hyderabad : The AICC preferred to snub the Telangana Rashtra Samithi leaders here on Tuesday by supporting the imposition of the ban on naxalites and also leaving the decision of parting ways "to the wisdom of the TRS".

(2966) Bangalore : Some of the Congress leaders, who had criticised Chief Minister N. Dharam Singh for his soft attitude towards the Janata Dal (Secular) leaders, have clarified that they are neither against his stewardship of the Government nor against the coalition arrangement.

(2967) New Delhi : The Bharatiya Janata Party's central disciplinary committee on Tuesday recommended the "expulsion" of senior leader Madan Lal Khurana from the party for six years.

(2968) Thiruvananthapuram : The Opposition Left Democratic Front (LDF) would work to strengthen the three-tier local bodies and bring more transparency and social accountability in their functioning, according to the LDF manifesto for the September 24-26 local bodies elections.

(2969) New Delhi : The Left parties on Tuesday decided to protest the hike in petrol and diesel prices and asked the State units to mobilise people against the move.

(2970) Gulbarga : Basavaraj Ingin, vice-president of the State unit of the Janata Dal (United), on Tuesday accused former Prime Minister and President of the Janata Dal (Secular) H.D. Deve Gowda of indulging in poaching other parties and attempting to break the Janata Dal (U) by luring senior party leaders and legislators with promises of making them Ministers.

(2971) Mysore : The former Deputy Chief Minister Siddaramaiah has categorically ruled out joining the Congress. "Neither have I submitted an application to the Congress party nor have I met senior Congress leaders in that regard," Mr. Siddaramaiah clarified at a meet the press programme organized by the Mysore District Journalists' Association here on Tuesday.

(2972) Thiruvananthapuram : The Congress spokesman M.M. Hassan has regretted that the people who had left the Congress to join the Democratic Indira Congress (Karunakaran) had landed in the backyard of the Left Democratic Front (LDF).

(2973) Thiruvananthapuram : Congress (S), a long-time partner in the Opposition LDF, stayed away from the LDF State committee meeting here on Tuesday in protest against what it termed the Front leadership's discriminatory attitude towards it. Congress(S) State president Ramachandran Kadannappalli left here for Kannur on Monday night after handing over a letter to LDF convener Paloli Mohammed Kutty expressing dismay at what he termed the rough treatment being meted out to traditional allies even while the Front leadership accommodated the demands of the Democratic Indira Congress (Karunakaran). The LDF convener, however, told reporters after the LDF meeting that some of Mr. Kadannappalli's concerns had already been addressed and that any outstanding issue would be resolved in a day or two.

(2974) Thiruvananthapuram : Left parties and trade unions have termed the Central Government decision to hike petroleum product prices a major blow to Kerala.

(2975) New Delhi : The Bharatiya Janata Party said on Tuesday that it would launch a nation-wide agitation against the "unreasonable" hike in the prices of petrol and diesel. It would hold demonstrations in all State capitals and district headquarters on Wednesday and Thursday.

(2976) New Delhi : The National Democratic Alliance on Tuesday drew the Election Commission's attention to "certain glaring violations" of the model code of conduct by Bihar Governor Buta Singh, in making political appointments on Saturday last, the day the poll schedule was announced. In a memorandum, it sought cancellation of the appointments.

(2977) Mumbai : Ever since Kohinoor Mills No 3, one of the defunct textile units at Dadar here, was bought for Rs. 421 crores by Shiv Sena leader Manohar Joshi's son and others, questions have been raised how the party justified the purchase, given that it opposed the sale of mill land in the past, and how this will affect its image as a "sons of the soil" organisation.

(2978) Mumbai : Expelled Shiv Sena leader and Maharashtra Revenue Minister Narayan Rane on Tuesday founded a new trade union with former Sainiks. He said workers were under a renewed threat after globalisation and many trade unions were not really working for the benefit of people.

(2979) New Delhi : Education Ministers from the Bharatiya Janata Party-ruled States walked out of the meeting of the Central Advisory Board of Education (CABE) on Tuesday to protest against Union Human Resource Development Minister Arjun Singh putting the National Curriculum Framework (NCF) up for discussion without incorporating their suggestions.

(2980) Chennai : The Janata Party president, Subramanian Swamy, on Tuesday condemned the decision to raise the prices of petrol and diesel. "India's petrol prices are already among the world's highest as a ratio of per capita income," he said in a statement. Fifty four per cent of the petrol prices were taxes of the Government.

(2981) New Delhi : The news of expulsion of former Delhi Chief Minister and senior BJP leader Madan Lal Khurana might have brought cheer to his rivals but it's certainly not good news for the faction-ridden party that is struggling to regain a stronghold in city politics. Not only would this action anger the Capital's dominant Punjabi community, it could also force Mr. Khurana to form a regional front damaging the saffron party.

(2982) Tambaram : The Marumalarchi Dravida Munnetra Kazhagam (MDMK) leader, Vaiko, on Tuesday charged Chief Minister Jayalalithaa with failing to uphold political decency and culture by not receiving Prime Minister Manmohan Singh at the Chennai airport, during his recent visit to the city.

09-09-2005

(2983) Hyderabad : The Chief Minister, Y. S. Rajasekhara Reddy, will not lead the Congress campaign in the civic elections, but only "monitor and interact" with the party workers and leaders through video-conferencing.

(2984) Hyderabad : The Telugu Desam Party has charged the Congress with holding out threats and forcing party candidates to withdraw from contesting municipal elections besides working for their disqualification wherever they were strong.

(2985) Hyderabad : The Telugu Desam Party has demanded an apology from the Chief Minister, Y. S. Rajasekhara Reddy, and action against officials following confirmation by the National Human Rights Commission (NHRC) that 2,227 tribals have died of malaria and other communicable diseases in Visakhapatnam .

(2986) Sangareddy : Unable to face mounting pressure from friendly parties and different sections of people, the Congress party is resorting to physical attacks on political opponents through killer gangs, TRS leader and Union Minister A. Narendra alleged here on Thursday.

(2987) Vizianagaram : The Telugu Desam Party, district unit has promised transparency, selfless service, accountability to people and also a code of conduct for councillors and chairperson for effective functioning.

(2988) New Delhi : A statement issued by the former Prime Minister, Atal Bihari Vajpayee, on Thursday criticising the expulsion of the senior leader, Madan Lal Khurana, from the Bharatiya Janata Party triggered a chain of events, throwing the party into turmoil. This comes eight days ahead of the BJP's national executive committee meeting in Chennai.

(2989) Chitradurga : H.D. Deve Gowda, former Prime Minister and President of Janata Dal (Secular), has asked the State Government to divide the quota for backward classes to help the most backward communities which have not benefited from the reservation system.

(2990) Hassan : Despite instructions from the Karnataka Pradesh Congress Committee (KPCC), many Congress leaders in the district have decided to participate in the Swabhimani Samavesha to be held here on September 26.

(2991) Madikeri : The Bharatiya Janata Party (BJP) is leaning more towards secularism by ignoring the interests of the Hindus, State president of the Shiv Sena, Pramod Mutalik, alleged here on Thursday.

(2992) Chitradurga : H.D. Deve Gowda, former Prime Minister and president of Janata Dal (Secular), has asked the Karnataka Government to divide the quota for backward classes to help the most backward communities which have not benefited from the reservation system.

(2993) Thiruvananthapuram : Leader of the Opposition V.S. Achuthanandan has urged the Government not to sign the Memorandum of Understanding (MoU) with the Dubai Internet City (DIC) since it contained several provisions detrimental to the State's interests.

(2994) Thiruvananthapuram : Convener of the Left Democratic Front (LDF) Paloli Mohammed Kutty has said that the LDF Government had refused to give in to the Asian Development Bank's condition that the State must go in for cut in staff strength if it wanted the bank's loan.

(2995) Thiruvananthapuram : The Congress Working Committee Member A. K. Antony appears to be ploughing a lonely furrow when it comes to the question of the former Congress veteran K. Karunakaran's return to the Congress fold. Knowing fully well that he was alone on this issue, Mr. Antony once again made an appeal to Karunakaran and his men to return home. Addressing presspersons soon after moving into his new office in the KPCC, Mr. Antony pointed out that Karunakaran and his men, had they continued in the party, would have had a major say in seat sharing and would have taken away more than 50 per cent. However, the new party was forced to run from one CPI (M) office to another seeking seats to contests.

(2996) New Delhi : Expelled BJP leader and former Delhi Chief Minister Madan Lal Khurana on Thursday accused party president L.K. Advani of adopting a "dictatorial attitude" in dealing with party matters and charged those surrounding him with giving wrong advice to him that had turned the BJP from a "family unit into a private limited company." The rally to express solidarity and support to Mr. Khurana saw a huge turnout with three Delhi BJP legislators and local party leaders turning up at the venue defying the party directive.

(2997) Patna : Communist Party of India (CPI) general secretary A.B. Bardhan on Thursday criticised the Congress for its "politics of threats, intimidation and ultimatums." He warned that if the Lok Jan Shakti Party (LJP) leader and Steel Minister, Ram Vilas Paswan, was shown the door, the United Progressive Alliance would be weakened.

(2998) New Delhi : The contours for the Bihar Assembly elections appear to have been drawn with the Lok Janshakti Party (LJP) getting the backing of three of the four Left parties supporting the United Progressive Alliance (UPA) to contest separately, even as the Rashtriya Janata Dal (RJD) on Thursday hinted that the LJP should leave the UPA coalition if it was forming a third political alternative.

(2999) New Delhi : Infighting within the Delhi unit of the Congress is all set to intensify as five Members of Parliament and two former DPCC presidents on Thursday called on the party general secretary in charge of Delhi affairs, Ashok Gehlot, and demanded "removal" of Chief Minister Sheila Dikshit, claiming that her continuation in office was causing immense damage to the image of the party and the Government.

(3000) Chandigarh : Twenty seven-year-old Deepender Singh Hooda, son of the Haryana Chief Minister, Bhupinder Singh Hooda, will be the Congress nominee for the Rohtak Lok Sabha seat, which was vacated after the latter got elected as MLA from the Kiloi Vidhan Sabha constituency in May this year.

(3001) Bhopal : Madhya Pradesh Congress Committee general secretary and spokesman Manak Agrawal has targeted the State Minister for Public Works Department, Kailash Vijayvargiya, for the alleged bungling in distribution of social security pension by the Indore Municipal Corporation during his tenure as Mayor-in-Council between 1998 and 2004.

(3002) Chennai : The Bharatiya Janata Party on Thursday criticised the Dravida Munnetra Kazhagam and the Left on the issue of hike in prices of petrol and diesel.

(3003) Chennai : Tamil Nadu Congress Committee president G.K. Vasan on Wednesday asked the State Government whether it was ready to reduce sales tax on petroleum products so as to lessen the burden on the common man following the price hike.

(3004) Chennai : The Dravida Munnetra Kazhagam president, M. Karunanidhi, on Thursday said that the Jayalalithaa Government had increased bus fares heavily in 2001itself and had placed a huge burden on the people.

(3005) Chennai : Chief Minister Jayalalithaa on Tuesday flayed the United Progressive Alliance Government for its decision to increase the price of petrol and diesel. She made it clear that her Government would not revise the bus fare though the diesel price hike would mean an additional burden of Rs. 122.5 crores per annum for the State Transport Corporations (STCs).

(3006) Villupuram : Pattali Makkal Katchi founder S.Ramadoss has accused the Chief Minister Jayalalithaa of pursuing "politics of convenience" in regard to the Sethu Samudhram Ship Channel Project.

10-09-2005

(3007) Hyderabad : The BJP State unit has assured the urban electorate water, shelter, health facilities, comprehensive development, besides good governance, in its manifesto for the municipal elections.

(3008) New Delhi : Several rounds of meetings at the houses of the former Prime Minister, Atal Bihari Vajpayee, and Bharatiya Janata Party president L.K. Advani here on Friday failed to resolve the crisis in the party resulting from Mr. Vajpayee's public disapproval of the expulsion of senior leader Madan Lal Khurana.

(3009) Bangalore : The Congress's stand on its members attending the AHINDA (federation of backward classes, minorities and Dalits) conventions organised by former Deputy Chief Minister Siddaramaiah is likely to be spelt out before the next convention in Hassan on September 26.

(3010) Hassan : More than three lakh people will participate in the Swabhimani Samavesha to be held in Hassan on September 26 and a reception committee has been formed for organising the same. This will be different from other conventions as problems pertained to farming sector will be discussed at length, former Deputy Chief Minister Siddaramaiah has said.

(3011) Kannur : Communist Party of India (Marxist) State secretary Pinarayi Vijayan said on Friday that the leader of the Democratic Indira Congress (Karunakaran) K. Karunakaran could not now be faulted for his past stand as a Congressman on Emergency introduced by the then Congress Prime Minister Indira Gandhi with the support of the Congress.

(3012) Thiruvananthapuram : The Democratic Indira Congress (Karunakaran) has proposed to set up a manifesto audit system to examine whether promises in election manifestoes are fulfilled. It has also promised to set up popular vigilance committees to check proliferation of corruption in the local bodies.

(3013) Thiruvananthapuram : Democratic Indira Congress (Karunakaran) president K. Muraleedharan said here on Friday that his party had got a honourable treatment from the Left Democratic Front (LDF) compared with that the former Chief Minister K. Karunakaran and his supporters had received from the Congress High Command. Addressing a press conference marking the release of his party's manifesto for the local body election, he said his party was fairly happy with the seat sharing with LDF . "We might not have got seats commensurate to our strength. But we are satisfied with what we got in the interest of a larger secular democratic alliance," he said.

(3014) Thrissur : The Deputy Leader of the CPI in the Lok Sabha C. K. Chandrappan, MP and the Leader of the Legislature party K. P. Rajendran, MLA, have criticised the UDF Government on the alleged mishandling of flood relief operations and the Smart City project.

(3015) Thiruvananthapuram : The UDF election manifesto has promised to make Kerala a zero-poverty territory. "Total literacy - zero poverty" is the slogan it has coined for the local body elections.

(3016) New Delhi : Efforts are under way to bring back the Kerala Congress (B) of R. Balakrishna Pillai to the United Democratic Front (UDF), Kerala Pradesh Congress Committee (KPCC) president Ramesh Chennithala said here on Friday. A meeting between the two parties would be held on Monday.

(3017) New Delhi : The All India Congress Committee (AICC) plenary session is likely to be postponed if there is no change in the schedule for the Bihar Assembly elections. Indications to this effect were given by the party's senior leadership even as general secretaries met here on Friday to discuss the arrangements being made for the plenary now scheduled between October 20 and 22 in Hyderabad.

(3018) New Delhi : There is no need for any United Progressive Alliance constituent, which stays away from the secular alliance being stitched up for the Bihar Assembly elections, to leave the ruling coalition at the Centre, the Congress clarified on Friday.

(3019) New Delhi : The Nationalist Congress Party (NCP) on Friday met Chief Election Commissioner B.B. Tandon to press for rescheduling the coming Bihar Assembly elections. Instead of a four-phase poll, the NCP has suggested a three-phase election beginning on November 12 and ending November 19 with November 15 as the second day of polling.

(3020) Patna : Lok Jan Shakti Party chief and Union Steel Minister Ram Vilas Paswan said on Friday that he was continuing in the United Progressive Alliance because he had helped constitute it and there was no need for the Congress to issue any "threat" to him.

(3021) New Delhi : Former Maharashtra Chief Minister Narayan Rane and former Rajya Sabha MP Sanjay Nirupam - who left the Shiv Sena earlier this year to join the Congress - have found a berth in the reconstituted Maharashtra Pradesh Congress Committee (MPCC).

(3022) New Delhi : With former Chief Minister Madan Lal Khurana taking up cudgels against the Bharatiya Janata Party high command, a move has been set in motion to put in place a third alternative in Delhi. Amid speculation about realignment of political forces, leaders of Janata Dal (S) and the Nationalist Congress Party held parleys with Mr. Khurana to work out modalities for putting in place a Third Front.

(3023) Patna : The CPI (ML) on Friday strongly asked LJP chief and Union Minister Ramvilas Paswan to decide his steps and oppose Congress in the coming Assembly elections in the State to pave the way for the formation of a "Third Front" in Bihar.

(3024) Chennai : Though the Centre had declared Tamil as a classical language, Tamils have not achieved their full victory, said Dravida Munnetra Kazhagam president M. Karunanidhi here on Friday.

(3025) Coimbatore : The pact the Sri Lankan Prime Minister, Mahinda Rajapakse, has entered into with the Janatha Vimukthi Peramuna (JVP) for the Presidential elections in the island nation will go against the Tamils, Marumalarchi Dravida Munnetra Kazhagam general secretary Vaiko said here on Friday.

11-09-2005

(3026) Hyderabad : The CPI (M) MP, M. Babu Rao, has alleged that most of the State Governments are following the World Bank diktats to obtain loans, which indirectly led to privatisation of public undertakings.

(3027) Hyderabad : The Congress, the Left parties and the BJP have sharply criticised the launching of the Telangana Jagarana Sena, an outfit of the Telangana Rashtra Samithi, by drawing parallels with the Rashtriya Swayamsevak Sangh (RSS).

(3028) Hyderabad : The Left parties - the Communist Party of India and the Communist Party of India (Marxist) - have refuted reports that they had entered into an understanding with the Telugu Desam Party for the civic elections.

(3029) Hyderabad : APCC president K. Keshava Rao has called upon Telugu Desam Party president N. Chandrababu Naidu to "join hands with the Congress in ushering in clean politics" and set an example to the rest of the country.

(3030) Nizamabad : Bharatiya Janata Party (BJP) State general secretary K. Lakshman has accused the Telangana Rashtra Samithi (TRS) of trying to gain political mileage by provoking regionalism.

(3031) Hyderabad : The Telangana Jagarana Sena (TJS), an outfit floated by the Telangana Rashtra Samithi (TRS) "to counter anti-Telangana forces", was formally launched here on Saturday with a full-fledged training camp with lathi-wielding cadres giving a demonstration to their leaders.

(3032) Thrissur : Leader of the Opposition V. S. Achuthanandan has made it clear that there is no question of withdrawing the cases filed by him against the Democratic Indira Congress leader K. Karunakaran in the controversial Palm oil deal and against the Kerala Congress (B) leader R. Balakrishna Pillai in the Edamalayar dam scam.

(3033) New Delhi : The crisis in the Bharatiya Janata Party, arising out of the expulsion of senior leader Madan Lal Khurana, has brought into the open the differences between the top two - the former Prime Minister, Atal Bihari Vajpayee, and BJP president L.K. Advani. Despite a number of meetings here on Saturday, the deadlock could not be broken.

(3034) New Delhi : The Bharatiya Janata Party on Saturday renewed its demand that Bihar Governor Buta Singh should be dismissed before polling in the State scheduled to start from October 18.

(3035) Bangalore : The former Prime Minister H.D. Deve Gowda has demanded suitable changes in the reservation policy for the backward classes to ensure social justice and fair play.

(3036) Bangalore : Former Deputy Chief Minister Siddaramaiah on Saturday said he needs at least three months to chalk out a course of action against his ouster and he can decide only after touring all constituencies and interacting with leaders and workers supporting social justice espoused by the federation of minorities, backward classes and dalits' federation (AHIND).

(3037) Gulbarga : Maruti Manpade, member of the Communist Party of India (Marxist) State Secretariat, on Saturday urged the State Government to order a resurvey of the areas submerged in the Bennethora major irrigation projects and revise the compensation package.

(3038) Gulbarga : The district unit of the Janata Dal (United) on Saturday issued an ultimatum to the State Government to lay the foundation stone for the building of the circuit Bench of the Karnataka High Court here before November 1 failing which it warned that the members of the party will commit self-immolation.

(3039) Hubli : Leader of the Opposition in the Legislative Assembly B.S. Yediyurappa on Saturday suggested that issues of importance to the State should be kept outside the purview of partisan politics.

(3040) Hubli : Leader of the Opposition in the Legislative Assembly B.S. Yediyurappa on Saturday chose to be non-committal on the alternatives available in the event of the fall of the present coalition Government in the State, which he considered quite imminent.

(3041) Chitradurga : Leader of the Opposition in the Legislative Council D.H. Shankaramurthy has termed the Upper Bhadra Project an eyewash.

(3042) Thiruvananthapuram : BJP State president P. S. Sreedharan Pillai said on Saturday that Kerala might turn into another West Bengal if the voters were not vigilant.

(3043) Coimbatore : The former Prime Minister, H.D. Deve Gowda, on Saturday criticised the United Progressive Alliance Government at the Centre for the frequent hikes in the price of petroleum products.

(3044) New Delhi : The Nationalist Congress Party (NCP) received a boost in the North-East with the former Manipur Chief Minister, Radha Binod Koijam, joining the party here on Saturday.

(3045) Dhanbad (Jharkhand) : The CPI(M) on Saturday made it clear that it would not forge any alliance with the Congress in the coming Assembly elections in Bihar.

(3046) New Delhi : The Nationalist Congress Party said on Saturday that there was no need for Ram Vilas Paswan to leave the Government in case the Lok Jan Shakti Party eventually decided to contest the Bihar Assembly elections separately.

(3047) New Delhi : The Leader of the Opposition in the Standing Committee of the Municipal Corporation of Delhi, Vijender Kumar Gupta, has written to the Central Vigilance Commission objecting to the Delhi Government's decision to hand over street lighting along with immovable property of the civic body to the Capital's private power distribution companies without obtaining approval of the MCD House.

(3048) New Delhi : The Delhi Pradesh Congress Committee is virtually being run single-handedly by its president, Ram Babu Sharma. The reason: the party leadership has not yet given the green signal for constitution of a new team of office-bearers even 11 months after Mr. Sharma was installed as the new president replacing Chaudhary Prem Singh.

(3049) Pondicherry : The Pondicherry DMK youth wing president and MLA, R. Siva, has called upon the Centre to include Pondicherry and Karaikal districts under the National Rural Employment Guarantee Scheme as it would be of help for the jobless youth.

(3050) Pondicherry : Pattali Makkal Katchi parliamentary party leader M. Ramadass has urged Lt. Governor M.M. Lakhera to issue an order ensuring job reservation for the most backward classes in the Union Territory.

(3051) Lucknow : The Congress today blamed the Mulayam Singh Yadav Government for playing with the lives of the people by not allowing the use of a helicopter provided by the party for aerial fogging in those areas infested by Japanese Encephalitis (JE) in eastern Uttar Pradesh.

(3052) Chennai : The Dravida Munnetra Kazhagam president, M. Karunanidhi, on Saturday flayed the State Government for not conducting elections to the primary agricultural cooperative banks during its present tenure.

(3053) Chennai : When AIADMK general secretary and Chief Minister Jayalalithaa declared here on September 5 that "America has been acclaimed as the land of opportunities and the All India Anna Dravida Munnetra Kazhagam is also the home of opportunities," she dropped a hint about what was in store for partymen.

12-09-2005

(3054) Hyderabad : The Andhra Pradesh Congress Committee president, K. Keshava Rao on Sunday said the party would tackle the problem of party rebels in several municipalities and corporations and ensure that they did not mar the chances of official nominees.

(3055) Hyderabad : The Left parties have reacted strongly to the "hijacking" of the Telangana armed struggle by the BJP and Telangana Rashtra Samithi (TRS) and said they had no claim to its celebration whatsoever.

(3056) Hyderabad : The Telugu Desam Party on Sunday exuded confidence that it would bag at least 75 per cent of the seats in the municipal elections.

(3057) Srikakulam : The senior TDP leader and Srikakulam MP, Kinjarapu Yerrannaidu, has said that the Congress has no moral right to ask for votes in the municipal elections. Addressing a press conference at the party office here on Saturday evening, Mr.Naidu, along with other TDP leaders including ZPP chairman,Y.V.Suryanarayana, and former Minister G.Appalasuryanarayana said that the Congress had not completed even a single development scheme during its 16 months in office. It was because of the fear of defeat that the Congress had opted for indirect elections. He recalled some instances where the Congress MPs and MLAs were present while scrutiny of nominations was taking place. Never in the history of the country were such instances witnessed, he said.

(3058) Hyderabad : The Andhra Pradesh Chief Minister Y. S. Rajasekhara Reddy on Sunday said the Telangana Rashtra Samithi (TRS) had parted ways with the Congress "due to a misunderstanding" but it would not have any impact on the party's prospects in the municipal elections.

(3059) Thiruvananthapuram : The Congress leaders will hold talks with the Kerala Congress (B) leader R. Balakrishna Pillai on Monday to clear the way for his return to the United Democratic Front (UDF).

(3060) New Delhi : There was no immediate end in sight to the Bharatiya Janata Party's ongoing crisis, ostensibly related to the expulsion of party leader Madan Lal Khurana, who received the orders on Saturday night.

(3061) Madhepura : Taking on RJD chief Lalu Prasad in his stronghold, Lok Jan Sakthi Party chief Ram Vilas Paswan on Sunday said Mr. Prasad would barely get 25 seats in the Bihar Assembly polls. He asked the Congress to snap alliance with the RJD or it would be reduced to a "zero" in the State.

(3062) Bangalore : The city unit of the Bharatiya Janata Party (BJP) has criticised Chief Minister N. Dharam Singh for his refusal to take the criticism by representatives of the information technology sector "in a positive way" and failing to make a commitment to address the issues raised by them.

(3063) Bangalore : Shiv Sena on Sunday chose Bangalore, where Chhatrapathi Shivaji spent his childhood, for its formal launch. The venue was the Gosai Mutt in Gavipuram Guttahalli, which is associated with the name of Shahaji Bhonsle, father of Shivaji.

(3064) Bellary : N. Pratap Reddy, General Secretary of State unit of Janata Dal (S), has endorsed the views of his party president, H.D. Deve Gowda, on reclassification of reservation to backward classes. This, he told presspersons here on Sunday, would ensure that the purpose for which reservation had been made was achieved.

(3065) Bijapur : Leader of the Opposition in Legislative Assembly B.S. Yediyurappa will stage a demonstration at the Alamatti dam site in protest against the Union Government's partisan directive asking the State to maintain the water level in the dam at 509 metres till the end of September.

(3066) Challakere (Chitradurga) : The Congress on Sunday came down heavily on the recent proposal of the former Prime Minister H.D. Deve Gowda, President of the Janata Dal (Secular), to restructure the reservation policy.

(3067) Challakere (Chitradurga) : Minister for Water Resources M. Mallikarjun Kharge said on Sunday that the State Government will take measures to protect the interests of the State in getting its share of river waters.

(3068) Alappuzha : The UDF Government is trying to usurp the powers of the local bodies in the State that had been given to them by the previous LDF Government to ensure comprehensive development of the State, Leader of the Opposition V.S. Achuthanandan has said.

(3069) Thiruvananthapuram : CPI(M) State secretary Pinarayi Vijayan has said that anti-CPI(M) forces are raking up the Rajan case now not because of their opposition to Emergency, but on account of the stand being taken by the Democratic Indira Congress (Karunakaran) in the panchayat-municipal elections.

(3070) Lucknow : Apprehending that international terrorism had the potential to start another world war, former Prime Minister Atal Bihari Vajpayee on Sunday said the world would have to unite in order to wipe out this problem from its roots.

(3071) Patna : The Bihar unit of the Bharatiya Janata Party (BJP) tentatively decided to field candidate for 105 seats in coming Assembly elections to facilitate the NDA to formthe government, State BJP president Sushil Kumar Modi said here on Sunday.

(3072) Cuttack : The Communist Party of India (CPI) has called upon all parties, irrespective of their affiliations, to oppose the MoU signed between the Orissa Government and South Korean steel major POSCO for setting up a steel plant at Paradeep.

(3073) New Delhi : The Communist Party of India (Marxist) on Sunday said the United Progressive Alliance Government should "firmly rebuff" the U.S. demand that India give up the gas pipeline project with Iran and join hands with it in pressuring Teheran into halting its nuclear programme. Also, the Government should "consider whether its recent enthusiasm for allying with the U.S. as a strategic partner is serving the country's interests."

(3074) Neemuch (MP) : Bharatiya Janata Party president L. K. Advani lashed out at the Centre for revoking POTA saying the move by the UPA Government was drawn from "vote-bank politics."

(3075) Lucknow : Days after publicly questioning Bharatiya Janata Party chief L.K. Advani's expulsion of senior party leader Madan Lal Khurana, former Prime Minister Atal Bihari Vajpayee said here on Sunday there were no differences between them and the two were still good friends.

(3076) Guwahati : The supporters of expelled Asom Gana Parishad leader and former Assam Chief Minister Prafulla Kumar Mahanta on Sunday claimed they were the real AGP and vowed to demonstrate their strength at a two-day convention on September 14 and 15.

(3077) Lucknow : Taking umbrage at Uttar Pradesh Chief Minister Mulayam Singh Yadav's reported statement that Sonia Gandhi owed her position in the UPA to the Samajwadi Party, the Congress today said the SP had always made attempts to strike at the AICC chief and the party.

(3078) Chennai : In a rare show of unity, Congress leaders appeared on a common platform here on Sunday and vowed to help the party occupy the numero uno position in the State's politics.

(3079) Tuticorin : Minor differences among constituents of United Progressive Alliance over issues such as increase in fuel price will not affect the Manmohan Singh Government which will complete its term, MDMK leader Vaiko told reporters here on Sunday.

13-09-2005

(3080) Hyderabad : The Bharatiya Janata Party has termed as "irresponsible" the Union Minister, A.Narendra's statement that the TRS cadres, if necessary, would take up AK-47s for achieving separate Telangana.

(3081) Hyderabad : A writ petition filed by Telugu Desam Party (TDP) challenging the orders providing voting rights to the MLAs and MPs while electing chairpersons of the municipal bodies was admitted by the High Court on Monday.

(3082) Hyderabad : The Telangana Rashtra Samiti president and Union Minister, K. Chandrasekhara Rao, on Monday questioned the Telangana Congress leaders campaign in the region wondering with what face they would seek votes in the municipal elections.

(3083) Vijayawada : TDP senior leader and former Minister Yanamala Ramakrishnudu has accused the ruling Congress party of spreading misinformation over the allotment of land to IMG in the State capital. The Government has cleared many mega projects but is "creating a controversy over IMG probably because the latter has refused to pay bribe," he said.

(3084) Vizianagaram : Telugu Desam Party deputy leader in the Assembly K. Kala Venkata Rao has asked Chief Minister Y.S. Rajasekhara Reddy to take up drought relief works in the three north coastal districts on a war-footing as farm workers, especially from Vizianagaram and Srikakulam, are migrating to other districts in search of employment.

(3085) Kadapa : Congress leaders on Monday charged their Telugu Desam Party counterparts with lodging 'false' complaints with the Election Commission that TDP candidates were abducted by ruling party members and demanded that the EC initiate action against the complainants.

(3086) Hyderabad : The Andhra Pradesh Congress Committee chief, K. Keshava Rao, has linked his job to the outcome of the municipal elections and has asked whether the Telugu Desam Party (TDP) is prepared to respond in the same manner.

(3087) Thiruvananthapuram : The Kerala Congress (B) found its way back into the UDF camp, with its leader R. Balakrishna Pillai making a formal announcement on Monday about his decision to return to the fold. Mr. Pillai's return to the UDF camp had been in the air for the last few weeks. The matter was confirmed on Monday at a special meeting between him and Kerala Pradesh Congress Committee president Ramesh Chennithala in the presence of Chief Minister Oommen Chandy.

(3088) New Delhi : The Bharatiya Janata Party on Monday evening revoked the expulsion order served on its Delhi leader, Madan Lal Khurana, after he wrote to president L.K. Advani expressing "regret" for his public statements against him and withdrawing them unconditionally.

(3089) Bangalore : Karnataka Pradesh Congress Committee President M. Mallikarjun Kharge has said that the plea of the Janata Dal (Secular) leader H.D. Deve Gowda to reduce the reservation for Kuruba and Idiga castes in the larger interests of other backward classes has put the coalition Government in a fix.

(3090) Hassan : General Secretary of the State unit of the Bharatiya Janata Party (BJP) Kailas said here on Monday that the party is not against its party workers taking part in the AHIND (Kannada acronym for backward classes and minorities) convention to be held in Hassan on September 26.

(3091) Mangalore : "My intention is to reach the benefits of social empowerment programmes including reservation to less fortunate communities of the society," former Prime Minister H.D. Deve Gowda said on Monday. Speaking at a press conference here, Mr. Deve Gowda said he has written to Chief Minister N. Dharam Singh about the need to divide and re-classify the 2A category for reservation in education and employment.

(3092) Mysore : The former Prime Minister and Janata Dal (Secular) President, H.D. Deve Gowda, has taken note of the drinking water crisis plaguing Mysore and directed the officials concerned to solve the problem within a week.

(3093) Santhemaralli (Chamarajanagar Dt.) : Karnataka Pradesh Congress Committee President and Water Resources Minister M. Mallikarjuna Kharge has said that the Congress is determined to take up the Kabini second stage project to irrigate drought-prone areas in Chamarajanagar district.

(3094) Bangalore : Three leaders who have been expelled from the Janata Dal (Secular) said the continuance of the coalition Government in Karnataka is against the interests of the people of the State as former Prime Minister H.D. Deve Gowda and a section of the Congress led by Chief Minister N. Dharam Singh are only interested in holding on to power.

(3095) Thiruvananthapuram : Leader of the Opposition V. S. Achuthanandan has accused the Congress of having joined forces with the BJP in the panchayat-municipal elections to make up for the erosion in its support base.

(3096) Thiruvananthapuram : The return of Kerala Congress (B) leader R Balakrishna Pillai to the United Democratic Front (UDF) camp once again proves the impenetrability of the bipolar coalition system in Kerala. Both Mr. Pillai and the Congress leadership appear to have realised the political advantages of working together.

(3097) New Delhi : The Rashtriya Janata Dal, the Congress and the Nationalist Congress Party on Monday decided to approach the coming Bihar Assembly polls on the basis of an agreed common minimum programme and conduct joint campaigns.

(3098) Vellore : Volunteers of the Pattali Makkal Katchi staged a novel protest in front of the taluk office in Katpadi on Monday protesting against the Vellore Institute of Technology for "ignoring aspirants from

Tamil Nadu and Vellore district and admitting candidates from other States and countries and collecting huge donations." They also demanded that the VIT hand over to the Tamil Nadu Government, the `poromboke' land it had "encroached."

14-09-2005

(3099) Hyderabad : The Congress Party has taken serious view of the 'intemperate and lowly language' of the two Union Ministers, K. Chandrasekhara Rao and A. Narendra, and is planning to take up the issue with the AICC president, Sonia Gandhi and the Prime Minister, Manmohan Singh.

(3100) Hyderabad : The Congress has promised round-the-clock drinking water supply soon in all the municipalities in the State in its election manifesto for the municipal elections. Better roads, sanitation, housing and livelihood for the poor are the other promises.

(3101) Hyderabad : The Telugu Desam Party polit bureau member, T. Devender Goud, on Tuesday said the party would keep its options open for the election of mayor/chairperson to Municipal Corporations and Councils.

(3102) Tirupati : The Congress Chief Whip, N. Kirankumar Reddy, on Tuesday sought a CBI probe into the sale of 400 acres of land in Hyderabad to IMG Academies Bharata (P) Ltd, allegedly for a throwaway price by the Chandrababu Naidu Government for setting up a sports academy. Mr Reddy, however, evaded a reply to the TDP's rebuttal of the charge and that the Congress was free to get a probe conducted by Interpol into the 'deal' if it wished.

(3103) Kadapa : The Telugu Desam Party will extend 5 per cent political reservations to minorities, if it regained power, the TDP President, N. Chandrababu Naidu, asserted on Tuesday.

(3104) Kadapa : Former Chief Minister N. Chandrababu Naidu's charges against the Kadapa Mayor candidate of Congress, P. Ravindranath Reddy, did not behove his stature, PCC member Makam Ashok Kumar alleged on Tuesday.

(3105) Patna : Rashtriya Janata Dal (RJD) chief Lalu Prasad Yadav kick-started the campaign for the Assembly polls here on Tuesday.

(3106) Thrissur : In a sensational disclosure, State president of the Bharatiya Janata Party (BJP) P. S. Sreedharan Pillai has said that the presidents of the nine District Congress Committees (DCC) had approached his party for tie-ups in the ensuing local body elections.

(3107) Bangalore : The former Congress Minister Kagodu Thimmappa on Tuesday joined issue with Janata Dal (Secular) President H.D. Deve Gowda on the latter's proposal to restructure the reservation policy and said the Government cannot suo motu change the percentage of reservation for different castes. It can only be done with the consent of the State's permanent Backward Classes Commission.

(3108) Hassan : Leader of the Opposition in the Legislative Council D.H. Shankaramurthy here on Tuesday claimed that Cauvery Neeravari Nigam Ltd., which is to implement the Upper Bhadra Project, is working on an alternative proposal, which is under the consideration of the technical subcommittee of the nigam.

(3109) Hubli : H. Vishwanath, Congress leader and one of the key activists of AHIND movement in the State, on Tuesday dubbed the letter written by the former Prime Minister, H.D. Deve Gowda, seeking internal reservation among backward classes as nothing but a political gimmick.

(3110) Udupi : The former Prime Minister, H.D. Deve Gowda, has made it clear that he and his party were in favour of the proposed thermal power plant to be set up by Nagarjuna power company at Yellur-Santhur in Udupi district.

(3111) Panaji : Describing the recent amendment to the MLAs Pension Bill, which would allow the pension of some senior MLAs to exceed their salaries at the time of their retirement, as absurd, the Opposition Bharatiya Janata Party (BJP) has resolved to approach the Governor S.C. Jamir seeking not to give his assent to the Bill. The Leader of the Opposition, Manohar Parrikar, has demanded that the Bill be allowed to lapse, as the amendment had been passed in the recent budget session of the Assembly while the Opposition was absent. He said it would allow some of the ruling MLAs and the Chief Minister Pratapsing Rane to draw more pension than their salary.

(3112) Bangalore : The Janata Party and the Bharatiya Janata Party (BJP) have plans to forge a third front in Tamil Nadu ahead of the Assembly elections.

(3113) Banaglore : In a significant development, the former Deputy Chief Minister Siddaramaiah held talks with Chief Minister N. Dharam Singh for 45 minutes at the latter's official residence here on Tuesday.

(3114) Kozhikode : After courting controversy over his statements regarding the role of the Democratic Indira Congress (Karunakaran) leader K. Karunakaran during the Emergency, CPI (M) State secretary Pinarayi Vijayan on Tuesday said that the onus of the dark days of the period would live with Mr. Karunakaran till he dies. Mr. Karunakaran was the Home Minister when the police excesses were rampant during that period in the State, said the CPI (M) leader whose coalition, Left Democratic Front (LDF), had forged a tactical seat sharing adjustment with the DIC (K) for the three-tier local body polls.

(3115) Panaji : Even as the ruling coalition appears to be against the new international airport at Mopa in north Goa and the demand for the civilian use of the Dabolim international airport in south Goa intensifies, the Opposition Bharatiya Janata Party (BJP) has called for use of both airports keeping in mind the massive tourism inflow anticipated by the State.

(3116) Gandhinagar : The Opposition Congress on Tuesday took up in the Gujarat Assembly the case of a ruling BJP MLA, who allegedly threatened to "self-immolate" herself if the Narendra Modi Government did not stop "victimising" her. Immediately after question hour, Congress member Chandrika Chudasma sought Speaker Mangaldas Patel's permission to raise the issue of BJP MLA Ramila Desai's alleged threat. Ms. Desai had also reportedly told Mr. Modi about the "threatening calls" she was receiving for supporting the dissidents.

(3117) Patna : Terming as "eyewash" RJD president Lalu Prasad's assertion that he would take up the issue of reservation for Dalits in the private sector, the Lok Jan Shakti president, Ram Vilas Paswan, on Tuesday said the former's "love" for Dalits at the time of polls was a "farce and politically motivated."

(3118) New Delhi : The Left parties have decided to take up with the United Progressive Alliance issues such as rise in prices of oil, privatisation of water supply, coming World Trade Organisation meeting and foreign direct investment in the retail sector.

(3119) Chitrakoot : Trying once again to cobble together a third front, Uttar Pradesh Chief Minister Mulayam Singh Yadav on Tuesday said his party was willing to work with all those who believed in socialism to emerge as a national alternative.

(3120) New Delhi : The Bharatiya Janata Party's national executive committee meeting, starting in Chennai on September 16, will attempt to shift the focus from internal bickering to the differences within the United Progressive Alliance and among its supporting parties.

(3121) New Delhi : The Delhi unit Bharatiya Janata Party president Harsh Vardhan on Tuesday termed the Congress Government's drive against faulty electronic electricity meters as a big farce aimed at befooling consumers.

(3122) Lucknow : The helicopter arranged by the Congress for aerial fogging in the Japanese Encephalitis (JE) infested areas of Rae Bareli and Gorakhpur, continues to be the centre of controversy between the party and the Uttar Pradesh Government.

(3123) Chennai : A large number of activists belonging to the Communist Party of India (Marxist) including State unit secretary N. Varadarajan and legislators of the party, courted arrest on Tuesday by staging a State-wide picketing. They were demanding among other things radical land reform measures, streamlining of the public distribution system and implementation of the employment guarantee scheme in all the districts.

15-09-2005

(3124) Anantapur : The Congress Government in the State has scripted a plan to reverse the people's mandate in the municipal elections with indiscriminate use of money and muscle power, the TDP president and Leader of the Opposition, N. Chandrababu Naidu, alleged here on Wednesday.

(3125) Hyderabad : The Telangana Regional Congress Coordination Committee (TRCCC), which strongly supported the demand of the Telangana Rashtra Samithi (TRS) prior to the Assembly elections, has now decided to seek its expulsion from the UPA Government.

(3126) Hyderabad : The State committee of the CPI(M) has attributed the frequent outbursts of the Telangana Rashtra Samiti leaders against other parties to their efforts to cover up the party's inefficiency.

(3127) Warangal : The Telangana Rasthra Samithi (TRS) is not dependent on Congress, but it is the Congress that is dependent on the TRS and other constituents, said the TRS president K Chandrasekhara Rao.

(3128) Warangal : Senior Congress leader and Andhra Pradesh State Road Transport Corporation chairman G. Prakash Rao has lashed out at TRS president K. Chandrasekhar Rao and accused him of deceiving employees and students of Telangana.

(3129) Mahabubnagar : Launching a scathing attack on Telangana Rashtra Samiti leaders, the CPI national council member and MP, Suravaram Sudhakar Reddy said that K. Chandrasekhar Rao and A. Narendra should remember that they are enjoying Ministerial berths in the Union Cabinet because of the Left parties' support.

(3130) New Delhi : Prime Minister Manmohan Singh's reported remarks to the U.S. President, George W. Bush, in New York has created a controversy here with senior leaders in the Bharatiya Janata Party, the Congress and the Communist Party of India joining issue.

(3131) Guwahati : The Asom Gana Parishad formally split on Wednesday with the founder-president and former Chief Minister Prafulla Kumar Mahanta floating a new regional outfit. The resolution to form the Asom Gana Parishad (Progressive) was adopted at a two-day political convention, which began here. The party would have the original flag of the AGP when its was launched on August 14, 1985 at Golaghat. The flag was modified in 1996 after the merger of the Natun Asom Gana Parishad with the AGP.

(3132) Thiruvananthapuram : Kerala Pradesh Congress Committee president Ramesh Chennithala on Wednesday lashed out at the CPI (M) for seeking the shortest route to power by forging an unholy alliance with the Democratic Indira Congress (K), led by K. Karunakaran, and discarding its long-standing ideological values.

(3133) Alamatti (Bijapur District) : The farmers' rally organised by the Bharatiya Janata Party here on Wednesday vowed to safeguard the interests of State with regard to Alamatti water.

(3134) Thiruvananthapuram : Communist Party of India (CPI) State secretary Veliyam Bhargavan on Wednesday said Bharatiya Janata Party

(BJP) State president P.S. Sreedharan Pillai's statement that nine DCC presidents had sought his party's support in the local body elections was an official confirmation of the State-wide ties between the UDF and BJP.

(3135) Thiruvananthapuram : The Bharatiya Janata Party (BJP) manifesto for the forthcoming elections to the local bodies in the district proposes a metro rail scheme for the capital city and a regulatory mechanism to curb the growth of high-rise buildings.

(3136) Thiruvananthapuram : Communist Marxist Party (CMP) leader and Minister for Cooperation M. V. Raghavan on Wednesday asked the CPI(M) whether it had become politically so bankrupt as to defend K. Karunakaran, whom it had all along held responsible for the Emergency excesses in the State.

(3137) Malappuram : Confuse, if you cannot convince someone. The Indian Union Muslim League (IUML) seems to have adopted the dictum in dealing with the Sunni group led by Kanthapuram A.P. Aboobacker Musaliar.

(3138) Bhubaneswar : The Communist Party of India on Wednesday demanded cancellation of the Memorandum of Understanding (MoU) signed between the Orissa Government and the Korean steel-maker, Pohang Steel Company (POSCO), for the setting up of a 12-million tonne capacity steel plant near Paradip.

(3139) Kolkata : Ridiculing the assurance that the interests of farmers would be safeguarded in any move to set up new industries in the State, Trinamool Congress chief Mamata Banerjee said here on Wednesday that they were a part of a design to "hoodwink" people on the hidden intentions of the Communist Party of India (Marxist) to acquire agricultural land for industrial purposes and real-estate.

(3140) Chennai : The Bharatiya Janata Party, which witnessed a series of controversies over the last three months, conceded on Wednesday that the recent happenings in the party had caused "some dent" to its image.

(3141) New Delhi : The Delhi Pradesh Bharatiya Janata Party president, Harsh Vardhan, on Wednesday demanded resignation of Chief Minister Sheila Dikshit saying she had been continuously misleading the people and telling lies on privatisation of power during the last three years.

(3142) Gandhinagar : The concluding day on Wednesday of the three-day truncated session of the Gujarat Assembly witnessed ugly scenes, repeated adjournments, eviction of the Opposition members, a "mock" session and even a protest walkout by a ruling party member.

(3143) Bhopal : Senior BJP leader Uma Bharti, who is also the party's Bihar poll campaign in charge, on Wednesday claimed that the Congress and the RJD were facing an adverse situation in that State due to actions of the UPA that was already fraught with internal contradictions.

(3144) Chandigarh : Reacting strongly to the demand for setting up of a Legislative Assembly for the Union Territory of Chandigarh, Shiromani Akali Dal president Parkash SIngh Badal on Wednesday said that his party would oppose any attempt at diluting Punjab's "inalienable claim" on its capital.

(3145) Chennai : The Chief Minister and All India Anna Dravida Munnetra Kazhagam general secretary, Jayalalithaa, on Wednesday said the goal of her political life was to raise the living standards of the people.

(3146) Madurai : Actor Vijaykanth formally launched his political party, the "Desiya Murpokku Dravida Kazhagam," in Madurai on Wednesday.

16-09-2005

(3147) Hyderabad : The State council of the Communist Party of India (CPI) has decided to take up the "violent and abusive" remarks made by Union Minister A. Narendra with the Centre through the party's national executive.

(3148) Hyderabad : The Bharatiya Janata Party (BJP) has asked the Government to order a Central Bureau of Investigation (CBI) inquiry into all the land allotments made to private companies and institutions by the previous Telugu Desam regime as well as the present Government.

(3149) Hyderabad : The Telugu Desam Party has urged the State Election Commission (SEC) to stop all television advertisements sourced to the Government regarding Rajiv Griha Kalpa and Rajiv Yuva Shakti and recover the costs incurred on them since August 28 from the Congress.

(3150) Kurnool : TDP president N. Chandrababu Naidu has asked the Congress Government not to indulge in mudslinging against predecessors over allotment of land to M/s IMG Bharata's international sports academy.

(3151) Sadasivapet (Medak Dt.) : Telangana Rashtra Samithi leader and Union Minister, K.Chandrasekhar Rao, alleged that the Congress, which had benefited by the alliance with his party during the Assembly elections, is now trying to cut the oxygen line to the TRS. Addressing a public meeting in Sadasivapet after an impressive road show, Mr Chandrasekhar Rao said that the people of Telangana had lost faith in the Andhra rulers and it was high time the wish of 3.5 crore people was respected and a separate Telangana created.

(3152) Kadapa : Telugu Desam Party leaders on Thursday alleged that Chief Minister Y.S. Rajasekhara Reddy had a chequered history of betraying Congress in several elections and has no moral right to criticise his predecessor N. Chandrababu Naidu.

(3153) Tuni (East Godavari Dt.) : Pradesh Congress Committee president K. Keshava Rao has opined that private armies and killings in the name of 'kobras' should end in the State.

(3154) New Delhi : The Congress party has asked its Andhra Pradesh State unit leaders to exercise restraint and not join issue with the Telangana Rashtra Samiti leaders in the wake of the ongoing war of words between the two.

(3155) Bangalore : Terming religious conversion as an attack on the sovereignty and security of the country, the all-India secretary of Vishwa Hindu Parishad Mohan Joshi has demanded that the Centre and the States enact laws to ban it.

(3156) Bellary : Thimmaiah, Vice-President of the BJP SC Morcha, has condemned the former Prime Minister, H.D. Deve Gowda, for seeking the reclassification of reservations to ensure that the benefits reach all backward classes.

(3157) Mangalore : Rajya Sabha MP and former President of Karnataka Pradesh Congress Committee B. Janardhana Poojary said he will moot a constitutional amendment in the next parliament session to increase the percentage of reservation to 80 per cent for all categories while keeping 20 per cent for the general category.

(3158) Kolkata : The three constituents of the ruling Left Front - the Revolutionary Socialist Party [RSP], the Communist Party of India [CPI] and the All India Forward Bloc [AIFB] - will submit next week their reply to a note from Chief Minister Buddhadeb Bhattacharjee, clarifying the State Government's plans for industrial growth in the State.

(3159) Chennai : The Bharatiya Janata Party is hoping that its national executive committee meeting starting here on Friday will help give it the push it needs in the south where at least three, possibly four, States are expected to go to the polls next year.

(3160) Bhabua : Asserting that he was keeping away from the RJD-led alliance for the Bihar polls for reasons of "ideological" differences, Lok Jan Jan Shakti Party president Ram Vilas Paswan said the day the Rashtriya Janata Dal agreed to make a Muslim Chief Minister "I will walk along with it.

(3161) New Delhi : The Communist Party of India has asked the Centre to review its decision to form a corporation by merging all mints and security presses and warned that trade unions will agitate against it.

(3162) New Delhi : Congress MP Rahul Gandhi has said there was "no trace of governance" in Bihar, now under Central rule.

(3163) Guwahati : The Asom Gana Parishad (AGP) on Thursday denied a split in the party and said that the AGP (Progressive) formed by "some expelled partymen" would have no impact on it.

(3164) New Delhi : Delhi Bharatiya Janata Party president Harsh Vardhan on Thursday asked the residents of Delhi to boycott the "drama" of the drive to test electricity meters by the Delhi Government and the Delhi Electricity Regulatory Commission. He exhorted them to start a movement to reclaim crores of rupees that the power distribution companies had charged them by installing fast-running meters.

(3165) New Delhi : When The Bharatiya Janata Party chose to protest the fact that Prime Minister Manmohan Singh had made a reference to Atal Bihari Vajpayee's opposition to the India-United States nuclear agreement in his meeting with President George W. Bush in New York, it perhaps did not realise the party spokesperson being fielded was somebody least suited to accuse anybody of discussing "domestic politics" on "foreign soil."

(3166) Bhopal : The Madhya Pradesh Women's Congress president, Shobha Oza, and the All-India Women's Congress Secretary, Shobhna Shah, on Thursday presented before journalists an 18-year old married woman who was allegedly kidnapped and gang-raped at Sarai Segran village near Rewa on the midnight of August 31-September 1. Ms. Oza and Ms. Shah returned here on Thursday after visiting Sarai Segran village.

(3167) Pondicherry : The Pattali Makkal Katchi (PMK) parliamentary party leader M. Ramadass has charged the Pondicherry Government with continuously neglecting the Most Backward Classes (MBCs), in sanctioning reservation for them in jobs.

(3168) Chennai : The women's wing of the Dravida Munnetra Kazhagam (DMK) on Thursday held a massive rally under the leadership of the party president, M. Karunanidhi, to highlight the demand for 33 per cent reservation for women in Parliament and legislature.

(3169) Chennai : The Marumalarchi Dravida Munnetra Kazhagam (MDMK), which had been spearheading the ideals of late Anna, would continue to protect and stand by his principles, said the party general secretary, Mr. Vaiko here on Thursday.

(3170) Villupuram : On the birth anniversary of the former Chief Minister, C.N. Annadurai, Chief Minister Jayalalithaa has taken a stance against his avowed ideals and principles, according to S. Ramadoss, founder of Pattali Makkal Katchi.

17-09-2005

(3171) Hyderabad : The Congress Legislature Party (CLP) has ridiculed the TDP president, N. Chandrababu Naidu's appeal to people to vote for his party in the civic elections asking him to explain the need for voters to choose his party.

(3172) Hyderabad : The CPI (M) State secretary, B.V. Raghavulu, has lashed out at the main political parties for keeping the real issues on the backburner in the municipal elections.

(3173) Hyderabad : Notwithstanding the tough posture adopted on the issue of a separate State and asking its cadre to defeat the Congress, the Telangana Rashtra Samiti has fielded only 696 candidates in 932 wards in the 31municipalities in the region.

(3174) Karimnagar : The Telangana Rashtra Samithi president and Union Minister for Labour, K Chandrasekhar Rao has said that the people of Telangana would again teach a fitting lesson to the Telugu Desam Party which is going with the slogan of integrated Andhra Pradesh in the municipal elections.

(3175) Srikakulam : "The TDP is a one-man show. It is run as business organization by the party president, N. Chandrababu Naidu," said the Minister for Revenue and Relief, Dharmana Prasada Rao, here on Friday.

(3176) Vijayawada : Finance Minister K. Rosaiah said here on Friday that the Congress Legislature Party (CLP) was provoked to talk about the IMG Bharata land deal, though it was not an election issue. The Telugu Desam Party (TDP) president N. Chandrababu Naidu was making "baseless allegations" against the State Government during his roadshows in the last 15 days. Addressing a press conference at Andhra Ratna Bhavan, Mr. Rosaiah derided the contention of Mr. Naidu that sports facilities in the State were handed over to the IMG only to promote sporting activity. "Is making good sportsmen in the State our priority when we don't have proper sanitation, drainage and other amenities in several towns and villages? How can they assign the facilities, including Lal Bahadur Stadium, which are worth hundreds of crores, to a company for 45 years with free electricity and water? What is the urgency to take a decision after the dissolution of the Assembly? Why did not the TDP Government think of this 15-year rule? I don't want to talk about the deals that are under review. We remained silent until a learned leader like Yanamala Ramakrishnudu made wild allegations," he pointed out.

(3177) Vijayawada : The Communist Party of India will not enter into any local adjustments with the Telugu Desam Party or the Telangana Rashtra Samithi for electing chairman or Mayor after the municipal elections. The State secretariat will take decisions on issues related to adjustments wherever there is no pre-poll tie-up case by case.

(3178) Vijayawada : Local leadership will be empowered to initiate disciplinary action against candidates contesting against official nominees of the Congress party or its allies, says the Andhra Pradesh Congress Committee president, K. Keshava Rao.

(3179) Kadapa : Congress leaders on Friday invited their Telugu Desam Party (TDP) counterparts for a public debate at the national, State or district-level on the welfare of minorities.

(3180) Sangareddy : TDP president Nara Chandrababu Naidu has warned the Congress not to provoke TDP by attacking its cadre. He said this while speaking to reporters on the outskirts of Ramayampet during the daylong road show in Medak district on Friday.

(3181) Mancherial (Adilabad Dt.) : The Telangana Rashtra Samiti (TRS) president and Union Labour Minister K. Chandrasekhara Rao on Friday refuted the Congress and Telugu Desam Party (TDP) charge on his party's links with naxalites. He said the stand of his party on the issue was clear in that the TRS desired peace through talks.

(3182) Sangareddy : Union Minister and TRS leader A.Narendra said that TRS would reserve the decision of post-poll alliance with Congress till the results of the elections are out.

(3183) Chennai : Bharatiya Janata Party president L.K. Advani on Friday unleashed a no-holds-barred attack on the United Progressive Alliance Government, describing Manmohan Singh as the "weakest Prime Minister in the country's history," even as he underplayed squabbles in the BJP and took care to mention its "symbiotic relationship" with the Rashtriya Swayamsevak Sangh.

(3184) New Delhi : The Supreme Court on Friday allowed 'One Earth One Life,' an organisaton of environmentalists, to implead itself in the special leave petitions (SLPs) filed by the former Kerala Forest Minister K.P. Viswanathan and the State seeking expunging of certain remarks made by the Kerala High Court while declining anticipatory bail in a smuggling case.

(3185) Chennai : The Tamil Nadu Legislative Assembly, which initiated suo motu privilege proceedings against Tamil biweekly, Kumudham Reporter, has been restrained by the Madras High Court from proceeding further in the matter.

(3186) Bijapur : Leader of the Opposition in the Legislative Assembly B.S. Yediyurappa on Wednesday condemned Deputy Chief Minister M.P. Prakash's criticism of information technology (IT) companies for not contributing to flood relief measures.

(3187) Shimoga : The MLA from Shimoga and State BJP General Secretary, K.S. Eshwarappa, said here on Friday that the President of the Janata Dal (S) and former Prime Minister, H.D. Deve Gowda, seems to have become desperate following the AHIND conventions if the manner in which he has raised the reservation bogey for backward classes is any indication. Addressing a press conference, he said what Mr. Deve Gowda had been doing was only shedding of crocodile's tears. He said if he had genuine concern for the backward classes he could have done something to set right the injustice done to these classes when he was the Chief Minister and also when he became Prime Minister. Mr. Eshwarappa asked where was the need for Mr. Deve Gowda to raise the question of inner reservation for backward classes when there is a permanent commission to look into the grievances of these classes. He also criticised the former Deputy Chief Minister Siddaramaiah for his repeated complaint that injustice had been done to the backward classes.

(3188) Thiruvananthapuram : CPI(M) Deputy Legislature Party Leader Kodiyeri Balakrishnan on Friday said that the Left had not forgotten the Emergency or the then Government or K. Karunakaran's role in it.

(3189) Chennai : L.K. Advani could make an announcement on quitting as Bharatiya Janata Party president at the end of the three-day national executive committee meeting, which opened here on Friday. Sources in the senior leadership said he could make the announcement and that some leaders were told about it before they left Delhi for Chennai.

(3190) New Delhi : The Janata Dal (United) on Friday urged Congress MP Rahul Gandhi to demand the resignations of Prime Minister Manmohan Singh, United Progressive Alliance Chairperson Sonia Gandhi and Rashtriya Janata Dal president Lalu Prasad as a follow-up to his recent remarks, in an interview to a weekly, on the lack of governance in Bihar.

(3191) New Delhi : The Congress on Friday announced that its Hyderabad plenary in October has been postponed in view of the Bihar elections.

(3192) New Delhi : Communist Party of India (Marxist) general secretary Prakash Karat on Friday said India-Iran relations could not be held hostage to the United States. He asked the United Progressive Alliance Government to act in India's interest and pursue an independent foreign policy.

(3193) New Delhi : The Congress on Friday asserted that the party MP, Rahul Gandhi, did not give any interview to a newsweekly and disputed the contents presented from a "casual conversation," stating it contained several discrepancies and misquotes.

(3194) Pondicherry : Chief Minister N. Rangasamy has said that a special Cabinet meeting will be held soon under his chairmanship to discuss the plea for reservation for the Most Backward Classes (MBCs) in jobs in the Union Territory. Mr. Rangasamy announced this at a meeting the Pattali Makkal Katchi (PMK) parliamentary party leader, M. Ramadass, had with him here on Friday.

(3195) Pondicherry : The Tamil Nadu PWD Minister, O. Paneerselvam, has said that Tamil Nadu was attracting a large number of foreign investors and also entrepreneurs from other States to launch their projects because of peaceful environment available for industrial activities in the State.

(3196) Chennai : The Dravida Munnetra Kazhagam (DMK) has betrayed farmers in southern districts as the Union Ministry of Forests and Environments, under the control of the party's ministers, had filed an affidavit in the Supreme Court supporting the Kerala Government in the Mullaperiyar Dam issue, Janata Party president Subramanian Swamy alleged on Friday.

(3197) Chennai : The Marumalarchi Dravida Munnetra Kazhagam (MDMK) will always remain dedicated to the cause of protecting Tamils and their identity and opposing Hindi hegemony, party general secretary Vaiko said here on Friday.

(3198) Chennai : The Bharatiya Janata Party's strategy for Tamil Nadu is to move the organisation forward in its endeavour to provide a nationalist platform for the people of the State, party vice-president M. Venkaiah Naidu said here on Friday.

18-09-2005

(3199) Guntur : The Congress Party is violating the model code of conduct by resorting to misuse of official machinery during the campaign for the municipal elections, alleged the Telugu Desam Party (TDP) leader, Yanamala Ramakrishnudu.

(3200) Guntur : The Communist Party of India (Marxist) has found fault with the Rajiv Gruhakalpa scheme of the State Government and has demanded reworking of the scheme, whereby only house sites are given to the beneficiaries.

(3201) Ongole : The Andhra Pradesh Congress Committee president, K. Keshava Rao, has ridiculed the Telugu Desam Party for its failure to prove any of its corruption charges against the Congress Government in the construction of irrigation projects.

(3202) Visakhapatnam : Telugu Desam Party (TDP) president N. Chandrababu Naidu has alleged that "it is Chief Minister Y.S. Rajasekhara Reddy's family that is running the State," and that his party will continue its fight to protect democracy.

(3203) Vizianagaram : The TDP president, N. Chandrababu Naidu, has charged Congress leaders of Parvathipuram and Bobbili with coercing TDP contestants for establishing family rule. This was done in 26th ward in Parvathipuram to install Minister for Forest, S. Vijaya Rama Raju's sister as chairperson in the council, he said on Saturday.

(3204) New Delhi : Even as the Finance Minister, P. Chidambaram, has again reiterated that "no scam is in the offing", the CPI Member of Parliament, Gurudas Das Gupta, on Saturday sought a thorough probe into the stock market boom as the Sensex was touching new highs each day `in utter disregard' of the country's economic fundamentals.

(3205) Chennai : The Bharatiya Janata Party's political resolution adopted here on Saturday charged the United Progressive Alliance Government with practising "minorityism" to the extent that it could once again nurture the kind of Muslim separatism which led to the creation of Pakistan.

(3206) Chennai : The Bharatiya Janata Party on Saturday condemned the fatwa issued by some Muslim clerics against Sania Mirza's tennis attire.

(3207) Hubli : Working President of the State unit of the Janata Dal (Secular) H.D. Kumaraswamy on Saturday indicated that the party is likely to take a decision on the expulsion of Siddaramaiah at the executive meeting to be held on September 22.

(3208) Kochi : Leaders of CPI (ML) Red Flag said here on Saturday that the former senior Congress leader and former Chief Minister K. Karunakaran and his trusted police officers cannot be absolved of the charges of Emergency excesses.

(3209) Kozhikode : Indian Union Muslim League State general secretary and former Industries Minister P.K. Kunhalikutty has ruled out any "tactical alliance" with the CPI(M) or any truck with the BJP in the ensuing local body elections.

(3210) Thiruvananthapuram : The Leader of the Opposition V.S. Achuthanandan says that though several issues extraneous to the contest at the grassroots might have cropped up during the last few weeks, the fight in the panchayat-municipal elections is all about two contrary approaches to development, the one being put forth by the Left Democratic Front with its emphasis on self-reliant development at the local level to support the overall growth of the State and that put forward by the United Democratic Front with its emphasis on big and glamorous projects and neglect of the local bodies. Excerpts from an interview:

(3211) Thiruvananthapuram : State secretary of the Communist Party of India (CPI) Veliyam Bhargavan has said that K. Karunakaran was to blame for Regional Engineering College student Rajan's arrest during the Emergency, but has pointed out that the issue was being raked up now only to isolate Mr. Karunakaran politically.

(3212) Thiruvananthapuram : BJP spokesman B. K. Sekhar reiterated here on Saturday that the BJP did not have any secret or open understanding with either of the two fronts in the State. Addressing a press conference here, the spokesman said the allegation made by CPI (M) leader Kodiyeri Balakrishnan that there was a secret understanding with the UDF was baseless. The party only had local adjustments, and that too with constituents of both the fronts.

(3213) Chennai : Bharatiya Janata Party president Lal Krishna Advani on Saturday heaped praise on the leadership of the former Prime Minister, Atal Bihari Vajpayee.

(3214) Chennai : The Bharatiya Janata Party-ruled Governments may introduce the Value Added Tax in a couple of months. The party would like Tamil Nadu and Uttar Pradesh also to go in for it.

(3215) Chandigarh : While the Communist Party of India (Marxist) has favoured a wider trilateral cooperation and understanding among India, China and Russia, to check the growing trend of creating a unipolar comity of nations, it understands that there is no scope for a strategic axis, especially in the present international scenario.

(3216) New Delhi : The Janata Dal (United) has said that the Congress MP, Rahul Gandhi's interview to Tehelka weekly on the "sorry state of affair in Bihar and Uttar Pradesh" was "formal" and that "there was nothing casual about it."

(3217) Chandigarh : Communist Party of India (Marxist) general secretary Prakash Karat said on Saturday that the party had decided to support the Rashtriya Janata Dal in the coming Bihar Assembly elections, to keep "communal forces" at bay.

(3218) Pondicherry : The president of Pondicherry State committee of the Janata Dal (Secular) E.Ganesan has called upon the Union Territory Administration to intervene immediately and take over the private medical colleges here that were ignoring the government orders and also court directives on pattern of admission they should adopt to enable students to do MBBS course in the institutions.

(3219) New Delhi : Congress president Sonia Gandhi on Saturday approved the names of office-bearers and members of the Executive Committee of the party's West Bengal and Himachal Pradesh units.

(3220) Tirunelveli : The State Government, which is announcing "glow-warm schemes" in the final phase of its tenure, is inciting fishermen and others against development schemes sponsored by the Centre in Tamil Nadu such as the Sethusamudram Ship Channel Project, "as it is keen that credit should not go to the United Progressive Alliance Government," Dravida Munnetra Kazhagam president M. Karunanidhi has alleged.

19-09-2005

(3221) Guntur : The Congress party is committed to all-round development of the State and it will not hesitate to rectify any mistake committed by the previous Government, party Municipal Elections Publicity Committee chairman Ghattamaneni Adiseshagiri Rao has said.

(3222) Hyderabad : The Telangana Rashtra Samiti (TRS) has clarified that like other parties, it was not seeking a mandate from voters directly on the issue of separate Telangana in the municipal poll.

(3223) Hyderabad : The Finance Minister, K. Rosaiah, has said the Congress party has been forced by the Telugu Desam to hit back at the latter's continued tirade that the Y. S. Rajasekhara Reddy's Government is corrupt.

(3224) Vijayawada : State secretary of the Communist Party of India (Marxist) B.V. Raghavulu on Sunday sought to clarify that the party had severed its ties with the Telugu Desam Party and would not forge an alliance with the party even in future.

(3225) Visakhapatnam : Minister for Sports and Culture M. Satyanarayana Rao on Sunday accused Union Minister for Labour and Telangana Rashtra Samiti president K. Chandrasekhar Rao of indulging in a double game.

(3226) Warangal : The Bharatiya Janata Party (BJP) would emerge as a deciding force in the ensuing municipal elections in the State, said senior BJP leader Bandaru Dattatreya.

(3227) Kadapa : The Congress characterised municipal elections as a referendum on the 16-month rule of Chief Minister Y.S. Rajasekhara Reddy and the party would reorient its policies in case of an adverse public mandate, APCC vice-president and observer Mohd. Jani asserted on Sunday.

(3228) Rajahmundry : The TDP president, N. Chandrababu Naidu, has alleged that there is no protection even for IPS officers in the State. He made the remark at a press conference on Sunday while referring to a report on a letter written by an IPS officer to the Chief Secretary seeking protection.

(3229) Sangareddy : Union Minister and Telangana Rashtra Samithi leader A. Narendra apprehends threat to his life and that of party president K. Chandrasekhar Rao from the 'Cobra' gangs.

(3230) Kadapa : A pamphlet brought out by Kadapa Muslim Committee at the behest of Telugu Desam Party (TDP) had distorted historical facts to hoodwink minorities, Congress leaders alleged on Sunday.

(3231) Miryalaguda (Nalgonda) : The Telangana Rastra Samiti president K. Chandrasekhar Rao has asked the Congressmen to ensure the victory of his party in the municipal elections to prove that they are sincere towards the cause of Telangana.

(3232) Chennai : A first rate crisis stared the Bharatiya Janata Party in the face here on Sunday when party president L.K. Advani announced in a concluding statement that he would demit office in December at the BJP national council session in Mumbai that would also mark the end of the party's silver jubilee celebrations.

(3233) Patna : The Former Bihar Chief Minister, Jagannath Mishra, on Sunday termed as "absurd, imaginary and based on hearsay" the allegations against Indira Gandhi and his elder brother, late Lalit Narain Mishra, by a former Soviet archivist that they had received money from the KGB.

(3234) New Delhi : The Congress and the Communist Party of India have dismissed reports in a book that the parties and their leaders received funds from the erstwhile Soviet Union intelligence agency, KGB.

(3235) New Delhi : The Communist Party of India on Sunday announced that it would go with the Lok Jan Shakti Party and other Left parties in the coming Assembly elections in Bihar polls by offering a secular alternative.

(3236) Chennai : That the "war" within the BJP and in the larger Sangh Parivar was not about to end soon became clear when serious attempts were made by elements close to Mr. Advani to convey to the press that the former Prime Minister, Atal Bihari Vajpayee, had seen Mr. Advani's concluding statement and approved it in advance.

(3237) Bangalore : Leaders, who work to ensure that their children will inherit their reigns of power, will do anything to satisfy their selfish ends.

(3238) Alappuzha : Leader of the Opposition V.S. Achuthanandan has said that the United Democratic Front (UDF) was trying to "intimidate" the Left Democratic Front (LDF) by raising the issue of seat adjustments with Democratic Indira Congress (Karunakaran) (DIC-K) and the entry of former Union Minister P.C. Thomas into the Kerala Congress (Joseph).

(3239) Thiruvananthapuram : Congress(S) State president Ramachandran Kadannappally has said that his party does not propose to go in for a public spat over the differences between his party and the LDF leadership in connection with the allocation of seats to the Democratic Indira Congress (Karunakaran).

(3240) Thiruvananthapuram : Kerala Congress (B) leader R. Balakrishna Pillai has alleged that political parties had set up an unhealthy trend of promoting communal feelings in the local bodies elections.

(3241) Kanhangad : Democratic Indira Congress (Karunakaran) leader K. Karunakaran said here on Sunday that Communist Party of India (CPI) State secretary Veliyam Barghavan's statement on Emergency period was an affront to the former Chief Minister the late C. Achutha Menon and his party.

(3242) Chennai : Bharatiya Janata Party president L.K. Advani will stay on as the Leader of the Opposition in the Lok Sabha even after he quits the party post in December.

(3243) Chennai : The Bharatiya Janata Party on Sunday demanded that the Central Government take steps for formulating a common strategy to tackle the problem of naxalism.

(3244) Chennai : The Rashtriya Swayamsevak Sangh has reacted with political correctness to the announcement from Bharatiya Janata Party chief L.K. Advani that he would quit the party office in December.

(3245) New Delhi : The Congress on Sunday said the decision of Bharatiya Janata Party president L.K. Advani to quit his post was not a surprise while the Communist Party of India said the announcement would not end its internal squabbles.

(3246) New Delhi : The Communist Party of India on Sunday urged the Centre to tackle the problem of naxalites on the socio-economic front rather than treating it as one related to law and order.

(3247) Shimla : Once a decider of politics in Himachal Pradesh, but now surviving as a non-entity after rejoining the Congress, Pandit Sukh Ram, was somewhat revived today by the Pradesh Congress Committee when his son, Anil Sharma, was made one of the six general secretaries of the State Congress.

(3248) Chennai : The State unit of the Communist Party of India (CPI) on Sunday welcomed the Rs. 645-crore debt relief package announced by Chief Minister Jayalalithaa.

20-09-2005

(3249) Anantapur : Results of the current municipal elections will have a far-reaching impact on the political scenario in the State, the CPI (M) Rajya Sabha member, P. Madhu, has observed.

(3250) Eluru : The Telugu Desam Party (TDP) president, N. Chandrababu Naidu, on Monday visualised polarisation of political parties with the twin principles of reforms and secularism as the basis.

(3251) Guntur : The Bharatiya Janata Party will decide who should be the chairperson in a majority of the municipalities in the State, the former Union Minister, U. Krishnamraju, said here on Monday.

(3252) Mahabubnagar : The Union Minister for Coal and Mines Dasari Narayan Rao said on Monday that Congress alone had a comprehensive action plan of the sustained development of urban areas.

(3253) Tenali : Some mistakes were committed during the erstwhile Telugu Desam Party regime but the party had reviewed and rectified them, said the former Chief Minister, N. Chandrababu Naidu.

(3254) Sangareddy : The Telangana Rashtra Samithi (TRS) president K. Chandrasekhar Rao predicted a TRS-centred post poll political alignment in the State.

(3255) New Delhi : The Rashtriya Janata Dal (RJD) began on Monday seat-sharing talks with the Congress, the Communist Party of India (Marxist) and the Nationalist Congress Party (NCP), and decided to accommodate any other secular party desirous of joining the coalition for the Bihar Assembly elections.

(3256) Thiruvananthapuram : General secretary of the IUML P. K. Kunhalikutty has said that his party did not have any tactical alliance with either the Left Democratic Front or the Democratic Congress (Karunakaran) in the two-phase local bodies elections and is firmly in the UDF.

(3257) New Delhi : RJD chief Lalu Prasad on Monday told the Election Commission that he had neither violated the model code of conduct nor misused his official position in Bihar. - UNI

(3258) Bidar : Shiv Sena state unit president Pramod Mutalik said here on Monday that he will not contest an election. He said he will dedicate his life to protect Hindutva.

(3259) Gulbarga : Leader of Opposition in the Legislative Assembly B.S. Yediyurappa (Bharatiya Janata Party) on Monday took exception to the statements of Janata Dal (Secular) President and former Prime Minister H.D. Deve Gowda against him on the issue of storing water in the Alamatti dam.

(3260) Kottayam : The controversies surrounding the role of the former Chief Minister K. Karunakaran during the Emergency will in no way make any changes in the basic issues being taken up during the local body elections, Leader of the Opposition V.S. Achuthanandan said here on Monday.

(3261) Kozhikode : Democratic Indira Congress(Karunakaran) leader K. Karunakaran has said that but for the effective action taken against naxalites during the Emergency, the radical movement would have continued to let loose murderous violence in the State.

(3262) Kozhikode : Democratic Indira Congress (Karunakaran) leader K. Karunakaran has alleged that those who did not know the traditions of the Congress were now posing as Congressmen.

(3263) Thiruvananthapuram : State president of the BJP P. S. Sreedharan Pillai said here on Monday that the CPI (M) had used muscle power to prevent opposing parties from fielding their candidates in the panchayat elections.

(3264) Thrissur : Democratic Indira Congress (Karunakaran) (DIC(K) leader K. Muraleedharan on Monday said that members of his party will never return to the Congress.

(3265) Thrissur : District secretary of the Communist Party of India-Marxist (CPI-M) P.R. Rajan has said that his party has worked out only seat adjustments with the Democratic Indira Congress-Karunakaran (DIC-K) in the coming local-body elections.

(3266) New Delhi : The Congress on Monday rejected allegations that the erstwhile Soviet intelligence agency, KGB, funded party leaders and said the reports based on the book The Mitrokhin Archive Volume II -

the KGB and the World were "tendentious and mischievous. " But the Bharatiya Janata Party demanded that the Government order a thorough probe into the issue.

(3267) New Delhi : The All-India Forward Bloc said on Monday that the Justice M.K. Mukherjee Commission of Inquiry probing the disappearance of Netaji Subhas Chandra Bose would leave here for Moscow on Tuesday to examine archives. .

(3268) Jalandhar : The Communist Party of India on Monday reacted sharply to the CPI (M)'s suggestion that the United Progressive Alliance take action against Union Minister and Lok Jan Shakti Party chief Ram Vilas Paswan for contesting against the UPA partner, Rashtriya Janata Dal, in the Bihar Assembly polls. It said the alliance could not dictate a constituent's political posturing at the State level.

(3269) Chennai : The Bharatiya Janata Party vice-president, M. Venkaiah Naidu, on Monday asked the Union Government to respond to reports in a book that the Congress and its leaders received funds from the erstwhile Soviet Union intelligence agency, KGB.

(3270) Gandhinagar : Gujarat BJP president Vajubhai Vala has issued a suspension order and a show cause notice to a dissident member of the Assembly, Ramilaben Desai, who had levelled an allegation against Chief Minister Narendra Modi and two of his Cabinet colleagues.

(3271) Bhopal : The Bahujan Samaj Party president Mayawati on Monday accused the Centre as well as the Madhya Pradesh Government of neglecting the interests of the weaker sections of society. She also asked Dalits to unite for their economic and social advancement.

(3272) Kolkata : Veteran Marxist leader Jyoti Basu said on Monday that the Americans had funded Indira Gandhi and Congress to curb the Communists in India. He, however, was not sure whether the Congress and the CPI, which were "friendly" with the erstwhile Soviet Union, had received funds from the Soviet secret service KGB. "I can't say whether the KGB had provided funds to them. Both the CPI and the Congress had a good rapport with them [former Soviet Union]. But the CPI has already denied it," he told PTI here.

(3273) Chennai : Union Minister of State for Commerce and Industry E.V.K.S. Elangovan's demand for the resignation of Congress Legislature Party leader S.R.Balasubramoniyan has evoked widespread condemnation.

(3274) Chennai : States should be allowed to determine, on their own, the quantum of reservation in education and employment, Pattali Makkal Katchi founder S. Ramadoss said on Monday.

(3275) Belgaum : The former General Secretary of the Bharatiya Janata Party (BJP) and national executive member of Swadeshi Jagran Manch K.N. Govindacharya said here on Monday that there is no confrontation between BJP president L.K. Advani and the Rashtriya Swayamsevak Sangh (RSS).

21-09-2005

(3276) Karimnagar : The Andhra Pradesh Congress Committee president, K. Kesava Rao, has refused to comment on the alleged links of TRS and TJS with naxalites till he secures more information on it. However, he said that the TJS has Rashtriya Swayamsevak Sangh (RSS) orientation.

(3277) Karimnagar : The APCC president, K. Kesava Rao, has appealed to the former Chief Minister and Telugu Desam Party (TDP) president, N. Chandrababu Naidu, not to stoop down to making personal allegations and mudslinging against the Congress party.

(3278) Karimnagar : The Union Minister for Labour and TRS president, K. Chandrashekhar Rao, has clarified that they had constituted the Telangana Jagarana Sena (TJS) only to protect and safeguard the Telangana movement.

(3279) Kadapa : Congress leaders on Tuesday said the Telugu Desam Party (TDP) president, N. Chandrababu Naidu, was targeting the Chief Minister, Y.S. Rajasekhara Reddy, and Kadapa Mayor candidate, P. Ravindranath Reddy, in the name of alleged family rule during the former's State-wide election canvassing, as he found no fault with Congress policies.

(3280) Kochi : Even as a controversy over responsibility for the Emergency excesses is raging in the State and the civic election campaigns echo it, the Congress leader A.K. Antony has once again come to the defence of his political foe and Democratic Indira Congress (K) leader K. Karunakaran.

(3281) Jammu : The National Conference on Tuesday suggested initiation of talks with Hizb-ul Mujahideen chief Syed Salahuddin for resolution of the Kashmir issue.

(3282) New Delhi : Bihar will see a contest between the constituents of the United Progressive Alliance and its supporting parties, with the Lok Jan Shakti Party and three Left parties insisting on taking on both the Janata Dal (United)-Bharatiya Janata combine and the Rashtriya Janata Dal.

(3283) Mumbai : The Shiv Sena on Tuesday paid a fine of Rs. 20 lakhs, imposed on it by the Bombay High Court and upheld by the Supreme Court, for organising a bandh on July 30, 2003. A cheque for the amount was sent to the Maharashtra Chief Secretary - UNI

(3284) Mysore : Women activists of Bharatiya Janata Party's K.R. constituency on Tuesday staged a protest in front of lottery agencies against the sale of single and double digit as well as hourly lotteries.

(3285) Alappuzha : Democratic Indira Congress (Karunakaran) (DIC-K) president K. Muraleedharan has said that the Congress has conceded defeat even before polling for the local body elections is held.

(3286) Pathanamthitta : Kerala Pradesh Congress Committee (KPCC) president Ramesh Chennithala has alleged that the CPI(M) has lost its trustworthiness by aligning with the Democratic Indira Congress (Karunakaran), led by K. Karunakaran and P.C. Thomas who had won the Muvattupuzha Lok Sabha seat with the help of the Bharatiya Janata Party in the last general elections.

(3287) Thiruvananthapuram : State secretary of the CPI(M) Pinarayi Vijayan has said that there is no confusion among CPI(M) rank and file about the party stand on Emergency or its tactical adjustments with the Democratic Indira Congress (Karunakaran).

(3288) Thrissur : The CPI(ML) leader K.N. Ramachandran has said that the support being extended by the CPI(M) to the Manmohan Singh Government at the Centre is much more dangerous than the electoral tie-up that the party has entered into with the Democratic Indira Congress (DIC-K). "This is not to undermine the negative significance of K. Karunakaran who has been the sponsor of the anti-Communist coalitions in Kerala right from 1967. There have also been serious public indictments against Mr. Karunakaran for his role in the incidents like the murder of Azhikkodan Raghavan, Koothuparamba police firing and the Emergency excesses, including the custodial killing of Rajan and Vijayan," Mr. Ramachandran told The Hindu.

(3289) Kottayam : Giving clear indications of the extension of the crisis in the Bharatiya Janata Party's (BJP) national leadership to the State unit, the former State unit chief, C.K. Padmanabhan, has said that it is wrong for any outside agency to interfere in the day-to-day affairs of any political party.

(3290) New Delhi : The Congress-led Government here in the Capital was in the throes of another crisis on Tuesday with senior party leader and MLA S.C. Vats resigning as Chairman of the Public Accounts Committee in protest against "attempts" to "sabotage" the tabling of the PAC report in the monsoon session of the Delhi Assembly beginning this Thursday. The report is understood to have indicted the Sheila Dikshit Government over the issue of privatisation of power.

(3291) Bhopal : Senior Congress leader and Union Human Resource Development Minister Arjun Singh has asked all Congressmen in Madhya Pradesh to unite against the Bharatiya Janata Party. He said he would be forced to lead an agitation against the Madhya Pradesh Government from December 23 onward if it fails to solve the problems of slum dwellers of Bhopal who were being uprooted as part of a massive urban beautification drive.

(3292) Pondicherry : The founder-leader of the Puduchery Munnetra Congress (PMC) and former Minister of Pondicherry, P. Kannan, has said that Pondicherry Chief Minister N. Rangasamy did not attend several important meetings convened by the Centre to discuss and decide crucial issues. Failure even to send representatives of the Government meant Pondicherry lost several Centre-sponsored projects and funds for development, Mr. Kannan told a public meeting at Villianoor near here recently.

(3293) Chennai : All-India Congress Committee secretary K. Jayakumar has appealed to party leaders and cadres in Tamil Nadu to refrain from personal attacks, saying these would tarnish the party's image.

(3294) Chennai : The State executive of the Communist Party of India (Marxist) has urged the Central Government to take immediate steps to fill the vacancies in the posts of judges in Madras High Court.

22-09-2005

(3295) Guntur : The Congress and Telangana Rashtra Samiti (TRS) friendship will be short-lived given the way their leaders were abusing each other just before municipal elections, the Telugu Desam Party president, Nara Chandrababu Naidu, has predicted.

(3296) Hyderabad : A city court has admitted a private complaint against Telangana Rashtra Samithi (TRS) president and Union Labour Minister, K. Chandrasekhar Rao, and the Union Minister of State for Rural Development, A. Narendra, on the basis of their inflammatory speeches recently and referred it to the police to book a case.

(3297) Hyderabad : The Telugu Desam Party has topped the list of parties violating the model code of conduct in force for the municipal elections.

(3298) Sangareddy : TDP leader and former Minister, T. Devender Goud, alleged that the continuing bickering between the Congress and TRS has affected the development of Telangana in the past 16 months. Addressing a press conference here on Wednesday, Mr. Devender Goud said that the Congress government was wilfully diverting funds due for this region following the growing differences with the TRS. Works in all the Assembly segments represented by the TRS have come to a grinding halt in the Congress regime, he said. Mr. Goud said that the TDP would soon take up an agitation demanding completion of irrigation projects in Telangana region. Babu Mohan, in charge of Party campaign alleged that the local TRS MLA T. Jayaprakash Reddy was threatening TDP candidates. He said that TDP candidate from 16th ward Rahela Kidwai is missing and threatening calls to TDP candidates have become a regular feature.

(3299) Sangareddy : Andhra Pradesh Congress Committee (APCC) president K. Kesava Rao has asked the voters to keep in mind local problems like sanitation, drinking water and health, while they vote, as this is not an election for a change in Government.

(3300) Sangareddy : Union Minister and TRS leader A. Narendra has dared Chief Minister Y.S. Rajasekhara Reddy to arrest him and the party chief K. Chandrasekhara Rao. The Government will not succeed in its attempt to suppress the movement.

(3301) Bangalore : The dissident Janata Dal (Secular) leader Siddaramaiah has prepared himself for the worst - his expulsion from the party - on the eve of the crucial meeting of its executive committee organised by the dominant Deve Gowda group here on Thursday.

(3302) Alappuzha : The Communist Party of India (CPI) national executive committee member J. Chitharanjan has said that the reported statement of K. Karunakaran on a Left front led by him and Pinarayi Vijayan is only his wishful thinking.

(3303) Kollam : CPI(M) State secretary Pinarayi Vijayan has said that the results of the forthcoming elections would reveal that many local bodies would lack representations from the UDF. Addressing an LDF election campaign meeting here on Wednesday, Mr. Vijayan said that even religious heads, who were traditionally with the UDF, have quit the party.

(3304) Kollam : President of the Democratic Indira Congress (Karunakaran) K. Muraleedharan has said that further exchange of views between his party and the Left after the local body elections can result in the DIC becoming a constituent of the LDF.

(3305) Kottayam : Kerala Pradesh Congress Committee (KPCC) president Ramesh Chennithala said CPI(M) State secretary Pinarayi Vijayan owed an answer to the voters on whether he agreed wi th the opinion expressed by Lead er of the Opposition V.S. Achuth anandan that it would take long for the popular ire against Democratic Indira Congress-Karunakaran (DIC(K) leader K. Karunakaran to subside.

(3306) Pathanamthitta : Bharatiya Janata Party (BJP) national secretary L.Ganesh, who is in charge of the organisational affairs of the party in the State, has clarified that his party has made no formal electoral tie-up with any of the constituents of either the United Democratic Front (UDF) or the Left Democratic Front (LDF) in the local body elections.

(3307) Thiruvananthapuram : CPI(M) parliamentary party leader T.M. Thomas Isaac has alleged massive corruption in the implementation of the World Bank-aided Kerala State Transport Project (KSTP) and asked the Government to come clean on the entire project procedures.

(3308) New Delhi : There is no move by Bharatiya Janata Party leaders, either collectively or individually, to ask L.K. Advani to reconsider his decision to quit as president in December. Party spokesperson Sushma Swaraj said "no discussion took place" at an expanded meeting of general secretaries here on Wednesday on Mr. Adani's announcement made in Chennai.

(3309) New Delhi : With the Congress putting off its plenary session, the party leadership has to take a view on increasing voices from the State units to nominate members to the Congress Working Committee, instead of elections to the decision making body.

(3310) New Delhi : Delhi Bharatiya Janata Party president Harsh Vardhan on Wednesday demanded that the report of the Public Accounts Committee chaired by senior Congress legislator S.C. Vats be laid on the table of the Delhi Assembly and an enquiry be initiated against those held guilty according to the report.

(3311) New Delhi : The Congress and the Rashtriya Janata Dal have finalised the seat-sharing pact but have decided to hold back its formal announcement for strategic reasons.

(3312) New Delhi : The former Bihar president of the Rashtriya Janata Dal, Kamal Paswan, joined the Janata Dal (United) here on Wednesday in the presence of party president George Fernandes.

(3313) Mumbai : The Bharatiya Janata Party on Wednesday deposited Rs. 20 lakhs as damages towards the losses in Mumbai due to a bandh called by the party two years ago to protest the blasts at Ghatkopar in the metropolis. The Shiv Sena had deposited the amount on Tuesday.

(3314) Sitapur : Opposition Leader in the Uttar Pradesh Vidhan Sabha Lalji Tandon was on Wednesday barred from visiting tension-ridden Macherheta town in the district, where curfew was imposed after an incident of cow slaughter.

(3315) Chennai : The Congress Legislature Party on Wednesday criticised Union Minister of State for Industry and Commerce E.V.K.S. Elangovan for his remarks against CLP leader S.R. Balasubramoniyan.

(3316) Erode : Demanding the State that Tamil be implemented in all departments including the judiciary, and that lessons in schools be taught in Tamil medium and free education be given to all students till Class XII, the members of the Pattali Makkal Katchi and Viduthalai Siruthaigal Movement staged demonstration on Wednesday in Erode, Bhavani, Gobichettipalayam and Dharapuram near the respective Taluk offices, and attempted to picket in front of the offices. The police held the activists and registered cases against them. As many as 326 members were held, including Anthiyur PMK MLA S.R. Krishnan who participated in the demonstration in Bhavani.

23-09-2005

(3317) Guntur : The Bharatiya Janata Party (BJP) will emerge as a decisive force in the coming municipal elections as the middle class is vexed with the Congress Government, said the former Minister and BJP leader, Bandaru Dattatreya.

(3318) Nizamabad : The TRS president and Union Minister, K. Chandrasekhar Rao said that all parties were jealous of the Telangana Jagarana Sena and dubbed their comments against the Sena "baseless and unfounded".

(3319) Nizamabad : The Telangana Rashtra Samithi chief , K. Chandrasekhar Rao said that court cases were common against those striving towards a specific goal.

(3320) Tirupati : TDP president N. Chandrababu Naidu on Thursday rounded off his hectic campaign for the municipal elections with an impressive road-show in his home district of Chittoor, touching en route Chittoor, Punganur, Palamaner and Madanapalle towns in course of his 80-km whistle-stop campaign lasting seven hours.

(3321) Sangareddy : BJP State president N. Indrasena Reddy, has demanded that Chief Minister Y.S. Rajasekhara Reddy impress upon the Congress led UPA Government at the Centre to remove the TRS Ministers on whom the State Government had reportedly submitted a proof of having links with the Maoists.

(3322) Thiruvananthapuram : Democratic Indira Congress (Karunakaran) leader K. Karunakaran on Thursday laid out the road map for the post-election political moves by stating that his party would uphold its secular democratic credentials and would cooperate with all sections that prescribe to this platform.

(3323) Hassan : The preparatory meeting of AHIND (Alpasankhyataru, Hindulidavaru mathu Dalitaru) held in Holenarsipur, the hometown of the former Prime Minister and President of Janata Dal (Secular) H.D. Deve Gowda on Wednesday, turned out to be a rally. Former Deputy Chief Minister Siddaramiah, former Ministers H. Vishwanath and A. Nabi, former MP Kodandaramiah, MLAs Mahadevu and Venkatesh participated in the rally.

(3324) Bangalore : The Janata Dal (Secular) leadership has suspended the former Deputy Chief Minister Siddaramaiah from the primary membership of the party.

(3325) Kochi : Getting even with the CPI(M) over its allegation of the UDF's electoral understanding with the BJP in the civic elections, Kerala Pradesh Congress Committee (KPCC) president Ramesh Chennithala on Thursday said it was the CPI(M) that had gone for a clandestine tie-up with the BJP.

(3326) Kozhikode : The former Chief Minister A.K. Antony has accused the CPI(M) of adopting double standards in Kerala on the development agenda.

(3327) Kozhikode : Criticising the United Democratic Front (UDF) Government for its failure on all spheres of activity, Communist Party of India State secretary Veliyam Bhargavan has said that the State is going the Bihar way. The law and order situation had taken a backseat during the UDF regime, he told a Meet-the-Press organised at the Calicut Press Club here on Thursday.

(3328) Thiruvananthapuram : UDF convener P.P. Thankachan on Thursday said that the LDF-DIC(K) alliance would fall through under the strain of incompatibility.

(3329) Thiruvananthapuram : The BJP leader and former Union Minister O. Rajagopal has said that the CPI(M) State secretary Pinarayi Vijayan was trying to stoke communal passions with his campaign dubbing the BJP as the enemy of Islam. At a press conference here on Thursday, Mr. Rajagopal attacked Mr. Vijayan for 'distorting' the contents of a resolution passed by the BJP at its national executive meeting held in Chennai recently. Mr. Rajagopal referred to a statement made by Mr. Vijayan at a press meet that the BJP national executive had passed a resolution describing Islam as the party's 'prime enemy.'

(3330) Thiruvananthapuram : State secretary of the Revolutionary Socialist Party (RSP) T. J. Chandrachoodan has said that the local-level ties between the LDF and the Democratic Indira Congress(Karunakaran) is a short-term measure aimed at defeating the UDF comprehensively in the panchayat-municipal elections.

(3331) Thrissur : The Leader of the Opposition V.S. Achuthanandan has criticised Democratic Indira Congress (Karunakaran) chairman K. Karunakaran for 'defending' the cruelties committed by the police during the Emergency when he was Home Minister.

(3332) Kolkata : The Congress leadership in Kerala "has made a mockery of its national commitment to fight communalism" by taking the "shameful step" of entering into an electoral understanding with the Bharatiya Janata Party at many places for the elections to local bodies in that State, general secretary of the Communist Party of India (Marxist), Prakash Karat, said in a statement here on Thursday.

(3333) New Delhi : Janata Party president Subramanian Swamy on Thursday demanded a probe by a commission into allegations of KGB's links with the Congress.

(3334) New Delhi : A no-confidence motion against the Sheila Dikshit Government on the first day of the monsoon session of the Delhi Assembly was defeated by a voice vote but not before the opposition Bharatiya Janata Party forced two adjournments and stormed the well of the House alleging a multi-crore scam in the privatisation of power and demanding resignation of Chief Minister. All 20 BJP members were physically evicted from the House by marshals for disrupting the proceedings.

(3335) New Delhi : Seat-sharing talks for the Bihar Assembly elections between the Bharatiya Janata Party and the Janata Dal (United) broke down on Thursday after the JD(U) leaders insisted that the BJP "keep its promise" of giving it the seats won in February by Lok Jan Shakti Party candidates who have since joined the JD(U).

(3336) Villupuram : Chief Minister Jayalalithaa is insistent on re-introducing the POTA with a motive; for, she wants to settle scores with many persons before demitting office, according to S. Ramadoss, Pattali Makkal Katchi founder.

(3337) Bhopal New Delhi : As the stalemate continued on Thursday over the teachers' demand for "equal pay for equal work", the Leader of Opposition in the Madhya Pradesh Assembly, Jamuna Devi, lashed out at the BJP-led State Government saying that it was trying to crush the teachers' peaceful and democratic agitation.

(3338) Bhopal New Delhi : The Communist Party of India (Marxist) has demanded that the Madhya Pradesh Government hold negotiations with teachers and immediately release those arrested and accept their genuine demands.

(3339) Chennai : Former Chief Minister C.N. Annadurai was a democrat and did not indulge in "Machiavellian machinations," Dravida Munnetra Kazhagam treasurer Arcot N. Veerasamy has said.

(3340) Chennai : The Bharatiya Janata Party on Thursday criticised Dravida Munnetra Kazhagam president M. Karunanidhi for questioning the need for reviving the Prevention of Terrorism Act (POTA).

24-09-2005

(3341) Hyderabad : The Telugu Desam Party president, N. Chandrababu Naidu, has exuded confidence that people will give the party a clear mandate over the Congress if the municipal elections were free and fair.

(3342) Hyderabad : The Chief Minister, Y.S. Rajasekhara Reddy, has berated the Leader of the Opposition, N. Chandrababu Naidu, "for picking holes in the governance process every day."

(3343) Vijayawada : Secretary of the Bharatiya Janata Party (BJP), Bandaru Dattatreya, on Friday urged the State Election Commission to conduct the municipal elections in a free and fair manner.

(3344) Vijayawada : The State secretary of the Communist Party of India (CPI), K. Narayana, on Friday said that the statement of Defence Minister Pranab Mukherjee exposed the "hollowness" in the claims of Telangana Rashtra Samithi (TRS) president K. Chandrasekhar Rao on statehood to Telangana.

(3345) Sangareddy : The Telangana Rashtra Samithi will bring to the notice of Congress president, Sonia Gandhi the issue of cases against party President and Union Minister K. Chandrasekhar Rao immediately after elections to local bodies.

(3346) Kannur : Kerala Pradesh Congress Committee (KPCC) president Ramesh Chennithala said on Friday that the Communist Party of India (Marxist) was taking political revenge on senior leader K. Karunakaran by putting the blame on him for all the excesses occurred in the State over the last three decades.

(3347) Kannur : Communist Party of India-Marxist (CPI-M) State secretary Pinarayi Vijayan said here on Friday that the party took its political positions in response to the situation during a given period of time and not based on the history of any leader.

(3348) Bijapur : The former President of the Karnataka Pradesh Congress Committee V.S. Koujalgi said here on Friday that only the party High Command can decide whether to admit the former Deputy Chief Minister Siddaramaiah into its fold or not.

(3349) Hassan : Terming his suspension and that of the former Union Minister C.M. Ibrahim from the primary membership of the Janata Dal (Secular) unilateral and illegal, the former Deputy Chief Minister Siddaramaiah said on Friday that the action has no legal sanctity.

(3350) Palakkad : Leader of the Opposition V.S. Achuthanandan has asked the Democratic Indira Congress (Karunakaran) leader K. Karunakaran to "apologise to the people for the excesses he committed during the Emergency as the then Home Minister, respecting people's anger about the unfortunate incidents."

(3351) Malappuram : Democratic Indira Congress (Karunakaran) State president K. Muraleedharan said here on Friday that it was the Indian Union Muslim League (IUML) that took the initiative for a Congress-League-Bharatiya Janata Party (BJP) 'nexus' in the Vadakara and Beypore constituencies for the 1991 elections. The Congress had no role in that "unholy alliance, as those seats had been allotted to the IUML," Mr. Muraleedharan said.

(3352) New Delhi : The Congress on Friday criticised Lok Jan Shakti Party chief Ram Vilas Paswan for charting an independent course for October-November Bihar Assembly elections and accused him of "violating the coalition dharma."

(3353) New Delhi : It is not only the ordinary citizens but also the Municipal Corporation of Delhi that is feeling the heat of inflated power bills due to "fast running" electronic meters. At the MCD House meeting on Thursday, the opposition Bharatiya Janata Party councillors accused the Congress leadership in the civic body of failing to prevent public money from going into the hands of the private power distribution company in the form of inflated electricity bills.

(3354) New Delhi : The National Democratic Alliance partners, Bharatiya Janata Party and Janata Dal (United), are likely to have separate manifestoes for the Bihar Assembly polls.

(3355) Mumbai : The former Health Minister of Maharashtra, Daulatrao Aher, has quit the Bharatiya Janata Party, alleging that it gave posts to those who got him defeated in the last Assembly elections.

25-09-2005

(3356) Hyderabad : The Andhra Pradesh Congress Committee president, K. Keshava Rao, complimented the Government for the peaceful conduct of elections in 96 municipalities and 11 corporations in the State on Saturday.

(3357) Hyderabad : Former Union Finance Minister and Leader of Opposition in the Rajya Sabha, Jaswant Singh, has called upon young managers to be innovative and "think out of the box" to meet challenges.

(3358) Hyderabad : The Bharatiya Janata Party (BJP) has charged the Government with resorting to large-scale misuse of administrative machinery to ensure the victory of the Congress candidates in various municipalities and corporation across the State.

(3359) New Delhi : Taking a serious view of the explosive findings of the Public Accounts Committee (PAC) of the Delhi Assembly that money had reportedly influenced the process of privatisation of power distribution in the Capital and monetary benefits were extended to business houses and officials involved in the process, the Congress high command is understood to have sought a complete "status report" on the alleged multi-crore scam. According to highly placed sources, the idea is to find out to what extent the political leadership was involved in it.

(3360) Patna : The state is heading for a multi-cornered contest, with the Communist Party of India (Marxist-Leninist) on Saturday ruling out the possibility of the formation of a third front and deciding to go it alone in the coming Assembly elections.

(3361) Mysore : The former Minister of State for Textiles, Satish Jharkiholi, has made it clear that he will remain with the former Deputy Chief Minister, Siddaramaiah, "come what may."

(3362) Alappuzha : Leader of the Opposition V.S. Achuthanandan has said that the Left Democratic Front (LDF) will win hands down the local body polls held in eight districts from Thiruvananthapuram to Thrissur on Saturday.

(3363) Kozhikode : Kerala Pradesh Congress Committee president Ramesh Chennithala said here on Saturday that Communist Party of India-Marxist (CPI-M) State secretary Pinarayi Vijayan had confessed about indulging in parliamentary opportunism by admitting that his party's political positions were decided in response to the situation prevailing at a given time.

(3364) Kozhikode : Deputy Leader of the Opposition in the Assembly Kodiyeri Balakrishnan has said that the Left Democratic Front (LDF) will get more votes than those polled by it in 2000 in the ongoing elections to the grama, block and district panchayats, municipalities and five corporations.

(3365) Thrissur : Democratic Indira Congress-Karunakaran (DIC-K) chairman K. Karunakaran has said that the people are strongly opposed to the present United Democratic Front (UDF) Government, and that they are using the local-body elections to express that anguish through the ballot.

(3366) New Delhi : The Bharatiya Janata Party is to launch a nationwide agitation against the Congress and some Left parties for allegedly receiving funds from the KGB, intelligence agency of the erstwhile Soviet Union.

(3367) New Delhi : Even as Congress legislators watched everything in silence, it was left to Nationalist Congress Party (NCP) MLA Ramvir Singh Bidhuri to defend the role and prestige of former Prime Minister Indira Gandhi who was attacked by Bharatiya Janata Party members inside the Delhi Assembly over allegations that the former Prime Minister had links with the Russian intelligence agency KGB.

(3368) New Delhi : The Congress-Rashtriya Janata Dal-Nationalist Congress Party alliance in Bihar will set up a Commission to look into the socio-economic and educational backwardness of religious and linguistic minorities and grant them reservation benefits if voted to power.

(3369) New Delhi : Emphasising the need for "social control" on private educational institutions, Rajya Sabha member Sitaram Yechury demanded that the Government set up an independent regulator to monitor the working of private institutes to ensure equity in and access to education.

(3370) Chennai : The Rashtriya Swayamsewak Sangh (RSS) has moved the Madras High Court seeking to delete a lesson from the history book prescribed for Plus Two students as it "linked the murder of Mahatma Gandhi with the RSS."

(3371) Chennai : Dravida Munnetra Kazhagam president M. Karunanidhi has lauded the Opposition members of the Tamil Nadu Assembly for forcing the Government to withdraw the Madras University (Special Provisions) Bill within a day after its passage in the Assembly.

26-09-2005

(3372) Khammam : Telugu Desam Party president N. Chandrababu Naidu, who visited flood-affected areas in the district on Sunday, came down heavily on the Government for what he called its failure to rise to the occasion.

(3373) Rajahmundry : Peddapuram Congress MLA Thota Gopalakrishna has sent his resignation to Chief Minister Y. S. Rajasekhara Reddy on Sunday night, protesting against the alleged police lathicharge on him and his supporters.

(3374) New Delhi : Communist parties and some others have charged the Manmohan Singh Government with abandoning non-alignment and acting under pressure from the United States when it voted with the West at the board meeting of the International Atomic Energy Agency in Vienna to refer to the United Nations Security Council issues related to Iran's nuclear programme.

(3375) New Delhi : In an apparent disapproval of the Rashtriya Swayamsevak Sangh's insistence on sticking to its core ideology in the changing times, the former Prime Minister, Atal Bihari Vajpayee, said on Sunday that thinking was an evolutionary process that could not be curbed.

(3376) Bangalore : Water Resources and Transport Minister and Karnataka Pradesh Congress Committee President M. Mallikarjuna Kharge on Sunday said it is the Congress Government that helped slum-dwellers by giving them possession certificates.

(3377) Bangalore : A day ahead of the AHINDA convention in Hassan, the former Prime Minister H.D. Deve Gowda, and Finance and Industries Minister P.G.R. Sindhia questioned the suspended party leader Siddaramaiah's concern for other backward classes and his actions as the Finance Minister of the State.

(3378) Bangalore : The Janata Dal (Secular) President and former Prime Minister, H.D. Deve Gowda, has reminded his critics who are questioning his commitment to the cause of the slum dwellers and the downtrodden that it was when he was the Prime Minister that the National Slum Development Programme was taken up.

(3379) Hassan : Accusing the former Prime Minister and President of Janata Dal (Secular), H.D. Deve Gowda, of trying to weaken the Congress in the State by encouraging defection, senior Congress leader, R.L. Jalappa, MP, claimed that he and a few others were making every effort to foil such attempts of Mr. Deve Gowda.

(3380) Chitradurga : Deputy Chief Minister M.P. Prakash has defended the statement of the President of the Janata Dal (S) H.D. Deve Gowda and said that instead of looking at the proposed revision of reservation scheme in a political angle, it should be seen in a broader sense keeping in mind people, who are still suppressed in society.

(3381) Thiruvananthapuram : Leader of the Opposition V.S. Achuthanandan has accused the State Government of trying to sabotage the second phase of the local-body elections by using the police.

(3382) Thiruvananthapuram : Kerala Pradesh Congress Committee president Ramesh Chennithala, on Sunday, took exception to the statement of Leader of the Opposition V. S. Achuthanandan, criticising the State Government and the police.

(3383) Aurangabad : CPI(M) Polit Bureau member Sitaram Yechury on Sunday said some of the promises made in the common minimum programme had not been fulfilled by the Government.

(3384) Coimbatore : The Union Government should order a probe into the charges of KGB payoffs to political parties in Mitrokhin Archives Volume II as it is the Government's duty to ensure that the guilty are punished, Janata Party president Subramanian Swamy said here on Sunday.

(3385) New Delhi : The Janata Dal (United) and the Bhartiya Janata Party are yet to reach an understanding on eight constituencies in their seat-sharing arrangement for the Assembly polls in Bihar.

(3386) Mumbai : The Nationalist Congress Party has threatened to depose against 18 supporters of the newly-inducted Revenue Minister Narayan Rane facing the charge of murdering an NCP activist Satyavijay Bhise. The hearing begins in his home constituency Malvan in the Konkan region on Tuesday.

(3387) Ahmedabad : Bharatiya Janata Party president L. K. Advani on Sunday said his "historic" Ram rath yatra 15 years ago would be considered "complete" only when the temple was constructed in Ayodhya.

(3388) New Delhi : A nine-member delegation under the leadership of the Delhi Bharatiya Janata Party chief, Harsh Vardhan, called on the Lieutenant-Governor, B.L. Joshi, over the weekend and submitted a memorandum to him demanding a Central Bureau of Investigation enquiry into the controversial privatisation of the power distribution network in the Capital.

(3389) Bhopal : Former Speaker of Madhya Pradesh Assembly Shriniwas Tiwari on Sunday said the Congress would start a State-wide agitation demanding withdrawal of "false" cases against farmers for recovery of electricity bills.

(3390) Pondicherry : The secretary of the Pondicherry State committee of All India Anna Dravida Munnetra Kazhagam (AIADMK) and party legislator, A Anbalagan, has said that the World Bank had provided Rs 180 crores as assistance to Pondicherry Administration for various rehabilitation and housing facilities in tsunami hit fishermen villages in Pondicherry and Karaikal regions, but nothing had been done to construct houses out of this for the tsunami ravaged families.

27-09-2005

(3391) Hyderabad : APCC president K. Keshava Rao thanked the voters for delivering a verdict in favour of value-based politics while teaching a fitting lesson to those banking on negative campaign.

(3392) Hyderabad : The BJP admitted that the party could not achieve the expected result.

(3393) Hyderabad : AICC president Sonia Gandhi greeted Chief Minister Y.S. Rajasekhara Reddy on the triumph of the party in the polls.

(3394) Hyderabad : The Left parties have attributed the "lacklustre" performance of the TDP to effective coordination between the Congress and the Left. Though the TDP tried to "overreact" on issues, people did not believe it resulting in the landslide victory for the Congress-Left alliance.

(3395) Srikakulam : The TDP MP from Srikakulam, K. Yerrannaidu on Monday charged the Congress Government with making a mockery of democracy by importing Lalu Prasad Yadav's Bihar-type election process in Andhra Pradesh. Speaking to newsmen here on Monday, Mr. Yerrannaidu said, "Right at the beginning, Dr. Rajasejhara Reddy had chalked out a game plan to win elections by hook or by crook and stick to power. He has achieved his mission. It is a black day for democracy."

(3396) Hyderabad : Maintaining its winning run, the ruling Congress registered a landslide victory in the municipal elections held on September 24, leaving its main challenger, the Telugu Desam Party, a poor second.

(3397) Hassan : Janata Dal (Secular) President and former Prime Minister H.D. Deve Gowda became the favourite whipping boy at the AHINDA convention here on Monday with speaker after speaker accusing him of promoting dynastic rule and harming the interests of backward classes, minorities and Dalits.

(3398) Hyderabad : Chief Minister Y. S. Rajasekhara Reddy has termed his party's triumph in the civic elections as "a people's victory" and a positive vote for the Congress Government.

(3399) Bangalore : H.N. Ananth Kumar, Bharatiya Janata Party MP, on Monday accused Janata Dal (S) President H.D. Deve Gowda of misleading the people by pretending to champion the cause of the poor and the backward classes.

(3400) Davangere : The Janata Dal (Secular) President and former Prime Minister, H.D. Deve Gowda, on Monday expressed concern over what he termed "political murders" taking place in many parts of the State. He cautioned Chief Minister N. Dharam Singh that this trend, if it continues, may threaten the existence of the coalition Government in the State.

(3401) Kozhikode : The Democratic Indira Congress (Karunakaran) president K. Muraleedharan has said that his party leaders will work out modalities with the Left Democratic Front (LDF) leadership to share power at the civic bodies in the State.

(3402) Thiruvananthapuram : The CPI(M) leadership has alleged massive irregularities in the distribution of postal ballots and urged the State Election Commission to count all postal ballots submitted till 5 p.m. on Tuesday.

(3403) Nedumbassery : Chief Minister Oommen Chandy on Monday said the election-related violence reported from Kannur during the second phase of elections to local bodies was a blot on the State and stringent legal measures would be taken against those responsible irrespective of party affiliations.

(3404) New Delhi : The Bharatiya Janata Party and the Janata Dal (U) reached a seat-sharing agreement for the coming Bihar Assembly elections under which the former will contest 102 seats, three short of the number it fought last time. Working out the arrangement after a marathon meeting, the two NDA allies decided that the JD(U) will contest the rest of the 141 seats in the 243-member House.

(3405) New Delhi : The Congress on Monday defended India's vote against Iran in the International Atomic Energy Agency stating it took a stand based on independent assessment and national interest.

(3406) New Delhi : Bharatiya Janata Party leader Jaswant Singh on Monday described the Government's approach to the Iran nuclear issue as "perplexing" and its stand on a host of nuclear-related issues as "confusing." He demanded that the Prime Minister or the External Affairs Minister "explain" to the country the concerns, which made India vote with the European Union on the Iran nuclear issue, leading to a "major shift" in foreign policy.

(3407) Ahmedabad : Gujarat BJP president Vajubhai Vala has sought a detailed report about a convention of Dalits in Rajkot where party dissidents shared the platform with the Congress to denounce the Narendra Modi Government in the State.

(3408) New Delhi : Union Minister and Lok Janshakti Party (LJP) leader Ram Vilas Paswan on Monday ruled out any alliance with the Rashtriya Janata Dal (RJD) before or after the Bihar Assembly elections.

(3409) Patna : Lok Jan Shakti Party (LJP) chief and Union Steel Minister Ram Vilas Paswan is expected to announce his seat-sharing arrangement with the Communist Party of India (CPI), Revolutionary Socialist Party (RSP) and Forward Bloc (FB) in a day or two. Forty seats for CPI

(3410) New Delhi : The Polit Bureau of the Communist Party of India (Marxist) on Monday denounced the allegation against Pramode Dasgupta, one of the founding leaders of the party, in the book The Mitrokhin Archive and the Secret History of the KGB.

(3411) New Delhi : Deciphering the former Prime Minister, Atal Bihari Vajpayee, was as difficult as trying to get at the meaning of Tulsidas' Ram Charit Manas. "It takes time to understand Atalji's views. It is like reading Tulsidas' Ram Charit Manas, you can read a new meaning into it on each reading."

(3412) New Delhi : Senior leaders of Left parties have written to Prime Minister Manmohan Singh seeking his intervention over the issue of privatisation of water supply in the Capital and demanding that the loan application to the World Bank be withdrawn immediately.

(3413) New Delhi : Charging that a well planned conspiracy had been hatched at the behest of some property dealers and vested interests in the Delhi Government to delay the notification for regularising residential areas having more than 70 per cent industrial units, Nationalist Congress Party MLA Ramvir Singh Bidhuri on Monday alleged that "fraudulent investments" running into hundreds of crores of rupees had been made and a CBI inquiry should be ordered to bring out the truth.

(3414) Chandigarh : The Indian National Lok Dal (INLD) on Monday criticised the silence of the Haryana unit of the Congress and the Bhupinder Singh Hooda Government in raising issues concerning Haryana and getting a special package for the State from Prime Minister Manmohan Singh during his two-day visit to the State Capital.

(3415) Jaipur : Opposition Congress members disrupted the proceedings of the Rajasthan Assembly on the opening day of the monsoon session on Monday by creating a ruckus over allegations of gang-rape against a Cabinet Minister and his associates. The House was adjourned thrice amid the pandemonium that obstructed Question hour

(3416) Coimbatore : A single entrance test should be conducted for admission to all professional courses, Janata Party president Subramaniam Swamy said on Monday.

28-09-2005

(3417) Hyderabad : The Bharatiya Janata Party has decided not to support any other political party in the election to the post of civic chiefs on September 30.

(3418) Hyderabad : The Congress Legislature Party (CLP) has advised the TDP to replace its president, N. Chandrababu Naidu, with "someone who respects the people's mandate instead of allowing him to heap abuse on the voters every time he loses."

(3419) Hyderabad : The Finance Minister, K. Rosaiah, has asked Telugu Desam leaders, especially its president, N. Chandrababu Naidu, to maintain dignity while reacting to the poll outcome instead of blaming others for the rout.

(3420) Hyderabad : The Telugu Desam Party on Tuesday asked the Congress not to gloat over a "people's mandate" in the municipal elections, because, it was, in fact, "Congress-managed," the party said.

(3421) Hyderabad : In the first sign of trouble in the Telangana Rashtra Samithi after the municipal elections, two party MLAs have openly blamed the party president and Union Labour Minister K. Chandrasekhara Rao, and his Cabinet colleague, A. Narendra, for its miserable performance.

(3422) Vijayawada : The Congress will continue to treat the Telangana Rastra Samithi (TRS) as an ally, AICC general secretary Dijvijay Singh said here on Tuesday.

(3423) Vijayawada : Congress leaders of the coastal Andhra region used the visit of Congress president Sonia Gandhi to impress upon her the need to rein in TRS leaders, while projecting their hurt sentiments.

(3424) Vijayawada : She came, she saw and she went. The four-hour visit of Congress president Sonia Gandhi can only be described thus. No usual hoop-la preceded her visit, nor had it had any fizz. Local Congress leaders were bewildered as Ms. Gandhi never uttered a word to any of them throughout. Except for allowing lensmen to take a few snapshots from their designated enclosures, sleuths of the Special Protection Group (SPG) completely insulated her from media glare.

(3425) New Delhi : The Janata Dal (United) on Tuesday released its first list of 70 candidates for the Bihar elections, a day after it reached a seat-sharing pact with the Bharatiya Janata Party.

(3426) Thiruvananthapuram : In what may well be a pointer to the electoral mood of Kerala, the Left Democratic Front (LDF), led by the Communist Party of India (Marxist), has registered a landslide victory in the local body elections. LDF candidates won all the five city corporations, at least 33 out of the 52 municipalities, 13 of the 14 district panchayats and a majority of the 152 block panchayats and 999 grama panchayats.

(3427) Bangalore : Representatives of a number of backward classes who say they have been denied a fair share in the reservations for backward classes in employment and education called on the former Prime Minister H.D. Deve Gowda on Monday and sought his intervention for the introduction of specified reservation for each group.

(3428) Mysore : The Janata Dal (Secular) will not project a chief ministerial candidate when elections are held to the State Assembly, Working President of Janata Dal (S) H.D. Kumaraswamy said here on Tuesday.

(3429) Gadag : Karnataka Pradesh Congress Committee President and Water Resources Minister Mallikarjun Kharge on Tuesday asked the former Prime Minister H.D. Deve Gowda to desist from raising issues extraneous to the Common Minimum Programme of the coalition government.

(3430) Thiruvananthapuram : BJP State president P.S. Sreedharan Pillai announced here on Tuesday that an eight-member State-level core committee would decide the party's stand in local authorities where the party could influence the election of office-bearers.

(3431) Thiruvananthapuram : Kerala Pradesh Congress Committee (KPCC) president Ramesh Chennithala has said that the general contention of his party's opponents that the UDF would be routed has been proved wrong and the ruling coalition had proved that it continued to be a strong force despite the defeat it suffered in the local bodies elections.

(3432) Malappuram : The Indian Union Muslim League (IUML) has reason to celebrate, despite its poor show in Perinthalmanna, Ponnani and Tirur municipalities. The triumph of the IUML candidates in Malappuram and Manjeri was outstanding.

(3433) Thiruvananthapuram : The Left Democratic Front (LDF) leadership has described the Opposition alliance's "thumping victory" in the local body elections as a strong rebuff to the State-wide United Democratic Front-Bharatiya Janata Party tie-up and accused the United Democratic Front of having yielded ground to the BJP in its greed to gain control of the local bodies.

(3434) Chennai : The International Atomic Energy Agency (IAEA) resolution on Iran "merely asks the Director-General of the IAEA to interact and deal with the Iranian authorities further, and leaves it to the Board of the IAEA to decide the timing and content of the report required to be filed," the Janata Party president Subramanian Swamy said in a statement on Tuesday.

(3435) Patna : The RJD supremo and Railway Minister, Lalu Prasad, on Tuesday sewed up a seat-sharing alliance with the Congress, the CPI(M) and the NCP, "closing" the door on the LJP for the coming Assembly elections.

(3436) New Delhi : Abu Asim Azmi, Samajwadi Party leader and Rajya Sabha member, has urged Prime Minister Manmohan Singh to intervene and lift the ban on the Student Islamic Movement of India (SIMI) imposed in 2001.

(3437) New Delhi : The Rashtriya Swayamsevak Sangh asserted on Tuesday that its ties with the Bharatiya Janata Party were "normal" and its ideology was "not stagnant or inflexible."

(3438) Hyderabad : The Communist Party of India (Marxist) has demanded that the Centre come out with a clear stand that it will not associate itself with any U.S. move to refer the Iran nuclear issue to the United Nations Security Council.

(3439) Chandigarh : The Indian National Lok Dal (INLD) on Tuesday alleged gross violation of the Election Commission's instructions by the ruling Congress in Rohtak Lok Sabha constituency where a by-election is taking place on Wednesday.

(3440) Jaipur : The stalemate over an alleged sex scandal involving a Cabinet Minister continued for the second day of the Rajasthan Assembly's monsoon session on Tuesday. The Opposition Congress members staged a dharna in the House while demanding institution of a CBI inquiry into the incident and the Minister's resignation.

(3441) Tambaram : The general secretary of the Communist Party of India (Marxist), Prakash Karat, on Tuesday exhorted students to participate intelligently in the political process.

(3442) Madurai : The Communist Party of India (CPI) on Monday sought the Centre's intervention to resolve the boundary row between Karnataka and Tamil Nadu.

29-09-2005

(3443) Vijayawada : State secretary of the Communist Party of India (CPI) K. Narayana on Wednesday observed that the existing political scenario in the State was conducive for the Left parties to strengthen their base and emerge an alternative political front.

(3444) New Delhi : Virtually paving the way for the expulsion of the former Deputy Chief Minister Siddaramaiah and C.M. Ibrahim from the Janata Dal (Secular), the party's national Executive Committee on Wednesday approved their suspension from the party and authorised JD(S) President H.D. Deve Gowda to take "appropriate action" against those indulging in anti-party activities.

(3445) Hyderabad : The Telangana Rashtra Samithi (TRS) Legislature Party on Wednesday authorised party chief K. Chandrasekhar Rao to seek an explanation from the two MLAs for their outburst against the leadership and to initiate action against them as he deemed fit.

(3446) Thiruvananthapuram : Chief Minister Oommen Chandy announced here on Wednesday that the UDF would not seek the help of the BJP to take power in municipalities and panchayats that have hung councils.

(3447) Thiruvananthapuram : After conquering a majority of the urban local bodies, the Communist Party of India (Marxist)-led Left Democratic Front (LDF) is heading for a runaway victory in the grama panchayats in Kerala.

(3448) Kathmandu : A five-party delegation from India led by CPI (M) leader Sitaram Yechury was greeted with a black-flag demonstration and stone-pelting by hundreds of pro-monarchy activists upon its arrival here on Wednesday.

(3449) Bangalore : As the President of the State unit of the Congress and a few Ministers have "conceded" that developmental works have taken a back seat, the Government has no moral right to continue, Leader of the Opposition in the Legislative Assembly B.S. Yediyurappa has said.

(3450) Bangalore : The former Deputy Chief Minister Siddaramaiah has termed illegal the ratification of the suspension of the Vice-President of the Janata Dal (S) C.M. Ibrahim and himself by the executive committee of the party in New Delhi on Wednesday.

(3451) Gulbarga : The Communist Party of India (CPI) on Wednesday did not approve of the present combative stand of the Union Government to end the naxalite menace in the country and wanted it to tackle it as a socio-economic problem and introduce labour intensive and poverty alleviation programmes to wean away people from naxal influence.

(3452) Gulbarga : The Communist Party of India (CPI) on Wednesday came out strongly against what it called a major shift in foreign policy by the Congress-led United Progressive Alliance (UPA) Government.

(3453) Gulbarga : The State unit of the Janata Dal (United) on Tuesday criticised the decision of the Government to keep out flood relief works from the purview of the Transparency Act, and said this will lead to misappropriation of the relief amount released to the affected districts.

(3454) Haveri (Gadag Dt.) : While Chief Minister N. Dharam Singh and KPCC President M. Mallikarjun Kharge were circumspect, other

Congress leaders were unsparing in their criticism of H.D. Deve Gowda, President of the Janata Dal (S), here on Wednesday.

(3455) Thiruvananthapuram : BJP State president P.S. Sreedharan Pillai said here on Wednesday that the collapse of the United Democratic Front in the local body elections would help the BJP expand its sphere of influence.

(3456) Thiruvananthapuram : The Indian Union Muslim League (IUML) has rejected the offer of support of the Bharatiya Janata Party (BJP) to gain control of hung municipalities and panchayats.

(3457) Thiruvananthapuram : Democratic Indira Congress (K) leader K. Karunakaran on Wednesday said that a formal and full-fledged alliance with the CPI (M)-led LDF was being worked out in the run-up to the Assembly elections.

(3458) New Delhi : The Left parties on Wednesday registered their "strong protest" over India's vote against Iran at the International Atomic Energy Agency meeting and expressed apprehension that it would affect New Delhi's relations with Teheran.

(3459) Jaipur : The Rajasthan unit of the Congress has shown the door to the author of a controversial book on party president Sonia Gandhi. Pradesh Congress Committee president B.D. Kalla, who released the book, Sonia Gandhi and Indian Politics, on August 30 at his official residence here without seemingly knowing about its contents, announced the dismissal of Manchand Khandela, the author, here on Wednesday.

(3460) New Delhi : The Delhi Bharatiya Janata Party in separate letters to the Lieutenant-Governor, B. L. Joshi, and the Chief Minister, Sheila Dikshit, on Wednesday demanded that immediate action be taken to issue a notification to declaring all industrial units running in non-conforming areas of the city as regularised to provide relief to lakhs of people including labourers and unit owners.

(3461) Chennai : Janata Party president Subramanian Swamy and Bharatiya Janata Party vice-president M. Venkaiah Naidu have demanded a probe by a sitting Supreme Court Judge into the report "that the erstwhile Soviet agency KGB funded Congress and Communist Party leaders."

(3462) Chennai : DMK president M. Karunanidhi has demanded an enquiry into the authenticity of letters displayed by Food and Cooperation

Minister Pollachi V. Jayaraman on the floor of the Assembly on Tuesday, and into his charge that former DMK MP, the late C.T. Dandapani, had received money from a dismissed road mazdoor for getting him the job.

30-09-2005

(3463) Hyderabad : Chief Minister Y.S. Rajasekhara Reddy and APCC president K. Keshava Rao have analysed the party performance in the civic elections.

(3464) Hyderabad : The revolt within Telangana Rashtra Samiti (TRS) caused by the open criticism of the party leadership by two MLAs - Mandadi Satyanarayana Reddy and D. Srinivas Rao - subsided on Thursday after they offered an explanation to party president K. Chandrasekhar Rao.

(3465) Thiruvananthapuram : The Democratic Indira Congress (Karunakaran) president, K. Muraleedharan, today asserted the ties between his party and the LDF had got popular recognition going by the results of the local bodies elections.

(3466) Kathmandu : The visiting political delegation from India on Thursday expressed solidarity with Nepal's seven-party alliance fighting King Gyanendra's rule.

(3467) Bangalore : Former Union Minister C.M. Ibrahim, who has been dismissive of the action taken against him and former Deputy Chief Minister Siddaramaiah by the Janata Dal (Secular), on Thursday said their group will go ahead with a parallel national council meeting of the party here on Friday.

(3468) Hassan : Reacting to the recent "Swabhimani Samaavesha" organised by AHINDA (Alpasankhyataru, Hindulidavaru mathu Dalitaru) in Hassan, former MP and Janata Dal (Secular) leader H.K. Javare Gowda said that though organisers succeeded in "bringing" people to the convention, they failed in reaching the message and limited themselves to attacking former Prime Minister and party President H.D. Deve Gowda.

(3469) Hassan : Accusing the coalition Government of neglecting the irrigation sector, Leader of Opposition in the Legislative Assembly B.S. Yediyurappa on Thursday urged Chief Minister N. Dharam Singh to issue a White Paper on the progress of irrigation projects in the State.

(3470) Chikmagalur : D.H. Shankaramurthy, Leader of the Opposition in the Legislative Council, said here on Thursday that the Bharatiya Janata Party (BJP) was gearing up for mid-term elections in the State and was confident of securing a majority.

(3471) New Delhi : The national Executive Committee of the Janata Dal (Secular) on Wednesday expressed its "resentment" over India's vote in favour of the resolution tabled by the U.S. against Iran in the governing body meeting of the International Atomic Energy Agency. The JD(S) is extending outside support to the United Progressive Alliance (UPA) Government.

(3472) New Delhi : A day after the Left parties registered a strong protest over the vote against Iran in the International Atomic Energy Agency (IAEA), the Communist Party of India (Marxist) held Prime Minister Manmohan Singh responsible for taking a major step affecting the country's independent policy and its status in the non-aligned movement.

(3473) New Delhi : A perusal of the full transcript of the September 8 hearings into the Indo-U.S. nuclear deal conducted by the House International Relations Committee (HIRC) makes it clear that for both the Congressmen and testifying State Department officials, India's Iran policy was key to the agreement.

(3474) New Delhi : The Bharatiya Janata Party on Thursday accused the Left of having called a general strike without any real issue.

(3475) New Delhi : The Communist Party of India (Marxist) on Thursday termed the victory of the Left Democratic Front in local body elections in Kerala as a "strong rejection of the Oommen Chandy Government and its misrule."

(3476) Srinagar : Making out a strong case for giving a "safe passage" to hundreds of Kashmiri youth waiting across the Line of Control, a number of MLAs on Wednesday urged the Union Government to facilitate their return to allow them to lead a peaceful life. CPI (M) Sstate secretary and MLA Kulgam M. Y. Tarigami, who moved a resolution in the State Assembly, maintained that the ongoing peace process was incomplete without the return of these youth who had been lured in early 1990s for acquiring arms and ammunition training in "Azad Kashmir".

(3477) Jaipur : Former Chief Minister Ashok Gehlot has sought a probe into the hospitality extended by the Rajasthan Government to the

MLAs from Jharkhand during their sojourn here in March this year. There seems to be a link between the allegation of rape against a Cabinet Minister in Rajasthan and the "entertainment" of the MLAs who were brought here prior to the Bharatiya Janata Party proving its majority in Jharkhand, he said.

01-10-2005

(3478) Hyderabad : The TDP has lost the chairmanship of all nine municipalities where it emerged as the single largest party (as against places where it got absolute majority).

(3479) Hyderabad : The Congress swept the elections to the posts of Mayor and Municipal Chairperson along expected lines but floor-crossing in defiance of party whips and adjournment of the special meetings in four places marred the process on Friday.

(3480) Bangalore : The Janata Dal (Secular) formally split on Friday with the faction headed by the former Deputy Chief Minister Siddaramaiah "removing" Janata Dal (Secular) national President H.D. Deve Gowda, State unit President N. Thippanna and Working President H.D. Kumaraswamy from their posts.

(3481) Thiruvananthapuram : The Left Democratic Front (LDF) has virtually cleared the way for power sharing with the Democratic Indira Congress (Karunakaran) in the local bodies by deciding to allow LDF panels at the lower level to take appropriate decision in the matter depending on local needs.

(3482) Kathmandu : India should continue arms embargo on Nepal to pressure King Gyanendra to restore multiparty democracy in the Himalayan Kingdom, according to visiting Indian political leaders.

(3483) Bangalore : A.K. Antony, All-India Congress Committee General Secretary in charge of the State, who arrived here on Friday afternoon to review the performance of the Congress Ministers, said the coalition Government is not a permanent arrangement. However, he has hastened to add that the Congress is committed to the continuation of the arrangement in the interest of the people.

(3484) Bangalore : Former Union Minister C.M. Ibrahim, who was appointed "President" of the Janata Dal (Secular) by the faction headed by former Deputy Chief Minister Siddaramaiah, has said party conventions will be held in Chitradurga, Mysore, Gulbarga, and Belgaum.

(3485) Bangalore : Samajwadi Party General Secretary and MP Amar Singh said on Friday described the administration by the Congress-led coalition governments at the Centre and in Karnataka as "chaotic."

(3486) Bangalore : The Siddaramaiah faction of the Janata Dal (Secular) has taken the first step to building a case before the Election Commission of India to claim that it is "legitimate JD(S)."

(3487) Mysore : Former Prime Minister H.D. Deve Gowda has ridiculed his "expulsion" from the Janata Dal (Secular) by the party faction led by ousted Deputy Chief Minister Siddaramaiah and expressed "happiness" over the development.

(3488) Shimoga : General Secretary of the State unit of the Samajwadi Party Madhu Bangarappa said here on Friday that the party will give more opportunities to newcomers to serve it in various capacities.

(3489) Torangal (Bellary Dist.) : President of the Karnataka Pradesh Congress Committee (KPCC) Mallikarjun Kharge said on Thursday that the trading of charges and counter charges by the coalition partners are not sending the wrong signals to the people and party supporters.

(3490) Kochi : A meeting of the district-level leaders of the BJP here to assess the post-poll scenario has decided to extend issue-based support to the local governing councils.

(3491) Thiruvananthapuram : Democratic Indira Congress (Karunakaran) (DIC-K) leader K. Karunakaran has come out strongly against the UPA Government's Iran policy urging Prime Minister Manmohan Singh to explain to the nation why India had deviated from its time tested policy.

(3492) Thrissur : The Kerala Congress(M) district committee has accused the Congress of "pursuing strategies to ruin" the partners of the United Democratic Front (UDF) in the just-concluded local body elections.

(3493) Patna : Rashtriya Janata Dal chief and Railway Minister Lalu Prasad on Friday said his party was ready to accept the verdict of the Supreme Court in the Bihar Assembly dissolution case but would go ahead with the present election process.

(3494) Kolkata : The Polit Bureau member of the Communist Party of India (Marxist), Jyoti Basu, criticised the United Progressive Alliance (UPA) Government here on Friday for its "failure" to ensure proper implementation of the Common Minimum Programme (CMP). The Left parties should take up the matter with the UPA, he said.

(3495) Chandigarh : Former Haryana Chief Minister and Indian National Lok Dal (INLD) chief Om Parkash Chautala on Friday hit out at "the miserly increase" in the minimum support price for rabi crops announced by the Union Government.

(3496) Bhopal : The Leader of the Opposition in the Madhya Pradesh Assembly, Jamuna Devi, lashed out at the ruling Bharatiya Janata Party on Friday describing the national Dalit convention the latter has planned here on Saturday as an attempt to mislead the people. It was also to divert people's attention away from the atrocities being committed on Dalits and Scheduled Tribes in the State, she added.

(3497) Pondicherry : The member of the executive committee of the Tamil Nnadu CPI (M), T. Murugan, has urged the Lt Governor to order a CBI probe into the modalities adopted by the Administration over the years in holding departmental examinations for recruitment or promotion of employees to various posts.

(3498) Dehra Dun : Congress president Sonia Gandhi's letter to Chief Ministers of Congress-ruled states to curb unnecessary expenditures including air travel and limit the practice of granting ministerial status to party workers has evoked much cheer from the party workers and the general public while sending the over 120 beneficiaries of Government largesse into a panic.

02-10-2005

(3499) Hyderabad : The Telugu Desam Party has come to the conclusion that "indirect elections, misuse of official machinery, terror tactics and allurements by the Congress" are the main reasons for its poor showing in the municipal polls.

(3500) Thiruvananthapuram : In what amounts to justification of the local-level tactical tie-up between the LDF and the Democratic Indira Congress (Karunarkaran) in the local body elections, Leader of the

Opposition V. S. Achuthanandan has said the tie-up was in keeping with the Opposition's policy to utilise the services of anyone who opposes the misrule of the UDF Government.

(3501) Chandigarh : Deepinder Singh Hooda, the 27-year-old US-returned son of Haryana Chief Minister Bhupinder Singh Hooda, made history of sorts on Saturday by winning the prestigious Lok Sabha by-election from Rohtak with a massive margin of 231,958 votes. He trounced his nearest BJP rival, Abhimanyu, while Indian National Lok Dal candidate Balwan Singh Suhag, who finished third, lost his security deposit.

(3502) New Delhi : The Janata Dal (Secular) is all set to expel former Deputy Chief Minister Siddaramaiah and former Union Minister C.M. Ibrahim for continuing to indulge in "anti-party" activities. Mr. Siddramaiah and Mr. Ibrahim convened a meeting in Bangalore on Friday after their suspension from the party.

(3503) Kozhikode : The Indian Union Muslim League (IUML) leadership has vowed not to accept support from the Bharatiya Janata Party (BJP) to come to power in local self-governments.

(3504) Chennai : The Dravida Munnetra Kazhagam president and Democratic Progressive Alliance leader in Tamil Nadu, M. Karunanidhi, on Saturday called for ending the "politicisation of women's self-help groups" in the State.

(3505) Bangalore : A.K. Antony, General Secretary of the All-India Congress Committee in charge of the State, has expressed satisfaction with the overall performance of the Government led by Chief Minister N. Dharam Singh. However, he has said its performance in social sectors and its efforts to improve infrastructure in Bangalore are not up to the mark.

(3506) Bangalore : The President of the Janata Dal (Secular) State unit, N. Thippanna has suspended from the party the former Ministers Satish Jarkiholi and H.C. Mahadevappa and H.Y Meti, K. Venkatesh, Manchanahalli Mahadev, M.K. Somashekar and B.R. Patil, MLAs, for participating in a meeting called by a faction headed by the former Deputy Chief Minister Siddaramaiah in Bangalore on Friday.

(3507) Bangalore : The Congress High Command, through A.K. Antony, AICC General Secretary in-charge of Karnataka affairs, has sent a message to all Congress leaders in the State that there is no question of leadership change now and the party would like to continue with the understanding with the Janata Dal (Secular).

(3508) Mysore : Senior Bharatiya Janata Party leader K.S. Eshwarappa has urged the coalition partners, Congress and Janata Dal (Secular), which are independently carrying out an appraisal of their Ministers, to make the findings of the exercise public.

(3509) Kozhikode : M.P. Veerendrakumar, MP, Janatadal (Secular) State president, has demanded that Chief Minister Oommen Chandy relinquish his post following the debacle of the Congress-led United Democratic Front (UDF) in the local body polls in the State.

(3510) Kozhikode : State president of the Bharathiya Janata Party P. S. Sreedharan Pillai on Saturday claimed that his party had won in 573 seats in the recent elections to local government bodies and not 312 as stated by Kerala Pradesh Committee chief Ramesh Chennithala.

(3511) Pathanamthitta : The Bharatiya Janata Party (BJP) has expressed the view that the Congress and the Communist Party of India (Marxist) could very well follow their policy of friendship at the national level in the State too, if they wished to avoid administrative stalemate in several local bodies that have a hung verdict in the just-concluded local body elections.

(3512) Thiruvananthapuram : CPI(M) State secretary Pinarayi Vijayan on Saturday came down heavily on the "murder" of a youth at the Fort police station allegedly following use of third degree torture. He said Chief Minister Oommen Chandy should give up the Home portfolio owning moral responsibility for the incident.

(3513) Thiruvananthapuram : Kerala Pradesh Congress Committee (KPCC) spokesman M.M. Hassan, MLA, has charged the workers of the CPI(M) with resorting to violence against Congress workers in different parts of the State after the local body poll results.

(3514) Thrissur : The Congress leader V.M. Sudheeran has said that the low voting percentage in the just-concluded local bodies elections is a reflection of people's loss of faith in the present political system and parties.

(3515) Guwahati : Tension prevailed in Garo Hills of Meghalaya on Saturday though no untoward incident was reported from the two districts, where nine persons died in police firing on Friday.

(3516) Bhopal : A conference of the Chief Ministers of BJP-ruled States will be convened soon to evaluate the work done for weaker sections, party president L.K. Advani said on Saturday.

(3517) Patna : The senior JD (U) leader and NDA's Chief Ministerial candidate, Nitish Kumar, on Saturday maintained that his party would come out with its own manifesto on October 4 because of "ideological differences" with the BJP.

(3518) Bombay : Clashes have erupted between the Shiv Sena and its former leader and Maharashtra Revenue Minister Narayan Rane, who is allegedly trying to take away members of the party unions.

(3519) New Delhi : The seven-member political delegation that visited Nepal to express solidarity with the people in the struggle for restoration of democracy said here on Saturday that efforts would intensify next month.

(3520) New Delhi : Bahujan Samaj Party (BSP) president Mayawati on Saturday called upon Dalits, minorities and backward sections to unite under a single nationwide platform well ahead of the next elections.

(3521) New Delhi : Claiming that there had been bungling to the tune of crores of rupees in privatisation of power in Delhi, BJP Pradesh president Harsh Vardhan has demanded that the Director of the Central Bureau of Investigation, Uma Shankar Mishra, raid all the offices of the three power companies in Delhi and seize the records and computers and get them examined.

(3522) New Delhi : The running battle between the Delhi Pradesh Congress Committee and the Delhi Government shows no sign of a ceasefire. In a strongly worded letter to Chief Minister Sheila Dikshit, DPCC president Ram Babu Sharma has accused her Government and the Industry and Labour Minister, Mangat Ram Singhal, of tarnishing the image of the party and dragging the office of the Lieutenant-Governor into controversy by issuing irresponsible statements.

(3523) Pondicherry : The Pondicherry Pradesh Congress Committee president, P. Shanmugham, has said that the constitution of the party's committees at the block, district and State levels would be completed in a month's time.

(3524) Lucknow : At least six youth Congress workers were injured as the police lobbed tear gas shells and resorted to mild force to disperse the activists gheraoing the Uttar Pradesh Assembly here on Saturday.

(3525) Dehra Dun : The Congress nominee and former Minister Surendra Singh Negi on Saturday won the Kotdwar Assembly by-election defeating his nearest rival, Anil Baluni of the Bharatiya Janata Party, by 7900 votes. The other candidates, including those fielded by the Uttarakhand Kranti Dal (Airi), Uttarakhand Kranti Dal (Democratic) and the Samajwadi Party, lost their security deposits.

(3526) Chennai : Results of local body elections in Kerala and Andaman and Nicobar Islands have come as a morale booster for Bharatiya Janata Party, which had been desperately searching for one in the last few months.

(3527) Chennai : The Tamil Nadu Congress Committee (TNCC) president, G.K. Vasan, has criticised the State Government for not taking effective steps for implementing the scheme "Education for all up to Eighth Standard before 2010."

03-10-2005

(3528) Hyderabad : The APCC president, K. Keshava Rao, has lashed out at Guntur Congress MP, Rayapati Sambasiva Rao, for attributing caste motives to him in the selection of mayoral candidate for the Guntur Municipal Corporation.

(3529) Vijayawada : The public debate on Pulichintala project organised by the Government at Jaggayyapet witnessed heated exchanges between Adviser to Government (Irrigation) P. Sitapati Rao and BJP State secretary N.V.S.S. Prabhakar on Sunday.

(3530) New Delhi : Bharatiya Janata Party president L.K. Advani demanded on Sunday that the Government come out with a white paper on the role of foreign intelligence agencies and order a judicial inquiry on the allegations in The Mitrokhin Archive II.

(3531) New Delhi : On Saturday the Prime Minister was asked about CPI(M) leader Prakash Karat's sharp criticism on India's Iran vote. If Dr.

Manmohan Singh seemed to shrug off the personal attack by citing the Gita, it was because a day earlier the Congress leadership had totally endorsed the United Progressive Alliance Government decision to vote against Iran in Geneva.

(3532) Bangalore : For people of Swagath slum in Tilaknagar here, Gandhi Jayanthi was a special occasion.

(3533) Bangalore : Even as AICC General Secretary A.K. Antony left Bangalore after reviewing the performance of his party Ministers, Janata Dal (Secular) President H.D. Deve Gowda has taken the stand that only Chief Minister N. Dharam Singh has the constitutionally approved right to review the performance of his Ministers irrespective of their party affiliation.

(3534) Bangalore : The former Chief Minister Siddaramaiah has put on the backburner all speculations of his joining the Congress by claiming that his faction of the Janata Dal (Secular) is the real Janata Dal (S).

(3535) Dharwad : Chief Minister N. Dharam Singh on Sunday denied there was dissidence in the State unit of the Congress and that any demand had been made for change in leadership during the visit of A.K. Antony, AICC General Secretary in charge of Karnataka, to Bangalore.

(3536) Thiruvananthapuram : CPI(M) State secretary Pinarayi Vijayan has asked the Government to construct a house and provide a compensation of Rs. 10 lakhs to the family of Udayakumar who was 'tortured to death' at the Fort police station here.

(3537) Bangalore : Janata Dal (Secular) leader H.D. Deve Gowda has said the coalition Government in Karnataka emerged stronger thanks to the political maturity of Congress president Sonia Gandhi, who has not been swayed, so far, by the disinformation campaign launched by a section of her partymen here.

(3538) Patna : The senior Janata Dal (United) leader Nitish Kumar was cautious regarding campaigning by BJP leaders for the NDA in the coming Bihar Assembly elections.

(3539) New Delhi : The Bharatiya Janata Party leader and MLA from Saket, Vijay Jolly, has in a letter to the Municipal Commissioner, Rakesh Mehta, pleaded that the demolition drive in Sainik Farms be stopped and a fresh affidavit be filed in the Delhi High Court stating the recommendations of the Nanavati Commission and requesting the Court to treat Sainik Farms at par with other unauthorised colonies in the Capital.

(3540) Chennai : Dravida Munnetra Kazhagam president M. Karunanidhi on Sunday charged Chief Minister Jayalalithaa with "double standard and hypocrisy" over the proposed meeting in the Nehru Stadium.

04-10-2005

(3541) Hyderabad : BJP national secretary Bandaru Dattatreya has urged Chief Minister Y.S. Rajasekhara Reddy to bring pressure on the Centre for setting up an IIT at Basar.

(3542) Hyderabad : Differences in the Telangana Rashtra Samiti (TRS) have come to the forefront, with the Union Minister A. Narendra blaming a section of his party leaders for gunning for him over his statements during the municipal election campaign.

(3543) Hyderabad : Members belonging to the Telangana Rashtra Samithi (TRS) stalled the proceedings of the Assembly for one and a half hours on Monday protesting against a Government order issued for increased diversion of Krishna waters to Rayalaseema.

(3544) Haveri : Minister for Rural Development and Panchayat Raj Basavaraj Horatti said on Sunday that the Janata Dal (Secular) is ready for fresh elections, if the Congress wants it.

(3545) Kochi : Cooperation Minister M.V. Raghavan has said that the United Democratic Front (UDF) and the Congress should open the doors to those who have left the party and the Front.

(3546) Kottayam : The recent Panchayati Raj elections have proved that Bharatiya Janta Party (BJP) is a deciding factor in the State politics, said BJP president P.S. Sreedharan Pillai.

(3547) Thiruvananthapuram : The Democratic Indira Congress (Karunakaran) has decided to confirm its slot in the democratic secular and socialist platform in its bid to gain entry into the Left Democratic Front (LDF) in time for the local bodies elections. The DIC(K) has decided not to vote for either the UDF or the BJP and ensure that the two do not get a chance to rule in hung local bodies.

(3548) New Delhi : The Congress on Monday sharply criticised the Mulayam Singh Government in Uttar Pradesh, where several schoolchildren fell unconscious at a function on Gandhi Jayanti at Kanpur.

(3549) New Delhi : The Bharatiya Janata Party has demanded the recall of Bihar Governor Buta Singh, who, it said, made "all types of unfounded charges against the National Democratic Alliance in general and its Chief Ministerial candidate Nitish Kumar in particular".

(3550) New Delhi : The Left parties will mobilise public opinion and launch a national campaign for an independent foreign policy.

(3551) Mumbai : The Congress and the Nationalist Congress Party (NCP) which share power in Maharashtra and at the Centre clashed here openly on Monday with the newly inducted Congress Minister, Narayan Rane, alleging that the NCP had a hidden understanding with his erstwhile party, the Shiv Sena, and the State police.

(3552) New Delhi : The Samajwadi Party on Monday urged the United Progressive Alliance Government to reverse its stand on Iran at the forthcoming meeting of the International Atomic Energy Agency's Board of Governors in November.

(3553) Pondicherry : Opposition Leader and Dravida Munnetra Kazhagam State unit convener R. V. Janakiraman has blamed the union territory Government for "lack of programmes and plans to develop Karaikal" on the same lines as other regions.

05-10-2005

(3554) Hyderabad : The State Bharatiya Janata Party has expressed satisfaction at the party's performance in municipal elections saying it has a secured sizable chunk of votes, though it was unable to win many seats.

(3555) Hyderabad : The Telangana Rashtra Samithi and the Telugu Desam joined hands in the Assembly on Tuesday to criticise Chief Minister, Y. S. Rajasekhara Reddy for ordering the discharge capacity at Pothyreddypadu head regulator of the Srisailam dam to be increased.

(3556) Shillong : NCP leader Purno A Sangma on Tuesday said he would resign as Member of Parliament from the Tura parliamentary constituency by next Tuesday to protest the "brutal" police action on "innocent" students in his constituency.

(3557) Bangalore : State Bharatiya Janata Party (BJP) leaders on Tuesday said they are ready to face elections to the taluk and zilla panchayats. The party's convention of slum dwellers and backward classes to be held here on October 28 will help galvanise the organisation.

(3558) Davangere : Shamanur Shivashankarappa, MLA and Karnataka Pradesh Congress Committee Treasurer, on Tuesday denied that wants Chief Minister N. Dharam Singh replaced.

(3559) Kolar : If the former Deputy Chief Minister Siddaramaiah joins the Republican Party of India (RPI), he will be made the Chief Minister, if the party is voted to power, said Ramados Athawale, MP and party president.

(3560) New Delhi : The Bharatiya Janata Party on Tuesday warned the Government against any move to scuttle its demand for a judicial inquiry into allegations that several Government officials and Ministers had been on the payrolls of the Russian intelligence agency, KGB, as revealed by the "Mitrokhin papers".

(3561) Kolkata : The Communist Party of India (Marxist) has retained the Asansol Lok Sabha seat, the byelection to which was held on September 28.

(3562) New Delhi : The Left parties on Tuesday sought the intervention of United Progressive Alliance (UPA) chairperson Sonia Gandhi for early enactment of a national slum law.

(3563) Mumbai : After a telephonic talk with the new Revenue Minister, Narayan Rane, on Tuesday, the Maharashtra Deputy Chief Minister, R.R. Patil, denied that he had had any problem with his new colleague in the coalition Government.

(3564) New Delhi : Delhi Pradesh Congress Committee president Ram Babu Sharma, Chief Minister Sheila Dikshit, her two ministerial colleagues A.K. Walia and Arvinder Singh Lovely, along with six sitting Lok Sabha members and 14 other Congress legislators figure among the list of 66 AICC delegates cleared for Delhi by Congress president Sonia Gandhi.

(3565) Patna : JD(U) today reiterated for establishing rule of law in the state and assured to provide reservation to the Dalit Muslims and Christians at par with Schedule Castes once the NDA came to power here.

(3566) Patna : Firebrand BJP leader Uma Bharti on Tuesday downplayed the ideological differences with its ally JD(U) saying that this would not come in the way of NDA for providing a development-oriented government in Bihar which is committed to rooting out crime and corruption from the State.

(3567) Chennai : The Bharatiya Janata Party seems to be reconsidering its strategy of going it alone in the Assembly elections.

(3568) Chennai : The Pattali Makkal Katchi and the Dalit Panthers of India on Tuesday denied the charges of male chauvinism, moral policing and instigating the campaign against actress Kushboo for her comments on sexual practices.

06-10-2005

(3569) Hyderabad : A heated debate continued over the proposal to increase discharge capacity of Pothireddypadu regulator of Srisailam dam for the second day in the Assembly on Wednesday but this time marked by a face-off between Chief Minister Y. S. Rajasekhara Reddy and Leader of the Opposition N. Chandrababu Naidu.

(3570) Karimnagar : BJP leader Ch Vidyasagar Rao has said his party will not forge an alliance with the Telugu Desam Party in the future.

(3571) Kurnool : The national committee member of CPI K. Ramakrishna has urged the Government to make the necessary amendments in the GO no. 170 to allay the fears of Coastal Andhra and Telangana people over the Srisailam Right Main Canal proposal.

(3572) Bangalore : Braving a downpour, a large gathering of Bahujan Samaj Party supporters heard party leader Mayawati unleash her "anti-upper caste and Manuwadi" rhetoric and demand extension of the reservation policy to the private sector.

(3573) Bangalore : The Janata Dal (Secular) group led by the former Deputy Chief Minister Siddaramiah will fight the elections to the zilla and taluk panchayats and is yet to take a decision on entering into an understanding with any other party.

(3574) Bangalore : Three Congress leaders on Wednesday came out in defence of Governor of Maharashtra S.M. Krishna and questioned the propriety of Janata Dal (Secular) supremo H.D. Deve Gowda's statement that he had sought his help for retaining the chief ministership last year.

(3575) Belgaum : Working President of the State unit of the Janata Dal (Secular) H.D. Kumaraswamy has said that the party plans to adopt two villages in each taluk in the flood-affected districts of Belgaum, Bijapur, Bagalkot and Gulbarga.

(3576) Bijapur : Karnataka Pradesh Congress Committee President M. Mallikarjun Kharge said here on Wednesday that the party's aim is to form a Government on its own.

(3577) Thiruvananthapuram : Leader of the Opposition V.S. Achuthanandan has asked the Government to dismiss the police personnel found prima facie responsible for the death of Udayakumar while in the custody of the Fort Police in the city.

(3578) New Delhi : The Communist Party of India (Marxist) has demanded tabling of the Scheduled Tribes (Recognition of Rights) Bill in the winter session of Parliament.

(3579) New Delhi : Gujarat Chief Minister Narendra Modi will not campaign for the Bharatiya Janata Party-Janata Dal (United) alliance in Bihar, it was officially announced here.

(3580) Patna : Lok Jan Shakti Party chief and Union Steel Minister Ram Vilas Paswan on Wednesday stuck to his stand of having a Muslim as the next Chief Minister of Bihar citing that the Sikhs received justice after 21 years only because Manmohan Singh happened to be the Prime Minister.

(3581) New Delhi :A day after the Allahabad High Court quashed the Aligarh Muslim University (AMU) Amendment Act 1981 providing minority institution status to the university, the Congress on Wednesday said its minority character should be maintained and respected. The Bharatiya Janata Party welcomed the verdict, which also declared illegal the recent decision of the AMU to reserve seats in post-graduate medical courses for Muslims.

(3582) Mumbai : After losing Narayan Rane to the Congress, the Shiv Sena suffered another blow with the former Rajya Sabha MP and veteran leader, Satish Pradhan, joining the Nationalist Congress Party on Wednesday.

(3583) Pondicherry : R.V. Janakiraman, Leader of the Opposition in the Pondicherry Assembly and convenor of the State committee of Dravida Munnetra Kazhagam, has expressed shock at the "scant respect" the Congress Government was showing to the legislators.

07-10-2005

(3584) Hyderabad : Telugu Desam deputy leader T. Devender Goud locked horns with Chief Minister Y.S. Rajasekhara Reddy in the Assembly on Thursday over the alleged injustice to Telangana culminating in a sit-in by his party members near the podium.

(3585) Hyderabad : Telangana Rashtra Samithi MLA and former Transport Minister S. Santosh Reddy has dismissed as "a figment of imagination" reports that his relationship with the party leadership is strained.

(3586) Hyderabad : Telugu Desam Party members stalled proceedings in the Assembly on Thursday for half an hour by staging a dharna near the podium over the issue of release of funds for scholarships to backward class students.

(3587) Hyderabad : The Telangana Rashtra Samithi (TRS) has threatened to launch an agitation with the help of farmers if the Government does not withdraw its order increasing the discharge capacity of Pothireddypadu head regulator.

(3588) Hyderabad : The Chief Minister, Y. S. Rajasekhara Reddy, has urged Congress MLAs and party functionaries to gear up for the elections to cooperative bodies later this month.

(3589) New Delhi : United Progressive Alliance chairperson Sonia Gandhi has written to the four Left parties to consider returning to the UPA-Left Coordination Committee, as the Cabinet decision to offload equity in Bharat Heavy Electricals Limited has been "put in abeyance."

(3590) New Delhi : In the wake of reverses in the recent civic elections, Congress president Sonia Gandhi on Thursday asked the State Congress leadership to strengthen the party's organisational set-up to gear up for the Assembly polls scheduled to be held early next year.

(3591) Thiruvanathapuram : Democratic Indira Congress (Karunakaran) (DIC-K) president K. Muraleedharan has demanded a judicial probe or a CBI inquiry into the custodial death at the Fort police station here.

(3592) New Delhi : The Bharatiya Janata Party and the Congress on Thursday condemned the armed attack on BJP leader and former Union Minister Ravi Shankar Prasad at an election campaign meeting in Nokha, Bihar.

(3593) New Delhi : Congress president Sonia Gandhi has asked the leadership of States ruled by the party to strictly follow the 'code of austerity and ethics.' The issue is likely to figure prominently at the two-day conclave of Chief Ministers of Congress-ruled States beginning in Chandigarh on Friday.

(3594) New Delhi : Lack of a comprehensive hydrocarbon pricing policy has resulted in an acute shortage of cooking gas (liquefied petroleum gas) cylinders with the man on the street having to wait for 15 to 30 days to get a cylinder at black-market prices several hundred rupees higher than the notified price, the Bharatiya Janata Party said here on Thursday.

08-10-2005

(3595) Hyderabad : The CPI has decided to ask the Centre to constitute a Parliamentary committee to study the functioning of private medical colleges as well as the Medical Council of India (MCI).

(3596) Hyderabad : A meeting of the Telugu Desam Legislature Party (TDLP) here on Friday absolved party president N. Chandrababu Naidu of any blame for the drubbing the party received at the hands of the Congress in the recently- held municipal elections.

(3597) Hyderabad : Heated exchanges, a brief adjournment and walkout by Telugu Desam members marked the debate in the Assembly on Friday on the payment of Rs.11.67 crores as equity to Vashista Wahan company by the Government.

(3598) Chandigarh : Congress president Sonia Gandhi on Friday emphasised the need for the party leaving its "distinctive imprint" on coalition governments and making people aware of its contribution to the Common Minimum Programme (CMP).

(3599) Thiruvanathapuram : State president of the BJP Sreedharan Pillai has said that the State Election Commissioner (SEC) cannot dissolve the Palakkad municipal council if the latter failed to elect a chairman to head it.

(3600) Ahmedabad : Three senior BJP leaders, including former Chief Minister Keshubhai Patel resigned on Friday from the State election committee formed for local elections.

(3601) Chandigarh : Chief Minister Y.S. Rajasekhara Reddy on Friday claimed his Government had been successful in implementing a majority of promises made by the party during elections and was confident that it would cover over 95 per cent. Dr. Reddy, participating in the Congress Chief Ministers' conclave that began here, was closely questioned by Congress central leadership on some key areas like irrigation and welfare of weaker sections and fiscal management in the State.

(3602) Raichur : The Bharatiya Janata Party (BJP) has demanded the resignation of Water Resources Minister M. Mallikarjun Kharge owning moral responsibility for the breach in one of the gates of the Narayanpur Dam on Thursday. It has also urged the Government to order a thorough inquiry into the incident.

(3603) Kannur : Communist Party of India (Marxist) State secretary Pinarayi Vijayan said on Friday that the United Democratic Front (UDF) Government was no longer functioning as a Government for the people.

(3604) Thiruvananthapuram : Kerala Pradesh Congress Committee president Ramesh Chennithala has said that the election of presiding officers in the local bodies elections has exposed the LDF-BJP ties.

(3605) Chandigarh : Kerala Chief Minister Oommen Chandy has said the defeat of the Congress in the recent local bodies elections in the State should not demoralise the party cadre and asserted that the party will bounce back to power in the Assembly election due early next year.

(3606) Ahmedabad : BJP national president L.K. Advani has demanded "immediate recall" of the Bihar Governor, Buta Singh, in view of the Supreme Court ruling holding the dissolution of the earlier State Assembly unconstitutional.

(3607) Guwahati : The Asom Gana Parishad (AGP) on Friday revived its alliance with the Autnomous State Demand Committee (ASDC). They reached an understanding to work for an anti-Congress alliance in the May 2006 Assembly elections.

(3608) Chandigarh : The plenary session of the All-India Congress Committee will be held in January next, party president Sonia Gandhi said on Friday. She was delivering the inaugural address at the Congress Chief Ministers' conclave here. The session, scheduled for this month, was postponed in view of the Bihar Assembly elections.

(3609) Patna : The Rashtriya Janata Dal leader and Railway Minister, Lalu Prasad, on Friday said criminal cases should be filed against the BJP workers who had beaten unconscious the youth who fired at the election rally in Nokha as that the intention was to suppress evidence of the "raging differences within the Sangh parivar."

(3610) Chandigarh : Union Home Minister Shivraj Patil on Friday said the Government would prefer to decide the next course of action following the Supreme Court's judgment on the Bihar Assembly after consulting allies.

(3611) New Delhi : Constituents and supporting parties of the United Progressive Alliance (UPA) on Friday gave different responses to the Supreme Court interim order striking down the May 23 Presidential Proclamation dissolving the Bihar Legislative Assembly.

(3612) Mumbai : "I am not going to ask people to vote for me. I will just ask people to vote", says Priya Dutt, daughter of the late Union Minister for Sports and Youth Affairs Sunil Dutt, who died on May 25 last.

(3613) Patna : The RJD supremo and Railway Minister Lalu Prasad on Friday claimed that the Supreme Court verdict on the Bihar House dissolution vindicated the party stand as the dissolved House had not been revived and the election process not stopped.

(3614) New Delhi : The four Left parties supporting the Government are scheduled to meet on Monday to consider United Progressive Alliance (UPA) chairperson Sonia Gandhi's request to return to the UPA-Left Coordination Committee as the Cabinet's decision to offload equity in Bharat Heavy Electricals Limited (BHEL) had been "put in abeyance".

(3615) New Delhi : The Communist Party of India (Marxist) on Friday urged the Government to convey its disapproval of U.S. Ambassador David Mulford's statement that investors would consider its policy of not hiking foreign direct investment cap in insurance a "breach of faith."

(3616) New Delhi : Welcoming the Supreme Court verdict on Bihar, the Bharatiya Janata Party and its partner, the Janata Dal (United) on Friday said not only the Bihar Governor Buta Singh, but Prime Minister Manmohan Singh and Home Minister Shivraj Patil cannot escape responsibility for the unconstitutional dissolution of the Bihar Assembly on May 23.

(3617) Mumbai : CPI(M) general secretary Prakash Karat said here on Friday that the Supreme Court judgment on Bihar raised wider questions about the role of the office of Governor and called for an amendment to Article 356 of the Constitution that gives Governors "arbitrary and discretionary" powers to dissolve State Assemblies. Mr. Karat, visiting Mumbai for the first time since taking over as general secretary, was speaking to journalists at a "Meet the Press" programme organised by the Mumbai Marathi Patrakar Sangh.

(3618) New Delhi : The jumbo-sized list of All-India Congress Committee delegates for Delhi approved by party president Sonia Gandhi has come as a shot in the arm for the Delhi Pradesh Congress Committee president Ram Babu Sharma, loaded as it is with his loyalists, including Councillors. The list also has a fair share of paratroopers who have made it as delegates under the "AICC quota" but have little to do with city politics or the party.

(3619) Dehra Dun : Seven general secretaries of the State unit of the ruling Congress party here enjoying ministerial status as chairmen of different Corporations and Councils resigned on Friday in response to party president Sonia Gandhi's call to cut down unnecessary Government expenditure in party-ruled States.

09-10-2005

(3620) Hyderabad : The Congress and Telugu Desam Parties have blamed each other for wasting the Assembly time and not allowing important issues to come up for discussion. On the other hand, the Left parties held both of them responsible on the same count.

(3621) Hyderabad : For the sixth straight day on Saturday, the Assembly witnessed a heated debate on the Pothireddipadu head regulator of the Srisailam dam which marked by a dharna by the Telangana Rashtra Samithi (TRS) protesting against the damage it would cause to the region's interests.

(3622) Chandigarh : Congress president Sonia Gandhi on Saturday sought to know what development work was being undertaken by the party-led government in Andhra Pradesh and asserted the need for a 'more humane approach' to address one of the main causes for naxal violence.

(3623) Chandigarh : Congress president Sonia Gandhi on Saturday expressed satisfaction with Andhra Pradesh Chief Minister Y.S. Rajasekhara Reddy's presentation on the development projects undertaken by his Government especially in the backward Telangana region. "The issue came up for discussion at the meeting and the Chief Minister briefed at length on projects in Telangana. We are satisfied with what he said," Ms. Gandhi told reporters at the end of the two-day Chief Ministers' Conclave.

(3624) Chandigarh : Prime Minister Manmohan Singh on Saturday said the Government would wait for the detailed judgment of the Supreme Court in the Bihar Assembly dissolution case before offering any comment but justified the move as the "only practical course."

(3625) Bangalore : Karnataka Pradesh Congress Committee (KPCC) President M. Mallikarjun Kharge has ruled out the immediate reconstitution of the KPCC. There may be a minor reshuffle of office-bearers, he said here on Saturday.

(3626) Hassan : The State unit of the Bharatiya Janata Party (BJP) will launch a "Sangharsha Yatra" to highlight the failures of the coalition Government and neglect of development works in the past 18 months. The yatra, which is scheduled to commence from Kolar on October 14, will conclude in Gadag on October 23. As many as 38 leaders of the party will participate in it, Chikmagalur MLA and President of the Yuva Morcha C.T. Ravi said.

(3627) Thiruvananthapuram : Leader of the Opposition V. S. Achuthanandan has cautioned the Government against allowing private hospitals to conduct post-mortem examinations.

(3628) Chandigarh : Prime Minister Manmohan Singh on Saturday said the Congress must act as an interface between the Government and the people; explain its policies and alert the Government to its mistakes and faults. He asserted that the country would never question the party's patriotism. "I do sincerely believe the party must educate the people about the limitations under which a Government functions so that false expectations are not generated. Our people are patriotic. They understand what is in the best interests of the country. But this must be explained to them. Be it our economic policy, or our foreign policy, or our national security policy.

(3629) New Delhi : The Bharatiya Janata Party (BJP) on Saturday sought an apology from Prime Minister Manmohan Singh for "misleading" the people, Parliament and even the President on the Bihar situation while recommending the dissolution of the Assembly.

(3630) New Delhi : The Bharatiya Janata Party (BJP) on Saturday demanded an inquiry by the Central Bureau of Investigation into the attack on the former Union Minister, Ravi Shankar Prasad, during an election rally in Bihar on Thursday. Talking to reporters here, BJP leader Pramod Mahajan, who was with Mr. Prasad at the rally, said any inquiry by the State would not be fair as the administration and the police were "totally politicised." This could be gauged from the fact that a slip recovered from the pocket of the accused made the Home Secretary suggest that he was a Vishwa Hindu Parishad (VHP) activist.

(3631) New Delhi : The Supreme Court's interim order in the Bihar Assembly dissolution case has raised the issue of modification of Article 356 of the Constitution to check arbitrariness in the Governor's discretionary powers, the Communist Party of India (Marxist) said on Saturday

(3632) Hyderabad : CPI national secretary D. Raja on Saturday said the stability and longevity of the United Progressive Alliance Government at the Centre would depend on its adherence to the Common Minimum Programme.

(3633) New Delhi : The Lok Jan Shakti Party on Saturday described as "totally hollow and absurd" Bharatiya Janata Party spokesman Arun Jaitley's claim that the Supreme Court interim order striking down the May 23 Presidential Proclamation dissolving the Bihar Legislative Assembly was a "victory of constitutionalism."

(3634) New Delhi : Senior Congress leader and All-India Congress Committee secretary Jai Kishen on Saturday accused Bahujan Samaj Party leader Mayawati of being the enemy number one of the Dalits and charged her with exploiting their sentiments for fulfilling her political ambitions.

(3635) New Delhi : Demanding an inquiry by the Central Bureau of Investigation into alleged bungling by the Delhi Government in its computer education programme, Delhi Bharatiya Janata Party president Harsh Vardhan on Saturday said Chief Minister Sheila Dikshit, Education Minister Arvinder Singh Lovely and the State Director of Education had full knowledge of the scam but were avoiding an inquiry.

(3636) Pondicherry : The women's wing of the Pondicherry DMK has called upon the Centre to bring in without delay legislation to ensure a quota of 33 per cent for women in the total Parliament and Assembly constituencies. A resolution adopted at a meeting held under the chairmanship of the Leader of the Opposition R.V. Janakiraman here on Saturday also urged the Government to ensure that a special quota (30 per cent) for women was introduced in educational institutions and also in employment.

10-10-2005

(3637) Hyderabad : The Congress Legislature Party has accused the Telugu Desam Party of raking up the Pothireddypadu head regulator controversy to divert the attention of the House, when Congress members intended to raise the IMG Bharata land dealings.

(3638) Nalgonda : The floor leader of the Communist Party of India (Marxist), Nomula Narasimhaiah, has criticised the Congress Government for being "absolutely adamant" in withdrawing G.O. 170 which enables it to increase the capacity of Pothireddypadu head regulator to discharge 40,000 cusecs of Krishna water to the Rayalaseema region.

(3639) Nellore : BJP vice-president M. Venkaiah Naidu has described the recent Supreme Court ruling on the dissolution of the Bihar Assembly as 'historic.' Addressing a press conference on Sunday at Venkatachalasatram, 11 km. from here, he pointed that the interim judgement would act as a 'check' on the powers and responsibilities of Governors and frequent resort to the imposition of Article 356.

(3640) Visakhapatnam : The Communist Party of India (Marxist) on Sunday asked the State Government to cancel the memorandum of understanding (MoU) signed with the Jindal Group for setting up an alumina refinery and smelter plant in Visakhapatnam.

(3641) **Dhaka :** Bangladesh police on Sunday claimed to have arrested seven Indian nationals for allegedly entering the country without valid documents. The Indians, who included four women, were arrested on Friday on Sylhet-Tamabil Road. - PTI

(3642) **Bangalore :** Two days after Congress President Sonia Gandhi supported the continuance of the coalition government in the State, the question of the ratio of power sharing between the two ruling parties has come to the fore.

(3643) **Srinagar :** United Progressive Alliance (UPA) chairperson Sonia Gandhi on Sunday promised that the Central and State governments would reach out to the remote villages and provide necessary relief.

(3644) **Hubli :** Pralhad Joshi, BJP MP from Dharwad North, has demanded a judicial inquiry into the washing away of the crest gate at Narayanpur dam, a balancing reservoir of the Upper Krishna Project (UKP) across the Krishna.

(3645) **Hubli :** The coordination committee planned by the Congress and the Janata Dal (S) for the smooth functioning of the government is yet to materialise even 16 months after the Dharam Singh Ministry took office.

(3646) **Kottayam :** The various Kerala Congress factions on Sunday observed the founding day of the party.

(3647) **Palampur (H.P.) :** Bharatiya Janata Party president L. K. Advani on Sunday demanded Union Home Minister Shivraj Patil's resignation in the aftermath of the "latest judicial indictment" in the Bihar case.

(3648) **Kolkata :** Left leaders have said that the Centre's reported change of mind on the disinvestment of Bharat Heavy Electricals Limited (BHEL) would not be the sole criterion while taking a decision on United Progressive Alliance (UPA) chairperson Sonia Gandhi's request to return to coordination committee meetings.

(3649) **Patna :** BJP general secretary Arun Jaitley said on Sunday the least the Centre could do after the judicial order on dissolution of the Bihar Assembly was to recall Governor Buta Singh. However, its failure to do so led to suspicion that the Government feared reprisal from him.

(3650) New Delhi : The Samajwadi Party has said that it was "very disappointed" over the `lack of any action' by the Centre after the Supreme Court's verdict describing the dissolution of the Bihar Assembly as unconstitutional.

(3651) New Delhi : Stating that India would be much poorer without a free Press that has helped preserve the democratic way of life, Congress president Sonia Gandhi on Saturday said a constant questioning of what the Establishment says and does was natural and imperative. "It keeps the Government on its toes," she said.

(3652) New Delhi : Once again targeting the Congress-led United Progressive Alliance (UPA) Government, Communist Party of India general secretary A B Bardhan on Sunday asked the Centre to pay more attention towards improving economic relations with neighbouring countries and not just solely look towards the West.

(3653) Pondicherry : Pondicherry All-India Anna Dravida Munnetra Kazhagam unit secretary and legislator A. Anbalagan has alleged that the desilting work of the Bahoor big tank, which had been a main source of irrigation for the commune, had been done in a haphazard way.

(3654) Pondicherry : V. Narayanasamy, Congress MP, on Sunday called upon Pondicherry Chief Minister N. Rangasamy to furnish constituency-wise details of the number of youths given jobs in the four-and-half years of Congress rule in the Union Territory.

(3655) Jaipur : Three weeks after his letter apparently annoyed the RSS top brass, Rajasthan 20-point Programme Implementation Committee vice-chairman Chandraraj Singhvi was removed late on Saturday night and no reason assigned for the move.

(3656) Lucknow : The major alliance partner in the Uttar Pradesh Government, Rashtriya Lok Dal (RLD), on Sunday alleged ambiguity in the State reservation policy.

11-10-2005

(3657) Hyderabad : The BJP has asked the Government keep in abeyance the controversial GO 170 enhancing the discharge capacity of Pothireddypadu head regulator and convene an all-party meeting to discuss the "sensitive" issue.

(3658) Hyderabad : Buoyed by its performance in the recent municipal elections, the Communist Party of India is favouring continuance of its alliance with the CPI (M) and the Congress in the forthcoming cooperative elections.

(3659) Hyderabad : In a move that is likely to cause embarrassment to the Government, the Telangana Regional Congress Coordination Committee (TRCCC) has asked the Government to protect the interests of Telangana farmers before releasing water to the Rayalaseema region through Pothireddypadu Head Regulator. The TRCCC held a meeting on Monday to take stock of the political fall-out of the issue in the region as the Telangana Rashtra Samithi (TRS) has already announced an agitation over the issue.

(3660) Ongole : Finance Minister K. Rosaiah has asked the Telugu Desam Party to analyse the reasons for its debacle in the municipal elections instead of blaming voters.

(3661) Warangal : Having tasted defeat in the recent municipal elections, Telangana Rasthra Samithi (TRS) leaders are now engaged in 'introspection' exercise.

(3662) New Delhi : Former Lok Sabha Speaker and All India Trinamool Congress leader P.A. Sangma on Monday resigned from the 14th Lok Sabha. He represents the Tura Parliamentary constituency in Meghalaya.

(3663) Bangalore : Bharatiya Janata Party (BJP) General Secretary and MP H.N. Ananth Kumar said on Monday that the National Manuscripts Mission under the Union Ministry of Cultural Affairs, which had completed publication of 15,000 of one lakh manuscripts, is yet to take up the work of searching, deciphering and publishing 85,000 more manuscripts in Sanksrit and other languages.

(3664) Bangalore : A delegation of Janata Dal (Secular) leaders led by Deputy Chief Minister M.P. Prakash will soon meet Chief Minister N. Dharam Singh to communicate to him the party's displeasure over the delay in appointing chairpersons to various boards and corporations under the power-sharing agreement reached between the coalition partners.

(3665) Hubli : Pramod Mutalik, President, Shiv Sena, Karnataka unit, on Monday announced that if the stand taken by the central unit of the party poses a threat to the interests of Karnataka, then the State unit would go its own way.

(3666) Madikeri : Y.S.V. Datta, spokesman of the State Janata Dal (Secular), on Monday blamed the former Deputy Chief Minister Siddaramaiah for the confusion with regard to internal reservation in group 2 A as proposed by party President H.D. Deve Gowda.

(3667) Raichur : Members of the Samajwadi Party district unit staged a dharna here demanding that the Government order an inquiry into the washing away of a crest gate of the Narayanpur reservoir.

(3668) Kochi : The Bharatiya Janata Party (BJP) has demanded a re-investigation to bring out the truth related to the death of Rajan who died in police custody during the Emergency.

(3669) Thiruvanathapuram : Leader of the Opposition V.S. Achuthanandan has appealed to Governor R.L. Bhatia to initiate action against Chief Minister Oommen Chandy and his Cabinet colleagues for what he termed their 'violation' of the oath of office in their handling of lottery cases.

(3670) Thiruvanathapuram : Chief Minister Oommen Chandy has said that the Opposition Left Democratic Front (LDF) was ahead of the UDF by only 3.32 lakh votes if one were to go by the votes cast in the district panchayat, corporation and municipality wards in the just-concluded local body elections.

(3671) New Delhi : With Congress president Sonia Gandhi giving a "categorical commitment" of all assistance to the earthquake-affected people of Jammu and Kashmir, the Congress has decided to mount an elaborate relief and rehabilitation operation.

(3672) New Delhi : The Left parties along with the Samajwadi Party and the Janata Dal (Secular) on Monday decided to mobilise public opinion against the stand of the Manmohan Singh Government to vote against Iran in the International Atomic Energy Agency (IAEA).

(3673) New Delhi : The former Prime Minister, Atal Bihari Vajpayee, and BJP president L.K. Advani have written on Monday separate letters to Pakistan President Pervez Musharraf to express their grief at the tragedy that has struck Pakistan in the wake of Saturday morning's earthquake.

(3674) New Delhi : The Bharatiya Janata Party on Monday accused the Congress-led Delhi Government and the Municipal Corporation of Delhi of playing with the lives of Delhiites by not taking preventive measures to check the spread of dengue.

(3675) Chandigarh : The former Member of Parliament from Chandigarh and National Convener of the BJP Legal Cell, Satya Pal Jain, said here on Monday that the recent conclave of Congress Chief Ministers here was a "flop show" as it had miserably failed in coming out either with concrete proposals to solve the burning issues the country was facing today or finding any solution to any issue concerning the problems of the common man.

(3676) Pondicherry : The founder leader of the Puducherry Munnetra Congress and former Home Minister P. Kannan has appealed to President A.P.J. Abdul Kalam to dismiss the Congress Government, headed by N. Rangasamy, alleging that it had made "unconstitutional appointments" of officials to additional posts and allowed "corruption to rule the roost" in administration.

(3677) Chennai : The Pattali Makkal Katchi has called a meeting of educationists and legal experts here next week to work out a framework for fee structure to be adopted by professional colleges.

13-10-2005

(3678) Hyderabad : After much dillydallying, the executive of Telangana Rashtra Samithi (TRS) finally took shape with a large body comprising 87 members. The party's previous executive was dissolved over 20 months ago and had only the president and three chief coordinators at the helm since then.

(3679) Thiruvananthapuram : Leader of the Opposition V. S. Achuthanandan has urged the United Democratic Front (UDF) Government to avoid taking policy decisions since its tenure would come to a close in six months and there was the possibility of its decisions being overturned by the next Government.

(3680) Kollam : P.S. Sreedharan Pillai, State president of the BJP, has said that his party will not allow the CPI(M) to exploit the results of the local body elections to convert the State into another West Bengal.

(3681) Thiruvananthapuram : Former Union Minister O. Rajagopal said on Wednesday that the Congress-led United Democratic Front (UDF) was increasingly proving to be incapable to taking on the Left in Kerala.

(3682) Thiruvananthapuram : The Capital City Development Forum has accused Chief Minister Oommen Chandy of raising false claims to hoodwink the people and torpedo the development of Thiruvananthapuram.

(3683) Thiruvananthapuram : C.S. Sujatha, CPI(M) Member of Parliament from Alappuzha, has urged Prime Minister Manmohan Singh to drop the Pampa-Achencoil-Vaipar Link Canal Project aimed at diverting water from the two Kerala rivers to Tamil Nadu.

(3684) New Delhi : In a veiled criticism of the outgoing party chief L.K. Advani, senior BJP leader Pramod Mahajan on Wednesday said discipline could be brought back to the party if all decisions are taken collectively.

(3685) Mumbai : Shiv Sena chief Bal Thackeray on Wednesday nominated Sindhudurg district party president Parshuram Uparkar for the Malvan-Kankavali Assembly seat. Mr. Uparkar will be up against Maharashtra Revenue Minister Narayan Rane.

(3686) Chandigarh : In a significant development, the Congress high command has decided to retain the Haryana strongman, former Chief Minister Bhajan Lal, as president of the faction-ridden State unit of the party.

(3687) Bhopal : Describing speculations about a possible change of guard in Madhya Pradesh as "unalloyed rumours", the Chief Minister, Babulal Gaur, said here on Wednesday that there was scant need to pay attention to them.

(3688) Pondicherry : The lone Bharatiya Janata party legislator in the opposition in the Pondicherry Assembly, A. M. Krishnamurthy, has called upon the Chief Minister, N. Rangasamy, to drop his plan to associate the name of nominated legislators with government functions.

(3689) Chennai : The Janata Party is working for a third front in Tamil Nadu as an alternative to the Dravidian parties.

(3690) Salem : The mysterious fire in the office of Chennai Corporation Deputy Mayor 'Karate' R. Thiagarajan and the recent incidents connected with him indicate that "some powerful forces" in the State are making surreptitious efforts to suppress certain facts that may put persons in higher places under a cloud, Marumalarchi Dravida Munnetra Kazhagam leader Vaiko said on Wednesday.

14-10-2005

(3691) Hyderabad : The Congress and the Telugu Desam Party will make a joint plea to the Delimitation Commission at the second meeting in New Delhi on October 17 that the exercise be started from Srikakulam instead of Adilabad district.

(3692) Kadapa : CPI State Secretariat member T. Lakshminarayana on Thursday urged the Government to amend G.O. 170 regarding enhancement of capacity of Pothireddypadu head regulator.

(3693) Kadapa : Congress leaders on Thursday charged Opposition parties with politicising the capacity augmentation of Pothireddipadu head regulator and trying to jeopardise the irrigation interests of Rayalaseema region.

(3694) New Delhi : The Left parties will resume participation in Coordination Committee meetings with the United Progressive Alliance, now that UPA chairperson Sonia Gandhi has given the assurance, in writing, that the Government's decision to offload equity in Bharat Heavy Electricals Limited has been "put in abeyance".

(3695) Bellary : N. Thippanna, President of the State-unit of Janata Dal (Secular), has dubbed the "Sangharsha Yatra" of the Bharatiya Janata Party (BJP), a publicity stunt. "The party is not serious about several important issues, which, if implemented, can benefit the poor and the needy. Being in the Opposition, the BJP has failed to take up issues that need to be taken," he told presspersons in an informal chat here on Thursday. Responding to a question, Mr. Thippanna said that his party will be contesting in the taluk and zilla panchayat polls independently. His party is indeed gearing up for the polls, he added. Mr. Thippanna said that he has been holding meetings with party leaders of each district on the steps to be taken to strengthen the party. He added that he had met leaders of 18 districts.

(3696) New Delhi : A National Democratic Alliance delegation met President A.P.J. Abdul Kalam on Thursday evening and urged him to "advise the Prime Minister to tender his resignation owning moral responsibility" for the "fraud" on the Constitution played by the dissolution of the Bihar Assembly on May 23.

(3697) Ahmedabad : Bharatiya Janata Party president L.K. Advani on Thursday expressed confidence that his party's success in the civic elections in Kerala, Andhra Pradesh and Gujarat and the outcome of the Bihar Assembly elections next month would have a "revolutionary impact" on the national politics.

(3698) New Delhi :A day before the launch of his joint campaign with the CPI in Bihar, Ram Vilas Paswan, the Lok Janshakti Party (LJP) chief, held both the National Democratic Alliance (NDA) and the Rashtriya Janata Dal (RJD) responsible for the fresh Assembly polls in the State. However, the Union Minister did not seek the resignation of Bihar Governor Buta Singh as he was part of the Government at the Centre.

(3699) Kankavali : The Malvan-Kankavali Assembly constituency is all set for an electoral battle between former Sena leader Narayan Rane, now in the Congress, and Prashuram Uparkar, Zilla Parishad member of the Shiv Sena. While the Sena faces an uphill task, Mr. Rane has to deal with resistance from the local units of the Congress and the Nationalist Congress Party.

(3700) New Delhi : Delhi Bharatiya Janata Party president Harsh Vardhan on Thursday said the Delhi Government should take additional water from the Haryana Government to end the severe water scarcity here in the Capital.

(3701) Patna : Amid reports that the BJP had decided to send her to Madhya Pradesh as Chief Minister after the Bihar elections, firebrand BJP leader Uma Bharti on Thursday said that she had no knowledge of any such move.

(3702) Patna : Claiming that he found himself "stronger" in the wake of every discussion about a change of guard, the Madhya Pradesh Chief Minister on Thursday said he nursed no complaint against his predecessor, Ms. Bharti.

(3703) Pondicherry : The Secretary of the Pondicherry State committee of the all India Anna Dravida Munnetra Kazhagam, A.

Anbalagan, MLA has said that the "lack of trust between the Chief Minister and a section of his cabinet colleagues" had been dislocating work in key departments such as Local Administration Department in Pondicherry.

(3704) Pondicherry : Leader of the Opposition in the Pondicherry Assembly R.V. Janakiraman (Dravida Munnetra Kazhagam) has called upon the Administration to make public the full details of tsunami related relief and rehabilitation programmes implemented in the Union Territory.

(3705) Chennai : Panrutti S. Ramachandran has been appointed chairman of the presidium of the Desiya Murpokku Dravida Kazhagam, floated by Mr.Vijaykant recently.

(3706) Chennai : Pattali Makkal Katchi leader, S. Ramadoss, has criticised Chief Minister Jayalalithaa for organising the platinum jubilee celebration of the Tamil Nadu Public Service Commission which, he alleged, has been made defunct by the State Government.

(3707) Dharampuri : The Karnataka Government should cooperate with the Tamil Nadu Government for continuation of the ongoing development works in Hogenakkal, said BJP State president C.P. Radhakrishnan while inspecting the Island area here on Thursday.

15-10-2005

(3708) Hyderabad : Andhra Pradesh Congress Committee president K. Keshava Rao has taken exception to the remarks of Major Irrigation Minister Ponnala Lakshmaiah that the Government will not take back or alter its order increasing the discharge capacity of the Pothireddipadu head regulator.

(3709) Hyderabad : The State Committee of the CPI (M) has on Friday cautioned the State Government against taking unilateral decisions based on the massive mandate it got in the recent municipal elections.

(3710) Thiruvananthapuram : The CPI(M)-led Left Democratic Front (LDF) secured 49 per cent of the total votes polled in the just-concluded local body elections, up from 46 per cent votes secured in the 2004 Lok Sabha election, according to a poll review report adopted by the two-day CPI(M) State committee meeting that concluded here on Friday.

(3711) Chennai : Deputy Mayor 'Karate' R. Thiagarajan has been removed from the primary membership of the All-India Anna Dravida

Munnetra Kazhagam. The expulsion comes in the wake of his mysterious disappearance from the State.

(3712) New Delhi : In a letter to Rashtriya Swayamsevak Sangh chief K.S. Sudarshan, the former Madhya Pradesh Chief Minister, Uma Bharti, seems to have taken forward the battle against the RSS started by Bharatiya Janata Party president L.K. Advani. In Chennai last month, Mr. Advani criticised the mother organisation for the "impression" that no decision could be taken by the party without RSS approval.

(3713) Malur : The 10-day Statewide "Sangharsh Yatra" of the Bharatiya Janata Party with an agenda of removing the Congress-Janata Dal (Secular) coalition government was launched at Malur in Kolar district on Friday afternoon.

(3714) Thiruvananthapuram : District Congress Committee (DCC) president K. Mohankumar has accused the CPI(M) of trying to divert public attention from the development works taken up by the Government in view of the forthcoming Lok Sabha byelection.

(3715) Thiruvananthapuram : The Kerala Pradesh Congress Committee has asked the Oommen Chandy Government to rework its development priorities and focus more on the welfare of farmers, fisherfolk, workers in the traditional industries and other weaker sections of society even as it went in for big development projects.

(3716) Thiruvananthapuram : Leader of the Opposition V. S. Achuthanandan has urged the Government to immediately suspend the revenue recovery measures against farmers in Wayanad and to declare a moratorium on loans taken by farmers.

(3717) New Delhi : The Communist Party of India (Marxist) on Friday ridiculed those who accused it of "political immorality for seeking to blackmail the Manmohan Singh Government while supporting it" and asked the Centre not to brush aside the import of the workers' protest across the country against the Government's economic policies.

(3718) Patna : BJP president L.K. Advani on Friday launched a three-day campaign in Bihar, hoping that President A.P.J. Abdul Kalam would advise Prime Minister Manmohan Singh to resign on the issue of the dissolution of the State Assembly and recall Governor Buta Singh.

(3719) New Delhi : The Bharatiya Janata Party on Friday charged the Left parties with having a "destructive influence" on the economic policy of the United Progressive Alliance Government and "sabotaging" reforms.

(3720) New Delhi : The former Prime Minister, Atal Bihari Vajpayee, on Friday stated categorically that there was no question of interference by the Rashtriya Swayamsevak Sangh in the party's affairs. "Sangh hastakshep nahin karta (the Sangh does not interfere)," he said.

(3721) Chennai : Deputy Mayor R. Thiagarajan's dismissal from the All-India Anna Dravida Munnetra Kazhagam was on expected lines for most councillors, following the interviews with him in magazines and newspapers since he became "elusive" last month. But the move has given rise to the prospect of the elected council meeting under extraordinary circumstances.

(3722) Chennai : The Marumalarchi Dravida Munnetra Kazhagam has donated Rs. 5 lakhs to the Prime Minister's Relief Fund for relief in the quake-hit areas of Jammu and Kashmir and Pakistan.

(3723) Chennai : Tamil Nadu Congress Committee president G.K.Vasan has questioned the need for a new building for the Tamil Nadu Public Service Commission at a cost of Rs. 2.81 crore when there was a ban on recruitment for various posts in Government departments.

16-10-2005

(3724) Patna : The Congress-Rashtriya Janata Dal-led Secular Democratic Front in Bihar is not born out of political expediency, AICC president Sonia Gandhi said on Saturday.

(3725) Ahmedabad : Gujarat Chief Minister Narendra Modi led the Bharatiya Janata Party to an impressive victory in the elections to the Ahmedabad Municipal Corporation (AMC).

(3726) Thiruvananthapuram : Opposition Left Democratic Front (LDF) expects the Democratic Indira Congress (Karunakaran) to support it in the Thiruvananthapuram Lok Sabha by-election as well, LDF convener Paloli Mohammed Kutty said here on Sunday.

(3727) Bangalore : The State Congress leadership is attempting to placate party leaders and workers of Tumkur district, who revolted and resigned en masse from the party following "the sell out to Janata Dal (Secular) the post of president of the district cooperative milk union".

(3728) Gulbarga : Working President of the Siddaramaiah faction of the Janata Dal (Secular) B.R. Patil on Saturday said that the faction has held discussions with the Janata Dal (United), Left parties and the Bahujan Samaj Party for working out a tie-up for the zilla and taluk panchayat elections.

(3729) Thiruvananthapuram : Junior LDF partners, barring Kerala Congress (Joseph) gave a piece of their mind to the CPI(M) leadership at the LDF State committee meeting here on Saturday.

(3730) Thiruvananthapuram : Leader of the Opposition V. S. Achuthanandan has demanded the resignation of Water Resources Minister Thiruvanchoor Radhakrishnan in the light of the cancellation of the tender processes relating to the JBIC-aided drinking water supply scheme by the Kerala High Court.

(3731) New Delhi : The Bharatiya Janata Party (BJP) was on Saturday elated at its victory in the Ahmedabad Municipal Corporation elections.

(3732) New Delhi : Communist Party of India (Marxist) general secretary Prakash Karat said on Saturday his party would carry out an independent campaign against the Janata Dal (United)-Bharatiya Janata Party alliance in the Bihar Assembly elections. He issued a statement to this effect amid reports of differences between the CPI(M) and partners of the United Progressive Alliance (UPA) contesting the elections over a joint campaign.

(3733) New Delhi : The Janata Dal (Secular) has donated Rs. 5 lakhs each for the quake-affected people of Jammu & Kashmir and Pakistan-occupied Kashmir.

(3734) Guwahati : The former Lok Sabha Speaker, Purno Agitok Sangma, on Saturday said he had written to Congress president Sonia Gandhi, urging her to replace Meghalaya Chief Minister D. D. Lapang and restrain the Congress-led coalition from going ahead with ratification of the ordinance on amendment to the Meghalaya Board of School Education (MBOSE) Act in the Assembly.

(3735) New Delhi : Delhi Pradesh Congress Committee president Ram Babu Sharma along with Education Minister Arvinder Singh Lovely and Power Minister Haroon Yusuf met Congress president Sonia Gandhi separately on Friday amid reports of cracks in the Delhi Cabinet over the worrying power and water situation in the Capital during the festival month.

(3736) Jaipur : : Rajasthan's ruling Bharatiya Janata Party on Saturday said it has taken a serious view of internal dissensions and indicated disciplinary action could be taken against five ministers of the Vasundhara Raje Government and 10 party office- bearers who were critical of allotment of land for projects.

(3737) Chennai : Bharatiya Janata Party (BJP) general secretary Bandaru Dattreya, has criticised both the Central and State Governments for their failure to address the people's problems. Talking to newsmen here on Saturday, Mr. Dattreya said the United Progressive Alliance (UPA) Government at the Centre in which the Dravida Munnetra Kazhagam (DMK) was a major partner, had failed to control the prices of essential commodities.

(3738) Chennai : Dravida Munnetra Kazhagam president M. Karunanidhi on Saturday flayed Chief Minister Jayalalithaa for opposing the Rs.2,427-crore Sethusamudram Ship Channel Project (SSCP).

17-10-2005

(3739) Hyderabad : Bharatiya Janata Party national secretary B. Dattatreya has urged Chief Minister Y.S. Rajasekhara Reddy to convene an all-party meeting to discuss issues confronting women.

(3740) Hyderabad : The Telugu Desam has decided to launch an agitation to pressure the State Government to take up the Pranahita-Yellampalli project on the Godavari.

(3741) Bangalore : Janata Dal (Secular) President and former Prime Minister H.D. Deve Gowda may have given Infosys Chairman N.R. Narayana Murthy a patient hearing on Saturday, but he is sceptical about the latter's blueprint for the development of the State, and feels that the new mantra of shifting focus on urban-rural partnership is just old wine in new bottle.

(3742) Thiruvananthapuram : The leader of Democratic Indira Congress (Karunakaran) T.M. Jacob has asked the State Government to have the torture killing at the Fort police station probed by a sitting judge of the High Court.

(3743) Hyderabad : Fresh trouble is brewing in the Telangana Rashtra Samiti (TRS) with former Minister S. Santosh Reddy raising his voice against party president K. Chandrasekhara Rao, questioning his style of functioning and also his commitment to separate Telangana.

(3744) Bhopal : Pressure seems to be mounting on the ruling Bharatiya Janata Party in Madhya Pradesh, with many supporters of the former Chief Minister, Uma Bharti, expressing their solidarity with her on Sunday. Some even demanded a leadership change.

(3745) Bangalore : The former Prime Minister and Janata Dal (Secular) President H.D. Deve Gowda has ridiculed the Bharatiya Janata Party's State-wide Sangharsh Yatra, that began two days ago, to highlight the "failures of the coalition Government."

(3746) Hassan : Accusing former Prime Minister and President of Janata Dal (Secular) H.D. Deve Gowda of shielding corrupt Congress leaders, the Leader of Opposition in the Legislative Assembly B.S. Yediyurappa, here on Sunday,

(3747) Hubli : The zilla and taluk panchayat elections is some sort of a semi-final match between the Congress and the Janata Jal (S) who are vying with each other to strengthen their base and the Assembly elections which may follow as a consequence is going to be the final.

(3748) Yadgir (Gulbarga Dist.) : Chief Minister N. Dharam Singh on Sunday launched a frontal attack on the Bharatiya Janata Party leaders who are on the Sangarsha Yatra. He accused the BJP of pursuing divisive politics.

(3749) Toranagal (Bellary Dist.) : M. Mallikarjun Kharge KPCC President and Minister for Water Resources, while expressing concern over the World Bank report in the media feared that such distorted reporting would affect the image of the party and also that of the government.

(3750) Kannur : Democratic Indira Congress (Karunakaran) president K. Muraleedharan said on Sunday that moves were on by the United Democratic Front (UDF) and the Bharatiya Janata Party (BJP) to repeat their 'unholy' alliance in the coming byelection for the Thiruvananthapuram Lok Sabha seat.

(3751) Thiruvananthapuram : The Congress leader M.M. Hassan has urged the State Government to institute a comprehensive inquiry into the alleged flow of foreign funds into the State for the People's Plan Campaign and the charges of corruption in the implementation of the programme.

(3752) Alappuzha .: Supporters of Leader of the Opposition V.S. Achuthanandan in the CPI (M) Mararikkulam area committee are learnt to have voiced their

(3753) Ahmedabad : The Ahmedabad city district Congress president, Rajkumar Gupta, submitted his resignation from the post on Sunday accepting moral responsibility for the party's debacle in the municipal corporation elections.

(3754) Kolkata : The decision of the West Bengal State committee of the Communist Party of India (Marxist), authorising the party's State secretariat to intervene in the event of an elected representative of the party publicly criticising the official line as adopted at the party's State conference and the 18th party congress earlier this year, is significant on at least two counts.

(3755) Patna : BJP president L.K. Advani told presspersons here on Sunday that he would continue to further cultural nationalism whether or not he happened to be the party chief. He had been committed to the issue since the formation of the Jan Sangh in 1951 and would continue to do so.

(3756) New Delhi : The continued defiance of the former Madhya Pradesh Chief Minister, Uma Bharti, is expected to figure prominently at the next weekly meeting of the Bharatiya Janata Party general secretaries expected to take place on Monday or Tuesday.

(3757) Shimla : The recent declaration by Major Vijai Singh Mankotia of sending a list of 'corrupt' Ministers and MLAs to Congress President Sonia Gandhi has sent a chill down the spine of some top party leaders here.

(3758) Jaunpur : Former Uttar Pradesh Chief Minister and national vice-president of the Bharatiya Janata Party, Kalyan Singh today sought a probe by a sitting high rpt high Court judge in the recent communal violence in Mau district that has claimed three lives besides causing injuries to 28 others. Mr Singh, who along with two other senior State BJP leaders was stopped from going to Mau district by the police in Shahganj area of Jaunpur, accused Independent MLA Mukhtar Ansari of inciting violence.

(3759) Lucknow : The ruling Samajwadi Party and Congress have locked horns over what Uttar Pradesh Chief Minister Mulayam Singh Yadav has termed as a spate of PILs to destabilise his government.

(3760) Chennai : All-India Anna Dravida Munnetra Kazhagam general secretary Jayalalithaa on Sunday appealed to party activists to counter the Opposition campaign and strive to convert people's goodwill into votes.

(3761) Chennai : Dravida Munnetra Kazhagam president M. Karunanidhi on Sunday promised reservation in jobs for minorities, if the seven-party Democratic Progressive Alliance won the next Assembly elections.

(3762) Chennai : More than 200 Pattali Makkal Katchi members, including party president G.K. Mani, were arrested for staging a protest in front of the office of Kumudam Reporter, a Tamil magazine, on Sunday. They were protesting the publication of allegations made against the Union Health Minister, Anbumani Ramadoss, in connection with tsunami relief.

18-10-2005

(3763) Hyderabad : The Bharatiya Janata Party has challenged the Telugu Desam for an open debate on the construction of irrigation projects during its rule in Telangana.

(3764) Hyderabad : The CPI State Council on Monday severely criticised the Government's handling of discussions with JAC leaders of the APSRTC employees and faulted its response.

(3765) Hyderabad : The Telugu Desam Party has criticised Chief Minister Y.S. Rajasekhara Reddy's New Delhi visit, saying he chose to stay away from the State when it was plagued with several problems.

(3766) Hyderabad : The rumblings in the Telangana Rasthra Samithi (TRS) over the party's debacle in the recent municipal elections are slowly developing into dissident activity. Former Minister S. Santosh Reddy, who raised the banner of revolt against TRS president K. Chandrasekhara Rao, is planning a meeting of "well wishers of Telangana" on October 21 in Hyderabad.

(3767) Hyderabad : The Telangana Rashtra Samithi organised dharna near Collectorates in all Telangana districts, except Adilabad, on Monday to protest against GO 170, which seeks higher release of Krishna water from Pothireddypadu head regulator.

(3768) New Delhi : The Left parties on Monday asked the Government not to commit the country, without national consensus, on the World Trade Organisation at the December Hong Kong Ministerial round. They sought a white paper on the stand the Government proposes to take.In a note to the Government ahead of its meeting with Commerce Minister Kamal Nath, they said the negotiating position adopted by the Government in Hong Kong and its outcome would have a far-reaching and even irreversible, adverse consequences for the country's economy and polity, especially the working class and peasantry.

(3769) Hyderabad : Former Minister S. Santosh Reddy has been suspended from the Telangana Rasthra Samithi (TRS) by its president K. Chandrasekhara Rao in a sudden move on Monday night to pre-empt a larger revolt in the party against his leadership.

(3770) Bangalore : The Siddaramaiah group of the Janata Dal (Secular) on Monday urged the Congress High Command to remove Chief Minister N. Dharam Singh and "save" the Congress in the State.

(3771) Gulbarga : B.R. Patil, Working President of the Janata Dal (Secular) faction led by former Deputy Chief Minister Siddaramaiah, on Monday charged former Prime Minister H.D. Deve Gowda of blackmailing Chief Minister N. Dharam Singh by raising new issues. He said Mr. Deve Gowda's statement on the information technology (IT) industry and demand seeking details of the land allocated to IT major Infosys are a ploy to "further his political and selfish interests."

(3772) Shimoga : Leader of the Opposition in the Legislative Assembly B.S. Yediyurappa said here on Monday that the former Prime Minister and Janata Dal (Secular) President H.D. Deve Gowda should accept his challenge to participate in an open debate with the BJP leaders instead of making false and irresponsible statements against them.

(3773) Shimoga : Bharatiya Janata Party General Secretary and MP H.N. Ananth Kumar said here on Monday that the former Prime Minister and Janata Dal (Secular) President H.D. Deve Gowda has become a threat to the development of Karnataka if the stand taken by him on major issues is any indication.

(3774) Chikmagalur : BJP General Secretary H.N. Ananth Kumar said here on Sunday that the Datta Jayanti celebrations and the "Shoba Yatra" should be held as scheduled. Any attempt by the authorities to prevent it will amount to infringement on the constitutional right of citizens to practise their religion.

(3775) Davangere : "The coalition partners - the Janata Dal (Secular) and the Congress - are gripped by fear following the announcement of the elections to the zilla panchayats and taluk panchayats. It is impossible for them to continue in power after the elections as there will be differences between the two parties. The coalition Government's days are numbered," Leader of the Opposition in the Legislative Assembly B.S. Yediyurappa and H.N. Ananth Kumar, MP, have said.

(3776) Alappuzha : The Bharatiya Janata Party (BJP) State leadership is contemplating legal steps to restrain the Communist Party of India (Marxist) from spreading a misinformation campaign that the party has reached an understanding with the United Democratic Front (UDF) for the byelection from the Thiruvananthapuram Lok Sabha constituency, the BJP State president P.S. Sreedharan

(3777) Thiruvananthapuram : CPI State secretary Veliyam Bhargavan has said that the November 18 Lok Sabha byelection would be a referendum on the performance of the UDF Government.

(3778) Thiruvananthapuram : Former member of Parliament V. S. Sivakumar will be the Congress candidate for the byelection to the Lok Sabha from the Thiruvananthapuram constituency.

(3779) Thrissur : Democratic Indira Congress (Karunakaran) leader K. Karunakaran has categorically stated that he will not return to the Indian National Congress.

(3780) Kolkata : "All strategy minus tactics leads to sectarianism. All tactics minus strategy leads to opportunism. We will have to stay alert both against sectarianism and opportunism in our future struggles," Communist Party of India (Marxist) Polit Bureau member and West Bengal state secretary Anil Biswas said here on Monday on the occasion of the 86th foundation day of the Communist Party of India.

(3781) New Delhi : The Bharatiya Janata Party hopes to "double" along with the Janata Dal (United) the electoral victories in the first phase of polling for 58 Assembly seats in Bihar on Tuesday.

(3782) New Delhi : The Congress on Monday expressed concern over the continuing violence at Mau in Uttar Pradesh, and charged the Mulayam Singh Government with failing to restore normality.

(3783) New Delhi : The Bharatiya Janata Party on Monday expressed its disapproval of dissident activity spurred by the former Chief Minister, Uma Bharti, in Madhya Pradesh and made it clear that there was "no proposal for any change in the State leadership."

(3784) Bhopal : Madhya Pradesh Bharatiya Janata Party president Shivraj Singh Chauhan on Monday said that the party leadership would take a final decision on the demand for convening the State unit's Legislature Party meeting.

(3785) Pondicherry : The two All-India Anna Dravida Munnetra Kazhagam legislators, A. Anbalagan and A. Kasilingam, and the lone Bharatiya Janata Party MLA, A.M. Krishnamoorthy, walked out of the Assembly on Monday to protest against lack of measures by Government to tackle unemployment and other issues.

(3786) Chennai : All India Anna Dravida Munnetra Kazhagam (AIADMK) general secretary and Chief Minister Jayalalithaa on Monday said that the ruling party's alliance with the people was stronger than ever and it was already in readiness to face the poll.

(3787) Chennai : It was the turn of MDMK general secretary Vaiko to defend the use of English when, on Monday, he said, "We cannot forget that English is our window to the world and (its use) cannot be avoided. Even countries like China and Japan are now taking to English in a big way."

(3788) Chennai : "After her attempts to break the Democratic Progressive Alliance had failed, the Chief Minister is trying to weaken the DPA by levelling unfair allegations against leaders of the constituent parties. But her attempts will not succeed," said Dravida Munnetra Kazhagam president M. Karunanidhi here on Monday.

(3789) Chennai : Around 440 persons belonging to the Pattali Makkal Katchi were arrested in different parts of the State on Monday as they staged protest demonstrations for the second day against Kumudam Reporter, a Tamil magazine. Those arrested were remanded to custody, according to reports reaching the police here.

19-10-2005

(3790) Hyderabad : Former Uttar Pradesh Chief Minister and Bahujan Samaj Party president Mayawati has urged the Centre to direct the Andhra Pradesh Government to pass a resolution in the Assembly on creation of Telangana.

(3791) Hyderabad : The Telangana Rashtra Samithi (TRS) saw a "conspiracy" behind the developments in the party saying it came at a time when it had effectively taken the Pothireddypadu head regulator issue to people.

(3792) Hyderabad : The Bharatiya Janata Party has criticised the Government's stand that Pranahita, Dummagudem and Inchampally projects be taken up as national projects. It demanded an all-party meeting to discuss the issue.

(3793) Hyderabad : Telugu Desam president N. Chandrababu Naidu has condemned the attacks on houses of his party leaders by Congressmen and accused the ruling party of making a "mockery of democracy" in Chief Minister Y. S. Rajasekhara Reddy's own constituency - Pulivendula.

(3794) Hyderabad : At the end of a day of intense backroom activity on Tuesday, the Telangana Rashtra Samithi (TRS) is heading for a political crisis with partymen divided on the basis of their loyalty to president K. Chandrasekhara Rao. But, some party seniors are making hectic efforts to avoid a possible split in the party.

(3795) Kadapa : Two Congressmen were shot dead by the gunman of a Telugu Desam Party leader in a sudden eruption of violence and arson in Pulivendula, Andhra Pradesh Chief Minister Y. S. Rajasekhara Reddy's Assembly constituency, during filing of nominations for elections to Primary Agricultural Cooperative Societies (PACS) on Tuesday.

(3796) Kozhikode : Ending speculation on who will be the BJP candidate for the Thiruvananthapuram Lok Sabha byelection, State BJP president P. S. Sreedharan Pillai on Tuesday confirmed that it would be the senior leader C. K. Padmanabhan.

(3797) Bangalore : The Siddaramaiah group on Tuesday reiterated its claim to the Janata Dal (Secular) symbol and urged the State Election Commissioner to adjudicate the matter soon as the dates for the zilla and taluk panchayat elections have been announced.

(3798) Bellary : Karnataka Pradesh Congress Committee President M. Mallikarjun Kharge on Tuesday asserted that the Congress alone is capable of ruling the country and appealed to people to extend support to the party.

(3799) Bellary : Congress leaders who spoke at the district-level party workers' convention here on Tuesday, underlined the need for the district Congress leaders to remain united.

(3800) Chikmagalur : The battle lines are drawn at the Dattatreya Peeta in Bababudanagiri with the Vishwa Hindu Parishad (VHP) and the Bajrang Dal announcing their decision to hold Dattamala Abhiyana on Sunday.

(3801) Kochi : The Kerala Congress(Secular) leader P.C. George, MLA, has urged Chief Minister Oommen Chandy to relinquish the charge of the Home Ministry.

(3802) Kottayam : By unceremoniously dumping its chairman Eapen Varghese, the Kerala Congress(S) and its beleaguered legislature party leader P.C. George appear to have saved the outfit from a major crisis, for the present. The action from the leader of the LDF constituent is viewed in the political circles as a pre-emptive strike against the brewing discontent among a section of the party members who were plotting a major coup against Mr. George and his political line.

(3803) Kozhikode : K. Muraleedharan, president, Democratic Indira Congress (Karunakaran), has said the understanding the UDF and the BJP had struck in the recent panchayat elections will be extended to the next Assembly polls too.

(3804) Thiruvananthapuram : The ruling United Democratic Front (UDF) has alleged a conspiracy involving police personnel owing allegiance to the CPI(M) to defame the Oommen Chandy Government on the eve of the Thiruvananthapuram Lok Sabha byelection.

(3805) Thiruvananthapuram : The BJP leader O. Rajagopal on Tuesday demanded a judicial inquiry into the attack on the Bishop's House of Latin Catholic diocese at Neyyattinkara.

(3806) Neyyattinkara : Leader of the Opposition V. S. Achuthanandan has demanded an impartial inquiry into Monday's attack by miscreants on the Bishop House here and stern steps by the Government to prevent recurrence of such incidents in the future.

(3807) Thiruvananthapuram : State secretary of the CPI(M) Pinarayi Vijayan has strongly protested against the delay in nabbing those behind the attack on the Bishop's House at Neyyattinkara.

(3808) New Delhi : The Communist Party of India (Marxist) on Tuesday condemned the killing of Jammu and Kashmir Minister Ghulam Nabi Lone and the bid on party MLA Mohammed Yusuf Tarigami by militants in Srinagar.

(3809) Patna : BJP MP Jai Narain Nishad on Tuesday joined the Rashtriya Janata Dal and campaigned with its president and Railway Minister Lalu Prasad.

(3810) New Delhi : A determined bid is being made by Bharatiya Janata Party dissidents loyal to former Chief Minister Uma Bharati to force the party's central leadership to agree to a timetable for changing Madhya Pradesh Chief Minister Babulal Gaur. However, central party leaders indicated that nothing would be done; at least not before the Bihar elections are out of the way.

(3811) Pondicherry : Secretary of Pondicherry unit of the Communist Party of India (Marxist) V. Perumal has taken exception to the Pondicherry Congress Government's "silence" on the issue of civic polls, which has not been held for 35 years.

(3812) Chennai : Puthiya Thamizhagam president K. Krishnasamy has criticised the police for refusing permission to organise party conferences at Rajapalayam and Sankarankovil.

(3813) Chennai : The Pattali Makkal Katchi on Tuesday accused the All India Anna Dravida Munnetra Kazhagam Government of being vindictive to the party.

20-10-2005

(3814) Hyderabad : Succumbing to pressure from with and from political parties, the Congress Government has agreed to make suitable changes in its controversial order on increasing the discharge capacity of the Pothireddypadu head regulator.

(3815) Hyderabad : Left parties have urged the Government to resume talks with striking Joint Action Committee of RTC employees unions and warned that they will mobilise other like-minded parties for a broad-based agitation if the crisis is not resolved.

(3816) Hyderabad : Telugu Desam Party president N. Chandrababu Naidu has demanded a judicial enquiry into the violent incidents in Pulivendula leading to the arrest and booking of "fabricated case" against the State secretary Satish Kumar Reddy. Addressing a press conference, Mr. Naidu said while it was unfortunate that two Congress workers were killed, the Government and police acted with vengeance in filing a murder case against Mr. Reddy and two others. Mr. Reddy was falsely implicated saying he had snatched a gun from the gunman and fired at Congress workers and obtaining false dying declaration from a victim.

(3817) Hyderabad : Chief Minister Y. S. Rajasekhara Reddy has said the firing at Velpula in the Pulivendula Assembly constituency of Kadapa district on Tuesday was carried out by Telugu Desam Party State secretary S. V. Satish Kumar Reddy himself, killing two Congressmen, and not his gunman.

(3818) Tirupati : PCC spokesperson and Puttur MLA Gali Muddukrishnama Naidu on Wednesday launched a broadside at TDP president N. Chandrababu Naidu, saying he is pursuing a vilification campaign against Chief Minister Y.S. Rajasekhar Reddy with the sole intention of painting him black before national leaders and the national media.

(3819) Kadapa : The Telugu Desam Party is promoting factionalism and levelling baseless charges against Chief Minister Y.S. Rajasekhara Reddy, Congress leaders alleged on Wednesday.

(3820) Kadapa : Telugu Desam Party MLA of Kamalapuram G. Veerasiva Reddy raised the banner of revolt against TDP President N. Chandrababu Naidu on Wednesday accusing him of meting out injustice to the perennially drought-prone Rayalaseema region during his nine-year rule.

(3821) New Delhi : The Bharatiya Janata Party on Wednesday demanded the removal of Union Ministers Lalu Prasad and Jaiprakash Narayan Yadav, as they "are a threat to the free and fair electoral process" in Bihar.

(3822) Hyderabad : On another day of hectic political activity, the Telangana Rashtra Samithi (TRS) just about managed to bring about a temporary truce with sulking senior leader S. Santosh Reddy till the legislature party meeting, scheduled after completion of cooperative elections on October 26.

(3823) Bangalore : Some members of the KPCC (Karnataka Pradesh Congress Committee) Executive Committee are stated to have expressed their displeasure over the functioning of the Government and demanded that the Congress Ministers be assertive to strengthen the party, in view of the taluk and zilla panchayat elections.

(3824) Bangalore : H.D. Kumaraswamy, Working President of the Janata Dal (Secular) State unit, has said Governor of Maharashtra S.M. Krishna is welcome to return to State politics immediately and the Janata Dal (S) will meet his political challenge.

(3825) Gulbarga : The Republican Party of India (Atwale) on Wednesday urged thc State Government to initiate measures to end the social boycott imposed on a group of Dalit families in Alwata village in Srinivasapur taluk in Kolar district and provide adequate protection to the affected families immediately.

(3826) Gulbarga : The Republican Party of India (Athwale) has initiated discussions with like-minded parties on having a tie-up for the zilla and taluk panchayat elections scheduled to be held in December.

(3827) Hubli : B.S. Yediyurappa, Leader of the Opposition in the Legislative Assembly, on Wednesday said Assembly elections are likely to be held immediately after the panchayat polls.

(3828) Hubli : Leaders of the Bharatiya Janata Party, led by Jagadish Shettar, H.N. Ananth Kumar and B.S. Yediyurappa, made the best use of the stage set for Sangharsh Yatra here on Wednesday to continue their attack on the coalition Government partners in the State as well as at the Centre.

(3829) Thiruvananthapuram : The overall development of the constituency seems to be the major election plank for both the major fronts contesting the by-election to the Lok Sabha from Thiruvananthapuram.

(3830) Thiruvananthapuram : Democratic Indira Congress (Karunakaran) (DIC-K) leader K. Karunakaran has scoffed at the UDF high power committee's theory that a conspiracy involving pro-CPI(M) elements in the police force was on in the State to defame the Oommen Chandy Government.

(3831) Thiruvananthapuram : Democratic Indira Congress (Karunakaran) (DIC-K) president K. Muraleedharan has criticised the Government for its failure to nab those responsible for the attack on the Neyyattinkara Bishop's House even three days after the incident.

(3832) Thiruvananthapuram : Leader of the Opposition V. S. Achuthanandan has asked Chief Minister Oommen Chandy to immediately remove K.V. Joseph, public prosecutor in the sensational ice-cream parlour case, from the job and entrust the work to someone who could handle the case efficiently.

(3833) Chennai : The Communist Party of India on Wednesday criticised the Centre for giving up the "old policy of being with developing countries" by voting against Iran at the International Atomic Energy Agency.

(3834) Bhopal : The dissident BJP MLAs loyal to the former Madhya Pradesh Chief Minister, Uma Bharti, are in no mood to abandon their demand for a change of leadership in the State. But in deference to the party's wishes, they have chosen to put their demand on hold till the Bihar Assembly elections are over.

(3835) Kolkata : Seldom has a visit from a foreign business magnate to the city generated as much heat in political and administrative circles as that of Benny Santoso. The chief executive officer of the Indonesia-based

Salim Group is to arrive here on Thursday. Mr. Santoso is to discuss with Chief Minister Buddhadeb Bhattacharjee the future of the proposed projects in the State for which a Memorandum of Understanding was signed two months ago in Jakarta.

(3836) Chennai : Bharatiya Janata Party national secretary L. Ganesan on Wednesday criticised the promises made by some parties on reservation for Muslims.

(3837) Chennai : The Pattali Makkal Katchi on Tuesday accused the All India Anna Dravida Munnetra Kazhagam Government of being vindictive to the party.

(3838) Salem : All India Secretary of the BJP, Bandaru Dattatreya, on Wednesday welcomed the Election Commission directive to Electoral Registration Officers (EROs) in Tamil Nadu to file complaints against politicians who allegedly submitted applications in bulk, carrying bogus names, for inclusion in the electoral rolls.

21-10-2005

(3839) Hyderabad : Telangana Rashtra Samithi president K. Chandrasekhar Rao and rebel party MLA S. Santosh Reddy were busy with their respective camps ahead of the latter's meeting with 'like minded' supporters of separate Telangana in the city on Friday.

(3840) Vijayawada : Telugu Desam Party (TDP) president N. Chandrababu Naidu has said that the Government's 'Adarshanandhra Pradesh' scheme is yet another "drama" aimed at covering up its failure in fulfilling the aspirations of people.

(3841) Kadapa : TDP State Secretary S.V. Satish Kumar Reddy on Thursday alleged that he was implicated in a murder case at the behest of Chief Minister Y.S. Rajasekhara Reddy.

(3842) Mumbai : Actor and member of Parliament Govinda who has been shown in a video footage with Dawood Ibrahim, on Thursday denied that he had any links with the underworld don. He said he was being framed in a conspiracy by his rivals.

(3843) New Delhi : The Election Commission on Thursday issued notice to Lok Jan Shakti Party president and Union Minister Ram Vilas

Paswan for favouring a Muslim chief minister for Bihar during his poll campaign. He has been asked to reply by October 24.

(3844) Kadapa : TDP State Secretary and Pulivendula constituency incharge S.V. Satish Kumar Reddy, the main accused, and nine other accused persons among 16 TDP functionaries charged with murder in connection with the death of two Congressmen in opening of fire in Velpula village in Vemula mandal during cooperative elections on October 18, were remanded to judicial custody till November 3 by Pulivendula Magistrate Kanthimathi on Thursday.

(3845) Bangalore : The Congress has alleged that the Bharatiya Janata Party, the Janata Dal (Secular) and other parties are using the World Bank report as an instrument to damage the party's image and investment climate in the State.

(3846) Bangalore : The State unit of the Janata Dal (United) will urge Governor T.N. Chaturvedi to recommend the dismissal of the coalition Government and facilitate a CBI inquiry into the alleged irregularities by the S.M. Krishna Government as revealed in a World Bank report and the alleged irregularities in the Upper Krishna Project highlighted by the Estimates Committee of the tenth Legislative Assembly when the Janata Dal was in power.

(3847) Belgaum : The Bharatiya Janata Party (BJP) seems to have put itself in the election mode as the "Sangharsh Yatra" of the party, which reached here on Wednesday, called upon people to elect the party candidates in the coming zilla and taluk panchayat elections.

(3848) Palakkad : Democratic Indira Congress (Karunakaran) president K. Muraleedharan has alleged that Chief Minister Oommen Chandy is promoting "criminalisation" of the police and the Congress party.

(3849) Pathanamthitta : Communist Party of India (Marxist) leader and Co-operation Minister M.V. Raghavan has said that he would not rule out the possibility of a "Karunakaran effect" in the forthcoming byelections in Thiruvananthapuram.

(3850) New Delhi : The Bharatiya Janata Party on Thursday sought the resignation of film star and Congress M.P. from North Mumbai, Govinda, for his alleged links with underworld don Dawood Ibrahim after video footage aired by a private television channel showed them together at a party.

(3851) New Delhi : Accompanied by a large number of Delhiites and representatives of various citizens' groups, senior Bharatiya Janata Party leader Vijay Goel on Thursday staged a dharna at Delhi Jal Board's headquarters, Varunalaya, to oppose proposed privatisation of water distribution in the Capital.

(3852) Kolkata : West Bengal's main Opposition, the Trinamool Congress, failed to carry out its threat of laying siege on Thursday to parts of Kolkata to disrupt the visit of Benny Santoso, chief of the Indonesian major, Salim Group. He went ahead with his schedule and held a meeting with Chief Minister Buddhadeb Bhattacharjee to finalise the setting up of a Rs. 250-crore motorcycle manufacturing plant.

(3853) New Delhi : The Bharatiya Janata Party on Thursday asked the Election Commission to be more vigilant about "repeated" violations of the model code of conduct by the Rashtriya Janata Dal leaders, particularly Railway Minister Lalu Prasad, in Bihar.

(3854) Patna : The Rashtriya Janata Dal (RJD) on Thursday expressed surprise over the Election Commission's "silence on the brutal assault" on party MLA and candidate, Vijay Prakash, and an independent candidate, Ashok Ram, allegedly by police on Tuesday.

(3855) Chennai : The former Tamil Nadu Congress Committee president, Tindivanam K. Ramamurthy, has criticised the All-India Congress Committee and the State unit for "systematically denigrating Vanniyar community."

(3856) Villupuram : Those involved in "stuffing" electoral rolls, be they Ministers, should not be spared. All of them should be awarded jail terms, said S. Ramadoss, founder leader of the Pattali Makkal Katchi.

22-10-2005

(3857) Hyderabad : The Congress Legislature Party has termed the nine-day indefinite fast undertaken by former Minister Mudragada Padmanabham as a "drama" and ploy by the Telugu Desam to delay execution of irrigation projects.

(3858) New Delhi : The Hyderabad Plenary session of the All-India Congress Committee would be held between January 21 and 23, Andhra Pradesh Congress Committee president K. Keshava Rao said on Friday.

(3859) Hyderabad : The crisis in Telangana Rashtra Samithi (TRS) scaled new heights on Friday with its president and Union Labour Minister K. Chandrasekhar Rao and the rebel MLA S. Santosh Reddy expelling each other and the latter announcing that he represents the 'real' TRS.

(3860) Thiruvananthapuram : Kerala Pradesh Congress Committee (KPCC) president Ramesh Chennithala on Friday alleged that the CPI(M) was stoking communal passions, an action that would have far reaching consequences in a State known for its communal peace and amity.

(3861) Kannur : Communist Party of India (Marxist) State secretary Pinarayi Vijayan has said that there is discontent among inmates in jails in the State, even as he has dismissed as politically motivated an "intelligence finding" that an explosive situation existed in the prisons.

(3862) Bangalore : The Karnataka Pradesh Congress Committee (KPCC) on Friday accused the Bharatiya Janata Party (BJP) MP H.T. Sangliana of being a pawn in the hands of political forces inimical to Congress leaders, especially Maharashtra Governor S.M. Krishna, obliquely stating that he is acting at the behest of Janata Dal (Secular) leaders.

(3863) Bidar : The Alpasankhyataru Hindulidaru mattu Dalitaru (AHINDA) rally to be held in Basavakalyan on Sunday is gaining more significance after the former Union Minister V. Srinivas Prasad agreed to inaugurate it.

(3864) Bijapur : The Bharatiya Janata Party's "Sangarsha Yatra" concluded in Bijapur and Bagalkot districts on Thursday with a call to end the "misrule of the Congress-Janata Dal (Secular) coalition Government".

(3865) Gulbarga : The former Minister and Congress MLC B.K. Chandrashekar on Friday said that a mountain is being made of a mole about the World Bank report on corruption. He said that the real issues in the report are not being highlighted.

(3866) Thiruvananthapuram : Regional, caste and parochial considerations will not figure in the Thiruvananthapuram Lok Sabha byelection, Leader of the Opposition V.S. Achuthanandan has said.

(3867) New Delhi : The Bharatiya Janata Party has demanded a judicial inquiry into the violence in Karbi Anglong district of Assam by a sitting judge of a High Court and immediate relief and compensation to the victims.

(3868) New Delhi : Bharatiya Janata Party leader Uma Bharti has put on hold her battle for change of leadership in Madhya Pradesh till after the Bihar elections. "I will not speak about Madhya Pradesh till November 18," she told reporters after a meeting with Arun Jaitley, general secretary and in-charge of the State, here on Friday.

(3869) New Delhi : The former Prime Minister, Atal Bihari Vajpayee, said on Friday that old leaders in the Bharatiya Janata Party would go and new ones would take charge. "I have started realising that I am ageing fast. We grow old, people come and go, but we keep moving. What matters is walking together shoulder to shoulder."

(3870) New Delhi : Given the strong resentment prevailing among the Capital's citizens over the water and power crises in the city, the Congress Councillors on Friday warned the Congress high command that if steps were not taken to undo the damage caused by '"mishandling" of these issues by the Sheila Dikshit Government, the party would have to face the people's wrath in the next political battle.

(3871) Kalyan (Maharashtra) : Shiv Sena Chief Bal Thackeray on Thursday alleged that there was a deal between Congress president Sonia Gandhi and the former Maharashtra Chief Minister, Narayan Rane, who joined her party after he was expelled from the Sena.

(3872) Kolkata : The Communist Party of India (Marxist) leadership would like to see foreign capital flow into West Bengal for industrial growth and employment generation. This is in keeping with Chief Minister Buddhadeb Bhattacharjee's moves to bringin foreign direct investment (FDI) to provide a boost to industry.

24-10-2005

(3873) Hyderabad : A delegation of Telugu Desam Party (TDP) leaders on Sunday sought Governor Sushil Kumar Shinde's intervention for a judicial enquiry by a High Court judge into the violent incidents at Velpula in Pulivendula Assembly constituency in Kadapa district.

(3874) Nizamabad : Telangana Rashtra Samithi (TRS) district president and MLA E. Ravinder Reddy has made it clear that the party will not take any action against those who attended the meeting organised by expelled leader S. Santosh Reddy in Hyderabad.

(3875) Rajahmundry : Pradesh Congress Committee president K. Keshava Rao has opined that separate Telangana cannot be achieved with the efforts of the TRS alone.

(3876) Bhopal : The Madhya Pradesh Chief Minister, Babulal Gaur, has taken a tough stand against the State Ministers, who had joined the signature campaign last week to build pressure on the party leadership for his ouster, and warned that the Ministers who do not have faith in his leadership would be removed if they fail to apologise. Mr. Gaur was talking to journalists during his tour of Jhabua district in western Madhya Pradesh on Sunday.

(3877) Thiruvananthapuram : CPI State secretary Veliyam Bhargavan and Leader of the Opposition V.S. Achuthanandan have come down heavily on the alleged attempts of the United Democratic Front (UDF) and the Government to manipulate the voters' list in the Thiruvananthapuram Lok Sabha constituency.

(3878) New Delhi : The Congress on Sunday began the process of consultations on the change of guard in Jammu and Kashmir, with the party president Sonia Gandhi meeting the State Chief Minister Mufti Mohammed Sayeed.

(3879) Chirakoot : Breaking its month-long silence on BJP president L. K. Advani's charge that it was "remote-controlling" the party, the RSS on Sunday said it would speak to him about the issue. It also said that it expected Mr. Advani's successor to adhere to the Sangh's five-point guidelines on the way the party should be run.

(3880) Bellary : Bharatiya Janata Party general secretary and former Union Minister H.N. Ananth Kumar has described the outburst of the former Prime Minister H.D. Deve Gowda against Infosys chief mentor Narayana Murthy a "unwise."

(3881) Bidar : AHINDA will never be converted into a political party. It will act as a pressure group and make governments take steps for the welfare of the deprived classes, the former Deputy Chief Minister Siddaramaiah has said.

(3882) Bidar : The former Deputy Chief Minister Siddaramaiah said his party, which he refers to as the real Janata Dal (Secular), will field candidates in all seats in the zilla and taluk panchayat elections. "We have expelled (former Prime Minister) H.D. Deve Gowda and appointed C.M. Ibrahim as our National President. The former Minister Satish Jarkiholi as the State unit President. We have applied to the Central Election Commission State Election Commission for recognition as the real Janata Dal (S). We are expecting the decision soon," he said.

(3883) Bidar : The former Union Minister and Janata Dal (Secular) leader V. Srinivas Prasad inaugurated the Alpasankhyataru Hindulidavaru mattu Dalitaru (AHINDA) Swabhimani Chaitanya Yatra, the first in a series of rallies planned by the splinter group of Janata Dal (Secular), across the State in Basavakalyan on Sunday.

(3884) Raichur : H.D. Kumaraswamy, Working President of the State unit of the Janata Dal (Secular), has said that he is ready to offer his post in the party to the former Union Minister, Srinivas Prasad if he returns to his party and sorts out the differences.

(3885) Alappuzha : The State Government has failed to obtain from the Union Government an amount of more than Rs.100 crores that it had promised as aid to the next of kin of farmers who had committed suicide, the Leader of the Opposition V.S. Achuthanandan said.

(3886) Kozhikode : CPI (M) State secretary Pinarayi Vijayan said on Sunday that the United Progressive Alliance (UPA) Government at the Centre should desist from its move to subscribe to the imperialistic policies of the U.S. India had voted for a US-sponsored proposal against Iran at the International Atomic Energy Agency (IAEA) meeting at Vienna last month. India's stance revealed a big shift from its declared foreign policy of non-alignment, the Polit Bureau member said.

(3887) Thiruvananthapuram : The Left Democratic Front (LDF) district committee today accused Chief Minister Oommen Chandy and his Cabinet colleagues of misusing Government machinery to manipulate the voters' list and derail the forthcoming byelections to the Thiruvananthapuram Lok Sabha constituency.

(3888) Thiruvananthapuram : The Congress was a spent force in Kerala and only the Bharathiya Janata Party (BJP) could politically counter the Communist Party (Marxist) in the State, the BJP all-India vice-president, Venkaiah Naidu, has said.

(3889) Thiruvananthapuram : The KPCC general secretary Joseph Vazhackan on Sunday questioned the sincerity of the CPI(M) State secretary Pinarayi Vijayan's statement that the CPI(M) would not tolerate attacks on minorities.

(3890) Thiruvananthapuram : Democratic Indira Congress (DIC) leader K. Karunakaran has asked Chief Minister Oommen Chandy to give up the Home portfolio in the light of his 'failure' to check rise of criminality in the State and the attempted 'politicisation of the police force' by KPCC president Ramesh Chennithala.

(3891) Thiruvananthapuram : National politics and governance at the Centre will be the main plank of the Bharatiya Janata Party (BJP) in the byelection from the Thiruvananthapuram Lok Sabha Constituency, party's State president P.S. Sreedharan Pillai said here on Sunday.

(3892) Jalandhar : Lauding the Election Commission for directing the Bihar Police to book Union Minister Jai Prakash Narain Yadav, Bharatiya Janata Party president L.K. Advani on Sunday demanded his dismissal from the Cabinet for his alleged involvement in securing the "illegal" release of his brother Vijay Prakash. "No doubt that Election Commission has played a responsible role in first phase of the Bihar polls, due to which RJD candidate Vijay Prakash was arrested for carrying arms and liquor," Mr. Advani told reporters here.

(3893) Patna : Rashtriya Janata Dal chief Lalu Prasad on Sunday accused the Election Commission of discriminating against his party candidates and workers in Bihar.

(3894) Pondicherry : The convenor of the youth wing of the Pondicherry State unit of the Dravida Munnetra Kazhagam (DMK) R. Siva MLA, has called upon the Centre to implement the National Rural Employment Guarantee programme in Pondicherry, as that would go a long way in relieving the jobless youth of their hardship.

(3895) Pondicherry : Health Minister of Pondicherry E.Valsaraj has said that the steps were taken through various sources to generate awareness among the people about use of iodated salt.

(3896) Chennai : Marumalarchi Dravida Munnetra Kazhagam (MDMK) general secretary Vaiko on Sunday said his party would continue to support the just demands of the Muslims including reservation in jobs and education.

(3897) Chennai : Tamil Nadu Congress Committee (TNCC) president G.K. Vasanon Sunday accused the State Government of attempting to hoodwink farmers by making several announcements ahead of the Assembly elections.

25-10-2005

(3898) Hyderabad : The BJP has expressed doubts over the State Government's claim that it would complete eight irrigation projects by next kharif, conforming to the two-year deadline.

(3899) Hyderabad : Having tasted defeat in the municipal elections, the Telugu Desam Party (TDP) has decided to gear up for the coming panchayat polls to elect members of the Zilla and Mandal Parishad Territorial Constituencies.

(3900) Kurnool : Telugu Desam Party (TDP) leader and former legislator Byreddy Rajasekhar Reddy has said Rayalaseema requires more than G.O. 170 on the irrigation front.

(3901) Hyderabad : The Telangana Rashtra Samithi (TRS) has alleged a major conspiracy to split the party by the Congress, particularly Chief Minister Y.S. Rajasekhara Reddy and Adviser to the Government on Political Affairs K.V.P. Ramachandra Rao.

(3902) New Delhi : Two TRS MLAs - K. Lingayya and A. Chandrasekhar - on Monday charged Andhra Pradesh Chief Minister's advisor K.V.P. Ramachandra Rao with attempting to engineer a split in the party when it was facing a crisis.

(3903) Thiruvananthapuram : Kerala Pradesh Congress Committee (KPCC) general secretary M.I. Shanavas has denied the allegation of the Communist Party of India (Marxist) that the Congress is making efforts to tamper with the electoral rolls and that it convened a meeting of the office-bearers of the Police Association recently.

(3904) New Delhi : With just a week to go for transfer of power in Jammu and Kashmir, the Congress leadership continued the process of consultation, with party president Sonia Gandhi and Prime Minister Manmohan Singh meeting senior party leaders here on Monday.

(3905) Bangalore : Karnataka Pradesh Congress Committee President M. Mallikarjun Kharge on Monday ruled out postponement of zilla and taluk panchayat elections in view of the rain havoc in southern Karnataka.

(3906) Bangalore : The State BJP, which is unhappy over the steps taken by the Government to safeguard residential layouts from torrential rains, has put forth several suggestions, including seeking expertise from Mumbai which faced a similar disaster in the recent past.

(3907) Chikmagalur : Chikmagalur MLA and Bharatiya Janata Party (BJP) Yuva Morcha State unit president C.T. Ravi has criticised the Government for imposing restrictions on the "Dattamala Abhiyana," which concluded on Sunday.

(3908) Kozhikode : Leader of the Opposition V.S. Achuthanandan on Monday filed a petition before the Kozhikode Second Additional Sub-Court and Assistant Sessions Court praying that his arguments also be heard while taking up the petition filed by the special prosecutor in the Kozhikode ice-cream parlour case seeking to delete the name of Indian Union Muslim League (IUML) leader P.K. Kunhalikutty from the charge-sheet.

(3909) Kochi : Former Bharatiya Janata Party (BJP) general secretary and Hindutva ideologue K.N. Govindacharya has said that "distrust and the rupture of dialogue" between the "political leadership" (BJP) and the "mass base" (Rashtriya Swayamsevak Sangh) have led to the current conflict between the two.

(3910) Hyderabad : Impressed by the spread of micro-finance in the drought-prone districts of Andhra Pradesh, Congress MP Rahul Gandhi has asked Swayam Krushi Sangham (SKS) Microfinance to replicate the model in his constituency of Amethi in Uttar Pradesh.

(3911) New Delhi : The Supreme Court has directed the Centre to return the properties of the erstwhile raja of Mahmudabad to his son, raja

Mohammed Amir Mohammad Khan, 32 years after they were seized under the Enemy Property Act with Rs. 5 lakhs towards costs.

(3912) New Delhi : Holding the Centre and the Delhi Government directly responsible for the sharp increase in prices of onion and scarcity of gas cylinders, Delhi Bharatiya Janata Party president Harsh Vardhan on Monday demanded resignation of Union Agriculture Minister Sharad Pawar and Delhi Chief Minister Sheila Dikshit.

(3913) Bhopal : Madhya Pradesh Congress Committee president Subhash Yadav has written to Chief Minister Babulal Gaur drawing his attention to "failure" of the State Government to ensure an adequate supply of electricity and fertilizers to the farmers.

(3914) Dehra Dun : The Uttaranchal Assembly was adjourned sine die on Monday amid noisy scenes by the Bharatiya Janata Party and Bahujan Samaj Party members seeking a statement from the Government on alleged attempted rape of a minor girl student by the son of a Cabinet Minister.

26-10-2005

(3915) Hyderabad : The Congress has strongly denied the Telangana Rashtra Samithi leaders' charge that it has been trying to engineer a split in the TRS.

(3916) Hyderabad : P. Veerasiva Reddy, Telugu Desam MLA who hit headlines recently for his outbursts against his party president N. Chandrababu Naidu, met Chief Minister Y. S. Rajasekhara Reddy at the Secretariat on Tuesday but denied making efforts to join the Congress or showing leaning to it.

(3917) New Delhi : A Congress delegation from Kerala, led by Chief Minister Oommen Chandy, on Tuesday sought United Progressive Alliance (UPA) chairperson Sonia Gandhi's intervention in securing early Central assistance for pending projects in the State. Mr. Chandy also met Prime Minister Manmohan Singh with a similar demand.

(3918) New Delhi : Congress legislators and leaders in Jammu and Kashmir have demanded that the party take its turn to head the coalition government in accordance with an earlier agreement with the People's Democratic Party.

(3919) Alappuzha : The Congress has lost its upper-hand in the United Democratic Front (UDF) after the recent elections to the local bodies, the Democratic Indira Congress (Karunakaran) president, K. Muraleedharan, has opined.

(3920) New Delhi : The Bharatiya Janata Party on Tuesday accused the Centre of "callously representing" facts on allotment of government accommodation to politicians and individuals in the capital, following which the Supreme Court made strong observations against the "illegal" occupation.

(3921) New Delhi : The Samajwadi Party Members of Parliament will meet President Abdul Kalam here on Wednesday to protest against "misuse of Governors" by the ruling Congress Party at the Centre.

(3922) New Delhi : The Communist Party of India (Marxist) on Tuesday continued to debate whether the Information Technology sector be included in the essential services while emphasising that there could be no dilution of labour laws in it.

(3923) New Delhi : Delhi Bharatiya Janata Party president Harsh Vardhan announced on Tuesday that a delegation of the party would meet the President and demand fresh elections to the Delhi Assembly and the Municipal Corporation of Delhi as both the Delhi Government and the Congress-led Corporation had failed the people.

(3924) New Delhi : Delhi Pradesh Congress Committee president Ram Babu Sharma on Tuesday declared said had been assured by the Reliance Energy chairman, Anil Ambani, that the agitating erstwhile Delhi Vidyut Board employees who availed of the Voluntary Retirement Scheme (VRS) would be paid Rs. 6,000 in form of encouragement wages and ex-gratia before Diwali.

(3925) Bhopal : Madhya Pradesh Bharatiya Janata Party president Shivraj Singh Chauhan on Tuesday said that the nuclear agreement between India and the US had come within the purview of doubt due to populist statements emanating from America.

(3926) Jalandhar : The Punjab Government is raking up the issue of terrorism to divert the attention of people from its "failures" and "misgovernance," opposition leader and SAD chief Parkash Singh Badal on Tuesday alleged.

(3927) Jaipur : The Rajasthan Government intends to develop new industrial areas to speed up industrial growth and attract big investors to the State. The Industries Department has approved the proposals for establishing new industrial areas at the land measuring 4,546 acres.

(3928) Lucknow : The Congress on Tuesday slammed Samajwadi Party leader Amar Singh for his "derogatory"remarks on Uttar Pradesh Governor T V Rajeswar, saying they were an insult to the constitutional post.

(3929) Chennai : The Tamil Nadu Congress Committee president, G.K.Vasan, has appealed to the State Government to take adequate measures to provide relief measures to flood-affected people in the State.

27-10-2005

(3930) Hyderabad : The Congress has asserted that the Government has spent more than Rs. 2,990 crores in the last 20 months on irrigation projects in Telangana as against Rs. 2,400 crores on projects in Andhra and Rayalaseema regions.

(3931) Bangalore : Dispelling the image of his being an information technology (IT) industry-basher, former Prime Minister and Janata Dal (Secular) president H.D. Deve Gowda on Wednesday said he had taken several decisions as Chief Minister and Prime Minister to attract IT investment into the State. But he urged the industry to provide jobs to "talented young engineers" and "people who are uprooted in the process of land acquisition for setting up industries." He was addressing delegates at the inauguration of Bangalore IT.in here.

(3932) New Delhi : The Congress in Jammu and Kashmir is facing a revolt, with a large number of MLAs threatening to quit the Assembly rather than opting for status quo in the coalition arrangement.

(3933) Bangalore : Disturbed by the situation in some of the rain-hit areas of Bangalore, the former Prime Minister and President of the Janata Dal (Secular), H.D. Deve Gowda, has called for permanent measures to tackle the factors behind the floods in the city.

(3934) Bangalore : Tourism Minister D.T. Jayakumar on Wednesday made light of former Union Minister V. Srinivasa Prasad's apparent disenchantment with the Janata Dal (Secular) leadership and his criticism of Working President H.D. Kumaraswamy.

(3935) Kozhikode : Condemning the Government Order invalidating the election of a BJP councillor, S.R. Balasubramanian, as vice-chairman of the Palakkad municipal council, BJP State president P.S. Sreedharan Pillai on Wednesday said the action was illegal, undemocratic and the first step towards dissolving the elected municipal council.

(3936) Pathanamthitta : Democratic Indira Congress (Karunakaran) president K. Muraleedharan has alleged that the Chief Minister Oommen Chandy's reported statement that the Communist Party of India (Marxist) (CPI(M) was 'manipulating' a section of the police force against the Government was nothing short of a testimony to the latter's gross failure in handling the Home portfolio.

(3937) New Delhi : Communist Party of India (Marxist) Polit Bureau member Pinarayi Vijayan on Wednesday said the electoral understanding with the fledgling Democratic Indira Congress (Karunakaran) (DIC-K) in Kerala had worked to his party's benefit.

(3938) New Delhi : The Bharatiya Janata Party (BJP) has welcomed the Supreme Court judgment upholding the Gujarat Government's order banning the slaughter of bulls and bullocks. The Gujarat High Court in 1998 had held the order unconstitutional.

(3939) New Delhi : The Janata Dal (U) on Wednesday urged President A.P.J. Abdul Kalam to dismiss the Union Council of Ministers if Minister of State for Water Resources Jaiprakash Narain Yadav, against whom a non-bailable arrest warrant has been issued in a poll-related incident in Bihar, was not sacked.

(3940) New Delhi : Samajwadi Party MPs on Wednesday urged President A.P.J. Abdul Kalam to recall Uttar Pradesh Governor T.V. Rajeshwar "to protect and uphold" the dignity of the Constitution.

(3941) New Delhi : Accusing the Sheila Dikshit Government of being hand in glove with private power distribution companies, the Leader of the Opposition in the Delhi Assembly, Jagdish Mukhi, on Wednesday termed the removal of old electricity meters and installation of new electronic ones as "illegal", not mandated by any regulatory body or central authority.

(3942) Chennai : The AIADMK Government is committed to protecting the interests of minorities. The demand for reservation by

Muslims will be taken up with Chief Minister Jayalalithaa, three Ministers told an Ifthaar party here on Wednesday.

28-10-2005

(3943) Hyderabad : Accepting a resolution adopted at the rebel meeting of Telangana Rashtra Samithi (TRS) last week, S. Santosh Reddy has taken over as president of the breakaway faction of the party.

(3944) Rajahmundry : The Communist Party of India (CPI-M) State secretariat member and CITU state general secretary S. Veeraiah has said that the his party will not allow the United Progressive Alliance (UPA) Government to make amendments in labour laws, which will benefit multi-national companies.

(3945) New Delhi : Union Minister Ghulam Nabi Azad will be the new Chief Minister of Jammu and Kashmir. He will be the first Congress leader to occupy the top post in the State after three decades.

(3946) New Delhi : The Left parties on Thursday returned to the coordination committee with the United Progressive Alliance after a four-month gap. They conveyed opposition to the foreign direct investment in the retail sector and asked the Government to have an independent foreign policy, and in the case of Iran, abstain in case consensus was lacking in the International Atomic Energy Agency.

(3947) Bangalore : Leader of the Opposition in the Legislative Assembly B.S.Yediyurappa on Thursday demanded that a special session of the legislature be convened to discuss the floods in north Karnataka which inundated one lakh acres of land and to seek an explanation from the Government for its failure to release aid to the farmers and the bizarre conditions it had laid down to pay compensation.

(3948) Gulbarga : The Election Commission's refusal to allot the "woman carrying a bundle of grass" symbol will not affect our prospects, MLA B.R. Patil said in Gulbarga on Thursday.

(3949) Thiruvananthapuram : Democratic Indira Congress (Karunakaran) leader K. Karunakaran on Thursday asserted that the CPI (M) Polit Bureau had recognised his party as an ally.

(3950) Thiruvananthapuram : Revenue Minister and Kerala Congress (M) leader K. M. Mani on Thursday lashed out at the CPI (M) leadership for its decision to organise agitations in the Information Technology sector.

(3951) Thiruvananthapuram : Leader of the Opposition V. S. Achuthanandan has urged Prime Minister Manmohan Singh to block the merger of the Federal Bank and the Lord Krishna Bank and take steps for the takeover of the latter by a public sector bank.

(3952) New Delhi : The Indian National Lok Dal (INLD) on Thursday criticised the proposed move to set up a commission to resolve the long pending issue of construction of the Sutlej-Yamuna Link (SYL) canal.

(3953) Gandhinagar : The Bharatiya Janata Party has made impressive gains in local body elections in Gujarat. It has dethroned the Congress from most of the district, taluka panchayats and municipalities that went to the polls on Tuesday.

(3954) New Delhi : Congress leader Ghulam Nabi Azad, scheduled to take over as Chief Minister of Jammu and Kashmir on November 2, vowed to strengthen the peace process with Pakistan. He would supply aid to the quake-stricken region of the State before winter set in.

(3955) Bhopal : The stalemate over the leadership issue in Madhya Pradesh continues even as a battle of wits rages between dissident MLAs and those heading the ruling Bharatiya Janata Party organisation in the State.

(3956) Villupuram : The Pattali Makkal Katchi has blamed the Karnataka Government for the flood havoc in Tamil Nadu, caused by the sudden discharge of a large quantum of water into the Cauvery.

29-10-2005

(3957) Hyderabad : The Telugu Desam Party has challenged the Congress for a public debate on the relative performance of each other's Governments in the core sectors of irrigation, power, health, rural development, roads and infrastructure in Telangana.

(3958) Kakinada : A former MLA and the Organising Secretary of the district unit of the Telugu Desam Vanamadi Venkateswerarao has threatened to launch an agitation if the government did not withdraw its decision to set up a Maritime Board for administration of minor Ports.

(3959) New Delhi : The Legislature Party of the Congress in Jammu & Kashmir will meet on Sunday in Srinagar to formally elect Union Minister

Ghulam Nabi Azad as its leader ahead of his taking charge as Chief Minister on November 2. The election of the CLP leader will take place in the presence of the All-India Congress Committee general secretary in-charge of the State, Ambika Soni, and a senior leader Motilal Vora.

(3960) Gandhinagar : The Narendra Modi juggernaut continued to roll in Gujarat crushing the Congress challenge in the elections to local self-government bodies and silencing the Chief Minister's critics.

(3961) Hassan : The Bahujana Samaj Party (BSP) will not join hands with any political party for the taluk and zilla panchayat elections, the general secretary of the State unit of the party, Sreedhara Kalaveer, has said.

(3962) Panaji : Agriculture Minister Francisco alias Micky Pacheco, the disgruntled Nationalist Congress Party Minister in the Pratapsinh Rane Ministry, who had launched a tirade against him, ended up consolidating Mr. Rane's position.

(3963) Thiruvananthapuram : The Opposition Left Democratic Front (LDF) has accused the ruling United Democratic Front of attempting to win the Thiruvananthapuram Lok Sabha byelection with Bharatiya Janata Party (BJP) votes.

(3964) Srinagar : Following the nomination of Union Minister Ghulam Nabi Azad as the next Chief Minister of Jammu and Kashmir, hectic consultations have begun within the People's Democratic Party for the post of Deputy Chief Minister, held by the Congress for the past three years as part of the coalition arrangement.

(3965) Chennai : The Janata Party president, Subramanian Swamy, on Friday opposed the current peace talks with Pakistan saying a plan to withdraw from Siachen, and thereafter from Sir Creek, was in the offing in the name of "confidence building" measures.

(3966) Mumbai : The Shiv Sena has decided to field Madhukar Sarpotdar for the North-West Mumbai Lok Sabha constituency bypoll, party sources said. The seat has fallen vacant following the death of Sunil Dutt.

(3967) Pondicherry : Congress M.P., V. Narayanasamy, has called upon Left parties to abstain from protesting against the Centre permitting

Foreign Direct Investment (FDI) in the infrastructure development sector, telecommunication, aviation, insurance and other sectors as such an investment would help raise the economy of the country and also widen job opportunities.

(3968) Jaipur : Bharatiya Janata Party workers clashed among themselves inside the State party office on the Sardar Patel Marg here on Friday injuring about half a dozen persons. A police party, led by the Superintendent of Police, entered the office premises and took into custody 15 of the irate members. Two of the injured are now in hospital.

(3969) Lucknow : The ruling Samajwadi Party and the main opposition BJP received a setback in the recently-held Kshetra and Zila panchayat polls in Uttar Pradesh.

(3970) Chennai : DMK joint general secretary and former Mayor, M.K. Stalin has stated that the AIADMK government and the Chennai Corporation have failed in undertaking relief measures on a war-footing as city residents suffered untold misery in the recent rains.

30-10-2005

(3971) Hyderabad : Former Minister of State for Railways and Bharatiya Janata Party (BJP) national secretary B. Dattatreya has demanded a high-level enquiry into the Repalle-Secunderabad Delta Fast Passenger train accident as he feels that it could have been averted had the police provided information to railway authorities.

(3972) Tirupati : Telugu Desam Party president N. Chandrababu Naidu reportedly expressed his strong reservations over the partymen adopting a 'compromise formula' with the rival Congress contestants in the just-concluded PAC elections.

(3973) New Delhi : The Communist Party of India (Marxist) on Saturday said there were grounds to believe that the Uttar Pradesh Governor, T.V. Rajeshwar, has "overstepped the limits of his office." On certain issues such as assent to legislation passed by the Assembly, decisions concerning the universities of which he is the chancellor, dealings with officers of the State government and some other actions disregarding the State government's advice, there are grounds to believe that the Governor has overstepped the limits of his office," the party Polit Bureau said in a statement here.

(3974) Bangalore : A city civil court has decreed the ownership of the building on Racecourse Road housing the headquarters of the Janata Dal (Secular) in favour of the Congress. Presiding officer of the court Balakrishna passed the order on Friday.

(3975) Thiruvananthapuram : Democratic Indira Congress (Karunakaran) president K.Muraleedharan has directed the general secretaries to coordinate the campaign of LDF candidate Pannian Ravindran for the Thiruvananthapuram Lok Sabha byelection.

(3976) New Delhi : Senior Bharatiya Janata Party leaders led by former Delhi Chief Minister Madan Lal Khurana, former Union Minister Shatrughan Sinha and cricketer-turned-politician Kirti Azad on Saturday announced the formation of a non-political outfit, Poorvanchal Kranti Sangh, to take up issues facing the people of Bihar, eastern Uttar Pradesh, Jharkhand and West Bengal.

(3977) New Delhi : The Congress on Saturday denied it was a "non-contractual beneficiary" of the United Nations oil-for-food programme in Iraq as has been listed in the Volcker Committee report on the administration and management of the programme. The party is exploring the possibility of legal recourse under international law after examining the report in detail.

(3978) New Delhi : Stepping up pressure on the Manmohan Singh Government, the Committee for an Independent Foreign Policy led by the Left parties on Saturday demanded that India make amends next month for voting against Iran at the International Atomic Energy Agency meeting on September 24. "The issue comes up for voting at the IAEA meeting on November 24 and the United States would try and refer the case to the U.N Security Council. India should state that Iran has the right to develop nuclear energy in accordance with international norms. If necessary, India, along with other nations in the Non-Aligned Movement, should abstain from voting... ," Communist Party of India (Marxist) general secretary Prakash Karat said at a convention here.

(3979) New Delhi : The Janata Dal (United) on Saturday sought the resignation of Union External Affairs Minister Natwar Singh for his alleged involvement in the "kickbacks" in the Oil-for-Food programme of the United Nations as exposed by the Independent Inquiry Committee headed by Paul A. Volcker. "If he doesn't resign, he must be sacked," said party general secretary and spokesman Shambhu Srivastava here today.

(3980) New Delhi : Prime Minister Manmohan Singh, Home Minister Shivraj Patil, Lok Sabha Speaker Somnath Chatterjee and Opposition Leader L.K. Advani on Saturday expressed shock over the blasts here.

(3981) New Delhi : The Bharatiya Janata Party on Saturday demanded the immediate resignation of External Affairs Minister Natwar Singh after the disclosures in the Volcker Committee report listed him among the "non-contractual beneficiaries" of Iraqi oil sales in 2001 related to the United Nations Oil-for-Food scandal.

(3982) Madurai : The Prime Minister should order a "high-level enquiry" into the revelations about "non-contractual beneficiaries" of India in the Volcker Committee report, which probed the Iraqi oil sales in 2001 under the United Nations Oil-for-Food Programme, the president of the Janata Party, Subramanian Swamy, said here on Saturday.

(3983) Chennai : Congress president Sonia Gandhi has cleared an exhaustive list of office bearers for the Pondicherry Pradesh Congress Committee. P. Shanmugam continues as the president.

(3984) Chennai : The Marumalarchi Dravida Munnetra Kazhagam (MDMK) general secretary, Vaiko, on Saturday thanked the Prime Minister, Manmohan Singh, for the Government's decision to permit candidates to write Staff Selection Commission (SSC) examinations in any language mentioned in the Eighth Schedule of the Constitution.

31-10-2005

(3985) Hyderabad : Bharatiya Janata Party (BJP) secretary Bandaru Dattatreya has asked for the resignation of Union Railway Minister Lalu Prasad Yadav for not visiting the train accident site at Nagaram and making an "irresponsible" statement that it was caused by rain.

(3986) Nalgonda : Union Minister of State for Rural Development and Telangana Rashtra Samithi (TRS) leader A. Narendra has blamed the State Government for the rail tragedy at Valigonda in Nalgonda district on Saturday.

(3987) Kakinada : BJP State unit president N. Indrasena Reddy while expressing serious concern over the anti-national forces raising their ugly heads posing a threat to the national integrity and security, especially after repealing of the POTA, has demanded the Central Government to take urgent remedial measures. Addressing a press conference here on Sunday, he blamed the UPA Government for scrapping of important act such as 'POTA' and giving leverage to the anti-national forces to continue their activities. He said the Government alone should own the responsibility for the present state of affairs, especially to the recurrence of blasts in New Delhi.

(3988) Nagaram (Nalgonda dist.) : Telugu Desam Party president N. Chandrababu Naidu has demanded a judicial enquiry into the train accident caused by flash floods, saying coordination appeared to be lacking between the Railways and officials of Irrigation and other departments.

(3989) Kadapa : Kamalapuram TDP legislator G. Veerasiva Reddy on Sunday charged the party president N. Chandrababu Naidu with remaining a 'nominal head' and running the party at will bowing to pressure from a coterie of Telangana MLAs and leaders.

(3990) Bangalore : Last week's rain havoc should not be an impediment to the zilla and taluk panchayat elections scheduled for December, the former Prime Minister H.D. Deve Gowda has said, even as he is engaged in confabulations with the Janata Dal (Secular) rank and file from the districts, and legislators and ministers over the weekend to chalk out strategy for the campaign.

(3991) Bangalore : Leader of the Opposition in the Legislative Assembly B.S. Yediyurappa has said the BJP will approach the Supreme Court if the Government decides to postpone the zilla and taluk panchayat elections.

(3992) Bangalore : Janata Dal (Secular) President H.D. Deve Gowda on Sunday admitted that the parting of ways with the former Deputy Chief Minister Siddaramaiah and the move to suspend him and eight others had been a setback for the party-building exercise.

(3993) Hubli : Several activists of the Congress staged a protest here on Saturday condemning the action of Belgaum City Corporation in accepting a resolution to transfer Belgaum and nearby places to Maharashtra.

(3994) Thiruvananthapuram : United Democratic Front convener P.P. Thankachan has termed the CPI(M) stand on the Neyyatinkara Bishop's

House attack as hollow, besides accusing it of playing up the issue in the light of the Thiruvananthapuram Lok Sabha byelection.

(3995) Srinagar : Chief Minister-designate Ghulam Nabi Azad on Sunday met Governor Lt. Gen. (retd) S. K. Sinha to stake his claim to form a government. Earlier, he was elected leader of the Congress Legislature Party (CLP).

(3996) Srinagar : Jammu and Kashmir Finance Minister Muzaffar Hussain Baig is set to become the Deputy Chief Minister after being appointed leader of the legislature party of the People's Democratic Party. He will replace Mangat Ram Sharma.

(3997) New Delhi : The Bharatiya Janata Party on Sunday said that the Government would have to be clear in its action and on its policy against terrorism as the country appeared high on the agenda of terrorists.

(3998) New Delhi : Political parties have condemned Saturday's serial bomb blasts here with the Communist Party of India (Marxist) coming out strongly against the reprehensible acts of violence against the innocent. It asked the Government to take urgent steps to reassure the people that their safety and security would be ensured. The Government should spare no efforts to book the culprits of this heinous crime, the party said.

(3999) New Delhi : The Left parties said on Sunday that the Government should investigate the charges made by the U.N.-sponsored oil-for-food inquiry committee against External Affairs Minister Natwar Singh, the Congress and a number of Indian companies, but should gather additional evidence and details "before reaching any conclusions."

(4000) Madhubani (Bihar) : Former Bihar Chief Minister Rabri Devi on Sunday charged LJP president Ramvilas Paswan with "playing into the hands of RSS-led communal forces by trying to split Muslim votes" and said he would have to "satisfy himself with no more than half-a-dozen MLAs" in the current Assembly elections.

(4001) New Delhi : The Bharatiya Janata Party has called upon Delhi Chief Minister Sheila Dikshit to honour the October 26 judgment of the Supreme Court upholding the total ban on cow slaughter and also production, storage, sale or consumption of any product having any part of the body of cow in Delhi with immediate effect. Further, the party has called for a special session of the Legislative Assembly to immediately amend the Delhi Agricultural Cattle Prevention Act so that the sentiments of the majority community are respected.

(4002) New Delhi : The mortal remains of the Congress leader, H.K.L. Bhagat, who passed away in the Capital on Saturday after a prolonged illness, were consigned to flames at the Nigambodh Ghat here on Sunday in the presence of a large number of party workers and leaders.

(4003) New Delhi : Senior Bharatiya Janata Party leader and Leader of the Opposition in the MCD Standing Committee, Vijender Kumar, has demanded that the policy of conversion of rented and leasehold properties to freehold as passed by the Delhi Municipal Corporation should also include the rented residential properties including slum properties mainly inhabited by the weaker sections of society.

(4004) Pondicherry : The list of office bearers of the reconstituted Pondicherry Pradesh Congress committee under the leadership of P. Shanmugham which was released by AICC on Saturday 'maintains balance between rural and urban aspects' of the party.

(4005) Jaipur : The Rajasthan Pradesh Congress Committee has opposed the State Government's move to acquire farmlands on the outskirts of the Capital for the proposed IT Park, knowledge corridor and special economic zone. Crores of rupees had changed hands in the deals involving acquisition of farmers' land at throwaway prices to facilitate entrepreneurs, the PCC charged seeking a CBI enquiry into the deals.

(4006) Lucknow : BSP supremo Mayawati on Sunday claimed the Uttar Pradesh zila panchayat results were the people's mandate against the "corrupt and inefficient" Mulayam Singh Yadav Government.

(4007) Chennai : The Union Government's decision to declare Sanskrit also as a classical language, the status accorded to Tamil earlier, has triggered a fresh bout of debate among political parties in Tamil Nadu.

(4008) Madurai : The Bharatiya Janata Party has called for a "stringent anti-terrorism law".

01-11-2005

(4009) Hyderabad : The Bharatiya Janapa Party (BJP) has demanded all-party meetings at the mandal level to discuss flood relief in view of politics coming into play in assessing the crop damage.

(4010) Hyderabad : Telugu Desam Party (TDP) has announced suspension of its rebellious MLA from Kamalapuram in Kadapa district G. Veerasiva Reddy for indulging in anti-party activities.

(4011) Thiruvananthapuram : Democratic Indira Congress (Karunakaran) (DIC-K) leader K. Karunakaran has once again delineated his political line by highlighting his party's differences with the Congress on economic issues.

(4012) Thrissur : Congress leader Vayalar Ravi, MP, has raised doubts over the commitment of the Communist Party of India(Marxist) to public sector undertakings (PSUs) in the country.

(4013) New Delhi : The Congress on Monday rejected demand for an inquiry into the Volcker report that named External Affairs Minister K. Natwar Singh and the party as beneficiaries in the Oil-for-Food programme of Iraq under Saddam Hussein.

(4014) New Delhi : Congress president and United Progressive Alliance chairperson Sonia Gandhi on Monday warned the nation to beware of divisive forces that were trying to weaken the nation and putting hurdles in the path of its progress and development. "India today faces many challenges. Though we are moving ahead, there are certain forces that are creating problems and trying to undo the nation's growth."

(4015) New Delhi : The country is "disappointed" that Prime Minister Manmohan Singh has not asked External Affairs Minister Natwar Singh to resign and has instead given him a "clean chit" in the oil deals with Iraq, Bharatiya Janata Party general secretary Arun Jaitley said here on Monday.

(4016) Patna : Vijay Prakash, Rashtriya Janata Dal candidate in Bihar's Jamui constituency and brother of Union Minister Jai Prakash Narain Yadav, surrendered before a local court on Monday. He was allegedly released from police custody illegally on October 18.

(4017) Chandigarh : Rich tributes were paid to Indira Gandhi at a function organised by the Haryana unit of the Congress here on Monday. Chief Minister Bhupinder Singh Hooda described the late Prime Minister as "a millennium lady of the world" and appealed to the people to give a befitting reply to the forces of terrorism.

(4018) Chennai : Tamil Nadu Congress Committee president G.K. Vasan on Monday called upon the State Government not to move the

Supreme Court to challenge the recent order of the Madras High Court, ordering a CBI probe into the leak of question paper for selection of police constables.

03-11-2005

(4019) Hyderabad : The TDP has demanded the removal of Foreign Minister Natwar Singh from the Union Cabinet for being allegedly cited as a non-contractual beneficiary of the Iraq's Oil-for-Food programme and a high-level inquiry.

(4020) Hyderabad : A five-member Telugu Desam Party delegation led by MLA N. Janardhan Reddy has urged Chief Minister Y. S. Rajasekhara Reddy to inquire into the alleged irregularities in the implementation of irrigation projects in Mahabubnagar district particularly Kalwakurthy lift irrigation scheme.

(4021) Karimnagar : Bharatiya Janata Party State president N. Indrasena Reddy has alleged that both the Congress and the Telangana Rashtra Samithi are deceiving the people of Telangana with their "contradictory and false statements" on the formation of separate State.

(4022) Gulbarga : B.R. Patil, Working President of the Siddaramaiah faction of the Janata Dal (Secular), has taken exception to what he termed a deliberate insult to elected representatives by the Government by keeping them out of the Rajyotsava Day celebrations organised in the taluk headquarters on Tuesday.

(4023) Hubli : Jagadish Shettar, President of the State unit of the Bharatiya Janata Party, holds Chief Minister N. Dharam Singh, Minister for Agriculture K. Srinivasa Gowda, and Minister for Agricultural Marketing Prakash B. Hukkeri responsible for fall in the price of onion in the State. He urged the Government to initiate steps to ensure that onion growers get a reasonable price for their produce.

(4024) Thiruvananthapuram : RSP (B) legislator Shibu Baby John has taken the splinter party back to the UDF coalition. The move that had been initiated with the ouster of A. V. Thamarakshan as general secretary was formalised on Wednesday at a special convention here with the party's formal request to the UDF leadership seeking a re-entry into the coalition and the election of Mr. Baby John as its general secretary.

(4025) Thiruvananthapuram : Leader of the Opposition V. S. Achuthanandan has said that the LDF is not too worried about the Government ordering any type of investigation into the deal with SNC Lavalin for repair of the Pallivasal, Panniar and Shenkulam projects.

(4026) New Delhi : Dismissing as "total rubbish" the Volcker panel report which mentions his father and External Affairs Minister Natwar Singh as a "beneficiary" of Iraq's oil-for-food programme, Congress MLA Jagat Singh on Wednesday night said the owner of an Indian company which had allegedly paid surcharge to a Swiss firm to import oil from Iraq was his friend.

(4027) Kolkata : The Left Front in West Bengal has announced a series of demonstrations across the State including one around the Indian Air Force base in Kaliakunda in West Midnapore District in protest against the proposed India - United States joint military air exercises from November 7.

(4028) New Delhi : The Congress and the Rashtriya Janata Dal have demanded an apology from K.J. Rao, Special Adviser to the Election Commission, for "trying to humiliate a particular community."

(4029) New Delhi : AICC General Secretary, incharge of Bihar, Digvijay Singh has advised former Madhya Pradesh Chief Minister Uma Bharti not to indulge in show of her strength with the help of her supporting MLAs in the State but to keep mum for some days.

(4030) New Delhi : Congress president and United Progressive Alliance chairperson Sonia Gandhi has warned the nation to beware of divisive forces that were trying to weaken the nation and putting hurdles in the path of its progress and development.

(4031) Raipur: Senior Congress leader and former Chhattisgarh Chief Minister Ajit Jogi said today that there were strong indications that the RSS was actively participating in Salwa Judum - the ongoing anti-naxal campaign in the State's tribal Bastar region.

(4032) Chennai : The ruling All-India Anna Dravida Munnetra Kazhagam has lost no time in cashing in on the Chief Minister's Deepavali gift of daily water supply to Chennai.

(4033) Chennai : S. Thirunavakkarasar, member of the Bharatiya Janata Party (BJP) national executive and former Union Minister, said on Wednesday that his party was for all communities and it did not believe in "vote bank politics."

(4034) Chennai : Tamil Nadu Congress Committee president G.K. Vasan has urged the State Government to sanction funds for modernising the Cauvery system in the delta districts so that floodwaters are harnessed instead of being let into the sea.

04-11-2005

(4035) Hyderabad : Union Minister of State for Rural Development A. Narendra has denied that the Sangareddy MLA of Telangana Rashtra Samithi (TRS) T. Jayaprakash Reddy would quit the party in the wake of his outburst against his colleague, T. Harish Rao.

(4036) Hyderabad : A delegation of BJP, led by its national secretary, B. Dattatreya, has appealed to Home Minister K. Jana Reddy to ensure that Pallavi returned to her parents at least for 15 days. The parents of Pallavi, who accompanied the BJP leaders to the Minister, offered to give an undertaking that they would not interfere with the religious freedom of their daughter. Pallavi would be allotted a separate room at their house where she could offer prayers as per Islamic practice. She could decide on the choice of her religion within the fortnight, the delegation said.

(4037) Hyderabad : Expressing reservations over the proposed Rs.23,000- crore Adarsha Andhra Pradesh project to be launched next year, Communist Party of India (Marxist) secretary B.V. Raghavulu has sought clarifications from the Government on the modalities of funding.

(4038) Hyderabad : The Telugu Desam Party (TDP) has alleged a move to dilute the free power scheme going by Chief Minister Y.S. Rajasekhara Reddy's remarks that the scheme will be extended in the rabi to only those farmers who have installed capacitors to their pumpsets.

(4039) New Delhi : The Manmohan Singh Government and the Congress on Thursday got their act together on the controversial Volcker Committee report on oil-for-food contracts in Iraq. While the government announced that it would "go to the root" of the matter, the Congress said it would send legal notice to the parties concerned.

(4040) Bidar : The Janata Dal (Secular) will lead a delegation to former Prime Minister H.D. Deve Gowda and the State Government demanding shifting of the site of the proposed thermal power plant from Jewargi in Gulbarga district to Hallikhed (B) in Bidar.

(4041) Thiruvananthapuram : Central assistance is imperative for the development of the State and a candidate like V.S. Sivakumar should be elected from Thiruvananthapuram to wrest maximum assistance, Congress leader A.K.Antony has said.

(4042) Thiruvananthapuram : The Congress is all set to launch a campaign against the Communist Party of India-Marxist (CPI-M) in Kannur against what it alleges to be anti-democratic and fascist functioning styles of the latter that abrogated civil rights.

(4043) New Delhi : The Left parties on Thursday said the deepening military collaboration with the United States did not augur well for India's strategic interests and independent foreign policy. They welcomed the call given by the Left Front in West Bengal to hold demonstrations at Kalaikunda and other parts of the State on November 7.

(4044) New Delhi : Jammu and Kashmir National Panthers Party chief Bhim Singh has denied having seen External Affairs Minister Natwar Singh's name in a document related to Iraq's oil-for-food deal. He said accepting a commission under the United Nations programme, as revealed in the Volcker Committee report, was not "illegal" though it could be termed "immoral."

(4045) New Delhi : In a letter to Prime Minister Manmohan Singh on Thursday, the Bharatiya Janata Party demanded the immediate dismissal of Natwar Singh as External Affairs Minister, saying his continuation would be a "national embarrassment."

(4046) Kolkata : Communist Party of India (Marxist) workers staged demonstrations outside the Netaji Subhas Chandra Bose International airport here and the joint-user aerodrome at Bagdogra in north Bengal on Thursday. They were protesting against India-U.S. joint exercises, scheduled to begin at the Kalaikunda airbase on November 7.

(4047) Ayodhya : Exuding confidence that the National Democratic Alliance would come up trumps in Bihar, BJP election campaign in-charge Uma Bharti said on Thursday that JD-U leader Nitish Kumar would be the next Chief Minister if the alliance was able to drum up a majority in the Assembly.

(4048) Patna : Bharatiya Janata Party vice-president M. Venkaiah Naidu on Thursday demanded a categorical statement from the Congress on the Panthers Party chief Bhim Singh's claims of having seen External Affairs Minister K. Natwar Singh's name among the recipients of favours under the Oil-For Food programme during Saddam Hussein's reign in Iraq.

(4049) Lucknow : The Congress today slammed Uttar Pradesh Chief minister Mulayam Singh Yadav for 'appeasing' sugarmill owners, while at the same time failing to announce sugarcane prices.

(4050) Chennai : The All-India Anna Dravida Munnetra Kazhagam Government failed to implement over half-a-dozen schemes announced by it in 2001 to alleviate the water problem in Chennai Pattali Makkal Katchi founder S. Ramadoss alleged on Thursday.

05-11-2005

(4051) Anantapur : District Telugu Desam leaders have criticised the State Government's decision to deny free power to the farmers who will take up paddy cultivation in the rabi season.

(4052) Hyderabad : The Congress Legislative Party has accused the TDP and the BJP of taking farmers for a ride by demanding continuation of free power to the agricultural sector, which they had bitterly opposed while in power.

(4053) Hyderabad : Political parties across the spectrum and farmers organisations have criticised Chief Minister Y. S. Rajasekhara Reddy's "warning" to farmers that free power supply will be discontinued for paddy crop in the ensuing rabi if they do not avoid raising it under borewells and wells and fail to install capacitors.

(4054) Karimnagar : Government Whip D. Sridhar Babu has accused the Telugu Desam Party of neglecting irrigation projects in Telangana region during its regime and now shedding 'crocodile tears' to gain political mileage.

(4055) Bhadrachalam : The Government which was firm on going ahead with the original design of the Polavaram project would be undermining the special status enjoyed by the tribals under the scheduled area Regulation 1/70, said the CPI(M) State Secretary B. V. Raghavulu.

(4056) Kadapa : The Government was trying to implement the World Bank-guided reforms in the power and agriculture sectors in a veiled manner, CPI district Secretary G. Obulesu alleged on Friday.

(4057) Kakinada : Communist Party of India(Marxist) town unit leader and district secretary of the CITU Duvva Seshu Babji has blamed the Government for allegedly working against the interests of farmers with regard to acquisition of land for ONGC refinery and Special Economic Zone.

(4058) Sangareddy : Union Minister and TRS leader A. Narendra on Friday succeeded in bringing about temporary truce between the warring groups in the party by pacifying Sangareddy MLA T. Jayaprakash Reddy to continue in the party. After an hour of cajoling, both 'guru' and his prodigy addressed a joint press conference but with a different tenor.

(4059) New Delhi : The Congress on Friday continued its discussions on the political controversy it has been drawn into following the Volcker report. This even as the Manmohan Singh Government deliberated on the nature and scope of the probe it plans to conduct into the report.

(4060) New Delhi : Armed with an assurance from West Bengal Chief Minister Buddhadeb Bhattacharjee, the Centre on Friday decided to go ahead with the Indo-U.S. exercises at the Kalaikunda airbase from November 7.

(4061) New Delhi : Former Delhi Chief Minister Madan Lal Khuarna, who has been at loggerheads with the Bharatiya Janata Party leadership in Delhi and at the national level, announced on Friday his retirement from active politics and launched "Poorvanchal Kranti Sangh", a non-political outfit that will take up issues relating to the migrant population from Bihar, Jharkhand, eastern Uttar Pradesh and parts of West Bengal.

(4062) New Delhi : Nearly two weeks after a non-bailable warrant was issued, the police on Friday raided the official residence of Union Minister of State for Water Resource Development Jaiprakash Narayan Yadav here but returned empty-handed.

(4063) Hyderabad : Trouble is brewing afresh in the Telangana Rashtra Samiti with four party MLAs from Warangal district dashing off an open letter on Friday making critical references to party president K. Chandrasekhara Rao's style of functioning.

(4064) Bangalore : Former Union Minister V. Srinivasa Prasad, who has jumped on the AHINDA (federation of backward classes, minorities and Dalits), has confirmed his decision to quit the Janata Dal (Secular). He may rejoin to the Congress. But the Janata Dal (S) leadership is unfazed as it is being compensated by the entry of BJP member of the Rajya Sabha M. Rajasekhara Murthy.

(4065) Thiruvananthapuram : Kerala Pradesh Congress Committee (KPCC) media cell convener M. M. Hassan on Friday came out with a few posers to CPI(M) State secretary Pinarayi Vijayan on the SNC Lavalin deal, asking him to explain certain gaps in the issue relating to Canadian aid for Malabar Cancer Centre.

(4066) Thiruvananthapuram : BJP State president P.S. Sreedharan Pillai said here on Friday that the proposed Ordinance aimed at increasing Government control over the Travancore Devaswom Board (TDB) would infringe the rights of Hindus.

(4067) Mumbai : Three Shiv Sena MLAs, who are supporters of Revenue Minister Narayan Rane, were on Friday inducted into the Congress at a function presided over by Maharashtra Pradesh Congress Committee president Prabha Rau.

(4068) New Delhi : With the Bharatiya Janata Party increasing pressure on the Congress and External Affairs Minister Natwar Singh with regard to the Volcker Committee report, Communist Party of India general secretary A.B. Bardhan and the former Prime Minister, Chandra Shekhar, came out in support of Mr. Natwar Singh on Friday.

(4069) New Delhi : A meeting of senior Bharatiya Janata Party leaders chaired by party president L.K. Advani here on Friday gave the go-ahead to the party's strategy to push ahead aggressively with its demand for the immediate dismissal of External Affairs Minister Natwar Singh.

(4070) Kolkata : The Communist Party of India (Marxist) staged a demonstration outside the international airport here on Friday for the second consecutive day, even as two DC 10 aircraft of the United States Air Force arrived. On November 7 the Indo-U.S. joint military air exercises are scheduled to start at the Air Force [IAF] base in Kalaikunda in West Midnapore district.

(4071) New Delhi : With Delhi Pradesh Congress Committee president Ram Babu Sharma completing one year in office on Saturday, there is a general feeling among the cadres that despite the year witnessing an uneasy relationship between Mr. Sharma and Chief Minister Sheila Dikshit, he has been successful in restoring the party's supremacy and making its voice heard by its own Congress-led Government here.

(4072) Patna : Bharatiya Janata Party vice-president M. Venkaiah Naidu on Friday said he was not in the race for president and that L.K. Advani's successor would be chosen by consensus.

(4073) Jaipur : The prevailing uncertainty in the Bharatiya Janata Party, both in the State and at the national level, is seemingly prompting the party leadership in Rajasthan to try out new alignments. The State leaders are still at a loss to decipher the likely impact a new national president - who will take over once L.K. Advani, steps down by December - would have on the party organisation here, but the regional satraps are already flexing their muscles.

06-11-2005

(4074) Hyderabad : The Andhra Pradesh Congress Committee (APCC) has fully endorsed the appeal made by Chief Minister Y. S. Rajasekhara Reddy to the farmers to avoid paddy cultivation during rabi season and diversify to commercial crops.

(4075) Hyderabad : The Telugu Desam has threatened to launch an agitation if the Government imposes restrictions on paddy cultivation during rabi.

(4076) Hyderabad : Communist Party of India secretary K. Narayana has said that the crisis brewing in the Telangana Rashtra Samiti is the making of the top leadership and not due to encouragement of dissidence by outside forces.

(4077) Nalgonda : The Telugu Desam has decided to boycott the Government-sponsored open debate on the Alimineti Madhava Reddy Project (AMRP) to be held at the Collectorate here on Sunday.

(4078) Kakinada : Telugu Desam district unit official spokesman and former Minister Chikkala Ramachandra Rao has criticised the Government for its decision not to allow paddy as the second crop under borewells.

(4079) New Delhi : After two rounds of consultations between Prime Minister Manmohan Singh and Congress president Sonia Gandhi, the United Progressive Alliance Government is on the verge of instituting an independent inquiry into the Volcker Committee disclosures, according to informed sources.

(4080) Hyderabad : In the face of a fresh crisis triggered by four Telangana Rashtra Samithi (TRS) MLAs from Warangal, the party leadership promptly got down to fire fighting on Saturday.

(4081) Kannur : Kerala Pradesh Congress Committee (KPCC) president Ramesh Chennithala has said that the 'terror situation' created by the Communist Party of India (Marxist) in Kannur district is an affront to a civilised society.

(4082) Thiruvananthapuram : State secretary of the CPI Veliyam Bharghavan said here on Saturday that the UDF and the BJP were on a secret pact in the byelection to the Thiruvananthapuram Lok Sabha seat.

(4083) Bangalore: President of the State unit of the Janata Dal (United) B. Somashekar has said the party will take up the cause of the large number of people who have been duped by Viniv Inc. He has demanded an inquiry by the Central Bureau of Investigation to identify the "real culprits".

(4084) Gulbarga : The Bahujan Samaj Party has decided to go it alone in the elections to the zilla and taluk panchayats scheduled to be held in December. The party will release the final list of candidates for the elections in Gulbarga district on November 27.

(4085) Kozhikode : Dissidence is raising its hood again in the Indian Union Muslim League (IUML). In what is seen as yet another attempt to throw a challenge at the IUML leadership, a group of party activists will hold a meeting here on Sunday.

(4086) Pathanamthitta : In two separate statements, the Kerala Congress (M) and the Kerala Congress (Secular) have condemned the reported move by the Union Government to undertake the interlinking of the Pampa, Achencoil and Vaipar rivers.

(4087) Pathanamthitta : The Youth Congress(Indira) State general secretary Jose Kaleeckal has called for an impartial inquiry into the allegations levelled against Devaswom Minister K.C.Venugopal by the SNDP Yogam general secretary Vellappaly Natesan in connection with the proposed Sabarimala development project.

(4088) Nagpur : The Rashtriya Swayamsevak Sangh, which had recently engaged the Bharatiya Janata Party in an ideological "course correction" in the wake of the Jinnah controversy, said on Saturday that after the ascension to the top of leaders like Atal Bihari Vajpayee and L.K. Advani, collective leadership was sidelined in the party.

(4089) Chandigarh : The Shiromani Akali Dal has pointed towards "a strong Punjab dimension" to the multi-billion dollar "Oil for Food" scam involving the Congress party, with serious allegations against External Affairs Minister Natwar Singh.

(4090) New Delhi : The Bharatiya Janata Party's State unit on Saturday held a protest demonstration in the capital demanding the resignation of Union External Affairs Minister Natwar Singh. They burnt an effigy of Congress president Sonia Gandhi in front of the BJP headquarters here.

(4091) New Delhi : Jammu and Kashmir Panthers Party chairman Bhim Singh on Saturday denied that he had received either notice or a call for responses from the United Nations Committee that investigated the Iraq oil-for-food scandal.

(4092) New Delhi : Amid a raging political controversy over alleged pay-offs to External Affairs Minister Natwar Singh and the Congress during the Saddam Hussein regime, the Petroleum Minister in the previous NDA Government, Ram Naik, said on Saturday senior Iraqi officials had sought a "surcharge" for supplying crude oil to India under the U.N. food-for-oil programme in 2002.

(4093) Jaipur : Back on his home turf, Bharatpur in Rajasthan, for the first time after the controversy over the Volcker report broke out, External Affairs Minister Natwar Singh on Saturday refuted the charges of being a "non-contractual" beneficiary of Iraq's Oil-for-Food programme. "The allegations in the Volcker report are baseless," he said.

(4094) New Delhi : The Bharatiya Janata Party's Delhi unit on Saturday held a protest demonstration in the Capital demanding resignation of External Affairs Minister Natwar Singh. The protestors also burnt an effigy of Congress president Sonia Gandhi in front of the BJP headquarters at 11 Ashoka Road.

(4095) New Delhi : Asserting that party was supreme and partymen had to be given due respect, the Delhi Pradesh Congress Committee president, Ram Babu Sharma on Saturday declared that he would continue to scrutinise the actions of the Congress-led Government in Delhi on the issue of power, water and if need be even take up confrontation in the interests of the people.

(4096) Pondicherry: The secretary of the Pondicherry State committee of the All India Anna Dravida Munnetra Kazhagam (AIADMK) and party legislator, A. Anbalagan, has asked the administration to ban private practice by doctors working in government hospitals as their services, particularly those of specialists were not available at critical times. The Government could sanction an allowance for doctors as had been done in Central Government run hospitals such as JIPMER.

(4097) Jaipur : A consensus on how to go about tackling serious issues involving the party and the Government in Rajasthan eluded the meeting of the core group of the Bharatiya Janata Party here on Saturday. Chief Minister Vasundara Raje kept away from the meeting presided over by Kalraj Misra, BJP general secretary and party in-charge for Rajasthan affairs at the State unit BJP office. A scheduled programme at Salemabad in Ajmer district was attributed to Ms. Raje's absence.

(4098) Jaipur : There is a new landmark for the Communist movement in Rajasthan with the Communist Party of India (Marxist)'s own office here in the Capital getting ready for inauguration this coming week. At present, barring the good old Indian National Congress and the Communist Party of India (CPI) no other major political party has its own office premises here. Even the Bharatiya Janata Party, in power for the third time in the State, functions from a bungalow owned by the State Public Works Department.

(4099) Lucknow : The Congress on Saturday announced the names of candidates for the two Uttar Pradesh Assembly constituencies where by-polls will be held on December 2.

(4100) Mau (UP): Holding Chief Minister, Mulayam Singh Yadav, responsible for the death of 12 people in Mau riots, the BJP on Saturday asserted that a judicial probe should be conducted into last month's communal clashes.

(4101) Chennai : Tamil Nadu Congress Committee president G.K. Vasan has alleged irregularities in the distribution of relief materials to rain-affected people, forcing them to indulge in road rako and other forms of agitations.

(4102) Krishnagiri : DMK Deputy General Secretary M.K. Stalin demanded the constitution of an all-party committee to distribute relief to flood affected persons in Dharmapuri and Krishnagiri districts. The committee should provide compensation to all farmers and public who were affected by the recent floods, he said addressing presspersons here on Saturday.

07-11-2005

(4103) Hyderabad : The Congress Legislature Party has flayed the Telugu Desam's decision to launch an agitation against the Government's appeal to ryots to avoid paddy cultivation during the rabi season.

(4104) Hyderabad : The Bharatiya Janata Party has charged the Chief Minister Y.S. Rajasekhara Reddy and the Congress Party with not only reneging on promises, but also hitting farmers where it hurt them the most.

(4105) Hyderabad : Telugu Desam Party president N. Chandrababu Naidu on Sunday slammed the Government, charging Chief Minister Y.S. Rajasekhara Reddy with reneging on pre-poll promises.

(4106) Hyderabad : Senior Congress leader and APSRTC Chairman Gone Prakash Rao has threatened to float an outfit of likeminded persons to counter Telangana Rashtra Samiti president K. Chandrasekhara Rao's threat to repeat the violent 1969 separatist movement.

(4107) Hyderabad : Former CLP leader and Khairatabad MLA P. Janardhan Reddy has demanded that the post of Deputy Chief Minister be revived immediately and a senior leader from Telangana appointed to it.

(4108) Hyderabad : Four Telangana Rashtra Samithi (TRS) MLAs from Warangal who have created a flutter by shooting off an open letter protesting the style of functioning of party president, K. Chandrasekhara Rao continued to remain inaccessible to the leadership.

(4109) Hyderabad : The Telangana Rashtra Samiti (TRS) has threatened to launch direct action, involving farmers of Telangana, if the Government does not drop its plan to deny free power for the rabi crop.

(4110) Vijayawada : In a bid to increase its strength in the city, the Telugu Desam Party (TDP) urban unit has begun poaching into the ruling Congress party ranks.

(4111) Sangareddy : It now seems to be the turn of district-level TRS cadre to criticise their leader and Union Minister K. Chandrasekhar Rao.

(4112) New Delhi : The Centre on Sunday night appointed former diplomat Virendra Dayal as "special envoy" to liaise with the United Nations to "gather relevant materials including those on the unverified references in the [Volcker] Report regarding the involvement of Indian entities and individuals." A separate judicial probe will be announced on Monday.

(4113) Thiruvananthapuram : Communist Party of India (Marxist) State secretary Pinarayi Vijayan has demanded an inquiry by an Assembly committee into the allegations of graft in appointments in the Travancore Devaswom Board (TDB).

(4114) New Delhi : Controversial Rashtriya Janata Dal MP Mohammad Shahabuddin was sent on transit remand of two days after his bail plea was rejected by the Metropolitan Magistrate on Sunday.

(4115) Bangalore: The Bharatiya Janata Party (BJP) is in fear of losing its status as the official Opposition in the Legislative Council following the death of one of its leading lights and one among its senior members M.R. Tanga, who was its Deputy Leader in the House.

(4116) Bangalore : Members of the All-India Congress Committee (AICC) from the State on Sunday unanimously passed a resolution authorising President Sonia Gandhi to constitute the Congress Working Committee (CWC) as required under article 19 of the party constitution.

(4117) Bangalore: Three Congress leaders have sought to make up for the general silence of the party Ministers and leaders on the H.D. Deve

Gowda vs. S.M. Krishna-N.R. Narayana Murthy debate by deploring the fact that it has become personalised and accusations are being levelled.

(4118) Bellary : Leaders of the AHINDA movement who are on a State-wide tour as part of the "Swabhimana Yatra," mounted a scathing attack on the former Prime Minister and Janata Dal (Secular) President H.D. Deve Gowda and accused him of being against Dalits, the backward classes and minorities.

(4119) Thiruvananthapuram : KPCC general secretary M.I. Shanavas has accused the CPI(M) of whipping up communal passions with an eye on the byelection to the Lok Sabha from the Thiruvananthapuram constituency.

(4120) Thiruvananthapuram : The Democratic Indira Congress (Karunakaran) leader T.M. Jacob has said that the Government is withdrawing police cases registered against operators of unauthorised lotteries.

(4121) Thiruvananthapuram : The LDF and the UDF are cheating the people of Thiruvananthapuram by putting up rival candidates for the Lok Sabha bypoll here, BJP leader O. Rajagopal has said.

(4122) New Delhi : The Bharatiya Janata Party (BJP) on Sunday demanded registration of cases against those named in the Volcker committee report. "The findings of the Volcker committee report are sufficient for a strong prima facie case because under the Foreign Contribution Regulation Act (FCRA), no person or political party can accept foreign contributions," BJP general secretary Arun Jaitley told a news conference here.

(4123) Gandhinagar : The police have registered a case of rioting against the Leader of the Opposition in the Gujarat Assembly, Arjun Modhvadia, and 50 other Congress leaders, including four MLAs,for allegedly ransacking the house of a Minister.

(4124) New Delhi : Chhatisgarh Congress Leader Ajit Jogi on Sunday came out in support of External Affairs Minister K. Natwar Singh and attacked the National Democratic Alliance for demanding Mr. Singh's resignation on the basis of the Volcker Committee report.

(4125) Chennai : Dravida Munnetra Kazhagam (DMK) president M. Karunanidhi on Sunday flayed the Bharatiya Janata Party (BJP) for demanding the resignation of External Affairs Minister K. Natwar Singh following the publication of the Volcker report.

(4126) Patna : External Affairs minister Natwar Singh on Sunday received a strong backing from Rashtriya Janata Dal president Lalu Prasad who said Singh should not resign on the "baseless" allegations.

(4127) Patna : The arrest of Rashtriya Janata Dal MP Md. Shahabuddin and the resignation of Union Minister Jai Prakash Narain Yadav seem to have puzzled the National Democratic Alliance leaders about their timing and motives, notwithstanding strong words from RJD supremo and Railway Minister Lalu Prasad.

(4128) Hyderabad : Andhra Pradesh Chief Minister Y.S. Rajasekhara Reddy has condemned the "politically motivated" campaign by the Bharatiya Janata Party (BJP) and a few other Opposition parties against External Affairs Minister K. Natwar Singh.

(4129) Kolkata : Elaborate security arrangements have been made around the Indian Air Force's Kalaikunda base in West Bengal in view of the threat of widespread demonstrations by ruling Left Front supporters against the Indo-U.S. joint exercises, scheduled to be held from November 7-19.

(4130) New Delhi : Janata Party president Subramanian Swamy said on Sunday that he had filed complaints with the Central Bureau of Investigation (CBI), the Directorate of Revenue Intelligence (DRI) and the Union Home Ministry to initiate action against the Congress and External Affairs Minister K. Natwar Singh on the basis of the findings of the Volcker Committee report which probed the United Nations oil-for-food programme in Iraq.

(4131) New Delhi : The continued squabbling within the Bharatiya Janata Party at the national level is having an adverse impact on the functioning of the party and the morale of its cadres in Delhi. The lack of support from the national leadership to agitational programme of the party and its inability to reach out to the people of the Capital on important issues like the power and water and the recent price rise could affect the party's chances in any future electoral battle, feel political observers here.

(4132) Jaipur : Former Rajasthan Chief Minister and Congress general secretary Ashok Gehlot on Sunday said only an enquiry would establish the authenticity of the charges in the Volcker Committee report. "What is going on at present is a media trial," he said.

(4133) Dehra Dun : The N D Tiwari-led Uttaranchal Government today came under attack from ruling Congress MLAs over the issue of rehabilitation of Tehri dam oustees, accusing him of adopting an insensitive attitude.

(4134) Chennai : A meeting of youth, student and volunteer wings of the Marumalarchi Dravida Munnetra Kazhagam (MDMK) here on Sunday demanded that the Centre and State Government create the infrastructure required to help unemployed youth earn a living.

(4135) Chennai : The Opposition have demanded judicial enquiry into the incident leading to the death of six women in Vyasarpadi on Sunday.

(4136) Chennai : The Pattali Makkal Katchi founder, S. Ramadoss, on Saturday said the State Government should make public the names of those responsible for the excesses committed by the Special Task Force, formed to nab the forest brigand Veerappan, and pay compensation to the victims as recommended by the Justice Sadashiva panel.

08-11-2005

(4137) Hyderabad : Three Telangana Rashtra Samithi (TRS) MLAs called on Chief Minister Y.S. Rajasekhara Reddy at the Secretariat on Monday raising several eyebrows.

(4138) Hyderabad : The Telugu Desam Party has faulted the Government for acting hastily with regard to providing 5 per cent reservations to Muslims, and favoured backwardness to be the yardstick for introducing them while the BJP has described the quashing of the ordinance by the Andhra Pradesh High Court as a "slap on the face of the Government."

(4139) Nizamabad : Former Minister and expelled leader from the Telangana Rashtra Samithi (TRS) S. Santosh Reddy has welcomed the present developments in the TRS and described them as a good sign. It will augur well for the Telangana movement, he opines.

(4140) Ongole : CPI State council member P. Lakshminarayana has asked the Government to convene an all-party meet to discuss the far-reaching changes it proposed in village administration and panchayat elections.

(4141) Visakhapatnam : Several Congress leaders on Monday asked the State Government to augment the public distribution system (PDS) by supplying essential commodities to pink card-holders.

(4142) Anantapur : The district unit of Telugu Desam Party (TDP) on Monday criticised the State Government stating that it had issued an ordinance on five per cent reservation to Muslims knowing well that it would not stand the legal and constitutional testimony. The High Court order quashing Muslim reservation had proved that the Government had assured reservation only to deceive the community.

(4143) Patna : A Siwan district court, on Monday, remanded Rashtriya Janata Dal MP Md. Shahabuddin to 14 days judicial custody at the Central Jail, Bhagalpur.

(4144) New Delhi : The two-pronged attack begun on Monday morning by the National Democratic Alliance to take forward its 'Natwar Singh must go' stand on the Volcker Committee report bore fruit by evening when Mr. Singh was divested of the External Affairs portfolio.

(4145) Bangalore: Leader of the Opposition in the Legislative Assembly B.S. Yediyurappa has warned the Government that victims of the heavy rain and floods in urban and rural areas will revolt against it if it fails to give them immediate relief without waiting for Central assistance.

(4146) Bangalore : The Karnataka High Court on Monday ordered issue of notice to the former Prime Minister H.D. Deve Gowda and the Election Commission on a petition by C.M. Ibrahim, former Union Minister, against the grant of the Janata Dal (Secular) flag and symbol to the faction led by Mr. Deve Gowda.

(4147) Hubli : The former Deputy Chief Minister Siddaramaiah has asserted that the financial health of the State remains good despite claims to the contrary made by some leaders of the Janata Dal (S).

(4148) Nanjangud : Working President of the Janata Dal (Secular) H.D. Kumaraswamy said here on Monday that the party will contest all seats in the ensuing zilla panchayat elections and workers at the grassroots level are being galvanised for the purpose.

(4149) New Delhi : The Janata Dal (Secular), headed by the former Prime Minister H.D. Deve Gowda, on Monday told the Election Commission that there was no split in the party since none of the members had been "expelled."

(4150) Kannur : Leader of the Opposition V.S. Achuthanandan has said that the State Government's educational policy of protecting the interests of private managements will reverse the progress of the State.

(4151) Kozhikode : A convention called by a group of Indian Union Muslim League (IUML) dissidents here on Sunday formed an organisation named CH Secular Forum.

(4152) Kozhikode : Leader of the Opposition V.S. Achuthanandan has said that only through concerted and organised protests will the huge mass of employees, in different sectors, be able to earn benefits and sustain them.

(4153) Pathanamthitta : A.K. Antony, MP, has called upon Congress workers to strive for unity in the party.

(4154) Thiruvananthapuram : The Left Democratic Front (LDF) has alleged that a conspiracy had been hatched at the "highest level" of the Government to shield the real culprits behind the attack of the Bishop House at Neyyattinkara on October 17.

(4155) Thiruvananthapuram : The former Electricity Minister Kadavoor Sivadasan on Thursday said that CPI (M) State secretary Pinarayi Vijayan was blaming the UDF Government for inaction in the SNC Lavalin case as he was finding it difficult to take on his colleague V. S. Achuthanandan in the party.

(4156) Thiruvananthapuram : President of the Democratic Indira Congress (Karunakaran) K. Muraleedharan on Monday alleged that the State Government was planning to give sanction to 3,000 unaided schools soon after the Lok Sabha byelection on November 18.

(4157) Aluva : On the anniversary of the October Revolution, a new party named Marxist Communist Party of India (United) was launched here on Monday evening.

(4158) Jaipur: Communist Party of India (Marxist) general secretary Prakash Karat on Monday expressed concern over the increasing "interference" by the United States in India's internal issues. "India is too big a country to be cowed down by the U.S. pressure. We should use our strength to protect the sovereignty of India," he told a public meeting here on the occasion of the inauguration of the newly-built office building of the party.

(4159) New Delhi : The Communist Party of India (Marxist) on Monday termed as a "necessary step" the appointment of Justice R.S. Pathak to look into the issues arising out of the Volcker Committee report and of Virendra Dayal to collect facts and information regarding the references to India in it.

(4160) New Delhi : The Congress on Monday sought a set of papers from United Nations Secretary-General Kofi Annan on the Volcker Committee report and related issues.

(4161) Kolkata : As jets belonging to the United States Air Force and the Indian Air Force (IAF) thundered overhead, supporters of Left parties who had congregated at a site adjoining the IAF base at Kalaikunda in the West Midnapore district waved black flags and shouted slogans on Monday protesting the joint air exercises, COPE India 05, which got underway there in the morning. The exercises will continue till November 19.

(4162) Kolkata : On a day when Left protests marked the commencement of Indo-U.S. military exercises, West Bengal Chief Minister Buddhadeb Bhattacharjee said the State wanted U.S. capital, knowledge and its universities but it was against its weaponry.

(4163) Jaipur: The Communist Party of India (Marxist) on Monday questioned the motive with which the United Nations had set up the Paul Volcker Committee to inquire into the oil-for-food programme in Iraq under the Saddam Hussein regime. "The Volcker Committee itself was the creation of the United States and its Right wing allies who were opposed to the oil-for-food programme," CPI (M) general secretary Prakash Karat said. "Now they want to project the whole programme as a corrupt scheme," he said.

(4164) New Delhi : Delhi Pradesh Congress Committee president Ram Babu Sharma on Monday handed over Rs. 71 lakhs as the party's contribution towards the relief fund for the earthquake victims of Jammu and Kashmir to the All-India Congress Committee treasurer, Moti Lal Vora.

(4165) Bhopal : The Congress party held protest demonstrations across 487 blocks of Madhya Pradesh on Monday to protest against "failure" of the Bharatiya

(4166) Jaipur: In a novel initiative, former Rajasthan Chief Minister and Congress general secretary Ashok Gehlot on Sunday collected Rs.16 lakhs towards relief for the earthquake-affected people in Jammu and Kashmir.

(4167) Chennai : Communist Party of India (Marxist) State secretary N. Varadarajan on Monday said the Government's "failure" to make proper arrangements for distribution of flood relief had resulted in the death of six women in a stampede at Vyasarpadi here on Sunday.

(4168) Chennai : The Dravida Munnetra Kazhagam on Monday demanded formation of State and district level all-party committees to oversee distribution of relief to the flood affected.

09-11-2005

(4169) Anantapur : The cries of hunger and suicide by farmers have become routine in Anantapur district due to severe drought year after year, CPI (M) Rajya Sabha member P. Madhu has observed.

(4170) Hyderabad : Even as the four defiant Telangana Rashtra Samiti MLAs from Warangal continued to adopt a tough posture and refused to yield to pleas from party leaders, Union Minister of State for Rural Development, A. Narendra, is likely to visit Warangal on Wednesday to find a way to end the crisis.

(4171) Hyderabad : The Majlis-e-Ittehadul Muslimeen has planned to hold a protest meeting in connection with the quashing of the Government Order on reservations for Muslims in jobs and educational institutions by the High Court. The meeting will be held at the Khilwat ground near Charminar next Sunday.

(4172) Karimnagar : The Telugu Desam Party has asked the State Government not to divert Godavari water from Telangana region to other parts of the State and take up the Yellampalli, SRSP flood canal, Devadula, Pranahita and Inchampalli projects to provide irrigation to Telangana.

(4173) Visakhapatnam : Speakers at the Communist Party of India (CPI) anniversary celebrations here on Monday dwelt at length on the influence of the Russian revolution in October 1917, which triggered the struggle against poverty, corruption, social oppression and economic imbalance in many parts of the world.

(4174) Kadapa : Farmers led by Bharatiya Janata Party leader K. Balachandra Reddy launched a 100-km padayatra from Proddatur town to Kadapa Collectorate on Tuesday, demanding increase in capacity of the Pothireddipadu head regulator to 75,000 cusecs.

(4175) Kadapa : CPI functionaries staged dharna before the Collectorate on Tuesday demanding expeditious disbursement of relief to flood-hit families in Kadapa town.

(4176) Bangalore: The Bharatiya Janata Party has named leaders in districts to make preparations for its campaign for the zilla and taluk panchayat elections.

(4177) Gulbarga : The Janata Dal (United) on Monday alleged that an Andhra Pradesh-based seed company was using children as bonded labourers in agricultural lands taken on lease by them in the villages in Sedam taluk.

(4178) Hubli : The former Deputy Chief Minister Siddaramaiah on Tuesday termed the critical remarks made by Finance Minister P.G.R. Sindhia as not only irresponsible but also uncalled for.

(4179) Mangalore : Karnataka Pradesh Congress Committee (KPCC) President M. Mallikarjun Kharge said here on Tuesday that the Congress had given land ownership rights to tenants in the coastal and Malnad regions by implementing the Land Reforms Act. He said families, which benefited from the initiative, must remember this.

(4180) Tumkur : Senior Congress leaders here on Tuesday called for an end to coalition politics which, they said, is "harming the interests of the State."

(4181) Karwar : The former Deputy Chief Minister Siddaramaih has alleged that the former Prime Minister and Janata Dal (Secular) President H.D. Deve Gowda has been trying to create rift among leaders of AHINDA (Alpasankyataru, Hindulidavaru mattu Dalitaru) movement to destroy it.

(4182) Thiruvananthapuram : President of the Kerala Pradesh Congress Committee (KPCC) Ramesh Chennithala on Tuesday alleged that the CPI (M) leadership, under its State secretary Pinarayi Vijayan, was bent on converting Kannur into a terror district. He also accused Mr.Vijayan of criminalising politics in the State and spreading the Kannur brand of violence to other parts of the State.

(4183) Thiruvananthapuram : Leader of the Opposition V.S. Achuthanandan has taken strong exception to the Forest Department's failure to initiate stern action against a city hotel that had advertised the sale of dishes made of game meat.

(4184) Thiruvananthapuram : KPCC president Ramesh Chennithala on Tuesday gave a clean chit to Tourism Devaswom Minister K.C. Venugopal in the controversy relating to the BOT proposal for Sabarimala development. He also welcomed the Government's decision to put off temporarily the recruitment in the Tranvancore Devaswom Board.

(4185) Thiruvananthapuram : Congress(S) State president Ramachandran Kadannappally has said that his party is firmly with the Opposition Left Democratic Front (LDF).

(4186) New Delhi : The Opposition on Tuesday sharpened its attack on the Congress with National Democratic Alliance (NDA) convenor and Janata Dal (United) president George Fernandes demanding the resignation of Sonia Gandhi as chairperson of the National Advisory Council in the wake of the Volcker report on the Oil-for-Food scandal. "If Natwar Singh deserved to be deprived of his portfolio, surely, Sonia Gandhi cannot hold on to her responsibilities currently supported by the public exchequer," Mr. Fernandes told a press conference here.

(4187) New Delhi : Bharatiya Janata Party general secretary Arun Jaitley on Tuesday charged the United Progressive Alliance Government with trying to do a "cover-up job" to prevent the truth from coming out about "involvement" of the former External Affairs Minister, Natwar Singh, and the Congress in the oil-for-food programme.

(4188) Kolkata : West Bengal Chief Minister Buddhadeb Bhattacharjee on Tuesday criticised Left Front demonstrators, who on Monday blocked the arterial VIP Road to protest against the India-U.S. air exercise at Kalaikunda air base. Mr. Bhattacharjee said the protesters had not acted responsibly.

(4189) New Delhi : The Left parties, increasing their pressure on the Government ahead of the next month's World Trade Organisation ministerial conference in Hong Kong, have decided to organise a campaign on the basis of a note they had submitted to the Government.

(4190) Chandigarh : Though Delhi is the main scene of action over the fall out of the Volcker Committee report sparks are flying in Punjab's political arena as well. While Chief Minister Amarinder Singh has rubbished the allegations against his family, the Shiromani Akali Dal has sought a "deeper probe" in the light of "fresh evidence."

(4191) New Delhi : Union Minister K. Natwar Singh said on Tuesday that he would not succumb to allegations levelled against him by the Opposition and respond to them in Parliament. A day after he was relieved of his charge as the External Affairs Minister, in the wake of the Volcker Committee report that made a reference to him in the oil-for-food contracts in Iraq, Mr. Singh said he was happy that the Centre had instituted an inquiry into it.

(4192) Shimla : The Himachal unit BJP president and Rajya Sabha member Suresh Bhardwaj has demanded a comprehensive CBI probe into the "appointments on chits" scam instead of a vigilance enquiry.

(4193) Pondicherry: Leader of the Opposition in the Pondicherry Assembly, R.V. Janakiraman (Dravida Munnetra Kazhagam), has urged the Government to raise the cash relief proposed for the rain-ravaged families in Pondicherry and Karaikal regions from Rs. 500 to 1000.

(4194) Jaipur: The Congress has held the "neglect '' of the energy sector by the Bharatiya Janata Party-led Government in the State responsible for the current power crisis in Rajasthan. The BJP Government, which assumed office two years ago, has not done anything to improve the power generation capacity in the State, instead energy losses from theft and leakages have gone up, the Congress has alleged. The party has threatened to launch an agitation if the power situation does not improve during the current rabi season.

(4195) Jaipur: Rajasthan Chief Minister Vasundhara Raje greeted Bharatiya Janata Party president L.K. Advani on his 79th birthday on Tuesday. On behalf of Ms.Raje, Rajasthan's Resident Commissioner in Delhi, Neelkamal Darbari, presented a bouquet to Mr.Advani at his official residence on Prithviraj Road in New Delhi.

(4196) Cuddalore : The Communist Party of India (Marxist) has alleged that the authorities had underplayed the recent flood damage to create an impression that the situation was under control.

(4197) Chennai : Communist Party of India (Marxist) general secretary Prakash Karat said on Tuesday that his party did not accept the Volcker Committee's findings at face value.

10-11-2005

(4198) Hyderabad : The State unit of the BJP has criticised both the Congress and Telugu Desam Party for adopting different and contradictory stands on irrigation projects, use of river waters and fiscal reforms while in power and out of it. It objected to the TDP decision to organise protest on the irrigation projects and accused it of rousing people for political gains.

(4199) Hyderabad : The Congress Legislature Party (CLP) has taken objection to humiliation of Warangal Collector Benhur Mahesh Ekka allegedly by TDP leaders saying such a bad treatment of a tribal official invited severe action.

(4200) Hyderabad : TDP president N. Chandrababu Naidu on Wednesday evening avoided attending the wedding of son of Home Minister K. Jana Reddy, ostensibly to register his protest against the arrest of party's deputy leader T. Devender Goud and others in Adilabad.

(4201) Srikakulam : TDP MLA and its deputy leader in the Asssembly Kimidi Kala Venkata Rao on Wednesday charged the Y.S. Rajasekhara Reddy Government with following fascist methods to browbeat opposition leaders, citing the arrest of TDP leaders in Warangal as an example.

(4202) Warangal : The rebel MLAs of the Telangana Rasthra Samithi (TRS) have reiterated that they will not join any other party, including the Congress, and demanded that party president K. Chandrasekhara Rao say openly whether the issues being raised by them are irrelevant.

(4203) Adilabad : Rumours are rife about the likelihood of Union Labour Minister and Telangana Rashtra Samithi (TRS) president K. Chandrasekhar Rao and Union Minister of State for Rural Development A. Narendra resigning their posts to "strengthen the party," according to sources.

(4204) Kadapa : Telugu Desam Party leaders on Wednesday charged Chief Minister Y.S. Rajasekhara Reddy with inciting regional conflicts over utilisation of Krishna water in the State.

(4205) Karimnagar : The Warangal district police with the help of the Karimnagar police arrested five TDP senior leaders- TDLP deputy leader T. Devender Goud, former Minister Kadiam Srihari, legislators Errabelli Dayakara Rao and Sana Maruthi and former Minister S. Veugopala Chary- near the NTPC, Ramagundam, on Wednesday evening.

(4206) Chennai : The Pattali Makkal Katchi (PMK), which is campaigning against the concept of unbridled freedom enjoyed by self-financing engineering colleges while giving admissions and fixing the fee structure, has come up with an alternative legislation on private professional educational institutions.

(4207) Mangalore : B. Janardhana Poojary, Rajya Sabha member and former president of Karnataka Pradesh Congress Committee, on Tuesday urged naxalites to lay down arms and join mainstream society.

(4208) Mysore : Former Union Minister V. Srinivas Prasad has announced his decision to quit the Janata Dal (Secular).

(4209) Chikmagalur : Chief Minister N. Dharam Singh has said that the proposed "surrender package" for Maoists is only for fresh recruits and not for hardcore naxalites who have committed heinous offences.

(4210) Kannur : The Left Democratic Front (LDF) has accused the United Democratic Front (UDF) of trying to tarnish the image of Kannur through a campaign that the Communist Party of India-Marxist (CPI-M) is making the district a land of terror. The LDF says it is prepared to face an independent inquiry into the allegation.

(4211) Thiruvananthapuram : Leader of the Opposition V.S. Achuthanandan has alleged a major bid by the R.P. Goenka group to sell thousands of acres of land that the erstwhile Travancore sovereign had allotted on lease to Malayalam Plantations Limited for cultivating tea and cashew.

(4212) Nedumbassery : Janata Party president Subramaniam Swamy has asked Sonia Gandhi to step down as chairperson of the United

Progressive Alliance in the wake of the Volcker Report on the United Nations' Oil-For-Food-Programme.

(4213) Jaipur: The former Foreign Minister and BJP leader, Jaswant Singh, on Wednesday accused the UPA Government of "twisting and ridiculing" the foreign policy in a bid to "protect" a political party named in the Volcker Committee report as a beneficiary of Iraqi oil pay-offs.

(4214) Chandigarh/New Delhi : Prime Minister Manmohan Singh on Wednesday denied that the Government had delayed action against the former External Affairs Minister, Natwar Singh, in the wake of references in the Volcker Committee report on the oil-for-food contracts in Iraq, even as the Congress rejected a suggestion by the Opposition that Sonia Gandhi should resign as chairperson of the National Advisory Council.

(4215) New Delhi : With the Union Cabinet all set to finalise the terms of reference of the Justice R.C. Pathak inquiry into the Volcker Committee's allegations, the BJP demanded on Wednesday that the probe must not be confined to the role of Hamdan Exports and should be armed with all the powers of a statutory inquiry.

(4216) New Delhi : Delhi Chief Minister Sheila Dikshit's meeting with Congress president Sonia Gandhi on Tuesday morning before her departure for Spain sparked off rumours in political and administration circles about Ms. Dikshit's future in Delhi and her possible induction into the Union Cabinet. At the end of the day, it turned out to be nothing but speculation.

(4217) Pondicherry: The secretary of the Pondicherry unit of the Communist Party of India (Marxist) V. Perumal has asked the Government to translate all the announcements made for relief measures in rain-hit areas into action.

(4218) Chennai : A group of eight young American political leaders, sponsored by the American Council of Young Political Leaders (ACYPL), met Dravida Munnetra Kazhagam president M. Karunanidhi and TNCC president G.K. Vasan, as part of their understanding of the politics and issues in this region.

(4219) Salem : The Salem district unit of the Janata Dal (Secular) criticised the State Government for not taking any serious steps on the requests seeking appointment of an IAS officer as Commissioner of the Salem Corporation.

11-11-2005

(4220) Hyderabad : The Telugu Desam Legislature Party on Thursday said the arrest of the party leaders reminded it of Emergency days when the Government tried to control people and their right to expression.

(4221) Hyderabad : The State BJP and several Backward Classes organisations have demanded withdrawal of G.O. 23 deleting some communities from the BC list.

(4222) Hyderabad : In what appears to be a relief for the Telangana Rashtra Samiti, rebel MLAs who took pot-shots at the party president, K. Chandrasekhar Rao's style of functioning, have decided to participate in the 'rasta roko' programme in protest against the Government's decision on free power during rabi at all divisional headquarters in Telangana on Friday.

(4223) Hyderabad : The Congress Legislature Party (CLP) has accused the Telugu Desam Party (TDP) of trying to derive political mileage by blaming Chief Minister Y. S. Rajasekhara Reddy for the arrest of TDP leaders in connection with the alleged abuse of Warangal Collector Benhur Ekka.

(4224) Khammam : The CPI has resolved to intensify its agitation to mount pressure on the Government for construction of the Dummugudem lift scheme on the Godavari and for opposing large-scale displacement by the proposed Polavaram project on the same river.

(4225) Vijayawada : A delegation of the Telugu Desam Party (TDP) submitted a memorandum to district Collector Navin Mittal, demanding payment of compensation to farmers in the flood-hit areas in the district.

(4226) Sangareddy : Peeved by stubborn attitude of the party president, T. Jayaprakash Reddy, Sangareddy MLA, on Thursday said that he would take the issue to people of Telangana. However he did not elaborate on how he plans to do it.

(4227) Warangal : All the 14 TDP leaders who have been arrested or who have surrendered on the basis of a case filed against them by the police following the filing of a complaint by the Warangal Collector charging them with obstructing officials on duty have been granted bail except Mandava Venkateswar Rao who is yet to present himself before the Magistrate concerned.

(4228) Bangalore: The resignation of the Bharatiya Janata Party member M. Rajasekhara Murthy from the Rajya Sabha brings to an end perhaps the longest period of political brinkmanship.

(4229) Gulbarga : The Republican Party of India (Atwale) has completed one round of discussions with like-minded parties, including the Janata Dal (Secular) faction led by the former Deputy Chief Minister Siddaramaiah, the Samajwadi Party and the Janata Dal (United), for working out an alliance to contest the coming elections to the zilla and taluk panchayats.

(4230) Madikeri: The two-year wait for C.S. Arun Machaiah, MLC, a youth leader who represents the local bodies in Kodagu, is over as he is set to join the Janata Dal (S) at its national executive in Bangalore on Sunday.

(4231) Mysore : The former Minister M. Shivanna has claimed that the Congress will gain from the rift in the Janata Dal (Secular) on account of the action against the former Deputy Chief Minister Siddaramaiah by the party.

(4232) Kozhikode : A revolt has broken out in Congress(S). State president Ramachandran Kadannappally has been sacked from his post for campaigning for the LDF candidate in the byelection from Thiruvananthapuram Lok Sabha constituency, flouting the decision of the party working committee to boycott LDF campaign.

(4233) Thiruvananthapuram : State president of the BJP P. S. Sreedharan Pillai on Thursday said the decision of the Congress to call a 'Pouravakasa Samrakshana Sangamam' (Save Citizen's Rights Meet) in Thiruvananthapuram on Friday "should rank as the biggest joke of the year."

(4234) Thiruvananthapuram : Deputy general secretary of the Communist Party of India D. Raja has said that though the Left is ready for a dialogue with the Government on the sale of a small portion of the stake in non-Navaratna public sector units, this should not be construed as some commitment on the issue.

(4235) New Delhi : The Congress Steering Committee on Thursday mourned the death of former President K.R. Narayanan and conveyed its condolences to his wife Usha Narayanan and the other members of his family.

(4236) Bhopal : Following the high-pitched demand raised by a section of MLAs led by former Chief Minister Uma Bharti for immediate removal of Chief Minister Babulal Gaur, majority of ruling party legislators have now taken the stand that the party should settle the leadership issue once for all and without any delay.

(4237) Cheenai : The State council of the Communist Party of India (Marxist) has urged the State Government to constitute an all-party committee to supervise and expedite flood relief works in the city and in other affected areas in the State.

(4238) Chennai : The group of young political leaders from the United States, who are here as part of an American Council of Young Political Leaders (ACYPL) team, on Thursday met Marumalarchi Dravida Munnetra Kazhagam general secretary Vaiko and visited a home for HIV/AIDS children.

12-11-2005

(4239) Hyderabad : Telangana Rashtra Samithi (TRS) workers organised dharna and staged rasta roko at various centres in Telangana districts on Friday in protest against the move of the Government to discontinue free power scheme in the rabi.

(4240) Karimnagar : "Is it right to arrest all the Telugu Desam Party leaders when one of the leaders abuses the Warangal district Collector?" questioned Minister for Sports and Culture M. Satyanarayana Rao here on Friday.

(4241) Hyderabad : Telugu Desam Party (TDP) leaders said they would not be cowed down by "intimidatory tactics" adopted by Government.

(4242) Puttaparthi : Meanwhile, APCC president K. Keshava Rao has said that TRS president and Union Minister K. Chandrasekhar Rao has no sincerity in the movement for separate Telangana.

(4243) Hyderabad : Expelled Telangana Rashtra Samithi (TRS) MLA S. Santosh Reddy was re-inducted into the party amid high drama here on Friday.

(4244) **Bangalore:** The former Prime Minister H.D. Deve Gowda has said that the real intention of the Siddararamaiah group in filing an application before the Election Commission to be recognised as the real Janata Dal (Secular) is to create confusion in the minds of the party workers and the people.

(4245) **Bangalore:** The first-ever plenary session of the Janata Dal (Secular), preceded by a meeting of the national executive of the party, is to be held here over the weekend. At the session, the party will declare that it is the "real JD(S)", and former Deputy Chief Minister Siddaramaiah's supporters are a splinter group.

(4246) **Bidar:** The Janata Dal (United) will enter into pre-poll alliances with the former Deputy Chief Minister Siddaramaiah's faction of the Janata Dal (Secular), the Samajwadi Party, the Bahujan Samaj Party and the Sarvodaya Karnataka Party for the zilla and taluk panchayat elections. "That means any party excluding the coalition partners and the Bharatiya Janata Party," vice-president of the party's State unit Basavaraj Ingin told presspersons here on Friday. He said the Janata Dal (U) will not enter into an alliance with the Congress, the Deve Gowda faction of the Janata Dal (S) or the BJP, as they are "anti-progress."

(4247) **Hassan :** Underlining the importance of introducing reservation in the private sector, the former Prime Minister and Janata Dal (Secular) President H.D. Deve Gowda said it is imperative for both the Union and State governments to take a policy decision in this regard.

(4248) **Hubli :** Jagadish Shettar, President of the State unit of the Bharatiya Janata Party, has asked Finance Minister P.G.R. Sindhia to resign in view of his recent comments regarding the budget tabled by former Deputy Chief Minister Siddaramaiah.

(4249) **Madikeri:** The Kodagu Janata Dal, led by former Minister, M.C. Nanaiah, has decided to align with the Janata Dal (S) Siddaramaiah group, and the one led by C.S. Arun Machaiah, MLC, to contest the forthcoming zilla and taluk panchayat elections. It was decided at a meeting in Gonicoppa on Friday, sources told The Hindu on Friday. Mr. Nanaiah told presspersons that the decision was taken based on the opinion of his supporters to keep away from the BJP and the Congress. The Nanaiah group would contest six of the 29 zilla panchayat seats in the district. The candidates are Kallichanda Vishnu from Balele, A.S. Shantu Appaiah from Gonicoppa, Moinuddin from Kakotparambu, Kodira Praveen Chengappa from Kadnur, M.N. Subhash from Ammathi and Biddatanda Bopanna from Napoklu.

(4250) Chikmagalur : C.T. Ravi, MLA and president of the State unit of the BJP Yuva Morcha, has ridiculed Chief Minister N.Dharam Singh's surrender package for naxalites.

(4251) Kannur : Communist Party of India (Marxist) Polit Bureau member Brinda Karat said here on Friday that there was a need to put pressure on the United Progressive Alliance Government to bring in legislation to ensure that higher education came under social control.

(4252) Kochi : The Congress (S) has not split, N.U. Pradeep Kumar, general secretary of the party, told presspersons here on Friday.

(4253) Kochi : United Democratic Front (UDF) convener P.P. Thankachan has said that misleading information pertaining to the Lavalin case was being circulated by the Communist Party of India (Marxist) (CPI(M).

(4254) Kolkata : Veteran Marxist leader Jyoti Basu on Friday scoffed at a BJP demand that Congress president Sonia Gandhi be removed from the post of the Chairperson of the National Advisory Council in connection with the Volcker Report on the Iraqi oil-for-food scam.

(4255) New Delhi : The Congress on Friday continued its attack against the Mulayam Singh Yadav Government alleging that the law and order situation in the State had deteriorated.

(4256) Chapra : Congress president Sonia Gandhi on Friday alleged that the BJP-led National Democratic Alliance (NDA) regime had landed the country in a communal whirlpool.

(4257) Patna : BJP president L.K. Advani on Friday alleged that the United Progressive Alliance Government at the Centre had backtracked on its assurance to set up a judicial commission to go into the Volcker Report. He told reporters here that the Pathak Committee would not be able to do justice to the task.

(4258) New Delhi : The opposition Bharatiya Janata Party in the Municipal Corporation of Delhi has accused the ruling Congress of failing to provide uniforms and other articles meant for winter to almost 4 lakh children studying in municipal primary schools. Alleging gross negligence on the part of the municipal authorities, the BJP has demanded strict action against the Congress leaders in the civic body and the officials concerned.

(4259) New Delhi : The President has appointed Justice Subray Rama Nayak, Judge of the Karnataka High Court, as the new Chief Justice of the Chhattisgarh High Court with effect from the date he assumes charge of office.

(4260) Jaipur : The former vice-chairman of Rajasthan's 20-Point Programme Implementation Committee, Chandraraj Singhvi, joined the Bahujan Samaj Party on Saturday. Mr.Singhvi, who was expelled from primary membership of the Bharatiya Janata Party on charges of indiscipline last week, said he was quitting the BJP in "disgust".

(4261) Dehra Dun : With water level continuing to rise in Bhagirathi reservoir of 2400 mw Tehri hydel project, Uttaranchal NCP President Surya Kant Dhasmana today said rehabilitation work is far from over in Tehri district and the issue would be taken up at the Centre by party President Sharad Pawar.

(4262) Chennai : Congress Legislature Party (CLP) leader S.R. Balasubramoniyan on Friday pleaded with Governor Surjit Singh Barnala to seek a "status report" on the case relating to housebreaking at his Kilpauk residence on October 1.

(4263) Chennai : Tamil Nadu Congress Committee president G.K. Vasan has urged the State Government to sanction Rs. 5,000 per acre as compensation to delta farmers whose paddy crop has been lost in the recent rain.

13-11-2005

(4264) Karimnagar : APSRTC chairman Gone Prakash Rao has launched a scathing attack against former Minister and TDLP deputy leader T. Devender Goud for making false and baseless allegations against Chief Minister Y. S. Rajashekhara Reddy.

(4265) Vijayawada : Communist Party of India (CPI) floor leader in the Assembly Chada Venkata Reddy on Saturday felt that there was no difference between the Congress and the TDP in implementing reforms in the power sector. "The TDP has lost its ground in the State by implementing the reforms. Ironically, the Congress does not seem to have learnt any lessons from the TDP's experience," he said while addressing the first State-level conference of the AP Electricity Staff and Workers' Union (APES&WU), an affiliated body of the AITUC.

(4266) Visakhapatnam : Speakers at a round table on 'Comprehensive development of Visakhapatnam,' organised by the Communist Party of India (Marxist) on Saturday came out with several suggestions for achieving the goal.

(4267) Kakinada : Vociferous scenes were witnessed at the District Review Committee here on Saturday on the issue pertaining to acquisition of lands for the ONGC refinery and Special Economic Zone (SEZ).

(4268) Bangalore : The first plenary session of the Janata Dal (Secular), to be held here on Sunday, is expected to set the trend for a fresh round of political re-grouping. The party may spell out a new political and economic philosophy that is different from that of the United Progressive Alliance and the National Democratic Alliance.

(4269) Bangalore : The State unit of Janata Dal (United) has criticised the Government for fixing the base auction price of land and machinery of the New Government Electric Factory (NGEF) at Rs. 737 crores and demanded that the price be revised to Rs. 1,500 crores.

(4270) Bidar : Senior vice-president of the Janata Dal (United) Basavaraj Ingin has alleged that former Prime Minister H.D. Deve Gowda forced the Government to exclude north Karnataka districts from the National Horticulture Mission Authority's assistance scheme.

(4271) Shimoga : Leader of the Opposition in the Legislative Council D.H. Shankaramurthy said here on Friday that his party will put up an impressive show in the coming elections to the taluk and zilla panchayats.

(4272) Kozhikode : The Kozhikode district committee of the Kerala Pradesh Congress Minority Cell has submitted a memorandum to the Commission appointed by the Prime Minister to prepare a report on the social, economic and education status of Muslim Community in India, that the Muslims in Kerala, especially those in the Malabar region are backward in aspects of education and profession.

(4273) Thiruvananthapuram : R. Balakrishna Pillai has been re-elected the chairman of the Kerala Congress(B). The State committee, elected on the basis of the membership from 2005 to 2008, also elected Paul Joseph as the vice-chairman. The chairman later nominated K.B. Ganesh Kumar, C. Venugopalan Nair and K.G. Kuttan Nair as general secretaries and K.K. Cheriyan, K. Bhageerathan, Ajith Kumar, V.S. Manoj Kumar and Brijesh Abraham as secretaries. - Special Correspondent

(4274) **Thiruvananthapuram :** BJP vice-president M. Venkaiah Naidu on Saturday called for a criminal investigation into accusations against Union Minister Natwar Singh and the Congress in the Volcker Committee report.

(4275) **Thiruvananthapuram :** KPCC president Ramesh Chennithala has criticised the CPI(M) decision to organise employees in the IT sector on trade union basis.

(4276) **Thiruvananthapuram :** C.K. Padmanabhan, BJP candidate in the byelection from Thiruvananthapuram Lok Sabha constituency, is known for his moderate views and affable leadership. Hailing from a communist family, Mr. Padmanabhan plunged into right wing politics late in the sixties and rose to be president of the State unit of the BJP in 1998. The BJP chose him as the candidate after veteran O. Rajagopal, who had contested from Thiruvananthapuram constituency unsuccessfully three times, expressed his unwillingness to be a candidate. Mr. Padmanabhan spoke to The Hindu about his campaign and election plank a day after submitting his nomination. Excerpts from the interview.

(4277) **New Delhi :** The Bharatiya Janata Party (BJP) on Saturday said restraint should be maintained while commenting on the judiciary, the executive and the legislature.

(4278) **New Delhi :** PTL claimed their investigations revealed that data was transferred to one M/s Telequest Systems. One of the partners, Biplab Saha, who had been with M/s PTL since November 2001, was the team leader for data management. He left the company a few months before the loss was discovered.

(4279) **Madurai :** The Central Bureau of Investigation should file a first information report (FIR) on the references made in the Volcker Committee Report, said Janata Party president Subramanian Swamy here on Saturday.

(4280) New Delhi : The Bharatiya Janata Party has said the Justice Pathak Inquiry Authority, set up to probe payoffs in the oil-for-food programme, lacked adequate powers to collect evidence from outside India and hence, would never be able to substantiate conclusively whether any Indian entity had paid or received money pertaining to the two specified contracts in favour of the Congress or the former External Affairs Minister, Natwar Singh.

14-11-2005

(4281) Hyderabad : Andhra Pradesh Congress Committee president K. Keshava Rao has said that the party would join the anti-sorcery drive in rural areas of the State.

(4282) Hyderabad : The Telugu Desam Party has demanded that the Government take immediate steps to scrap its orders (GO Ms 23) issued to Backward Classes Commission to ascertain the status of certain BC communities, as it is aimed at delisting some of the communities from the BC list.

(4283) Hyderabad : The Congress Legislature Party (CLP) has accused Telugu Desam of shedding crocodile tears for backward classes, who were completely neglected during its nine-year rule.

(4284) Godavarikhani (Karimnagar) : The opposition Telugu Desam Party and the BJP representatives alleged neglect of irrigation projects in Telangana region by the State Government at an open debate organised to discuss about the progress of ongoing Yellampalli (Sripadasagar) project here at NTPC township on Sunday evening.

(4285) Lucknow : The Left parties on Sunday told the United Progressive Alliance (UPA) Government to change its stand on the Iran nuclear issue, or they would raise the matter in Parliament and put the "government in the dock."

(4286) Jammu : Bringing an end to several days of suspense, two MLAs of the Bhim Singh-led Jammu and Kashmir National Panthers Party are all set to form a separate outfit.

(4287) Hyderabad : The joy in the Telangana Rashtra Samithi over the return of expelled MLA S. Santosh Reddy to the party fold proved to be short-lived as eight other legislators plunged the party into a fresh crisis by shooting off an 'open letter' to party president K. Chandrasekhar Rao. They, in unequivocal terms, demanded his response publicly to issues raised in it.

(4288) Bangalore : The former Prime Minister H.D. Deve Gowda, who was on Sunday re-elected president of the Janata Dal (Secular), said that his party will not destabilise the coalition Government in Karnataka.

(4289) Bangalore : The Janata Dal (Secular) on Sunday reinforced its pro-rural, pro-grassroots image by announcing its policy to strengthen the "new radical politics" that argues for empowerment of the local bodies (the three tiers of the panchayat raj system).

(4290) Gulbarga : Chief Minister N. Dharam Singh on Sunday disputed the statement of Janata Dal (S) supremo H.D. Deve Gowda on coalition politics and maintained that the coalition arrangements at the Centre and in the State were functioning well.

(4291) Raichur : The Bahujan Samaj Party (BSP) has threatened to stage a dharna if the Government fails to initiate action to supersede the Raichur City Municipal Council within a week.

(4292) Tumkur : The Janata Dal (United) has accused the Congress, Janata Dal (Secular) factions and the Bharatiya Janata Party (BJP) of ignoring people's problems and going ahead with elections to zilla and taluk panchayats.

(4293) Thiruvananthapuram : Taking its anti-CPI(M) campaign a step further, the Congress-led United Democratic Front (UDF) on Sunday paraded 'victims of political violence in Kannur' at its Civil Rights Protection Conclave here.

(4294) Thiruvananthapuram : The Congress leader Vayalar Ravi, MP, has accused the CPI(M) of highhandedness in its functioning, acting as if elections are a cakewalk for the party and the Left Democratic Front.

(4295) Thiruvananthapuram : BJP leader Sushma Swaraj has said that the State Government should provide free medical aid to 15-month-old Reshmi who has been found to be HIV infected, allegedly after a blood transfusion given to her two days after her birth, at SAT Hospital here.

(4296) Chennai : Peter Alphonse, member of the Tamil Nadu Congress Committee, called the Right to Information Act an achievement of the United

Progressive Alliance government capable of charting out a new chapter of governance.

(4297) Chennai : Chairperson of the United Progressive Alliance Sonia Gandhi has expressed happiness over the completion of all formalities for declaring Tamil as a Classical Language.

15-11-2005

(4298) Hyderabad : TDP president and former Chief Minister N. Chandrababu Naidu called upon children to dream and work towards fulfilling their dreams.

(4299) Hyderabad : Telugu Desam Legislature Party (TDLP) has taken exception to the way Chief Minister Y. S. Rajasekhara Reddy had admonished irrigation engineers publicly while reviewing the works at Velugonda project in Prakasam district on Sunday.

(4300) Ongole : Bharatiya Janata Party State president N. Indrasena Reddy has criticised the Government for creating confusion among people with its hasty decisions on linking gas supply with ration cards, and on denying free power to farmers for raising paddy in the rabi season.

(4301) Vijayawada : The Communist Party of India (CPI) will insist that the United Progressive Alliance (UPA) Government implement the National Common Minimum Programme (NCMP) in its "letter and spirit" and that it consults the Left parties before taking decisions on related subjects in the winter session of Parliament, according to party's national secretariat member Suravaram Sudhakar Reddy.

(4302) Sangareddy : Dissident TRS legislators have decided to meet UPA chairperson Sonia Gandhi to find out her stand on the issue of statehood to Telangana.

(4303) New Delhi : Bharatiya Janata Party president L.K. Advani on Monday made it clear that he was firm on his decision to quit his post next month. - UNI

(4304) Bangalore : The Congress on Monday blamed its coalition partner in Karnataka, the Janata Dal (Secular), for the delay in obtaining clearance from the Union Government for the proposed Bangalore metro rail project.

(4305) Bellary : Anil Lad, Kudligi MLA, has expressed unhappiness over the treatment being meted out to him by State BJP leaders.

(4306) Gulbarga : The district unit of Janata Dal (United) on Sunday accused Chief Minister N. Dharam Singh of neglecting the Jewargi Assembly constituency, which has elected him to the Assembly for the last eight terms.

(4307) Hassan : Janata Dal (Secular) State Working President H.D. Kumaraswamy on Monday accused the Information Minister B. Shivaram of misusing the official machinery in Chikmagalur district to ensure the success of the Congress in the zilla and taluk panchayat elections.

(4308) Mangalore : Jagadish Shettar, President of the Bharatiya Janata Party (BJP) State unit, has expressed confidence that party workers will get their act together in the run-up to the zilla and taluk panchayat elections.

(4309) Alappuzha : A group of office-bearers of the Revolutionary Socialist Party in the district led by party central committee member V.Mohan Das has quit the party alleging that the State and the district leadership of the party were victimising party leaders and workers by raising baseless agitations.

(4310) Kozhikode : The annual general council meeting of the National Development Front (NDF) Keralam, held at Manjeri on November 12 and 13, has said that the Centre should take the initiative to reconstruct the Babri Masjid.

(4311) Kolkata : Anil Biswas, member of the Polit Bureau of the Communist Party of India (Marxist), filed a criminal defamation case here on Monday against Congress MP Adhir Chowdhury for comments about him made in an interview to a private television news channel in New Delhi.

(4312) New Delhi : The Bharatiya Janata Party on Monday demanded the resignations of Union Home Minister Shivraj Patil and Bihar Governor Buta Singh citing "complete failure" of the State Government under the President's rule to stop or tackle the naxalite attack at Jehanabad on Sunday.

(4313) New Delhi : Warning against violation of the guidelines on the code of ethics and austerity issued by the Delhi Pradesh Congress Committee, the Ethics Committee has asked all the party workers and leaders to come out with their annual assessments and valuation reports at the earliest and comply with the directives issued by Congress president Sonia Gandhi.

(4314) Lucknow : Uttar Pradesh Minister for Parliamentary Affairs and senior Samajwadi Party leader Mohammed Azam Khan today appealed to the Centre to restore the minority status of the Aligarh Muslim University.

(4315) Chennai : The Bharatiya Janata Party will raise the Volcker Committee report controversy in the coming winter session of Parliament, party vice-president M. Venkaiah Naidu, said on Monday.

(4316) Salem : Pattali Makkal Katchi (PMK) has warned that it had to resort to a series of agitations to protest the inordinate delay in sanctioning a school building for the Bharathinagar Maniyanur Panchayat Union School here.

(4317) Tuticorin : N. Varadharajan, State secretary of the CPI(M), said the party has a prima facie suspicion about the revelations of the Volcker Committee, which made references to the then External Affairs Minister Natwar Singh and the Congress as beneficiaries of the pay-offs in the United Nation oil-for-food programme in Iraq.

16-11-2005

(4318) Hyderabad : The BJP has demanded seizure of the passports of Congress president Sonia Gandhi and Union Minister Natwar Singh and booking of criminal cases against those involved in the oil-for-food scam.

(4319) Hyderabad : Telugu Desam Party leaders on Tuesday lambasted the Congress for failing to maintain law and order.

(4320) Warangal : Telangana Rasthra Samithi leaders have demanded that the four MLAs - Dugyala Srinivasa Rao, Mandadi Satyanarayana Reddy, B.S. Rani and K. Lakshma Reddy - elected on the party ticket, resign and get elected afresh.

(4321) Warangal : Rebel TRS MLA Dugyala Srinivasa Rao has said none of the TRS leaders has any moral right to demand his resignation, and reiterated that he will continue to be a member of the party.

(4322) Hyderabad : In a new twist to the on-going controversy in the Telangana Rashtra Samiti, a party MLA, Soyam Bapu Rao, has returned to the partyfold, and alleged that the dissident legislators have lured him to their camp with a promise of paying Rs. 30 lakhs.

(4323) Hyderabad : The State committee of the Communist Party of India (Marxist) has threatened to launch direct action and stall the works on Polavaram (Indirasagar) project by conducting indefinite picketing if the Government did not change its design, which was detrimental to the interests of tribals.

(4324) Thiruvananthapuram : Leader of the Opposition V. S. Achuthanandan on Tuesday said DIC(K) leader K. Karunakaran was just "doing his duty" by supporting the LDF candidate in the byelection in the Thiruvananthapuram Lok Sabha constituency.

(4325) New Delhi : Congress president Sonia Gandhi said on Tuesday that action would be taken against anyone found culpable by the R.S. Pathak Inquiry Authority. The Authority has been appointed by the Central Government to investigate the charges in the United Nations-appointed Volcker Committee Report on the Iraqi oil-for-food scandal.

(4326) Thiruvananthapuram : The Communist Party of India (Marxist) and the Communist Party of India have warned the Government of serious consequences if it votes in favour of referring the Iran nuclear issue to the U.N. Security Council at the November 24 meeting of the board of governors of the International Atomic Energy Agency (IAEA).

(4327) Bellary : Janardhan Reddy, president of the district unit of the Bharatiya Janata Party, accused Deputy Chief Minister M.P. Prakash of attempting to destabilise the party in the district.

(4328) Shimoga : President of the State unit of the Bharatiya Janata Party (BJP) Jagdish Shettar said here on Tuesday that his party is prepared to face mid-term Assembly elections if they become an eventuality.

(4329) Chikmagalur : Janata Dal (Secular) State unit Working President H.D. Kumaraswamy has reiterated that his party will support those who are opposing the implementation of the Upper Bhadra Project.

(4330) Thiruvananthapuram : General secretary of the CPI(M) Prakash Karat has said that victory of the LDF nominee in the Thiruvananthapuram Lok Sabha byelection is crucial in the current national context because it would strengthen the Left's ability to influence the policies of the UPA Government.

(4331) Hyderabad : The Bharatiya Janata Party will have a "new president in the New Year" and its three-day national convention, beginning in Mumbai on December 28, will decide on the successor to L.K. Advani. The convention will be preceded by a two-day national executive meeting.

(4332) New Delhi : Leader of Opposition L.K. Advani on Tuesday reiterated his earlier views that money power in politics should be curbed and one way would be to bring in public funding of elections.

(4333) New Delhi : The Communist Party of India (Marxist) on Monday said the Manmohan Singh Government should be able to adopt a position in consonance with the stand taken by a ministerial delegation of the Non-Aligned Movement that provides a framework for settling the Iran issue within the International Atomic Energy Agency.

(4334) New Delhi : The Leader of the Opposition in the Standing Committee of the Municipal Corporation of Delhi, Vijender Kumar Gupta, has urged the Lieutenant-Governor, B.L. Joshi, to conduct a CBI inquiry into the payment of Rs. 30 crores for construction of 1,000 porta cabin classrooms in the MCD schools.

(4335) Lucknow : The BJP today alleged that the communal riots in Mau have proved that Uttar Pradesh chief minister Mulayam Singh Yadav was not sensitive towards the sentiments of the majority community.

17-11-2005

(4336) Hyderabad : The Bharatiya Janata Party has demanded an enquiry by the Lok Satta into the allegations made by Telangana Rashtra Samiti MLA S. Bapu Rao that he was offered Rs. 30 lakhs to split the party at the behest of the Congress.

(4337) Hyderabad : Congress Legislature Party (CLP) has said the Telangana Rashtra Samiti had become a 'laughing stock' with its oft-repeated charge that Congress had encouraged dissident activity and engineered a split.

(4338) Hyderabad : Andhra Pradesh Congress Committee (APCC) president K. Keshava Rao on Wednesday said that some Telangana Rashtra Samiti legislators had approached him recently expressing their desire to join the party.

(4339) Hyderabad : Telugu Desam president N. Chandrababu Naidu on Wednesday reorganised the party's State committee by making it a jumbo 123 strong-body but without effecting any major changes.

(4340) Hyderabad : Close on the heels of the return of S. Santosh Reddy and Soyam Bapu Rao to the party, the Telangana Rashtra Samithi (TRS) has intensified efforts to woo the remaining dissident MLAs.

(4341) Warangal : Mild tension prevailed in the town with rival TRS groups clashing near the Kaloji Narayana Rao's statue.

(4342) Mettur : Actress Kushboo spent about two hours in judicial custody in II Judicial Magistrate court here on Wednesday, as angry Dalit Panthers and Pattali Makkal Katchi cadres shouted slogans outside, decrying her reported comments on chastity and status of women in society.

(4343) Bidar : Addressing presspersons, Karnataka Pradesh Congress Committee President M. Mallikarjun Kharge said the Congress has no plan to field candidates proposed by the Siddaramaiah faction of the Janata Dal (S) in the panchayat elections.

(4344) Gulbarga : Vittal Heroor, Janata Dal (Secular) MLC and President of the Karnataka Rajya Koli Samaja Jana Jagruti Mathu Horata Samiti, on Wednesday accused political parties in the State of not being committed to the inclusion of the Koli Samaj in the Scheduled Tribes list.

(4345) Hassan : The Congress, which fared badly in the elections to the Assembly and the Lok Sabha in 2004, is making an effort to give a befitting reply to the Janata Dal (Secular) in the elections to the zilla and taluk panchayats, according to Congress leaders. Hassan MLC S.M. Anand, former Revenue Minister H.C. Srikantaiah, and the former MP G. Puttaswamy Gowda addressed presspersons on different occasions in the past week and said that they are trying to enthuse party workers to put up a fight in these elections.

(4346) Hubli : H.N. Ananth Kumar, Bharatiya Janata Party General Secretary, has termed the setting up of an inquiry authority to look into the Volcker Committee Report and the statement of Congress President Sonia Gandhi in this regard as eyewash.

(4347) Hubli : B.S. Yediyurappa, Leader of the Opposition in the Legislative Assembly, on Wednesday urged the Government to seize the

"Resolution Book" of the Belgaum Municipal Corporation (BMC) and take disciplinary action against its Commissioner.

(4348) Panaji : Though the Bharatiya Janata Party (BJP) announced its support to the agitation against the controversial ordinance amending Town and Country Planning Act, it has said that it would not associate with any moves to disrupt the holding of the International Film Festival in the name of the agitation.

(4349) Thiruvananthapuram : The Democratic Indira Congress-Karunakaran (DIC-K), on Wednesday, petitioned the Election Commission, seeking a detailed examination of the election expenditure of the United Democratic Front candidate in the Lok Sabha byelection, V.S. Sivakumar.

(4350) New Delhi : With the campaign for the Bihar Assembly elections reaching its conclusion, the countdown for selecting a new Bharatiya Janata Party president is expected to begin. A meeting between outgoing BJP president L.K. Advani and Rashtriya Swayamsevak Sangh chief K.S. Sudarshan could take place as early as Friday.

(4351) New Delhi : The Bharatiya Janata Party has signalled that it will adopt an aggressive posture in Parliament when the winter session begins on November 23 by vociferously demanding the resignations of Congress president Sonia Gandhi from the office of chairperson of the United Progressive Alliance and of Natwar Singh as Cabinet Minister.

(4352) New Delhi : Increasing its pressure on the Manmohan Singh Government, the Left parties have given notices in the Lok Sabha seeking a discussion on the vote against Iran by India in the International Atomic Energy Agency.

(4353) Malvan : Shiv Sena chief Bal Thackeray on Wednesday called upon people here to take revenge against Revenue Minister Narayan Rane, who "stabbed him in the back," and defeat him in the Assembly by-election here, scheduled for November 19. "Teach Narayan Rane a lesson and settle the score. Aren't you going to punish him for stabbing me in the back?" Mr. Thackeray said at a public meeting.

(4354) New Delhi : Pointing an accusing finger at the Delhi Mayor, Satbir Singh, the BJP MLA from Saket, Vijay Jolly, on Wednesday demanded a CBI inquiry and resignation of the Mayor for allegedly being involved in a major building scam that has rocked the Saket Cultural Club adjoining PVR Anupam.

(4355) Coimbatore : Tamil Nadu Congress Committee president G.K. Vasan on Wednesday criticised the "slack" distribution of flood relief to the affected in the State.

(4356) Tiruchi : The district unit of the Communist Party of India has urged the State Government to take steps to provide adequate relief to the farming community in the district affected by heavy rains and floods recently.

18-11-2005

(4357) Eluru : CPI State secretary K. Narayana hardly finds a difference between Chief Minister Y.S. Rajasekhara Reddy and his bete noir and former Chief Minister N. Chandrababu Naidu with respect to replicating the World Bank model in the State.

(4358) Hyderabad : The Telangana Rashtra Samithi (TRS) has launched a frontal attack on the Congress and accused it of conspiring to weaken and split the party.

(4359) Hyderabad : The Congress has decided to counter the campaign launched by the Telugu Desam Party against the irrigation projects and expose the neglect of Telangana region during the last nine years of rule in the State.

(4360) Hyderabad : The Telugu Desam Party has demanded that the Central Bureau of Investigation immediately take into custody the prime accused in the Paritala Ravi murder case Julakanti Srinivas Reddy, alias Moddu Sreenu, who was accidentally caught after being injured in a bomb blast at a lodge on the city outskirts.

(4361) Hyderabad : The United Progressive Alliance (UPA) Government at the Centre has decided to bring in policy changes to make education affordable to the poor.

(4362) Hyderabad : Telangana Rashtra Samithi (TRS) MLA S. Santosh Reddy has said he is against the extended general body meeting of the party at Warangal on Saturday saying it would amount to a provocative step in view of the clashes between supporters of rebel MLAs and loyalists in the town on Wednesday.

(4363) Karimnagar : APSRTC Chairman Gone Prakash has asked TRS president and Union Minister K. Chandrasekhar Rao to disclose as to when he will secure separate Telangana.

(4364) Kurnool : TDP MLA from Pathikonda S.V. Subba Reddy has turned down the offer of being a member on the party district coordination committee.

(4365) Nizmababad : The Telugu Desam Party plans to take out a rally and later stage a dharna in front of the Collectorate to press for early completion of pending irrigation projects in Telangana and stoppage of alleged diversion of Godavari waters at the cost of the region here on November 28.

(4366) Tirupati : Chittoor, the home district of Telugu Desam president N. Chandrababu Naidu, walked away with a big chunk of posts in the reconstituted bodies of the party. Notable among those who got the plum posts were film actress R.K. Roja who has been made one of the Executive Secretaries of the state body. Another person to be named the executive secretary from the district is former minister B. Gopalakrishna Reddy.

(4367) Warangal : As the crisis in the Telangana Rashtra Samithi (TRS) seems to have reached a point of no return, academics and intellectuals, who have built up the movement from the grass-roots level, now prefer to remain mute spectators to the developments in the party.

(4368) Kochi : The Kochi Corporation and the Communist Party of India (Marxist), which is controlling the civic administration, have found most of the conditions laid down by the Asian Development Bank (ADB) unacceptable, even as the State Government is all set to receive the financial assistance from the Bank.

(4369) Bangalore : Leader of the Opposition in the Legislative Assembly B.S. Yediyurappa on Thursday demanded that Chief Minister N. Dharam Singh convene an all-party meeting to provide details on the status of the Bangalore International Airport and the Bangalore Metro Rail.

(4370) Bangalore : Minister for Primary Education Ramalinga Reddy said on Thursday that the Congress will not impose the candidate for Mayor on the corporators of the Bangalore Mahanagara Palike.

(4371) Bangalore : Taking a distinct line, the Communist Party of India (Marxist) has opposed any move to supersede the Belgaum City Corporation.

(4372) Bangalore : The Siddaramaiah faction of the Janata Dal (Secular) suffered a setback when the Karnataka High Court dismissed its plea for either freezing the party symbol or allotting it to them for the zilla and taluk panchayat elections in December.

(4373) Bidar : Congress leaders here on Wednesday converted a party workers' meeting into an election campaign rally.

(4374) Gulbarga : Members of the Republican Party of India (Atwale) on Thursday staged a dharna in front of the Deputy Commissioner's office here demanding action against those responsible for the attacks on Dalits in Mandya, Kolar and Gulbarga districts and seeking compensation to the affected families.

(4375) Tumkur : The former Gubbi MLA G.S. Shivananjappa, who has decided to leave the Janata Dal (Secular), said on Thursday that he would return to the Congress "if the Karnataka Pradesh Congress Committee President Mallikarjun Kharge promises to give him a high post."

(4376) Karwar : Samajawadi Party (SP) State unit President and Shimoga MP S. Bangarappa said his party will contest taluk and zilla panchayat elections in the State independently.

(4377) Kozhikode : Janata Dal (Secular) State president M.P. Veerendrakumar, MP, has asked the State Government not to yield to the conditions of the Asian Development Bank (ADB) such as phasing out of public taps and hiking water charges to avail of loans from the funding agency.

(4378) Thiruvananthapuram : Kerala Pradesh Congress Committee president Ramesh Chennithala has said that the Communist Party of India-Marxist (CPI-M) leadership was overrating the strength of the Democratic Indira Congress (Karunkaran) leader K. Karunakaran strength in Kerala politics, and the results of the Thiruvananthapuram Lok Sabha byelection would disprove that party's line.

(4379) Thiruvananthapuram : Communist Party of India-Marxist (CPI-M) State secretary Pinarayi Vijayan has alleged that the State Government's decision to hand over the inquiry into a case of molestation of a nursing student in Kottayam to a new team was meant to divert the focus of investigation. The move comes when the investigation under the Kottayam Superintendent of Police (SP) has made considerable progress.

(4380) New Delhi : A two-hour meeting between the former Prime Minister Atal Bihari Vajpayee and the Rashtriya Swayamsevak Sangh chief K.S. Sudarshan here on Thursday signalled the start of the process of consultations between senior Bharatiya Janata Party and RSS leaders on the selection of a new BJP president who will replace L.K. Advani by the end of this year.

(4381) New Delhi : Denying all allegations levelled against him by BJP MLA Vijay Jolly, Delhi Mayor Satbir Singh on Thursday stated that there was no land grabbing or illegal construction at the Saket Cultural Club in South Delhi and all dues of the Club have been paid and proper licences and permissions taken for various activities. "These charges are blatant lies and politically motivated. The fact is that since I took over as the Club's president, things have improved. And I still enjoy the confidence of the Club's executive committee," he claimed.

(4382) New Delhi : The Delhi Bharatiya Janata Party has asked the Delhi Government and Delhi Electricity Regulatory Commission to immediately replace over 10 lakh electronic meters that have been installed in residential premises across the Capital and to refund with interest the excess amount recovered from the consumers due to their fast running.

(4383) Bhopal : For over a month the State Capital has been witnessing hectic political activity over the demand for leadership change raised by legislators and State Ministers loyal to the former Chief Minister Uma Bharti. Now with the fourth and last phase of polling for the Bihar Assembly election just round the corner, the top State Bharatiya Janata Party leaders have started shifting camp to Delhi where the issue would be taken up on top priority after polling ends in Bihar on November 19.

(4384) Pondicherry : Founder of the Puduchery Munnetra Congress P. Kannan and thousands of party volunteers were arrested here on Thursday when they tried to picket the Assembly in protest against inadequate relief to rain-hit farmers and fishermen in Pondicherry and Karaikal.

(4385) Dharmapuri : The Dharmapuri unit of CPI has urged the district administration to provide adequate compensation to farmers affected by the recent rain in the district. In a statement here on Thursday, the district secretary of CPI P. Ilamparithi said that the district administration should provide compensation of Rs. 5,000 an acre for agricultural crops submerged in floodwater.

(4386) Mayiladuturai : All-India Anna Dravida Munnetra Kazhagam cadres, led by Sirkazhi MLA M. Chandramohan, blocked the car of Union Minister for Petroleum Mani Shankar Aiyar, squatting on the main road at Thenpaathi in Sirkazhi town for 20 minutes on Thursday afternoon.

19-11-2005

(4387) Hyderabad : Bharatiya Janata Party vice president M. Venkaiah Naidu termed the Centre's move on reservations for minorities in IIMs and IITs as "dangerous, divisive and one that would have far-reaching consequences."

(4388) Hyderabad : The CPI (ML) New Democracy has demanded boycott by the country of the World Trade Organisation (WTO) ministerial-level conference beginning in Hong Kong on December 8.

(4389) Hyderabad : The Telugu Desam Party (TDP) has charged the Government with washing off its hands in the Julakanti Srinivas Reddy alias Moddu Sreenu (prime accused in TDP MLA Partiala Ravi's murder) episode by conveniently passing it on to the CBI.

(4390) Hyderabad : Chief Minister Y. S. Rajasekhara Reddy has promised to examine if the Government can take steps legally or from police side, to trace out Pallavi of the old cty of Hyderabad, and facilitate her meeting with her parents.

(4391) Warangal : Of the four dissident MLAs, two are likely to come back into the TRS party's fold and the other two may face suspension at the proposed meeting on Saturday here at Warangal.

(4392) Bangalore : The Bharatiya Janata Party has described as "eyewash" Congress President Sonia Gandhi's "anger and hurt" over the way in which the exit of Natwar Singh as External Affairs Minister unfolded.

(4393) Madikeri : Virajpet MLA H.D. Basavaraj on Friday urged the State Government to introduce a Bill in the Legislative Assembly to accord rights over trees grown on their own lands to the landholders in Kodagu.

(4394) Mangalore : Those opposing the sops given to the IT industry do not know what will be the implications on the State if IT companies shift their base, B. Janardhana Poojary, MP, said on Friday.

(4395) Mangalore : The expansion of Mangalore airport and upgrading it into an international one has to become a people's movement or else the city in particular and the State in general will lose heavily, B. Janardhana Poojary, MP, said on Friday.

(4396) Tumkur : Senior Congress leaders in Tumkur district on Friday appealed to Chief Minister N. Dharam Singh and Karnataka Pradesh Congress Committee President M. Mallikarjun Kharge to end the alliance with the Janata Dal (Secular) in the Government.

(4397) Davangere : Karnataka Pradesh Congress Committee President M. Mallikarjun Kharge has reportedly directed all district units to give importance to the recommendations of block levels in selection of candidates for the taluk and zilla panchayat elections.

(4398) Thiruvananthapuram : The BJP has protested against the publication of a report in a Malayalam newspaper with the headline that the party had withdrawn from the contest in the bypoll from the Thiruvananthapuram Lok Sabha constituency during polling on Friday.

(4399) New Delhi : The central leadership of the Bharatiya Janata Party has begun discussions on a possible change of Chief Minister in Madhya Pradesh.

(4400) New Delhi : Former Petroleum Minister in the National Democratic Alliance Government Ram Naik knew as early as July 2002 that the then Iraqi President Saddam Hussein was asking for a surcharge on oil coupons under the oil-for-food programme controlled by the United Nations as part of the sanctions regime against Iraq.

(4401) New Delhi : The Left parties on Friday decided to keep the Iran nuclear issue in the spotlight at the United Progressive Alliance Coordination Committee meeting on Monday. They hope to get a clear signal from the Manmohan Singh Government ahead of the November 24 meeting of the International Atomic Energy Agency.

(4402) New Delhi : The Rashtriya Swayamsevak Sangh chief K.S. Sudarshan met Bharatiya Janata Party president L.K. Advani for nearly 90 minutes over lunch on Friday afternoon at Mr. Advani's residence taking forward the discussions between the RSS and BJP leaderships on the change of guard expected to take place in the party in December-end.

(4403) New Delhi : Describing the untimely death of an average of 29 cows per day in the cow shelters run by the Delhi Government as "cow slaughter", Delhi Bharatiya Janata Party president Harsh Vardhan has urged the Lieutenant-Governor, B.L. Joshi, to take stern action against the officers responsible for running these shelters.

(4404) Pondicherry : The Pondicherry State committee of the All-India Anna Dravida Munnetra Kazhagam has called upon the Election Commission to ensure that the order of the Commission delimiting the number of constituencies in the Union Territory was enforced for the next Assembly polls.

(4405) Chennai : Communist Party of India (Marxist) State secretary N. Varadarajan on Friday urged the Centre to pass the Scheduled Tribes (Recognition of Forest Rights) Bill, 2005 with necessary amendments in the coming session of Parliament.

20-11-2005

(4406) Anantapur : The Communist Party of India (CPI) on Saturday urged the State Government to find permanent solution to the woes of perennially drought-hit farmers of Anantapur district by completing the Handri-Neeva project with 100 tmcft capacity and allocating 10 tmcft water to Penna Ahobilam Balancing Reservoir.

(4407) Hyderabad : The Andhra Pradesh Congress Committee has termed as unfortunate the alleged tie-up between the CPI(M) and the TDP in the election of Chairman of the Khammam District Cooperative Central Bank.

(4408) Hyderabad : The Congress Legislature Party has advised Telugu Desam leaders to refrain from levelling wild charges against the police and dragging the name of Chief Minister Y.S. Rajasekhara Reddy in connection with the arrest of Julakanti Srinivasa Reddy alias Moddu Sreenu, the prime accused in Paritala Ravi murder case.

(4409) Hyderabad : Chief Minister Y. S. Rajasekhara Reddy has expressed displeasure at the CPI(M)-TDP combine bagging the chairman and vice-chairman posts in the Khammam District Cooperative Central Bank (DCCB).

(4410) Hyderabad : The Telugu Desam has urged the CBI to speed up investigation to establish truth and bring culprits involved in the murder of Paritala Ravi to book.

(4411) Hyderabad : Chief Minister Y.S. Rajasekhara Reddy and other senior Congress leaders on Friday paid glowing tributes to former Prime Minister Indira Gandhi on her 88th birth anniversary.

(4412) Warangal : The Telangana Rasthra Samithi (TRS) leadership has reiterated its appeal to rebel MLAs to return to the party fold and strengthen the Telangana movement, and not to fall prey to the forces that have been trying to weaken the movement.

(4413) Tirumala : Minister for Finance and Health K. Rosaiah on Saturday reiterated that there was no need for the Congress to encourage a split in the TRS.

(4414) Chennai : The scales seem to be tilting in favour of actors Kusbhoo and Suhasini, who had been at the receiving end for some time legally and otherwise, following the former's alleged remarks on pre-marital sex.

(4415) Bangalore : Deputy Chief Minister M.P. Prakash has spiked rumours that he is planning to join the Congress.

(4416) Bijapur : Independent MLA from Indi Ravikant Patil on Saturday gave a clear indication that he is likely to join the Janata Dal (Secular) shortly.

(4417) Gulbarga : The State unit of the Communist Party of India (Marxist) on Saturday charged the BJP with practicing opportunistic politics on the legislation to provide 33 per cent reservation to women in Parliament.

(4418) Madikeri : Defeats will not deter the Congress but will enable the party to go all out with a strong resolve to win, Chief Minister N. Dharam Singh said here on Saturday.

(4419) Madikeri : C.S. Arun Machaiah, MLC from Kodagu, who recently joined the Janata Dal (Secular), said here on Friday that he has no regrets and is happy to have joined a secular party, headed by the former Prime Minister H.D. Deve Gowda.

(4420) Mangalore : Janata Dal (Secular) President H.D. Deve Gowda said here on Saturday that if the Congress wants to end its ties with his party, it means that they (Congressmen) want to encourage the Bharatiya Janata Party (BJP) in the State.

(4421) Mangalore : The former Prime Minister H.D. Deve Gowda has said that Kudremukh Iron Ore Company Ltd. (KIOCL) should be allowed to continue mining at Kudremukh for some more time. The issue of whether mining in the area should be stopped as demanded by some or allowed to continue should be considered seriously in view of the naxalite influence in the Kudremukh National Park area, he said in a letter to Prime Minister Manmohan Singh.

(4422) Tumkur : The Communist Party of India (Marxist) on Saturday blamed the Bharatiya Janata Party (BJP)-led National Democratic Alliance (NDA) for the delay in passing the Women's Reservation Bill in Parliament.

(4423) Alappuzha : A large number of groups that had hitherto viewed Communist parties with suspicion were now extending support to the Left parties, CPI(M) State secretary Pinarayi Vijayan has said.

(4424) Alappuzha : CPI(M) State secretary Pinarayi Vijayan has said that the Rashtriya Swayamsevak Sangh (RSS) and the Bharatiya Janata Party (BJP) ditched C.K. Padmanabhan, BJP candidate in the bypoll for the Thiruvananthapuram Lok Sabha seat held on Friday, and canvassed votes for the United Democratic Front (UDF) candidate V.S. Sivakumar.

(4425) Kochi : Public sector units (PSUs) have an important role to play in the national economy and there should be a social commitment to retain them, said Vayalar Ravi, MP. Hire and fire policies cannot be accepted, he said while inaugurating a seminar on 'UPA Government and public sector,' organised by CITU as part of the convention of public sector employees here on Saturday.

(4426) Kollam : CPI State secretary Veliyam Bhargavan on Saturday urged Prime Minister Manmohan Singh to amend the labour laws of the country. He was inaugurating a public meeting here in connection with the 10th State conference of the Kerala Cooperative Employees Council (KCEC).

(4427) New Delhi : The Bharatiya Janata Party on Saturday night indicated to Lok Sabha Speaker Somnath Chatterjee that it would not hold up proceedings in the winter session of Parliament beginning on November 23.

(4428) Hyderabad : The Communist Party of India (Marxist) on Saturday called upon the student community to be vigilant and gear up to counter the efforts to commercialise and privatise the education sector.

(4429) Hyderabad : The CPI(M) Polit Bureau member and MP, Sitaram Yechury, has demanded that the Central Government introduce the women's reservation bill in the Parliament in the coming session instead of delaying its enactment in the name of obtaining a consensus on it.

(4430) New Delhi : Delhi Bharatiya Janata Party president Harsh Vardhan has accused the Delhi Government of betraying the industrialists of Delhi by declaring only 16 residential areas in the Capital as conforming industrial areas after promising them that all 23 industrial areas and all residential areas where industrial activity is taking place in over 70 per cent of the premises.

(4431) Jaipur : The Congress party has opposed sharp increases in the rates of clinical tests and fees for patient admission in Rajasthan's biggest hospital in the Government sector, Sawai Man Singh Hospital. The increases, made effective from Saturday, amount to a 15 per cent rise in the fees for clinical examinations while the rate for outdoor patient admission cards has gone up from Rs. 2 to Rs. 5.

21-11-2005

(4432) Hyderabad : Samajwadi party general secretary and MP Amar Singh on Sunday said though he had discussed several things with Telugu Desam Party president N. Chandrababu Naidu it was "too premature to say anything."

(4433) Hyderabad : Stung by Union Minister A. Narendra's harsh criticism against Chief Minister Y. S. Rajasekhara Reddy, the Congress hit back, saying time has come for people of Telangana to construct a "grave" for the Telangana Rashtra Samiti.

(4434) Hyderabad : Six of the seven rebel Telangana Rashtra Samiti (TRS) MLAs have described the Warangal meeting of the loyalists on Saturday as "provocative" and vowed to place the party issue before people.

(4435) Hyderabad : Andhra Pradesh Congress Committee (APCC) general secretary Danam Nagender and AICC secretary P. Sudhakar Reddy sought an unconditional apology from TRS leader, A. Narendra for his outburst against Chief Minister Y.S. Rajasekhara Reddy at the Warangal meeting.

(4436) Vijayawada : Central committee member of the Communist Party of India (Marxist) Tammineni Veerabhadram on Sunday said the party would organise padayatras in all districts to identify long-pending programmes and chalk out plans for the overall development of the districts.

(4437) Vijayawada : The poll outcome in Bihar would clearly be in favour of the National Democratic Alliance (NDA) besides marking the beginning of disintegration of the United Progressive Alliance Government at the Centre, BJP general secretary Pramod Mahajan said here on Sunday.

(4438) Warangal : While the leaders in TRS are engaged in levelling charges against each other of diluting the Telangana movement, the people in rural parts of the district say they are in confusion.

(4439) Kakinada : Mahila Congress workers who strived for the party would be given recognition and duly rewarded by giving them nominated posts, P. Venu Madhavi, secretary of the State Mahila Congress Committee, said on Sunday.

(4440) Warangal : The District Congress Committee (DCC) took strong objection to the remarks made by TRS leader A Narendra against Chief Minister Y.S. Rajasekhara Reddy.

(4441) Nizamabad : District Congress Committee president Gadugu Gangadhar expressed surprise at the language used by Mr. Narendra at the party meeting in Warangal against Chief Minister Y.S. Rajasekhara Reddy.

(4442) Sangareddy : Ridiculing T. Harish Rao for sitting on the floor during the TRS Warangal meeting, Sangareddy legislator T. Jayaprakash Reddy has described it as a drama by the former youth affairs minister.

(4443) Bangalore : Janata Dal (Secular) President and former Prime Minister H.D. Deve Gowda went all out to clear the air about rumours that Finance and Industry Minister P.G.R. Sindhia is allowing himself to be wooed by the Congress.

(4444) Gulbarga : The president of the Shiv Sena State unit, Pramod Mutalik, on Sunday said the party High Command had not barred him from speaking on the controversial resolution passed by the Belgaum City Municipal Corporation seeking merger of Marathi-speaking areas with Maharashtra and maintained that the State unit of the party opposed the demand for division of the State and also the resolution passed by the Belgaum City Municipal Corporation.

23-11-2006

(4445) Mysore : Former Deputy Chief Minister and Janata Dal (Secular) leader Siddaramaiah said here on Sunday that his group was ready for an alliance with the Janata Dal (U) in the zilla and taluk panchayat elections if the latter dissociated itself from the Bharatiya Janata Party.

(4446) Thiruvananthapuram : Joining issue with the Left Democratic Front (LDF) Opposition which had alleged that the United Democratic Front (UDF) had allied with the BJP in the Thiruvananthapuram Lok Sabha byelection, the senior BJP leader O. Rajagopal said the UDF candidate might have received the votes of RSS-BJP sympathisers in the byelection. "If UDF candidate V.S. Sivakumar had received RSS-BJP supporters' votes, it is mainly due to the campaign unleashed by the LDF that the UDF had entered into alliance with the BJP," Mr. Rajagopal told presspersons here on Sunday.

(4447) Thiruvananthapuram : Kerala Pradesh Congress Committee spokesperson M.M. Hassan has denied allegations that his party and the UDF had bought votes from the RSS and BJP.

(4448) New Delhi : Congress party leaders met Speaker Somnath Chatterjee on Sunday and promised him of complete cooperation in running the House in the winter session of Parliament beginning on November 23.

(4449) Hyderabad : The Communist Party of India (Marxist) wants the Centre to come out with an assurance that it will not support any U.S. move to refer Iran's nuclear programme to the Security Council.

(4450) New Delhi : India will not succumb to pressure from any country at the coming World Trade Organisation Ministerial Conference in Hong Kong next month, Commerce and Industries Minister Kamal Nath has assured the Left parties.

(4451) Patna : Railway Minister and Rashtriya Janata Dal chief Lalu Prasad on Sunday rubbished the exit polls and accused the media of campaigning against him.

(4452) Pondicherry : Pattali Makkal Katchi Parliamentary party leader M. Ramadoss has called upon the people to acquaint themselves fully with the contents of the Right to Information Act, 2005.

(4453) Pondicherry : Pattali Makkal Katchi Parliamentary party leader M Ramadoss has expressed surprise over absence of government functions to celebrate the World Fisheries Day on Tuesday.

(4454) Tirupattur : The agitation against "some persons who have expressed their views against the one man-one woman culture" of Tamil Nadu was spontaneous and not instigated by anyone, S. Ramadoss, founder of the Pattali Makkal Katchi said here on Sunday.

24-11-2005

(4455) Hyderabad : The Communist Party of India (CPI) has demanded that the Government initiate action against Congress leaders who are opposing the drive against encroachments in the Kolleru Lake.

(4456) Hyderabad: Senior Congress leader, G. Venkataswamy, said here on Wednesday that the issue of statehood for Telangana would be a time-consuming matter now.

(4457) Nalgonda : Telugu Desam politburo member and former Minister T .Devender Goud has charged Chief Minister Y. S. Rajasekhar Reddy with "deliberately discriminating" against irrigation projects in the Telangana region.

(4458) New Delhi : Efforts by the Congress-led United Progressive Alliance to find a way out for the introduction of the Andhra Pradesh Legislative Council Bill received a boost on Wednesday with the Communist Party of India indicating that it would not oppose the move to revive the second chamber in the State.

(4459) Patna : The first NDA Government of the Janata Dal (United) and the BJP with Nitish Kumar as Chief Minister will be sworn in at a public function at the Gandhi Maidan here on Thursday. BJP's State unit chief Sushil Kumar Modi will be the Deputy Chief Minister.

(4460) New Delhi : The Opposition has made up its mind to press for an adjournment motion demanding the resignation of Sonia Gandhi as chairperson of the United Progressive Alliance and of Natwar Singh from the Cabinet on the basis of the Volcker Committee Report. After a meeting of the Bharatiya Janata Party parliamentary wing and another session of National Democratic Alliance MPs here on Wednesday, the BJP deputy leader in the Lok Sabha, V.K. Malhotra, said an adjournment motion would be moved in the House and a motion under Rule 176 in the Rajya Sabha on Thursday.

(4461) Bangalore: The State unit of the Bharatiya Janata Party, apparently buoyed by the victory of the National Democratic Alliance in the Bihar Legislative Assembly elections, has decided to go it alone in the coming polls to zilla and taluk panchayats in Karnataka.

(4462) Bangalore : Three Congress leaders said on Wednesday that the Janata Dal (S) has intensified its attack on Congress seniors as it is wary of "the growing popularity" of the party under its new State unit President M. Mallikarjun Kharge.

(4463) Gulbarga : The State unit of the Communist Party of India (Marxist) on Wednesday termed the supersession of the Belgaum City Corporation autocratic and hasty and said it will result in frayed relations between Marathi- and Kannada-speaking people in the State and jeopardise the interests of Kannadigas in Maharashtra and other States.

(4464) Hassan : The Siddaramaiah faction of the Janata Dal (Secular) will contest more than 20 constituencies in the district in the zilla panchayat election to be held on December 19, spokesperson of the faction S.N. Manjunatha Datta said.

(4465) Madikeri : The Samajwadi Party will contest all the 1,050 zilla panchayat and 3,680 taluk panchayat seats in the State.

(4466) Mysore : The Congress convention here brought to the fore differences among the party leaders over efforts to bring leaders from other parties into the Congress.

(4467) Davangere : Siddeshwar, Davangere MP, has called upon Bharatiya Janata Party workers to project the failures of the Union and State governments and the achievements of the National Democratic Alliance Government.

(4468) Chikmagalur : M.P. Kumaraswamy, MLA, has denied reports that there are differences between him and BJP district unit President M.K. Pranesh.

(4469) Kottayam : State secretary of the CPI(M) Pinarayi Vijayan has scoffed at the allegation raised by Chief Minister Oommen Chandy to the effect that the LDF had a tacit understanding with the BJP in the byelection in the Thiruvananthapuram parliamentary constituency. He dubbed it as an "extreme position taken by him out of desperation. Such allegations would not be believed by the people," he added.

(4470) Thiruvananthapuram : K. P. Rajendran, legislature party leader of the CPI, has termed unconstitutional the conditions of the agreement between the State Government and the Asian Development Bank (ADB) for availing Rs.1,422.27 crores as loan for the sustainable urban development project.

(4471) Thiruvananthapuram : K. Karunakaran has once again proved his political currency in State's politics. The Thiruvananthapuram byelection result has virtually confirmed the formal entry of his party, the Democratic Indira Congress (Karunakaran), into the LDF and the only issue that remains to be decided is whether this would be the second slot.

(4472) Thiruvananthapuram : Chief Minister Oommen Chandy said here on Wednesday that the Democratic Indira Congress(Karunakaran) leader K. Karunakaran had played an important role in 'hijacking' BJP votes for the LDF in the Lok Sabha byelection from the Thiruvananthapuram constituency.

(4473) New Delhi: Railway Minister and Rashtriya Janata Dal chief Lalu Prasad said on Wednesday that he had his own doubts about the claims by Bihar chief minister-designate Nitish Kumar of providing good governance and improving the lot of the people in 90 days.

(4474) Chennai : Tamil Nadu Chief Minister Jayalalithaa on Wednesday greeted Janata Dal (United) leader Nitish Kumar on his leading the National Democratic Alliance to victory in the Bihar Assembly elections.

(4475) New Delhi : The Left Parties on Wednesday told the United Progressive Alliance Government to have a discussion in Parliament on the country's foreign policy with special focus on West Asia and on the outcome of the recent South Asian Association of Regional Cooperation (SAARC) summit.

(4476) Kolkata : Bihar Chief Minister-designate Nitish Kumar has invited Trinamool Congress leader Mamata Banerjee to attend the swearing-in ceremony of his ministry in Patna on Thursday.

(4477) Patna: The Rashtriya Janata Dal, voted out of power in the Bihar Assembly elections, is understood to have decided to elect former Chief Minister Rabri Devi head of its legislature group, paving the way for her to become Leader of the Opposition in the Assembly. Ms. Rabri Devi, who retained the Raghopur seat for the RJD by a meagre margin of 5,000 votes, told reporters here on Wednesday that the newly elected party MLAs would meet here on Friday to elect their leader.

(4478) Jaipur : The Communist Party of India has expressed concern over the Rajasthan Government's move to acquire farmland near the State Capital to facilitate big industrial houses setting up their units. "The proposal to acquire fertile agricultural land for industrial purposes was replete with corruption and anti-farmer attitude," the party said.

25-11-2005

(4479) Hyderabad : The Congress Legislature Party (CLP) has claimed that the Telugu Desam Party's cadre was falling apart after the party's wash-out in the cooperative polls and its debacle in the municipal elections earlier.

(4480) Hyderabad : The Telangana Rashtra Samithi (TRS) leadership has asked its party cadre to show restraint towards the seven dissident MLAs since they are very much part of the organisation.

(4481) Tirupati : The Bharatiya Janata Party took strong exception to the increasing interference by the Rajasekhara Reddy Government into the affairs of the TTD though it is supposed to be an autonomous institution governed by an independent Act of its own.

(4482) Warangal : The Congress Government is not only trying to fulfil the promises made by it but also that of the Telangana Rashtra Samithi (TRS), senior party leader Banda Prakash has said.

(4483) Bhadrachalam : The CPI will oppose the Polavaram project by all means if the project is to cost the very existence of the tribes, their culture and traditions along the course of Godavari in Kammam district, according to CPI state Secretary K. Narayana and party national council memer, Puvvada Nageswara Rao today. Addressing a public meeting

(4484) Bangalore : The academic-turned-Congress legislator B.K. Chandrashekar is of the view that Chief Minister N. Dharam Singh has not endorsed H.D. Deve Gowda's views on issues such as allotment of land to the IT giant Infosys and the proposed Bangalore metro rail.

(4485) Bangalore : The Bangalore city unit of the Bharatiya Janata Party has criticised the Bangalore Mahanagara Palike (BMP) for giving more attention to the development of parks and gardens instead of getting damaged roads repaired.

(4486) Bangalore : The Congress has said that it will go it alone in the zilla and taluk panchayat elections and no party has sought an alliance with it.

(4487) Bijapur : Deputy Chief Minister M.P. Prakash has said that AHINDA is being misused to criticise the former Prime Minister H.D. Deve Gowda and to glorify the former Deputy Chief Minister Siddaramaiah.

(4488) Alappuzha : Political parties here are issuing statements blaming each other for the execution of Ramankutty Maniappan, the Border Roads Organisation (BRO) employee who had been killed by the Taliban militia in Afghanistan.

(4489) Kannur : Former Chief Minister and Congress Working Committee member A. K. Antony called for a collective and peaceful movement to force the Communist Party of India (Marxist) to change what he termed its culture of violence.

(4490) Kannur : Kerala Pradesh Congress Committee (KPCC) president Ramesh Chennithala on Thursday said that the outcome of the Thiruvananthapuram Lok Sabha byelection laid bare the 'opportunistic'

stand of the Communist Party of India (Marxist) as it had resorted to communal and caste appeasement during the campaign and 'vote purchase.'

(4491) Thiruvananthapuram : CPI(M) district secretary M. Vijayakumar has said that V.S. Sivakumar, the UDF candidate for the recently held Lok Sabha byelection, had received 50,000 votes from BJP supporters. He levelled the charge at a press conference convened at the CPI(M) distrrct committee here on Thursday.

(4492) Thiruvananthapuram : Leader of the Opposition V. S. Achuthanandan has come down heavily on the Centre and the State Government for what he termed their "lax response" to Taliban militia's ultimatum to kill Ramankutty Maniappan. Mniappan's life could have been saved if the Centre had indicated that it was ready for negotiations with the Taliban on pulling out the Border Roads Organisation (BRO) from Afghanistan, he has said.

(4493) Kasaragod: Democratic Indira Congress (Karunakaran) (DIC(K) would jointly contest the coming Assembly elections in Kerala with the Left Democratic Front (LDF), its leader K Karunakaran said on Thursday.

(4494) Alappuzha : State secretary of the CPI(M) Pinarayi Vijayan has said that the failure of Minister of State for Foreign Affairs E. Ahamed to take necessary steps to save Ramankutty Maniappan from Taliban extremists was a disgrace to the whole State.

(4495) New Delhi: Members of Parliament belonging to the All-India Anna Dravida Munnetra Kazhagam on Wednesday sought the intervention of President A.P.J. Abdul Kalam for the dismissal of Union Finance Minister P. Chidambaram for alleged abuse of office in securing a Rs. 6 crore loan from a foreign institution to a company floated by his son and nephew.

(4496) New Delhi : The Bharatiya Janata Party on Thursday night deferred taking a decision on replacing the Madhya Pradesh Chief Minister Babulal Gaur, butindicated that the matter was very much on its agenda.

(4497) Patna : Senior Janata Dal (United) leader Nitish Kumar took over as the Chief Minister of Bihar on Thursday in front of a huge cheering crowd.

(4498) New Delhi : Delhi Bharatiya Janata Party president Harsh Vardhan on Thursday said he had written to the Chief Justice of India,

Justice Y.K. Sabharwal, requesting him to set up special fast track courts for disposal of cases relating to power, water and corruption so that they might be settled within 60 days.

(4499) Pondicherry: Founder of Pondicherry Munnetra Congress (PMC) and former Home Minister of Pondicherry P. Kannan has called upon President A.P.J. Abdul Kalam to intervene and dismiss the Rangasamy headed Congress Government in Pondicherry.

26-11-2005

(4500) Hyderabad : Khairatabad MLA (Congress) P. Janardhan Reddy has asked the Government to keep in abeyance the G.O. No.170 regarding the release of 40, 000 cusecs of water from Pothireddypadu Head Regulator to Rayalaseema. He has also sought a meeting of the MLAs concerned to prevent injustice to Telangana and Andhra regions.

(4501) Nellore: State Vice-President of Pradesh Congress party C.V. Sesha Reddy has charged the administration with slackness in extending necessary assistance to the rain-battered areas of Nellore district.

(4502) Vijayawada : Senior Congress leader and Kankipadu MLA Devineni Rajasekhar (Nehru) on Friday hailed the Operation Kolleru taken up by the Rajasekhara Reddy Government as the most laudable initiative with an aim to permanently solve the problems of farmers and save paddy crop from inundation. The removal of encroachments and handing over of all the lakebed area in fifth contour to the Forest Department would restore lost glory to the freshwater lake.

(4503) Visakhapatnam : Residents of VAMBAY Colony at Madhurawada poured their woes to leaders of Communist Party of India (Marxist) during the fifth day of the party's padayatra on Friday. Their problems mainly revolved around drinking water, power and means of livelihood.

(4504) Bijapur : The Janata Dal (S) group of the former Deputy Chief Minister Siddaramaiah will meet in Bangalore to decide on electoral understanding with the Congress for the panchayat elections.

(4505) Davangere : The Siddaramaiah group of the Janata Dal (Secular) will not merge with the Congress but will have an alliance with the party for the ensuing zilla and taluk panchayat elections, P. Kodandaramaiah, senior leader of the party, said.

(4506) Thiruvananthapuram : Leader of the Opposition V.S. Achuthanandan has accused the Government of stooping too low to save the former Industries Minister P.K. Kunhalikutty from the Kozhikode ice-cream parlour sex scandal case.

(4507) New Delhi : The Communist Party of India (Marxist) on Friday criticised the Bharatiya Janata Party-led Opposition for their continued disruption of Parliament proceedings, saying they were "making a mockery of this great institution."

(4508) New Delhi : If the Opposition-sponsored adjournment motion on the Volcker Committee Report is admitted and taken up on Monday, Lok Sabha proceedings will not be disrupted. This decision was taken at a meeting of National Democratic Alliance leaders here on Friday.

(4509) Patna : The former Bihar Chief Minister, Rabri Devi, was elected leader of the Rashtriya Janata Dal Legislature Party on Friday, thereby becoming the Leader of the Opposition in the Assembly.

(4510) New Delhi : Expressing disappointment over the Bihar election result, Congress president Sonia Gandhi on Friday said it was a "signal for secular forces to remain united" and more effectively propagate the principles of equity, democracy and development.

(4511) New Delhi : The Leader of the Opposition in the Delhi Assembly, Jagdish Mukhi, on Friday accused the Delhi Government and the Municipal Corporation of Delhi of misleading the Supreme Court about the operation of shops and commercial establishments in the Capital's residential areas. This had led to a situation where these establishments were faced with the threat of demolition, he added.

(4512) Jaipur : Former Rajasthan Chief Minister and Congress general secretary Ashok Gehlot on Friday charged that the Bharatiya Janata Party's attempts to stall Parliament proceedings over the Volcker Committee report were prompted by its own internal problems.

(4513) Chandigarh : The Indian National Lok Dal (INLD), which received a severe drubbing in the last Assembly elections and the Lok Sabha by-election not long ago, appears to be coming out of political hibernation if one goes by the big public response at the "first" political rally addressed by its chief Om Parkash Chautala at Sampla on Thursday.

(4514) Lucknow: Congress on Friday charged Uttar Pradesh Chief Minister Mulayam Singh Yadav with failing to take appropriate action against IPS officer D K Panda, who prefers dressing up like a woman in public.

27-11-2005

(4515) Hyderabad : The Congress Party will opt for a constitutional amendment to get over the legal problems in implementing the 5 per cent reservation for Muslims.

(4516) Hyderabad : Telugu Desam cadre has reportedly been given the go ahead by their party president N. Chandrababu Naidu to join the agitations organised by Left parties if they are invited.

(4517) Nalgonda : Tension prevailed in various villages in Tungaturthy Assembly constituency on Saturday as Telugu Desam activists tried to observe bandh demanding that the CBI arrest R. Damodar Reddy, Congress MLA "for his nexus" with Julakanti Sreenivasa Reddy alias Moddu Sreenu.

(4518) Sangareddy: The UPA Sub-Committee on Telangana will submit its report immediately after the current Parliament session, Union Minister and Telangana Rashtra Samithi (TRS) senior leader A. Narendra has said.

(4519) Kakinada : The district unit of the Telugu Desam Party has demanded an inquiry into alleged financial irregularities in the Municipal Corporation administration and on the inaction of the authorities concerned on the issue.

(4520) New Delhi : Shivraj Singh Chauhan will be the new Chief Minister of Madhya Pradesh. The BJP central parliamentary board's decision to replace Babu Lal Gaur with Mr. Chauhan ends the nearly month-long uncertainty in the State where the party swept to power two years ago.

(4521) Bangalore: Janata Dal (United) State unit President B. Somashekar and party Secretary General M.P. Nadagouda on Saturday called on State Election Commissioner M.R. Hegde and urged him to ensure that the elections to the taluk and zilla panchayats are conducted in a free and fair manner.

(4522) Shimoga : The former MLA from Shimoga H.M. Chandrashekharappa, who resigned from the Congress and joined the

Janata Dal (Secular) recently, said here on Friday that he decided to leave the Congress as he was disgusted with the groupism in the district unit of the party.

(4523) New Delhi : Chief Minister N. Dharam Singh on Saturday met Political Secretary to Congress President Ahmed Patel and Congress Working Committee member in-charge of Karnataka A.K. Antony and discussed the fresh move by a section of State Congress leaders to get the former Deputy Chief Minister and Janata Dal (Secular) rebel Siddaramaiah into the party on the ground that it would improve its prospects in the elections to the zilla and taluk panchayats slated for December.

(4524) Panaji : The Nationalist Congress Party (NCP), Goa unit, has called for the shifting of the International Film Festival of India (IFFI) in Goa to February, to coincide with the last day of the Carnival, to avert the congestion of the city during the peak tourist season of November-December.

(4525) Thiruvananthapuram : The CPI(M) State secretariat has begun a two-day meeting here marking the beginning of a protracted inner party exercise involving review of the LDF's performance in the just-concluded Thiruvananthapuram Lok Sabha elections and matters concerning the party organisation.

(4526) Thiruvananthapuram : Former member of the CPI(M) State committee V. B. Cherian has been elected State secretary of the Marxist Communist Party of India (United).

(4527) New Delhi : Congress president Sonia Gandhi on Saturday expressed her heartfelt condolences and empathy for the families of the victims who died in the Ramanathapuram bus tragedy due to unprecedented floods in Tamil Nadu. The flash floods have caused untold misery to human life and extensive damage to property, she said in her message. The Congress president requested the Centre to extend all possible assistance.

(4528) New Delhi : The 38th session of the All-India Trade Union Congress, first to be held in Delhi after Independence, saw fireworks on Saturday as senior Left leaders A.B. Bardhan and Gurudas Dasgupta denounced the economic and foreign policies of the United Progressive Alliance Government and warned that it should adhere to the Common Minimum Programme.

(4529) New Delhi : The BJP on Friday demanded a judicial inquiry into the recent communal clashes at Mau in Uttar Pradesh that left 20 persons dead.

(4530) Mumbai : In its first official reaction to the squabble between the Thackeray cousins, Uddhav and Raj, the Shiv Sena on Saturday said the issue could be resolved only by party supremo Bal Thackeray.

(4531) New Delhi : Congress president Sonia Gandhi on Saturday underscored the need to rise above factionalism and asked the new generation to stay away from selfish and group politics and put the interests of the country and society before one's own.

(4532) New Delhi : Delhi Bharatiya Janata Party president Harsh Vardhan has warned that the party would take to the streets in a big way if the running of shops and other commercial activities in the residential areas of the city is banned as that would render nearly seven lakh people unemployed.

(4533) New Delhi : Former Union Minister Omar Abdullah on Saturday called for changes in the United Nations, saying the world body has to represent the world of today and not the polarisation of the 1940s.

(4534) New Delhi : Criticising the recent decision of the Delhi Cabinet to raise the salary of the Chief Minister, the Ministers and MLAs by almost 100 per cent, senior Bharatiya Janata Party MLA Vijay Jolly described it as an "unpopular and cheap" move at a time when the common man was struggling to ensure a decent meal in view of all-round increase in prices of essential and other commodities.

(4535) Jaipur : The Rajasthan unit of the Congress has sought intervention by the Governor, Pratibha Patil, on the Government's decision to rename to the game sanctuary named after Rajiv Gandhi in Rajasthan. This decision was politically motivated, the party has said.

(4536) Chennai : The State secretary of the Communist Party of India (Marxist), N. Varadarajan, on Saturday said his party did not agree with the assessment of Dravida Munnetra Kazhagam (DMK) president M. Karunanidhi that involvement of "highly placed persons" in the Kushboo-Suhasini issue would result in a situation that would help the DMK "to nurture again a non-Brahmin movement."

(4537) Chennai : The Democratic Progressive Alliance on Friday requested the Centre to give the assistance requested by the State Government to tide over the flood situation in the State.

(4538) Chennai : The Marumalarchi Dravida Munnetra Kazhagam (MDMK) general secretary, Vaiko, on Saturday contributed Rs.10 lakhs to the Chief Minister's Public Relief Fund (CMPRF) for flood relief. He accused Chief Minister Jayalalithaa of "shirking her responsibilities" to gear up the administration to provide relief to the people in the affected areas.

28-11-2005

(4539) Hyderabad : The Congress Legislature Party has accused some Telugu Desam Party leaders of fanning regional sentiments and provoking people.

(4540) Hyderabad : The Telugu Desam Party has sought a white paper on issue of farmers' suicide and the steps taken by the Government to mitigate their suffering.

(4541) Hyderabad : Taking a serious view of the remarks made by Ch. Umesh Rao, the Telangana Rashtra Samiti State secretary and nephew of party chief K. Chandrasekhara Rao, the Disciplinary Action Committee has placed him under suspension for his anti-party action.

(4542) Visakhapatnam : The Communist Party of India (Marxist) has asked authorities concerned to pay special attention to development of gram panchayats, which have been merged with the Municipal Corporation under the Greater Visakha Project.

(4543) New Delhi : Peddapalli MP and Congress Parliamentary Party deputy leader G. Venkatswamy on Sunday accused the "Andhra lobby," including leaders of Left parties, of hampering the chances of formation of separate Telangana.

(4544) Narsaraopet (Guntur Dist) : A tense situation prevailed in the town on Sunday following district Telugu Desam Party leaders organising a 'rasta roko' along with the slain leader Anji Babu's body on the Palnadu Road in the city, blaming the Congress and police for the incident.

(4545) Thiruvananthapuram : Bharatiya Janata Party (BJP) secretary L. Ganesh arrived here on Sunday to decipher the reasons for the humiliating performance of the party candidate C.K. Padmanabhan in the Thiruvananthapuram Lok Sabha byelection.

(4546) Bijapur : Shiv Sena's State unit President Pramod Muthalik on Sunday gave enough indications that he may quit the party if it continues its hostile stand over the Belgaum issue and Kannadigas.

(4547) Mumbai : Raj Thackeray on Sunday resigned from his position as Shiv Sena leader and also as president of the Bharatiya Vidyarthi Sena (BVS), the party's student wing.

(4548) Mysore : All-India Progressive Janata Dal (AIPJD) leader and former Deputy Chief Minister Siddaramaiah on Sunday launched the party's campaign for the elections to the zilla and taluk panchayats and hinted at the possibility of an alliance with the Congress.

(4549) Bangalore : The Janata Dal (Secular) received a shot in the arm on Sunday with the entire Shimoga district unit of the Janata Party merging with it.

(4550) Bijapur : Shiv Sena's State unit president Pramod Muthalik on Sunday gave enough indications that he may quit the party if it continues its hostile stand over the Belgaum issue and Kannadigas.

(4551) Alappuzha : The CPI(M) is planning to grill the Union and State Governments in the coming days for its alleged inaction to take effective steps to save Ramankutty Maniappan, a Border Roads Organisation employee who had been executed by the Taliban militia in Afghanistan.

(4552) Ahmedabad : The former Union Minister for Disinvestment, Arun Shourie, on Sunday hit out at the Left parties, accusing them of following no ideologies or principles.

(4553) Mumbai: Shiv Sena executive president Uddhav Thackeray on Sunday night hit back at his estranged cousin Raj's revolt against his leadership saying he wondered if his (Raj's) remarks were drafted by expelled party leader and Congressman Narayan Rane.

(4554) New Delhi : Praising the National Cadet Corps (NCC) for its role in spreading social harmony and instilling values of character, courage and friendship among the younger generation, Congress president Sonia

Gandhi on Sunday said efforts should be made to make the organisation more appealing to the youth.

(4555) Bhopal: While protesting against the process whereby Mr Shivraj Singh Chauhan was elevated to the post of Madhya Pradesh chief minister, former chief minister Uma Bharti's dejected supporters - who had launched the state's change of guard campaign - have adopted a "wait-and-watch" policy and are avoiding any confrontation in the present situation.

(4556) Bhopal: The Madhya Pradesh Chief Minister, Babulal Gaur has sent in his resignation to the Bharatiya Janata Party Parliamentary Board and would be formally handing over his resignation to the State Governor after he returns to the State capital from tour.

(4557) Chennai : The controversy over actress Kushboo's remarks in an interview to a magazine about pre-marital sex and the support extended to her by fellow film star Suhasini has taken a new turn with the two Communist parties opposing DMK president Karunanidhi's view that the involvement of some influential people might help his party nurture an anti-Brahmin movement again.

(4558) Chennai : Dravida Munnetra Kazhagam president M. Karunanidhi on Sunday clarified that his remark on the protest against actress Khusboo was misquoted. The remark on the "Brahmin-non-brahmin" issue was made in jest by him after the press conference had concluded.

(4559) Cuddalore : Dravida Munnetra Kazhagam president M. Karunanidhi has justified the Tamil Nadu Government's demand for an increased quantum of flood relief from the Centre.

29-11-2005

(4560) Hyderabad : While welcoming the Government's action in ordering an enquiry into reports of suicides by farmers, senior Bharatiya Janata Party leader B. Dattatreya has condemned the statements of Ministers - N. Raghuveera Reddy, Ponnala Lakshmaiah and Mohd. Ali Shabbir.

(4561) Hyderabad : The Hyderabad unit of the Communist Party of India (Marxist) has embarked upon a 30-day 600-km walkathon in 100 divisions of the city to pressure the State Government to focus on developmental issues in slums.

(4562) Hyderabad : Suspended TRS leader Ch. Umesh Rao, who is the nephew of Union Minister K. Chandrasekhara Rao, has faulted the party leadership for acting 'unilaterally' and not following democratic norms.

(4563) Khammam : CPI State secretary K. Narayana and party National Council member Puvvada Nageswara Rao were among 3,000 partymen arrested during the day-long road blockade organised in the district on Monday opposing the large-scale submergence by the Polavaram project.

(4564) Kurnool : TDP district president K.E. Krishna Murthy has said the TDP would fight the ensuing mandal elections with all its might as the elections are considered crucial for its existence.

(4565) Nellore: District president of Telugu Desam Party (TDP) S. Chandramohan Reddy has charged the Government with being indifferent in providing necessary relief and rehabilitation to the people affected by the recent heavy rain in the district.

(4566) Nizamabad : The Telugu Desam Party has said that it will launch padayatra in Telangana villages to enlighten people on the injustice being meted out to the region in the construction of irrigation projects if the Congress Government fails to give up its "discriminatory" and "conspiratorial" stand on the backward region.

(4567) Hasanparthy (Warangal DT.) : There is no pomp and heraldry. There are no media managers. The padayatra being undertaken by the 50-year-old CPI (M) district secretary G. Nagaiah has already covered 13 mandals so far.

(4568) New Delhi : The Left parties on Monday firmly opposed any unilateral decision of the United Progressive Alliance Government to privatise the Mumbai and Delhi airports, the two major profit centres of a "consistently profit making" public sector undertaking without consulting its employees.

(4569) Bhopal : The former Madhya Pradesh Chief Minister, Uma Bharti, along with 16 MLAs,walked out of the BJP legislature party meeting here on Monday evening. Soon after, she began a march to Ayodhya, saying it was for the cause of "Ram and roti."

(4570) Bangalore : Even as the Siddaramaiah faction of the Janata Dal (S) has begun to call itself the All India Progressive Janata Dal, the Janata Dal (S), led by H.D. Deve Gowda, petitioned the State Election Commission on Monday against allotting election symbol to the former for the zilla and taluk panchayat elections. The petition has been filed by Y.S.V. Datta, General Secretary of the Janata Dal (S).

(4571) Thiruvananthapuram : 'Kesari', mouthpiece of the Rashtriya Swayamsevak Sangh (RSS), has termed 'disgraceful' the BJP's defeat in the just-concluded Thiruvananthapuram Lok Sabha byelection.

(4572) New Delhi : The Congress on Monday used the debate on the adjournment motion on the Volcker Report in the Lok Sabha to underscore the difference in its approach to allegations of corruption vis-a-vis the Bharatiya Janata Party-led National Democratic Alliance which refused to discuss the Tehelka scam in Parliament.

(4573) Bhopal : Madhya Pradesh BJP president Shivraj Singh Chauhan was elected legislature party leader here on Monday evening. He had the support of 154 of the 171 MLAs, who attended.

(4574) Kolkata: The ruling Left Front has reservations against the Election Commission order to delete from the electoral rolls the names of those against whom non-bailable warrants were pending for over six months.

(4575) Chennai : Janata Party president Subramanian Swamy has demanded that all papers connected with Volcker Committee Report relating to the oil-for-food programme of the United Nations for Iraq, particularly the documents connected with Indian beneficiaries, should be placed on the floor of the Lok Sabha.

(4576) Mumbai : Top Shiv Sena leaders met at party chief Bal Thackeray's residence, Matoshree, here on Monday to discuss the resignation of Raj Thackeray from organisational posts. The former Lok Sabha Speaker Manohar Joshi told the press in the afternoon that the meeting was in progress but nothing came of it yet. Soon after he and other leaders including Ramdas Kadam and Sena MLA Subhash Desai left the place.

(4577) New Delhi : Even before Shivraj Singh Chauhan could take office as new Chief Minister of Madhya Pradesh, accusations and counter accusations are flying around on the manner of decision making in the Bharatiya Janata Party. An internal battle has broken out.

(4578) New Delhi : Even as elections for the Municipal Corporation of Delhi are due only in early 2007, the daggers are already out and the blame game has begun. Afraid of a poor show at the hustings, the Delhi Pradesh Congress Committee and the Congress Councillors have warned the party high command that poor performance by the Administration coupled with increase in power and water charges would affect the party's chances in the civic polls.

(4579) Guwahati: Speaker Prithibi Majhi on Monday admitted a no-confidence motion jointly moved by the Asom Gana Parishad (AGP), BJP and the Autonomous State Demand Committee (ASDC) against the Tarun Gogoi-led Congress Government but disallowed an adjournment motion on the recent violence in Karbi Anglong.

(4580) Dehra Dun : The Bharatiya Janata Party on Monday launched a major offensive against the Narain Dutt Tiwari Government by asking it to resign before the Centre withdraws the "special status" granted to Uttaranchal by Atal Bihari Vajpayee when he was Prime Minister.

(4581) Chennai : The Bharatiya Janata Party reiterated on Monday that the Central Government should help Tamil Nadu in a "big way."

(4582) Chennai : The Tamil Nadu Congress Committee has urged the Tamil Nadu Government to set up all-party monitoring committee in all districts to oversee flood relief operations in the State.

(4583) Chennai : All-India Congress Committee secretary K.B. Krishnamurthi has blamed the poor infrastructure in the State, particularly in Chennai city, for the heavy flooding after the torrential rains.

(4584) Cuddalore : Bharatiya Janata Party leader Venkiah Naidu has demanded that the Centre immediately sanction Rs.1000 crore to help Tamil Nadu deal with the flood havoc.

(4585) New Delhi : Marumalarchi Dravida Munnetra Kazhagam leader Vaiko and four party MPs met Prime Minister Manmohan Singh on Monday and sought immediate release of Rs. 3,000 crores for Tamil Nadu which was devastated by the cyclone and floods.

30-11-2005

(4586) Hyderabad : Congress legislator P. Janardhan Reddy on Tuesday reiterated his plea for creation of Deputy Chief Minister post and earmarking it for Telangana region.

(4587) Hyderabad : Close on the heels of the IMG land imbroglio, Congress MLA P. Janardhana Reddy has demanded a CBI probe into the allotment of 520 acres of land in Manikonda and Nanakramguda to a Dubai-based real estate company at a 'throwaway price' by the Telugu Desam Government for setting up a golf course, convention centre, townships and tourist facilities.

(4588) Hyderabad : The Telugu Desam Party has demanded that Governor S. K. Shinde recall the remission granted to Congress leader Gouru Venkat Reddy convicted in murder cases and take action against police officers responsible for filing a factually incorrect report to favour him.

(4589) Hyderabad : The Telangana Rashtra Samiti has asked senior Congress leaders from Telangana to give concrete suggestions instead of lamenting about backwardness of the region.

(4590) Karimnagar : CPI floor leader in the Assembly Chada Venkat Reddy has endorsed the statement made by senior Congress leader and Peddapalli MP G Venkatswamy that Chief Minister Y. S. Rajasekhar Reddy, former Chief Minister N. Chandrababu Naidu, CPM leaders Sitaram Yechuri and B V Raghavulu were opposed to the formation of Telangana statehood.

(4591) Nizamabad : District Congress Committee president Gadugu Gangadhar has suggested to Telugu Desam Party leaders to do some introspection before criticising the Congress Government and Chief Minister Y.S. Rajasekhara Reddy regarding construction of projects in Telangana region.

(4592) Vijayawada : Rich aqua culture farmers, who are trying to exploit the natural wealth of Kolleru Lake, are also using poor farmers to shield themselves, according to CPI State secretary K. Narayana.

(4593) Hyderabad : In yet another twist to the crisis in the Telangana Rashtra Samiti (TRS), rebel MLAs have set a 48-hour deadline for party president K. Chandrasekhara Rao to publicly withdraw the charges levelled against them, failing which they have threatened to go ahead with meetings in all the Telangana districts.

(4594) New Delhi : The Bharatiya Janata Party's central leadership has given strong signals that it will adopt a hard stance against general secretary Uma Bharti and her supporters in Bhopal, where vandalism on Monday tarnished the party's image. The word is that she will be suspended from the party when the BJP parliamentary board meets on Wednesday; if that happens, it will be the second time in less then 13 months.

(4595) Thiruvananthapuram: The Democratic Indira Congress (Karunakaran) leader K. Karunakaran on Tuesday alleged that the Oommen Chandy Government was using three IAS officials to promote corruption in the remaining part of its term in office.

(4596) Bangalore : Chief Minister N. Dharam Singh has overruled those Congress leaders who are attempting to forge an alliance with the revived All-India Progressive Janata Dal (AIPJD) in the coming zilla and taluk panchayat elections and said the move does not have the approval of the party High Command.

(4597) Mangalore : The Dakshina Kannada district committee of the Bharatiya Janata Party (BJP) has urged the electorate to reject the Congress and Janata Dal (Secular) in the forthcoming elections to panchayat raj bodies in Karnataka.

(4598) Mysore : Janata Dal (Secular) Working President H.D. Kumaraswamy lashed out at the former Deputy Chief Minister and leader of the All India Progressive Janata Dal Siddaramaiah for "misleading" rural people with false assurances on free power and agricultural loans at 3 per cent interest.

(4599) Mysore : Beating the November 30 deadline to file nominations for the zilla and taluk panchayat elections, leaders of the Congress and the newly formed All India Progressive Janata Dal (AIPJD) led by the former Deputy Chief Siddaramaiah held several rounds of talks to finalise a seat-sharing arrangement in the district for the December 19 elections.

(4600) New Delhi: The controversial Belgaum City Corporation resolution on the merger of Belgaum and some other areas with neighbouring Maharashtra figured in the Lok Sabha on Tuesday. The House witnessed noisy scenes with Shiv Sena members opposing the issue raised by a member of the Bharatiya Janata Party (BJP).

(4601) Mumbai : Maharashtra Chief Minister Vilasrao Deshmukh on Tuesday said that he had written to Prime Minister Manmohan Singh seeking a meeting on the State's border row with Karnataka.

(4602) Bhopal : The former Madhya Pradesh Chief Minister, Uma Bharti, said on Tuesday that the Bharatiya Janata Party had been hijacked by a "group of four" who were dictating terms and bulldozing democratic traditions and the hopes and aspirations of the grass-roots level party workers.

(4603) New Delhi : An agreement was hammered out on Tuesday between the ruling and Opposition party members that the Lok Sabha would devote Wednesday to official legislative business and on Thursday discuss internal security, with reference to the recent bomb blasts in Delhi and the series of terrorist attacks in Jammu and Kashmir.

(4604) Bhopal : The Bharatiya Janata Party Parliamentary Board will meet at the party's central office in New Delhi at 12.30 p.m. on Wednesday to decide about the disciplinary action against the former Madhya Pradesh Chief Minister, Uma Bharti, for her repeated utterances before the media after the announcement of the selection of Shivraj Singh Chauhan as the next State Chief Minister.

(4605) Bhopal : Shivraj Singh Chauhan was on Tuesday sworn in Chief Minister of Madhya Pradesh. Governor Balram Jakhar administered the oath of office and secrecy to him at a special function held on the sprawling lawns of Raj Bhawan here.

(4606) New Delhi : The Bharatiya Janata Party on Tuesday sought to know whether the Government lodged any protest with Pakistan against its rolein the killing of Border Roads Organisation driver Ramankutty Maniappan in Afghanistan. BJP leader V.K. Malhotra raised the issue in the Lok Sabha during zero hour and cited reports, quoting National Security Adviser M.K. Narayanan, that Pakistan had a hand in the killing.

(4607) New Delhi The Delhi Bharatiya Janata Party on Tuesday called on the President, A.P.J. Abdul Kalam, and sought dismissal of the Sheila Dikshit Government for what it called "patronising and conniving with the private power distribution companies to loot the consumers". It also sought a CBI inquiry into the bungling that has taken plaee in privatisation of the power sector in the Capital and working of the companies during the past three years.

(4608) New Delhi : With all political parties joining hands to plead the case of farmhouse owners and those who have violated building norms by converting residential areas into commercial hubs, senior Congress leader and Kalkaji MLA Subhash Chopra has also joined the bandwagon. Mr. Chopra has written to Chief Minister Sheila Dikshit demanding that a meeting of the Congress Legislative Party (CLP) be convened to discuss the issue.

(4609) Pondicherry : The Pattali Makkal Katchi parliamentary party leader M. Ramadoss has urged Pondicherry Chief Minister N. Rangasamy to initiate steps to procure Veeranam water. Mr. Ramadoss said this could be done by diverting the lake's water into the Veedur dam so that farmers downstream in Pondicherry could benefit. In a release here on Monday, he highlighted the woes of the farmers in the villages of Sandhaipudukuppam, Suttukeni, Katterikuppam, Lingareddipalayam, Sethampakkam and Kumarapalayam.

(4610) Ghazipur / Lucknow : Krishnanand Rai, BJP MLA from the Mohammadabad Assembly constituency in Uttar Pradesh, and six others were shot dead on Tuesday broad- daylight by several gun toting men near Basheri village under the Bhanwarkot area of Ghazipur district, the police said.

(4611) Lucknow: Three leaders from Uttar Pradesh are in the run for the post of BJP president when present incumbent Lal Krishna Advani relinquishes charge next month.

(4612) Chennai : Dravida Munnetra Kazhagam president M. Karunanidhi on Tuesday accused communal forces of trying to exploit his comments on the Kushboo issue and said these efforts would not succeed.

(4613) Chennai : The Pattali Makkal Katchi founder, S. Ramadoss, on Tuesday rebutted the charge that he was against freedom of expression.

(4614) New Delhi: Union Railway Minister Lalu Prasad on Tuesday assured the general secretary of the Marumalarchi Dravida Munnetra

Kazhagam, Vaiko, that the Government would take immediate steps to fill the 1,500 vacancies in the Integral Coach Factory, Chennai.

(4615) New Delhi: The Tamil Nadu Congress Committee (TNCC) on Tuesday urged the Centre to take steps for early release of flood relief to the State.